Carry On

Carry On

Sound Advice from Schneier on Security

Bruce Schneier

WILEY

Carry On: Sound Advice from Schneier on Security
Published by
John Wiley & Sons, Inc.
10475 Crosspoint Boulevard
Indianapolis, IN 46256
www.wiley.com

Copyright © 2014 by Bruce Schneier

Published by John Wiley & Sons, Inc., Indianapolis, Indiana

Published simultaneously in Canada

ISBN: 978-1-118-79081-6
ISBN: 978-1-118-79083-0 (ebk)
ISBN: 978-1-118-79082-2 (ebk)

Manufactured in the United States of America

10 9 8 7 6 5 4 3 2 1

For general information on our other products and services please contact our Customer Care Department within the United States at (877) 762-2974, outside the United States at (317) 572-3993 or fax (317) 572-4002.

Wiley publishes in a variety of print and electronic formats and by print-on-demand. Some material included with standard print versions of this book may not be included in e-books or in print-on-demand. If this book refers to media such as a CD or DVD that is not included in the version you purchased, you may download this material at http://booksupport.wiley.com. For more information about Wiley products, visit www.wiley.com.

Library of Congress Control Number: 2013954201

Credits

Executive Editor
Carol Long

Project Editor
Tom Dinse

Senior Production Editor
Kathleen Wisor

Editorial Manager
Mary Beth Wakefield

Freelancer Editorial Manager
Rosemarie Graham

Associate Director of Marketing
David Mayhew

Marketing Manager
Ashley Zurcher

Business Manager
Amy Knies

Vice President and Executive Group Publisher
Richard Swadley

Associate Publisher
Jim Minatel

Project Coordinator, Cover
Katie Crocker

Proofreader
Nancy Carrasco

Indexer
Johnna VanHoose Dinse

Cover Image
Steve Woit

Cover Designer
Ryan Sneed

Contents

Introduction

I like writing essays. I like the length: 600 to 1,200 words is my personal sweet spot. I like the format: a tight argument designed to make a particular point. And I like the style: explaining complicated topics to a lay audience is something I do well. Books are long, both in actual words and in the time they take to write. But I can write an essay in a fit of inspiration in a morning, and get it published the next day if everything goes well.

Not that it always goes that well, of course. Some essays are harder to write than others, and some are *very* hard. I like to take a few days to consider an issue before I write about it, which means that mine is generally not the first essay on the Internet after a news event. Editors, of course, hate this. They want something that catches the current news cycle.

Still, writing is something I'm good at and something I do a lot of. Since 1992, I have written almost 500 essays, op-eds, and articles for a wide variety of publications. They're all on my website—www.schneier.com, if you don't already know—and a selection of them has been collected into two books. The first collection, *Schneier on Security*, covered essays from April 2002 to February 2008. This volume covers essays from March 2008 to June 2013.

Looking back at the entire body of work, I have some lessons, observations, and advice for others trying to get their own articles published. And while my writing is mostly about security, much of the advice is general.

- **Opinions are cheap.** Charles McCabe famously said, "Any clod can have the facts, but having opinions is an art." He's right, but it doesn't follow that any clod lacks an opinion. On the Internet, opinions are a dime a dozen. I rarely get paid for my essays. Oh, there were a few fun years where *Wired* paid me to write a regular column, but they eventually realized that it was cheaper to not bother paying me for them, since I was going to keep writing in any case. I'm not saying that it's impossible to get paid for writing opinions—of course it is—only that it's increasingly rare and difficult.

- **Persuading someone is hard—and rare.** My goal is to write persuasive essays, but I doubt they do a lot of actual persuading. More often, I'm writing to people who already agree with me, giving them new ways to think about the issue, or new words to use when doing their own persuading.

- **It's hard not to repeat yourself.** I write for many different audiences, often on very similar topics. And I often repeat myself. If I find a turn of phrase I like, I reuse it. If I have a perfect paragraph on a topic, I'm likely to use it again. I used to write restaurant reviews semiprofessionally, and would regularly complain about how few ways there are to say "this tastes good." It's not that bad in my security writing, but sometimes it feels as if it comes close.

- **Stories repeat.** Again and again, essays I wrote five or ten years ago suddenly become relevant after some news event. The essay I wrote about data mining in 2001 was important after the Boston Marathon bombing. The essay I wrote about fingerprint scanners in 1998 was important when Apple released an iPhone with a fingerprint scanner. The essay I wrote about Chinese cyberattacks in 2008 has been pertinent every couple of years since then. Drug testing in sports, TSA security, the value of privacy, ubiquitous surveillance, security against lone shooters: it all becomes relevant again after a news event. Sometimes I dust off an old essay, tack on a new introduction, and republish it. But most of the time I try for a new perspective. I don't like resaying old things, even if they are new again.

- **Editors rewrite.** Sometimes they only rewrite a little, but sometimes they rewrite a lot. Sometimes their rewrites are improvements, and sometimes they're just different. It's okay to push back on rewrites that don't improve your work. Once I refused to let a publication publish an essay of mine because they changed too much and wouldn't change things back. And there were a few times I wish that I'd yanked essays where the editors cut too much.

- **The headline isn't your problem.** As an essay writer, you don't get any say in your headline. If you're lucky, you'll get to see it before it's published, but you probably won't. The headline is how the publication entices readers to your essay. As such, it'll be more sensationalist than you want. Or it'll be simpler than you want. Or it'll be less descriptive than you want. Let it go—you can't change it.

- **Links rot.** It's frustrating, but they do. Links you include in essays you write today are likely to return "Page not found" errors a few years from now. For my last volume of essays, I included links at the end. I was going to do the same for this book, but link-checking showed that almost a tenth of them were already dead. These aren't ancient essays; the oldest are six years old and the newest are current.

- **Mistakes happen.** Don't be afraid to admit your mistakes. If you're going to write in anything resembling real time, your writing will sometimes contain errors—of fact, of logic, of conclusion, of opinion—of pretty much everything. When you do, admit them. Don't hedge. Don't mumble. Just admit them. You'll feel better, and your audience will respect you for it.
- **Opinions can change.** Don't be afraid to change your mind. If you're going to write over anything resembling a reasonable length of time, you're going to change your mind about some things. Maybe you'll discover new facts that cause you to reach different conclusions. Maybe you'll just think about things in a new light and reach different conclusions. That's fine. Just explain it. John Maynard Keynes said, "When the facts change, I change my mind. What do you do, sir?" Exactly.
- **You need to write in order to be read.** The world is full of people with great ideas who never make them available to the wider world. My first rule of writing is that you can't improve it until it's written down. So write that first draft; it's really the only way you'll see the weaker parts of your argument. (The world is also filled with people with terrible ideas who make them available to everyone—but that's a separate problem.)
- **Beta readers are important.** Cultivate a stable of them. The more people you have reading your essays before publication, the better your writing will be. Don't be afraid of criticism. Divorce your ego from your writing. That's the key for accepting criticism, and being able to process and use it; you can't let your ego interfere with hearing what your beta readers are telling you. The way I think of it is that people will criticize my work regardless, but if they criticize a draft, I have the opportunity to fix it before publication. Almost all of my essays have been improved by someone else's comments on an early draft, and some of my essays would have been terrible without those improvements.

When I write a book, it's easy to thank the people who read and commented on it. It's impossible to do the same with essays. So here, in this collection of essays, I would like to thank all the people who have read and commented on essay drafts: David M. Perry, Greg Guerin, Steve Bass, Bill Herdle, David Prentiss, Vicki Laidler, Stephen Leigh, Moshe Yudkowsky, Jon Callas, Doug Whiting, Stefan Lucks, and Jesse Walker. I apologize for any names I inadvertently omitted. I haven't kept a list, and I know I'm not remembering everybody.

So, welcome to my second collection of essays. I think there's something in here for everyone's tastes, as long as their tastes include security: technology and security, economics and security, psychology and security, politics and security. I'm still writing, and will probably publish a third volume of these in five or so years. Thanks for reading.

Bruce Schneier

The essays in this book previously appeared in various publications and may follow the usage conventions of the original publishers.

Carry On

The Business and Economics of Security

Consolidation: Plague or Progress

Originally published in Information Security, *March 2008*

This essay appeared as the second half of a point/counterpoint with Marcus Ranum.

We know what we don't like about buying consolidated product suites: one great product and a bunch of mediocre ones. And we know what we don't like about buying best-of-breed: multiple vendors, multiple interfaces, and multiple products that don't work well together. The security industry has gone back and forth between the two, as a new generation of IT security professionals rediscovers the downsides of each solution.

The real problem is that neither solution really works, and we continually fool ourselves into believing whatever we don't have is better than what we have at the time. And the real solution is to buy results, not products.

Honestly, no one wants to buy IT security. People want to buy whatever they want—connectivity, a Web presence, email, networked applications, whatever—and they want it to be secure. That they're forced to spend money on IT security is an artifact of the youth of the computer industry. And sooner or later the need to buy security will disappear.

It will disappear because IT vendors are starting to realize they have to provide security as part of whatever they're selling. It will disappear because organizations are starting to buy services instead of products, and demanding security as part of those services. It will disappear because the security industry will disappear as a consumer category, and will instead market to the IT industry.

The critical driver here is outsourcing. Outsourcing is the ultimate consolidator, because the customer no longer cares about the details. If I buy my network services from a large IT infrastructure company, I don't care if it secures things by installing the hot new intrusion prevention systems, by configuring the routers and servers as to obviate the need for network-based security, or if it uses magic security dust given to it by elven kings. I just want a contract that specifies a level and quality of service, and my vendor can figure it out.

IT is infrastructure. Infrastructure is always outsourced. And the details of how the infrastructure works are left to the companies that provide it.

This is the future of IT, and when that happens we're going to start to see a type of consolidation we haven't seen before. Instead of large security companies gobbling up small security companies, both large and small security companies will be gobbled up by non-security companies. It's already starting to happen. In 2006, IBM bought ISS. The same year BT bought my company, Counterpane, and last year it bought INS. These aren't large security companies buying small security companies; these are non-security companies buying large and small security companies.

If I were Symantec and McAfee, I would be preparing myself for a buyer.

This is good consolidation. Instead of having to choose between a single product suite that isn't very good or a best-of-breed set of products that don't work well together, we can ignore the issue completely. We can just find an infrastructure provider that will figure it out and make it work—who cares how?

Prediction: RSA Conference Will Shrink Like a Punctured Balloon

Originally published in Wired News, *April 17, 2008*

Last week was the RSA Conference, easily the largest information security conference in the world. More than 17,000 people descended on San Francisco's Moscone Center to hear some of the more than 250 talks, attend I-didn't-try-to-count parties, and try to evade over 350 exhibitors vying to sell them stuff.

Talk to the exhibitors, though, and the most common complaint is that the attendees aren't buying.

It's not the quality of the wares. The show floor is filled with new security products, new technologies, and new ideas. Many of these are products that will make the attendees' companies more secure in all sorts of different ways. The problem is that most of the people attending the RSA Conference can't understand what the products do or why they should buy them. So they don't.

I spoke with one person whose trip was paid for by a smallish security firm. He was one of the company's first customers, and the company was proud to parade him in front of the press. I asked him whether he walked through the show floor, looking at the company's competitors to see if there was any benefit to switching.

"I can't figure out what any of those companies do," he replied.

I believe him. The booths are filled with broad product claims, meaningless security platitudes and unintelligible marketing literature. You could walk into a booth, listen to a five-minute sales pitch by a marketing type, and still not know what the company does. Even seasoned security professionals are confused.

Commerce requires a meeting of the minds between buyer and seller, and it's just not happening. The sellers can't explain what they're selling to the buyers, and the buyers don't buy because they don't understand what the sellers are selling. There's a mismatch between the two; they're so far apart that they're barely speaking the same language.

This is a bad thing in the near term—some good companies will go bankrupt and some good security technologies won't get deployed—but it's a good thing in the long run. It demonstrates that the computer industry is maturing: IT is getting complicated and subtle, and users are starting to treat it like infrastructure.

For a while now I have predicted the death of the security industry. Not the death of information security as a vital requirement, of course, but the death of the end-user security industry that gathers at the RSA Conference. When something becomes infrastructure—power, water, cleaning service, tax preparation—customers care less about details and more about results. Technological innovations become something the infrastructure providers pay attention to, and they package it for their customers.

No one wants to buy security. They want to buy something truly useful—database management systems, Web 2.0 collaboration tools, a company-wide network—and they want it to be secure. They don't want to have to become IT security experts. They don't want to have to go to the RSA Conference. This is the future of IT security.

You can see it in the large IT outsourcing contracts that companies are signing—not security outsourcing contracts, but more general IT contracts that include security. You can see it in the current wave of industry consolidation: not large security companies buying small security companies, but non-security companies buying security companies. And you can see it in the new popularity of software as a service: Customers want solutions; who cares about the details?

Imagine if the inventor of antilock brakes—or any automobile safety or security feature—had to sell them directly to the consumer. It would be an uphill battle convincing the average driver that he needed to buy them; maybe that technology would have succeeded and maybe it wouldn't. But that's not what happens. Antilock brakes, airbags and that annoying sensor that beeps when you're backing up too close to another object are sold to automobile companies, and those companies bundle them together into cars that are sold to consumers. This doesn't mean that automobile safety isn't important, and often these new features are touted by the car manufacturers.

The RSA Conference won't die, of course. Security is too important for that. There will still be new technologies, new products and new startups. But it will become inward-facing, slowly turning into an industry conference. It'll be security companies selling to the companies who sell to corporate and home users—and will no longer be a 17,000-person user conference.

How to Sell Security

Originally published in CIO, May 26, 2008

It's a truism in sales that it's easier to sell someone something he wants than a defense against something he wants to avoid. People are reluctant to buy insurance, or home security devices, or computer security anything. It's not they don't ever buy these things, but it's an uphill struggle.

The reason is psychological. And it's the same dynamic when it's a security vendor trying to sell its products or services, a CIO trying to convince senior management to invest in security or a security officer trying to implement a security policy with her company's employees.

It's also true that the better you understand your buyer, the better you can sell.

Why People Are Willing to Take Risks

First, a bit about Prospect Theory, the underlying theory behind the newly popular field of behavioral economics. Prospect Theory was developed by Daniel Kahneman and Amos Tversky in 1979 (Kahneman went on to win a Nobel Prize for this and other similar work) to explain how people make trade-offs that involve risk. Before this work, economists had a model of "economic man," a rational being who makes trade-offs based on some logical calculation. Kahneman and Tversky showed that real people are far more subtle and ornery.

Here's an experiment that illustrates Prospect Theory. Take a roomful of subjects and divide them into two groups. Ask one group to choose between these two alternatives: a sure gain of $500 and 50 percent chance of gaining $1,000. Ask the other group to choose between these two alternatives: a sure loss of $500 and a 50 percent chance of losing $1,000.

These two trade-offs are very similar, and traditional economics predicts that whether you're contemplating a gain or a loss doesn't make a difference: People make trade-offs based on a straightforward calculation of the relative outcome. Some people prefer sure things and others prefer to take chances. Whether the outcome is a gain or a loss doesn't affect the mathematics and therefore shouldn't affect the results. This is traditional economics, and it's called Utility Theory.

But Kahneman's and Tversky's experiments contradicted Utility Theory. When faced with a gain, about 85 percent of people chose the sure smaller gain over the risky larger gain. But when faced with a loss, about 70 percent chose the risky larger loss over the sure smaller loss.

This experiment, repeated again and again by many researchers, across ages, genders, cultures and even species, rocked economics, yielded the same result. Directly contradicting the traditional idea of "economic man," Prospect Theory recognizes that people have subjective values for gains and losses. We have evolved a cognitive bias: a pair of heuristics. One, a sure gain is better than a chance at a greater gain, or "A bird in the hand is worth two in the bush." And two, a sure loss is worse than a chance at a greater loss, or "Run away and live to fight another day." Of course, these are not rigid rules. Only a fool would take a sure $100 over a 50 percent chance at $1,000,000. But all things being equal, we tend to be risk-averse when it comes to gains and risk-seeking when it comes to losses.

This cognitive bias is so powerful that it can lead to logically inconsistent results. Google the "Asian Disease Experiment" for an almost surreal example. Describing the same policy choice in different ways—either as "200 lives saved out of 600" or "400 lives lost out of 600"—yields wildly different risk reactions.

Evolutionarily, the bias makes sense. It's a better survival strategy to accept small gains rather than risk them for larger ones, and to risk larger losses rather than accept smaller losses. Lions, for example, chase young or wounded wildebeests because the investment needed to kill them is lower. Mature and healthy prey would probably be more nutritious, but there's a risk of missing lunch entirely if it gets away. And a small meal will tide the lion over until another day. Getting through today is more important than the possibility of having food tomorrow. Similarly, it is better to risk a larger loss than to accept a smaller loss. Because animals tend to live on the razor's edge between starvation and reproduction, any loss of food—whether small or large—can be equally bad. Because both can result in death, and the best option is to risk everything for the chance at no loss at all.

How to Sell Security

How does Prospect Theory explain the difficulty of selling the prevention of a security breach? It's a choice between a small sure loss—the cost of the security product—and a large risky loss: for example, the results of an attack on one's network. Of course there's a lot more to the sale. The buyer has to be convinced that the product works, and he has to understand the threats against him and the risk that something bad will happen. But all things being equal, buyers would rather take the chance that the attack won't happen than suffer the sure loss that comes from purchasing the security product.

Security sellers know this, even if they don't understand why, and are continually trying to frame their products in positive results. That's why you see slogans with the basic message, "We take care of security so you can focus on your business," or carefully crafted ROI models that demonstrate how profitable a security purchase can be. But these never seem to work. Security is fundamentally a negative sell.

One solution is to stoke fear. Fear is a primal emotion, far older than our ability to calculate trade-offs. And when people are truly scared, they're willing to do almost anything to make that feeling go away; lots of other psychological research supports that. Any burglar alarm salesman will tell you that people buy only after they've been robbed, or after one of their neighbors has been robbed. And the fears stoked by 9/11, and the politics surrounding 9/11, have fueled an entire industry devoted to counterterrorism. When emotion takes over like that, people are much less likely to think rationally.

Though effective, fear mongering is not very ethical. The better solution is not to sell security directly, but to include it as part of a more general product or service. Your car comes with safety and security features built in; they're not sold separately. Same with your house. And it should be the same with computers and networks. Vendors need to build security into the products and services that customers actually want. CIOs should include security as an integral part of everything they budget for. Security shouldn't be a separate policy for employees to follow but part of overall IT policy.

Security is inherently about avoiding a negative, so you can never ignore the cognitive bias embedded so deeply in the human brain. But if you understand it, you have a better chance of overcoming it.

Why Do We Accept Signatures by Fax?

Originally published in Wired News, *May 29, 2008*

Aren't fax signatures the weirdest thing? It's trivial to cut and paste—with real scissors and glue—anyone's signature onto a document so that it'll look real when faxed. There is so little security in fax signatures that it's mind-boggling that anyone accepts them.

Yet people do, all the time. I've signed book contracts, credit card authorizations, nondisclosure agreements and all sorts of financial documents—all by fax. I even have a scanned file of my signature on my computer, so I can virtually cut and paste it into documents and fax them directly from my computer without ever having to print them out. What in the world is going on here?

And, more importantly, why are fax signatures still being used after years of experience? Why aren't there many stories of signatures forged through the use of fax machines?

The answer comes from looking at fax signatures not as an isolated security measure, but in the context of the larger system. Fax signatures work because signed faxes exist within a broader communications context.

In a 2003 paper, *Economics, Psychology, and Sociology of Security*, professor Andrew Odlyzko looks at fax signatures and concludes:

> *Although fax signatures have become widespread, their usage is restricted. They are not used for final contracts of substantial value, such as home purchases. That means that the insecurity of fax communications is not easy to exploit for large gain. Additional protection against abuse of fax insecurity is provided by the context in which faxes are used. There are records of phone calls that carry the faxes, paper trails inside enterprises and so on. Furthermore, unexpected large financial transfers trigger scrutiny. As a result, successful frauds are not easy to carry out by purely technical means.*

He's right. Thinking back, there really aren't ways in which a criminal could use a forged document sent by fax to defraud me. I suppose an unscrupulous consulting client could forge my signature on a non-disclosure agreement and then sue me, but that hardly seems worth the effort. And if my broker received a fax document from me authorizing a money transfer to a Nigerian bank account, he would certainly call me before completing it.

Credit card signatures aren't verified in person, either—and I can already buy things over the phone with a credit card—so there are no new risks there, and Visa knows how to monitor transactions for fraud. Lots of companies accept purchase orders via fax, even for large amounts of stuff, but there's a physical audit trail, and the goods are shipped to a physical address—probably one the seller has shipped to before. Signatures are kind of a business lubricant: mostly, they help move things along smoothly.

Except when they don't.

On October 30, 2004, Tristian Wilson was released from a Memphis jail on the authority of a forged fax message. It wasn't even a particularly good forgery. It wasn't on the standard letterhead of the West Memphis Police Department. The name of the policeman who signed the fax was misspelled. And the time stamp on the top of the fax clearly showed that it was sent from a local McDonald's.

The success of this hack has nothing to do with the fact that it was sent over by fax. It worked because the jail had lousy verification procedures. They didn't notice any discrepancies in the fax. They didn't notice the phone number from which the fax was sent. They didn't call and verify that it was official. The jail was accustomed to getting release orders via fax, and just acted on this one without thinking. Would it have been any different had the forged release form been sent by mail or courier?

Yes, fax signatures always exist in context, but sometimes they are the linchpin within that context. If you can mimic enough of the context, or if those on the receiving end become complacent, you can get away with mischief.

Arguably, this is part of the security process. Signatures themselves are poorly defined. Sometimes a document is valid even if not signed: A person with both hands in a cast can still buy a house. Sometimes a document is invalid even if signed: The signer might be drunk, or have a gun pointed at his head. Or he might be a minor. Sometimes a valid signature isn't enough; in the United States there is an entire infrastructure of "notary publics" who officially witness signed documents. When I started filing my tax returns electronically, I had to sign a document stating that I wouldn't be signing my income tax documents. And banks don't even bother verifying signatures on checks less than $30,000; it's cheaper to deal with fraud after the fact than prevent it.

Over the course of centuries, business and legal systems have slowly sorted out what types of additional controls are required around signatures, and in which circumstances.

Those same systems will be able to sort out fax signatures, too, but it'll be slow. And that's where there will be potential problems. Already fax is a declining technology. In a few years it'll be largely obsolete, replaced by PDFs sent over e-mail and other forms of electronic documentation. In the past, we've had time to figure out how to deal with new technologies. Now, by the time we institutionalize these measures, the technologies are likely to be obsolete.

What that means is people are likely to treat fax signatures—or whatever replaces them—exactly the same way as paper signatures. And sometimes that assumption will get them into trouble.

But it won't cause social havoc. Wilson's story is remarkable mostly because it's so exceptional. And even he was rearrested at his home less than a week later. Fax signatures may be new, but fake signatures have always been a possibility. Our legal and business systems need to deal with the underlying problem—false authentication—rather than focus on the technology of the moment. Systems need to defend themselves against the possibility of fake signatures, regardless of how they arrive.

The Pros and Cons of LifeLock

Originally published in Wired News, *June 12, 2008*

LifeLock, one of the companies that offers identity-theft protection in the United States, has been taking quite a beating recently. They're being sued by credit bureaus, competitors and lawyers in several states that are launching class action lawsuits. And the stories in the media. . . it's like a piranha feeding frenzy.

There are also a lot of errors and misconceptions. With its aggressive advertising campaign and a CEO who publishes his Social Security number and dares people to steal his identity—Todd Davis, 457-55-5462—LifeLock is a company that's easy to hate. But the company's story has some interesting security lessons, and it's worth understanding in some detail.

In December 2003, as part of the Fair and Accurate Credit Transactions Act, or FACTA, credit bureaus were forced to allow you to put a fraud alert on their credit reports, requiring lenders to verify your identity before issuing a credit card in your name. This alert is temporary, and expires after 90 days. Several companies have sprung up—LifeLock, Debix, LoudSiren, TrustedID—that automatically renew these alerts and effectively make them permanent.

This service pisses off the credit bureaus and their financial customers. The reason lenders don't routinely verify your identity before issuing you credit is that it takes time, costs money and is one more hurdle between you and another credit card. (Buy, buy, buy—it's the American way.) So in the eyes of credit bureaus, LifeLock's customers are inferior goods; selling their data isn't as valuable. LifeLock also opts its customers out of pre-approved credit card offers, further making them less valuable in the eyes of credit bureaus.

And, so began a smear campaign on the part of the credit bureaus. You can read their points of view in this *New York Times* article, written by a reporter who didn't do much more than regurgitate their talking points. And the class action lawsuits have piled on, accusing LifeLock of deceptive business practices, fraudulent advertising and so on. The biggest smear is that LifeLock didn't even protect Todd Davis, and that his identity was allegedly stolen.

It wasn't. Someone in Texas used Davis's SSN to get a $500 advance against his paycheck. It worked because the loan operation didn't check with any of the credit bureaus before approving the loan—perfectly reasonable for an amount this small. The payday-loan operation called Davis to collect, and LifeLock cleared up the problem. His credit report remains spotless.

The Experian credit bureau's lawsuit basically claims that fraud alerts are only for people who have been victims of identity theft. This seems spurious; the text of the law states that anyone "who asserts a good faith suspicion that the consumer has been or is about to become a victim of fraud or related crime" can request a fraud alert. It seems to me that includes anybody who has ever received one of those notices about their financial details being lost or stolen, which is everybody.

As to deceptive business practices and fraudulent advertising—those just seem like class action lawyers piling on. LifeLock's aggressive fear-based marketing doesn't seem any worse than a lot of other similar advertising campaigns. My guess is that the class action lawsuits won't go anywhere.

In reality, forcing lenders to verify identity before issuing credit is exactly the sort of thing we need to do to fight identity theft. Basically, there are two ways to deal with identity theft: Make personal information harder to steal, and make stolen personal information harder to use. We all know the former doesn't work, so that leaves the latter. If Congress wanted to solve the problem for real, one of the things it would do is make fraud alerts permanent for everybody. But the credit industry's lobbyists would never allow that.

LifeLock does a bunch of other clever things. They monitor the national address database, and alert you if your address changes. They look for your credit and debit card numbers on hacker and criminal websites and such, and assist you in getting a new number if they see it. They have a million-dollar service guarantee—for complicated legal reasons, they can't call it insurance—to help you recover if your identity is ever stolen.

But even with all of this, I am not a LifeLock customer. At $120 a year, it's just not worth it. You wouldn't know it from the press attention, but dealing with identity theft has become easier and more routine. Sure, it's a pervasive problem. The Federal Trade Commission reported that 8.3 million Americans were identity-theft victims in 2005. But that includes things like someone stealing your credit card and using it, something that rarely costs you any money and that LifeLock doesn't protect against. New account fraud is much less common, affecting 1.8 million Americans per year, or 0.8 percent of the adult population. The FTC hasn't published detailed numbers for 2006 or 2007, but the rate seems to be declining.

New card fraud is also not very damaging. The median amount of fraud the thief commits is $1,350, but you're not liable for that. Some spectacularly horrible identity-theft stories notwithstanding, the financial industry is pretty good at quickly cleaning up the mess. The victim's median out-of-pocket cost for new account fraud is only $40, plus ten hours of grief to clean up the problem. Even assuming your time is worth $100 an hour, LifeLock isn't worth more than $8 a year.

And it's hard to get any data on how effective LifeLock really is. They've been in business three years and have about a million customers, but most of them have joined up in the last year. They've paid out on their service guarantee 113 times, but a lot of those were for things that happened before their customers became customers. (It was easier to pay than argue, I assume.) But they don't know how often the fraud alerts actually catch an identity thief in the act. My guess is that it's less than the 0.8 percent fraud rate above.

LifeLock's business model is based more on the fear of identity theft than the actual risk.

It's pretty ironic of the credit bureaus to attack LifeLock on its marketing practices, since they know all about profiting from the fear of identity theft. FACTA also forced the credit bureaus to give Americans a free credit report once a year upon request. Through deceptive marketing techniques, they've turned this requirement into a multimillion-dollar business.

Get LifeLock if you want, or one of its competitors if you prefer. But remember that you can do most of what these companies do yourself. You can put a fraud alert on your own account, but you have to remember to renew it every three months. You can also put a credit freeze on your account, which is more work for the average consumer but more effective if you're a privacy wonk—and the rules differ by state. And maybe someday Congress will do the right thing and put LifeLock out of business by forcing lenders to verify identity every time they issue credit in someone's name.

The Problem Is Information Insecurity

Originally published in Security Watch, *August 10, 2008*

Information insecurity is costing us billions. We pay for it in theft: information theft, financial theft. We pay for it in productivity loss, both when networks stop working and in the dozens of minor security inconveniences we all have to endure. We pay for it when we have to buy security products and services to reduce those other two losses. We pay for security, year after year.

The problem is that all the money we spend isn't fixing the problem. We're paying, but we still end up with insecurities.

The problem is insecure software. It's bad design, poorly implemented features, inadequate testing and security vulnerabilities from software bugs. The money we spend on security is to deal with the effects of insecure software.

And that's the problem. We're not paying to improve the security of the underlying software. We're paying to deal with the problem rather than to fix it.

The only way to fix this problem is for vendors to fix their software, and they won't do it until it's in their financial best interests to do so.

Today, the costs of insecure software aren't borne by the vendors that produce the software. In economics, this is known as an externality, the cost of a decision that's borne by people other than those making the decision.

There are no real consequences to the vendors for having bad security or low-quality software. Even worse, the marketplace often rewards low quality.

More precisely, it rewards additional features and timely release dates, even if they come at the expense of quality.

If we expect software vendors to reduce features, lengthen development cycles and invest in secure software development processes, it needs to be in their financial best interests to do so. If we expect corporations to spend significant resources on their own network security—especially the security of their customers—it also needs to be in their financial best interests.

Liability law is a way to make it in those organizations' best interests. Raising the risk of liability raises the costs of doing it wrong and therefore increases the amount of money a CEO is willing to spend to do it right. Security is risk management; liability fiddles with the risk equation.

Basically, we have to tweak the risk equation so the CEO cares about actually fixing the problem, and putting pressure on his balance sheet is the best way to do that.

Clearly, this isn't all or nothing. There are many parties involved in a typical software attack. There's the company that sold the software with the vulnerability in the first place. There's the person who wrote the attack tool. There's the attacker himself, who used the tool to break into a network.

There's the owner of the network, who was entrusted with defending that network. One hundred percent of the liability shouldn't fall on the shoulders of the software vendor, just as 100% shouldn't fall on the attacker or the network owner. But today, 100% of the cost falls directly on the network owner, and that just has to stop.

We will always pay for security. If software vendors have liability costs, they'll pass those on to us. It might not be cheaper than what we're paying today. But as long as we're going to pay, we might as well pay to fix the problem. Forcing the software vendor to pay to fix the problem and then pass those costs on to us means that the problem might actually get fixed.

Liability changes everything. Currently, there is no reason for a software company not to offer feature after feature after feature. Liability forces software companies to think twice before changing something. Liability forces companies to protect the data they're entrusted with. Liability means that those in the best position to fix the problem are actually responsible for the problem.

Information security isn't a technological problem. It's an economics problem. And the way to improve information technology is to fix the economics problem. Do that, and everything else will follow.

Security ROI: Fact or Fiction?

Originally published in CSO Magazine, *September 2, 2008*

Return on investment, or ROI, is a big deal in business. Any business venture needs to demonstrate a positive return on investment, and a good one at that, in order to be viable.

It's become a big deal in IT security, too. Many corporate customers are demanding ROI models to demonstrate that a particular security investment pays off. And in response, vendors are providing ROI models that demonstrate how their particular security solution provides the best return on investment.

It's a good idea in theory, but it's mostly bunk in practice.

Before I get into the details, there's one point I have to make. "ROI" as used in a security context is inaccurate. Security is not an investment that provides a return, like a new factory or a financial instrument. It's an expense that, hopefully, pays for itself in cost savings. Security is about loss prevention, not about earnings. The term just doesn't make sense in this context.

But as anyone who has lived through a company's vicious end-of-year budget-slashing exercises knows, when you're trying to make your numbers, cutting costs is the same as increasing revenues. So while security can't produce ROI, loss prevention most certainly affects a company's bottom line.

And a company should implement only security countermeasures that affect its bottom line positively. It shouldn't spend more on a security problem than the problem is worth. Conversely, it shouldn't ignore problems that are costing it money when there are cheaper mitigation alternatives. A smart company needs to approach security as it would any other business decision: costs versus benefits.

The classic methodology is called annualized loss expectancy (ALE), and it's straightforward. Calculate the cost of a security incident in both tangibles like time and money, and intangibles like reputation and competitive advantage. Multiply that by the chance the incident will occur in a year. That tells you how much you should spend to mitigate the risk. So, for example, if your store has a 10 percent chance of getting robbed and the cost of being robbed is $10,000, then you should spend $1,000 a year on security. Spend more than that, and you're wasting money. Spend less than that, and you're also wasting money.

Of course, that $1,000 has to reduce the chance of being robbed to zero in order to be cost-effective. If a security measure cuts the chance of robbery by 40 percent—to 6 percent a year—then you should spend no more than

$400 on it. If another security measure reduces it by 80 percent, it's worth $800. And if two security measures both reduce the chance of being robbed by 50 percent and one costs $300 and the other $700, the first one is worth it and the second isn't.

The Data Imperative

The key to making this work is good data; the term of art is "actuarial tail." If you're doing an ALE analysis of a security camera at a convenience store, you need to know the crime rate in the store's neighborhood and maybe have some idea of how much cameras improve the odds of convincing criminals to rob another store instead. You need to know how much a robbery costs: in merchandise, in time and annoyance, in lost sales due to spooked patrons, in employee morale. You need to know how much not having the cameras costs in terms of employee morale; maybe you're having trouble hiring salespeople to work the night shift. With all that data, you can figure out if the cost of the camera is cheaper than the loss of revenue if you close the store at night— assuming that the closed store won't get robbed as well. And then you can decide whether to install one.

Cybersecurity is considerably harder, because there just isn't enough good data. There aren't good crime rates for cyberspace, and we have a lot less data about how individual security countermeasures—or specific configurations of countermeasures—mitigate those risks. We don't even have data on incident costs.

One problem is that the threat moves too quickly. The characteristics of the things we're trying to prevent change so quickly that we can't accumulate data fast enough. By the time we get some data, there's a new threat model for which we don't have enough data. So we can't create ALE models.

But there's another problem, and it's that the math quickly falls apart when it comes to rare and expensive events. Imagine you calculate the cost—reputational costs, loss of customers, etc.—of having your company's name in the newspaper after an embarrassing cybersecurity event to be $20 million. Also assume that the odds are 1 in 10,000 of that happening in any one year. ALE says you should spend no more than $2,000 mitigating that risk.

So far, so good. But maybe your CFO thinks an incident would cost only $10 million. You can't argue, since we're just estimating. But he just cut your security budget in half. A vendor trying to sell you a product finds a Web analysis claiming that the odds of this happening are actually 1 in 1,000.

Accept this new number, and suddenly a product costing 10 times as much is still a good investment.

It gets worse when you deal with even more rare and expensive events. Imagine you're in charge of terrorism mitigation at a chlorine plant. What's the cost to your company, in money and reputation, of a large and very deadly explosion? $100 million? $1 billion? $10 billion? And the odds: 1 in a hundred thousand, 1 in a million, 1 in 10 million? Depending on how you answer those two questions—and any answer is really just a guess—you can justify spending anywhere from $10 to $100,000 annually to mitigate that risk.

Or take another example: airport security. Assume that all the new airport security measures increase the waiting time at airports by—and I'm making this up—30 minutes per passenger. There were 760 million passenger boardings in the United States in 2007. This means that the extra waiting time at airports has cost us a collective 43,000 years of extra waiting time. Assume a 70-year life expectancy, and the increased waiting time has "killed" 620 people per year—930 if you calculate the numbers based on 16 hours of awake time per day. So the question is: If we did away with increased airport security, would the result be more people dead from terrorism or fewer?

Caveat Emptor

This kind of thing is why most ROI models you get from security vendors are nonsense. Of course their model demonstrates that their product or service makes financial sense: They've jiggered the numbers so that they do.

This doesn't mean that ALE is useless, but it does mean you should 1) mistrust any analyses that come from people with an agenda and 2) use any results as a general guideline only. So when you get an ROI model from your vendor, take its framework and plug in your own numbers. Don't even show the vendor your improvements; it won't consider any changes that make its product or service less cost-effective to be an "improvement." And use those results as a general guide, along with risk management and compliance analyses, when you're deciding what security products and services to buy.

Social Networking Risks

Originally published in Information Security, *February 2009*

This essay appeared as the first half of a point-counterpoint with Marcus Ranum.

Are employees blogging corporate secrets? It's not an unreasonable fear, actually. People have always talked about work to their friends. It's human nature for people to talk about what's going on in their lives, and work is a lot of most people's lives. Historically, organizations generally didn't care very much. The conversations were intimate and ephemeral, so the risk was small. Unless you worked for the military with actual national secrets, no one worried about it very much.

What has changed is the nature of how we interact with our friends. We talk about our lives on our blogs, on social networking sites such as Facebook and Twitter, and on message boards pertaining to the work we're doing. What was once intimate and ephemeral is now available to the whole world, indexed by Google, and archived for posterity. A good open-source intelligence gatherer can learn a lot about what a company is doing by monitoring its employees' online activities. It's no wonder some organizations are nervous.

So yes, organizations should be concerned about employees leaking corporate secrets on social networking sites. And, as much as I hate to admit it, disciplinary action against employees who reveal too much in public is probably in order. But actually policing employees is almost certainly more expensive and more trouble than it's worth. And when an organization catches an employee being a bit too chatty about work details, it should be as forgiving as possible.

That's because this sort of openness is the future of work, and the organizations that get used to it or—even better—embrace it, are going to do better in the long run than organizations that futilely try to fight it.

The Internet is the greatest generation gap since rock and roll, and what we're seeing here is one particular skirmish across that gap. The younger generation, used to spending a lot of its life in public, clashes with an older generation in charge of a corporate culture that presumes a greater degree of discretion and greater level of control.

There are two things that are always true about generation gaps. The first is that the elder generation is always right about the problems that will result from whatever new/different/bad thing the younger generation is doing. And the second is that the younger generation is always right that whatever they're doing will become the new normal. These things have to be true; the older generation understands the problems better, but they're the ones who fade away and die.

Living an increasingly public life on social networking sites is the new normal. More corporate—and government—transparency is becoming the new normal. CEOs who blog aren't yet the new normal, but will be eventually. And then what will corporate secrecy look like? Organizations will still have secrets, of course, but they will be more public and more open about what they're doing and what they're thinking of doing. It'll be different than it is now, but it most likely won't be any worse.

Today isn't that day yet, which is why it's still proper for organizations to worry about loose fingers uploading corporate secrets. But the sooner an organization can adapt to this new normal and figure out how to be successful within it, the better it will survive these transitions. In the near term, it will be more likely to attract the next-generation talent it needs to figure out how to thrive. In the long term. . .well, we don't know what it will mean yet.

Same with blocking those sites; yes, they're enormous time-wasters. But if an organization has a problem with employee productivity, they're not going to solve it by censoring Internet access. Focus on the actual problem, and don't waste time on the particulars of how the problem manifests itself.

Do You Know Where Your Data Are?

Originally published in the Wall Street Journal, *April 28, 2009*

Do you know what your data did last night? Almost none of the more than 27 million people who took the RealAge quiz realized that their personal health data was being used by drug companies to develop targeted e-mail marketing campaigns.

There's a basic consumer protection principle at work here, and it's the concept of "unfair and deceptive" trade practices. Basically, a company shouldn't be able to say one thing and do another: sell used goods as new, lie on ingredients lists, advertise prices that aren't generally available, claim features that don't exist, and so on.

Buried in RealAge's 2,400-word privacy policy is this disclosure: "If you elect to say yes to becoming a free RealAge Member, we will periodically send you free newsletters and e-mails that directly promote the use of our site(s) or the purchase of our products or services and may contain, in whole or in part, advertisements for third parties which relate to marketed products of selected RealAge partners."

They maintain that when you join the website, you consent to receiving pharmaceutical company spam. But since that isn't spelled out, it's not really informed consent. That's deceptive.

Cloud computing is another technology where users entrust their data to service providers. Salesforce.com, Gmail, and Google Docs are examples; your data isn't on your computer—it's out in the "cloud" somewhere—and you access it from your web browser. Cloud computing has significant benefits for customers and huge profit potential for providers. It's one of the fastest growing IT market segments—69% of Americans now use some sort of cloud computing services—but the business is rife with shady, if not outright deceptive, advertising.

Take Google, for example. Last month, the Electronic Privacy Information Center (I'm on its board of directors) filed a complaint with the Federal Trade Commission concerning Google's cloud computing services. On its website, Google repeatedly assures customers that their data is secure and private, while published vulnerabilities demonstrate that it is not. Google's not foolish, though; its Terms of Service explicitly disavow any warranty or any liability for harm that might result from Google's negligence, recklessness, malevolent intent, or even purposeful disregard of existing legal obligations to protect the privacy and security of user data. EPIC claims that's deceptive.

Facebook isn't much better. Its plainly written (and not legally binding) Statement of Principles contains an admirable set of goals, but its denser and more legalistic Statement of Rights and Responsibilities undermines a lot of it. One research group who studies these documents called it "democracy theater": Facebook wants the appearance of involving users in governance, without the messiness of actually having to do so. Deceptive.

These issues are not identical. RealAge is hiding what it does with your data. Google is trying to both assure you that your data is safe and duck any responsibility when it's not. Facebook wants to market a democracy but run a dictatorship. But they all involve trying to deceive the customer.

Cloud computing services like Google Docs, and social networking sites like RealAge and Facebook, bring with them significant privacy and security risks over and above traditional computing models. Unlike data on my own computer, which I can protect to whatever level I believe prudent, I have no control over any of these sites, nor any real knowledge of how these companies protect my privacy and security. I have to trust them.

This may be fine—the advantages might very well outweigh the risks—but users often can't weigh the trade-offs because these companies are going out of their way to hide the risks.

Of course, companies don't want people to make informed decisions about where to leave their personal data. RealAge wouldn't get 27 million members if its webpage clearly stated "you are signing up to receive e-mails containing advertising from pharmaceutical companies," and Google Docs wouldn't get five million users if its webpage said "We'll take some steps to protect your privacy, but you can't blame us if something goes wrong."

And of course, trust isn't black and white. If, for example, Amazon tried to use customer credit card info to buy itself office supplies, we'd all agree that that was wrong. If it used customer names to solicit new business from their friends, most of us would consider this wrong. When it uses buying history to try to sell customers new books, many of us appreciate the targeted marketing. Similarly, no one expects Google's security to be perfect. But if it didn't fix known vulnerabilities, most of us would consider that a problem.

This is why understanding is so important. For markets to work, consumers need to be able to make informed buying decisions. They need to understand both the costs and benefits of the products and services they buy. Allowing sellers to manipulate the market by outright lying, or even by hiding vital information, about their products breaks capitalism—and that's why the government has to step in to ensure markets work smoothly.

Last month, Mary K. Engle, Acting Deputy Director of the FTC's Bureau of Consumer Protection said: "a company's marketing materials must be consistent with the nature of the product being offered. It's not enough to disclose the information only in a fine print of a lengthy online user agreement." She was speaking about Digital Rights Management and, specifically, an incident where Sony used a music copy protection scheme without disclosing that it secretly installed software on customers' computers. DRM is different from cloud computing or even online surveys and quizzes, but the principle is the same.

Engle again: "if your advertising giveth and your EULA [license agreement] taketh away don't be surprised if the FTC comes calling." That's the right response from government.

Be Careful When You Come to Put Your Trust in the Clouds

Originally published in the Guardian, *June 4, 2009*

This year's overhyped IT concept is cloud computing. Also called software as a service (Saas), cloud computing is when you run software over the Internet and access it via a browser. The salesforce.com customer management software is an example of this. So is Google Docs. If you believe the hype, cloud computing is the future.

But, hype aside, cloud computing is nothing new. It's the modern version of the timesharing model from the 1960s, which was eventually killed by the rise of the personal computer. It's what Hotmail and Gmail have been doing all these years, and it's social networking sites, remote backup companies, and remote email filtering companies such as MessageLabs. Any IT outsourcing—network infrastructure, security monitoring, remote hosting—is a form of cloud computing.

The old timesharing model arose because computers were expensive and hard to maintain. Modern computers and networks are drastically cheaper, but they're still hard to maintain. As networks have become faster, it is again easier to have someone else do the hard work. Computing has become more of a utility; users are more concerned with results than technical details, so the tech fades into the background.

But what about security? Isn't it more dangerous to have your email on Hotmail's servers, your spreadsheets on Google's, your personal conversations on Facebook's, and your company's sales prospects on salesforce.com's? Well, yes and no.

IT security is about trust. You have to trust your CPU manufacturer, your hardware, operating system and software vendors—and your ISP. Any one of these can undermine your security: crash your systems, corrupt data, allow an attacker to get access to systems. We've spent decades dealing with worms and rootkits that target software vulnerabilities. We've worried about infected chips. But in the end, we have no choice but to blindly trust the security of the IT providers we use.

Saas moves the trust boundary out one step further—you now have to also trust your software service vendors—but it doesn't fundamentally change anything. It's just another vendor we need to trust.

There is one critical difference. When a computer is within your network, you can protect it with other security systems such as firewalls and IDSs. You can build a resilient system that works even if those vendors you have to trust may not be as trustworthy as you like. With any outsourcing model, whether it be cloud computing or something else, you can't. You have to trust your outsourcer completely. You not only have to trust the outsourcer's security, but its reliability, its availability, and its business continuity.

You don't want your critical data to be on some cloud computer that abruptly disappears because its owner goes bankrupt. You don't want the company you're using to be sold to your direct competitor. You don't want the company to cut corners, without warning, because times are tight. Or raise its prices and then refuse to let you have your data back. These things can happen with software vendors, but the results aren't as drastic.

There are two different types of cloud computing customers. The first only pays a nominal fee for these services—and uses them for free in exchange for ads: e.g., Gmail and Facebook. These customers have no leverage with their outsourcers. You can lose everything. Companies like Google and Amazon won't spend a lot of time caring. The second type of customer pays considerably for these services: to salesforce.com, MessageLabs, managed network companies, and so on. These customers have more leverage, providing they write their service contracts correctly. Still, nothing is guaranteed.

Trust is a concept as old as humanity, and the solutions are the same as they have always been. Be careful who you trust, be careful what you trust them with, and be careful how much you trust them. Outsourcing is the future of computing. Eventually we'll get this right, but you don't want to be a casualty along the way.

Is Perfect Access Control Possible?

Originally published in Information Security, *September 2009*

This essay appeared as the second half of a point/counterpoint with Marcus Ranum.
Access control is difficult in an organizational setting. On one hand, every employee needs enough access to do his job. On the other hand, every time you give an employee more access, there's more risk: he could abuse that access, or lose information he has access to, or be socially engineered into giving that access to a malfeasant. So a smart, risk-conscious organization will give each employee the exact level of access he needs to do his job, and no more.

Over the years, there's been a lot of work put into role-based access control. But despite the large number of academic papers and high-profile security products, most organizations don't implement it—at all—with the predictable security problems as a result.

Regularly we read stories of employees abusing their database access-control privileges for personal reasons: medical records, tax records, passport records, police records. NSA eavesdroppers spy on their wives and girlfriends. Departing employees take corporate secrets.

A spectacular access control failure occurred in the UK in 2007. An employee of Her Majesty's Revenue & Customs had to send a couple of thousand sample records from a database on all children in the country to National Audit Office. But it was easier for him to copy the entire database of 25 million people onto a couple of disks and put it in the mail than it was to select out just the records needed. Unfortunately, the discs got lost in the mail, and the story was a huge embarrassment for the government.

Eric Johnson at Dartmouth's Tuck School of Business has been studying the problem, and his results won't startle anyone who has thought about it at all. RBAC is very hard to implement correctly. Organizations generally don't even know who has what role. The employee doesn't know, the boss doesn't know—and these days the employee might have more than one boss—and senior management certainly doesn't know. There's a reason RBAC came out of the military; in that world, command structures are simple and well-defined.

Even worse, employees' roles change all the time—Johnson chronicled one business group of 3,000 people that made 1,000 role changes in just three months—and it's often not obvious what information an employee needs until he actually needs it. And information simply isn't that granular. Just as it's much easier to give someone access to an entire file cabinet than to only the particular files he needs, it's much easier to give someone access to an entire database than only the particular records he needs.

This means that organizations either over-entitle or under-entitle employees. But since getting the job done is more important than anything else, organizations tend to over-entitle. Johnson estimates that 50 percent to 90 percent of employees are over-entitled in large organizations. In the uncommon instance where an employee needs access to something he normally doesn't have, there's generally some process for him to get it. And access is almost never revoked once it's been granted. In large formal organizations, Johnson was able to predict how long an employee had worked there based on how much access he had.

Clearly, organizations can do better. Johnson's current work involves building access-control systems with easy self-escalation, audit to make sure that power isn't abused, violation penalties (Intel, for example, issues "speeding tickets" to violators), and compliance rewards. His goal is to implement incentives and controls that manage access without making people too risk-averse.

In the end, a perfect access control system just isn't possible; organizations are simply too chaotic for it to work. And any good system will allow a certain number of access control violations, if they're made in good faith by people just trying to do their jobs. The "speeding ticket" analogy is better than it looks: we post limits of 55 miles per hour, but generally don't start ticketing people unless they're going over 70.

News Media Strategies for Survival for Journalists

Originally published in Twin Cities Daily Planet, *November 14, 2009*

Those of us living through the Internet-caused revolution in journalism can't see what's going to come out the other side: how readers will interact with journalism, what the sources of journalism will be, how journalists will make money. All we do know is that mass-market journalism is hurting, badly, and may not survive. And that we have no idea how to thrive in this new world of digital media.

I have five pieces of advice to those trying to survive and wanting to thrive: based both on experiences as a successful Internet pundit and blogger, and my observations of others, successful and unsuccessful. I'll talk about writing, but everything I say applies to audio and video as well.

One, be interesting. Yes, that's obvious. But the scale is different now. It used to be you could be interesting in aggregate; a few interesting articles or features could carry an entire publication. Now every single piece of writing has to be interesting; otherwise, it won't get read, passed around, or linked to. Have something to say. Pick a niche you can become known for.

Two, be entertaining. Interesting isn't enough; you have to entertain people as well. Internet readers live in a world where millions of things are constantly vying for their attention. Only the best individual pieces of content thrive in this environment. Often, "best" means "most entertaining." Opinions are dime a dozen on the Internet; you need to make sure yours are worth your readers' time.

Three, be engaging. Readers want to be engaged. They want to be part of a community. They want to engage, with each other as well as with you, on their own terms. Engagement might involve comment or discussion areas, or ways people can follow your work. Anything that limits engagement inhibits community. What this means depends on context; sometimes you have to allow community to develop naturally, even if it's in ways you don't like. Sometimes you need to censor off-topic comments to prevent hateful or annoying commenters from driving others away. In general, though, you should allow anonymous comments. You should make your interface as easy as possible to use. You should reply to your readers. And you shouldn't treat your readers solely as marketing opportunities. The more your writing fosters engagement, the more popular it will be.

Four, be available. Readers need to be able to interact with your writing on their own terms. This means you can't make it difficult for them to find and link to your content. Make sure your content is accessible by any and every Internet device out there. Never take your old writing off the Internet. Never change your URLs. Never make it hard for them to find or link to a URL . Never put your writing behind a paywall. You're part of an ecosystem now; fail to play by the rules and you quickly become isolated.

Five, be agile. The Internet changes all the time; what's true today might not be true in two years. Don't lock yourself in to a particular look, or a particular web technology. Simple interfaces are better than flashy complicated ones; I don't care what your ad agency tells you. Agility applies to making money, too. We have no idea what financial models will thrive in the future, but it seems likely that it will be a portfolio of different things. You'll be more likely to write for different publications. You'll be more likely to figure out cross subsidies, so that some things pay for the others. I have a free blog and a free monthly newsletter, and charge for books, speaking engagements, and consulting. Your mix will be different. If you're lucky, everything you do will augment everything else.

Revolutions are scary times. The old crumbles around us, and we have no idea what—if anything—will be built on its ruins. Remember, though, that human nature doesn't change. People will always gravitate to the interesting, entertaining, engaging, and available, and the agile will be the first on the scene.

Security and Function Creep

Originally published in IEEE Security & Privacy, *January/ February 2010*

Security is rarely static. Technology changes the capabilities of both security systems and attackers. But there's something else that changes security's cost/ benefit trade-off: how the underlying systems being secured are used. Far too often we build security for one purpose, only to find it being used for another purpose—one it wasn't suited for in the first place. And then the security system has to play catch-up.

Take driver's licenses, for example. Originally designed to demonstrate a credential—the ability to drive a car—they looked like other credentials: medical licenses or elevator certificates of inspection. They were wallet-sized, of course, but they didn't have much security associated with them. Then, slowly, driver's licenses took on a second application: they became age-verification tokens in bars and liquor stores. Of course the security wasn't up to the task—teenagers can be extraordinarily resourceful if they set their minds to it—and over the decades driver's licenses got photographs, tamper-resistant features (once, it was easy to modify the birth year), and technologies that made counterfeiting harder. There was little value in counterfeiting a driver's license, but a lot of value in counterfeiting an age-verification token.

Today, US driver's licenses are taking on yet another function: security against terrorists. The Real ID Act—the government's attempt to make driver's licenses even more secure—has nothing to do with driving or even with buying alcohol, and everything to do with trying to make that piece of plastic an effective way to verify that someone is not on the terrorist watch list. Whether this is a good idea, or actually improves security, is another matter entirely.

You can see this kind of function creep everywhere. Internet security systems designed for informational Web sites are suddenly expected to provide security for banking Web sites. Security systems that are good enough to protect cheap commodities from being stolen are suddenly ineffective once the price of those commodities rises high enough. Application security systems, designed for locally owned networks, are expected to work even when the application is moved to a cloud computing environment. And cloud computing security, designed for the needs of corporations, is expected to be suitable for government applications as well—maybe even military applications.

Sometimes it's obvious that security systems designed for one environment won't work in another. We don't arm our soldiers the same way we arm our policemen, and we can't take commercial vehicles and easily turn them into ones outfitted for the military. We understand that we might need to upgrade our home security system if we suddenly come into possession of a bag of diamonds. Yet many think the same security that protects our home computers will also protect voting machines, and the same operating systems that run our businesses are suitable for military uses.

But these are all conscious decisions, and we security professionals often know better. The real problems arise when the changes happen in the background, without any conscious thought. We build a network security system that's perfectly adequate for the threat and—like a driver's license becoming an age-verification token—the network accrues more and more functions. But because it has already been pronounced "secure," we can't get any budget to re-evaluate and improve the security until after the bad guys have figured out the vulnerabilities and exploited them.

I don't like having to play catch-up in security, but we seem doomed to keep doing so.

Weighing the Risk of Hiring Hackers

Originally published in Information Security, *June 2010*

This essay previously appeared as the first half of a point-counterpoint with Marcus Ranum.

Any essay on hiring hackers quickly gets bogged down in definitions. What is a hacker, and how is he different from a cracker? I have my own definitions, but I'd rather define the issue more specifically: Would you hire someone convicted of a computer crime to fill a position of trust in your computer network? Or, more generally, would you hire someone convicted of a crime for a job related to that crime?

The answer, of course, is "it depends." It depends on the specifics of the crime. It depends on the ethics involved. It depends on the recidivism rate of the type of criminal. It depends a whole lot on the individual.

Would you hire a convicted pedophile to work at a day care center? Would you hire Bernie Madoff to manage your investment fund? The answer is almost certainly no to those two—but you might hire a convicted bank robber to consult on bank security. You might hire someone who was convicted of false advertising to write ad copy for your next marketing campaign. And you might hire someone who ran a chop shop to fix your car. It depends on the person and the crime.

It can get even murkier. Would you hire a CIA-trained assassin to be a bodyguard? Would you put a general who led a successful attack in charge of defense? What if they were both convicted of crimes in whatever country they were operating in? There are different legal and ethical issues, to be sure, but in both cases the people learned a certain set of skills regarding offense that could be transferable to defense.

Which brings us back to computers. Hacking is primarily a mindset: a way of thinking about security. Its primary focus is in attacking systems, but it's invaluable to the defense of those systems as well. Because computer systems are so complex, defending them often requires people who can think like attackers.

Admittedly, there's a difference between thinking like an attacker and acting like a criminal, and between researching vulnerabilities in fielded systems and exploiting those vulnerabilities for personal gain. But there is a huge variability in computer crime convictions, and—at least in the early days—many hacking convictions were unjust and unfair. And there's also a difference between someone's behavior as a teenager and his behavior later in life. Additionally, there might very well be a difference between someone's behavior before and after a hacking conviction. It all depends on the person.

An employer's goal should be to hire moral and ethical people with the skill set required to do the job. And while a hacking conviction is certainly a mark against a person, it isn't always grounds for complete non-consideration.

"We don't hire hackers" and "we don't hire felons" are coarse generalizations, in the same way that "we only hire people with this or that security certification" is. They work—you're less likely to hire the wrong person if you follow them—but they're both coarse and flawed. Just as all potential employees with certifications aren't automatically good hires, all potential employees with hacking convictions aren't automatically bad hires. Sure, it's easier to hire people based on things you can learn from checkboxes, but you won't get the best employees that way. It's far better to look at the individual, and put those check boxes into context. But we don't always have time to do that.

Last winter, a Minneapolis attorney who works to get felons a fair shake after they served their time told of a sign he saw: "Snow shovelers wanted. Felons need not apply." It's not good for society if felons who have served their time can't even get jobs shoveling snow.

Should Enterprises Give In to IT Consumerization at the Expense of Security?

Originally published in Information Security, *September 2010*

This essay appeared as the second half of a point/counterpoint with Marcus Ranum.

If you're a typical wired American, you've got a bunch of tech tools you like and a bunch more you covet. You have a cell phone that can easily text. You've got a laptop configured just the way you want it. Maybe you have a Kindle for reading, or an iPad. And when the next new thing comes along, some of you will line up on the first day it's available.

So why can't work keep up? Why are you forced to use an unfamiliar, and sometimes outdated, operating system? Why do you need a second laptop, maybe an older and clunkier one? Why do you need a second cell phone with a new interface, or a BlackBerry, when your phone already does e-mail? Or a second BlackBerry tied to corporate e-mail? Why can't you use the cool stuff you already have?

More and more companies are letting you. They're giving you an allowance and allowing you to buy whatever laptop you want, and to connect into the corporate network with whatever device you choose. They're allowing you to use whatever cell phone you have, whatever portable e-mail device you have, whatever you personally need to get your job done. And the security office is freaking.

You can't blame them, really. Security is hard enough when you have control of the hardware, operating system and software. Lose control of any of those things, and the difficulty goes through the roof. How do you ensure that the employee devices are secure, and have up-to-date security patches? How do you control what goes on them? How do you deal with the tech support issues when they fail? How do you even begin to manage this logistical nightmare? Better to dig your heels in and say "no."

But security is on the losing end of this argument, and the sooner it realizes that, the better.

The meta-trend here is consumerization: cool technologies show up for the consumer market before they're available to the business market. Every corporation is under pressure from its employees to allow them to use these new technologies at work, and that pressure is only getting stronger. Younger employees simply aren't going to stand for using last year's stuff, and they're not going to carry around a second laptop. They're either going to figure out ways around the corporate security rules, or they're going to take another job with a more trendy company. Either way, senior management is going to tell security to get out of the way. It might even be the CEO, who wants to get to the company's databases from his brand new iPad, driving the change. Either way, it's going to be harder and harder to say no.

At the same time, cloud computing makes this easier. More and more, employee computing devices are nothing more than dumb terminals with a browser interface. When corporate e-mail is all webmail, corporate documents are all on GoogleDocs, and when all the specialized applications have a web interface, it's easier to allow employees to use any up-to-date browser. It's what companies are already doing with their partners, suppliers, and customers.

Also on the plus side, technology companies have woken up to this trend and—from Microsoft and Cisco on down to the startups—are trying to offer security solutions. Like everything else, it's a mixed bag: some of them will work and some of them won't, most of them will need careful configuration to work well, and few of them will get it right. The result is that we'll muddle through, as usual.

Security is always a tradeoff, and security decisions are often made for non-security reasons. In this case, the right decision is to sacrifice security for convenience and flexibility. Corporations want their employees to be able to work from anywhere, and they're going to have loosened control over the tools they allow in order to get it.

The Vulnerabilities Market and the Future of Security

Originally published in Forbes, *May 30, 2012*

Recently, there have been several articles about the new market in zero-day exploits: new and unpatched computer vulnerabilities. It's not just software companies, who sometimes pay bounties to researchers who alert them of security vulnerabilities so they can fix them. And it's not only criminal organizations that pay for vulnerabilities they can exploit. Now there are governments, and companies who sell to governments, who buy vulnerabilities with the intent of keeping them secret so they can exploit them.

This market is larger than most people realize, and it's becoming even larger. Forbes recently published a price list for zero-day exploits, along with the story of a hacker who received $250K from "a US government contractor." (At first I didn't believe the story or the price list, but I have been convinced that they both are true.) Forbes published a profile of a company called Vupen, whose business is selling zero-day exploits. Other companies doing this range from startups like Netragard and Endgame to large defense contractors like Northrop Grumman, General Dynamics, and Raytheon.

This is very different than in 2007, when researcher Charlie Miller wrote about his attempts to sell zero-day exploits; and a 2010 survey implied that there wasn't much money in selling zero days. The market has matured substantially in the past few years.

This new market perturbs the economics of finding security vulnerabilities. And it does so to the detriment of us all.

I've long argued that the process of finding vulnerabilities in software systems increases overall security. This is because the economics of vulnerability hunting favored disclosure. As long as the principal gain from finding a vulnerability was notoriety, publicly disclosing vulnerabilities was the only obvious path. In fact, it took years for our industry to move from a norm of full-disclosure—announcing the vulnerability publicly and damn the consequences—to something called "responsible disclosure": giving the software vendor a head start in fixing the vulnerability. Changing economics is what made the change stick: instead of just hacker notoriety, a successful vulnerability finder could land some lucrative consulting gigs, and being a responsible security researcher helped. But regardless of the motivations, a disclosed vulnerability is one that—at least in most cases—is patched. And a patched vulnerability makes us all more secure.

This is why the new market for vulnerabilities is so dangerous; it results in vulnerabilities remaining secret and unpatched. That it's even more lucrative than the public vulnerabilities market means that more hackers will choose this path. And unlike the previous reward of notoriety and consulting gigs, it gives software programmers within a company the incentive to deliberately create vulnerabilities in the products they're working on—and then secretly sell them to some government agency.

No commercial vendors perform the level of code review that would be necessary to detect, and prove mal-intent for, this kind of sabotage.

Even more importantly, the new market for security vulnerabilities results in a variety of government agencies around the world that have a strong interest in those vulnerabilities remaining unpatched. These range from law-enforcement agencies like the FBI and the German police who are trying to build targeted Internet surveillance tools, to intelligence agencies like the NSA who are trying to build mass Internet surveillance tools, to military organizations who are trying to build cyber-weapons.

All of these agencies have long had to wrestle with the choice of whether to use newly discovered vulnerabilities to protect or to attack. Inside the NSA, this was traditionally known as the "equities issue," and the debate was between the COMSEC (communications security) side of the NSA and the SIGINT (signals intelligence) side. If they found a flaw in a popular cryptographic algorithm, they could either use that knowledge to fix the algorithm and make everyone's communications more secure, or they could exploit the flaw to eavesdrop on others—while at the same time allowing even the people they wanted to protect to remain vulnerable. This debate raged through the decades inside the NSA. From what I've heard, by 2000, the COMSEC side had largely won, but things flipped completely around after 9/11.

The whole point of disclosing security vulnerabilities is to put pressure on vendors to release more secure software. It's not just that they patch the vulnerabilities that are made public—the fear of bad press makes them implement more secure software development processes. It's another economic process; the cost of designing software securely in the first place is less than the cost of the bad press after a vulnerability is announced plus the cost of writing and deploying the patch. I'd be the first to admit that this isn't perfect—there's a lot of very poorly written software still out there—but it's the best incentive we have.

We've always expected the NSA, and those like them, to keep the vulnerabilities they discover secret. We have been counting on the public community to find and publicize vulnerabilities, forcing vendors to fix them. With the rise of these new pressures to keep zero-day exploits secret, and to sell them for exploitation, there will be even less incentive on software vendors to ensure the security of their products.

As the incentive for hackers to keep their vulnerabilities secret grows, the incentive for vendors to build secure software shrinks. As a recent EFF essay put it, this is "security for the 1%." And it makes the rest of us less safe.

So You Want to Be a Security Expert

Originally published in Krebs on Security, *July 12, 2012*

This essay originally appeared as part of a series of advice columns on how to break into the field of security.

I regularly receive e-mail from people who want advice on how to learn more about computer security, either as a course of study in college or as an IT person considering it as a career choice.

First, know that there are many subspecialties in computer security. You can be an expert in keeping systems from being hacked, or in creating unhackable software. You can be an expert in finding security problems in software, or in networks. You can be an expert in viruses, or policies, or cryptography. There are many, many opportunities for many different skill sets. You don't have to be a coder to be a security expert.

In general, though, I have three pieces of advice to anyone who wants to learn computer security.

Study. Studying can take many forms. It can be classwork, either at universities or at training conferences like SANS and Offensive Security. (These are good self-starter resources.) It can be reading; there are a lot of excellent books out there—and blogs—that teach different aspects of computer security out there. Don't limit yourself to computer science, either. You can learn a lot by studying other areas of security, and soft sciences like economics, psychology, and sociology.

Do. Computer security is fundamentally a practitioner's art, and that requires practice. This means using what you've learned to configure security systems, design new security systems, and—yes—break existing security systems. This is why many courses have strong hands-on components; you won't learn much without it.

Show. It doesn't matter what you know or what you can do if you can't demonstrate it to someone who might want to hire you. This doesn't just mean sounding good in an interview. It means sounding good on mailing lists and in blog comments. You can show your expertise by making podcasts and writing your own blog. You can teach seminars at your local user group meetings. You can write papers for conferences, or books.

I am a fan of security certifications, which can often demonstrate all of these things to a potential employer quickly and easily.

I've really said nothing here that isn't also true for a gazillion other areas of study, but security also requires a particular mindset—one I consider essential for success in this field. I'm not sure it can be taught, but it certainly can be encouraged. "This kind of thinking is not natural for most people. It's not natural for engineers. Good engineering involves thinking about how things can be made to work; the security mindset involves thinking about how things can be made to fail. It involves thinking like an attacker, an adversary or a criminal. You don't have to exploit the vulnerabilities you find, but if you don't see the world that way, you'll never notice most security problems." This is especially true if you want to design security systems and not just implement them. Remember Schneier's Law: "Any person can invent a security system so clever that she or he can't think of how to break it." The only way your designs are going to be trusted is if you've made a name for yourself breaking other people's designs.

One final word about cryptography. Modern cryptography is particularly hard to learn. In addition to everything above, it requires graduate-level knowledge in mathematics. And, as in computer security in general, your prowess is demonstrated by what you can break. The field has progressed a lot since I wrote this guide and self-study cryptanalysis course a dozen years ago, but they're not bad places to start.

When It Comes to Security, We're Back to Feudalism

Originally published in Wired, *November 26, 2012*

Some of us have pledged our allegiance to Google: We have Gmail accounts, we use Google Calendar and Google Docs, and we have Android phones. Others have pledged allegiance to Apple: We have Macintosh laptops, iPhones, and iPads; and we let iCloud automatically synchronize and back up everything. Still others of us let Microsoft do it all. Or we buy our music and e-books from Amazon, which keeps records of what we own and allows downloading to a Kindle, computer, or phone. Some of us have pretty much abandoned e-mail altogether. . . for Facebook.

These vendors are becoming our feudal lords, and we are becoming their vassals. We might refuse to pledge allegiance to all of them—or to a particular one we don't like. Or we can spread our allegiance around. But either way, it's becoming increasingly difficult to not pledge allegiance to at least one of them.

Feudalism provides security. Classical medieval feudalism depended on overlapping, complex, hierarchical relationships. There were oaths and obligations: a series of rights and privileges. A critical aspect of this system was protection: vassals would pledge their allegiance to a lord, and in return, that lord would protect them from harm.

Of course, I'm romanticizing here; European history was never this simple, and the description is based on stories of that time, but that's the general model.

And it's this model that's starting to permeate computer security today.

I Pledge Allegiance to the United States of Convenience

Traditional computer security centered around users. Users had to purchase and install anti-virus software and firewalls, ensure their operating system and network were configured properly, update their software, and generally manage their own security.

This model is breaking, largely due to two developments:

1. New Internet-enabled devices where the vendor maintains more control over the hardware and software than we do—like the iPhone and Kindle; and
2. Services where the host maintains our data for us—like Flickr and Hotmail.

Now, we users must trust the security of these hardware manufacturers, software vendors, and cloud providers.

We choose to do it because of the convenience, redundancy, automation, and shareability. We like it when we can access our e-mail anywhere, from any computer. We like it when we can restore our contact lists after we've lost our phones. We want our calendar entries to automatically appear on all of our devices. These cloud storage sites do a better job of backing up our photos and files than we would manage by ourselves; Apple does a great job keeping malware out of its iPhone apps store.

In this new world of computing, we give up a certain amount of control, and in exchange we trust that our lords will both treat us well and protect us from harm. Not only will our software be continually updated with the newest and coolest functionality, but we trust it will happen without our being overtaxed by fees and required upgrades. We trust that our data and devices won't be exposed to hackers, criminals, and malware. We trust that governments won't be allowed to illegally spy on us.

Trust is our only option. In this system, we have no control over the security provided by our feudal lords. We don't know what sort of security methods they're using, or how they're configured. We mostly can't install our own security products on iPhones or Android phones; we certainly can't install them on Facebook, Gmail, or Twitter. Sometimes we have control over whether or not to accept the automatically flagged updates—iPhone, for example—but we rarely know what they're about or whether they'll break anything else. (On the Kindle, we don't even have that freedom.)

The Good, the Bad, and the Ugly

I'm not saying that feudal security is all bad. For the average user, giving up control is largely a good thing. These software vendors and cloud providers do a lot better job of security than the average computer user would. Automatic cloud backup saves a lot of data; automatic updates prevent a lot of malware. The network security at any of these providers is better than that of most home users.

Feudalism is good for the individual, for small startups, and for medium-sized businesses that can't afford to hire their own in-house or specialized expertise. Being a vassal has its advantages, after all.

For large organizations, however, it's more of a mixed bag. These organizations are used to trusting other companies with critical corporate functions: They've been outsourcing their payroll, tax preparation, and legal services for decades. But IT regulations often require audits. Our lords don't allow vassals to audit them, even if those vassals are themselves large and powerful.

Yet feudal security isn't without its risks.

Our lords can make mistakes with security, as recently happened with Apple, Facebook, and Photobucket. They can act arbitrarily and capriciously, as Amazon did when it cut off a Kindle user for living in the wrong country. They tether us like serfs; just try to take data from one digital lord to another.

Ultimately, they will always act in their own self-interest, as companies do when they mine our data in order to sell more advertising and make more money. These companies own us, so they can sell us off—again, like serfs—to rival lords. . . or turn us into the authorities.

Historically, early feudal arrangements were ad hoc, and the more powerful party would often simply renege on his part of the bargain. Eventually, the arrangements were formalized and standardized: both parties had rights and privileges (things they could do) as well as protections (things they couldn't do to each other).

Today's Internet feudalism, however, is ad hoc and one-sided. We give companies our data and trust them with our security, but we receive very few assurances of protection in return, and those companies have very few restrictions on what they can do.

This needs to change. There should be limitations on what cloud vendors can do with our data; rights, like the requirement that they delete our data when we want them to; and liabilities when vendors mishandle our data.

Like everything else in security, it's a trade-off. We need to balance that trade-off. In Europe, it was the rise of the centralized state and the rule of law that undermined the ad hoc feudal system; it provided more security and stability for both lords and vassals. But these days, government has largely abdicated its role in cyberspace, and the result is a return to the feudal relationships of yore.

Perhaps instead of hoping that our Internet-era lords will be sufficiently clever and benevolent—or putting our faith in the Robin Hoods who block phone surveillance and circumvent DRM systems—it's time we step in in our role as governments (both national and international) to create the regulatory environments that protect us vassals (and the lords as well). Otherwise, we really are just serfs.

You Have No Control Over Security on the Feudal Internet

Originally published in Harvard Business Review, *June 6, 2013*

Facebook regularly abuses the privacy of its users. Google has stopped supporting its popular RSS feeder. Apple prohibits all iPhone apps that are political or sexual. Microsoft might be cooperating with some governments to spy on Skype calls, but we don't know which ones. Both Twitter and LinkedIn have recently suffered security breaches that affected the data of hundreds of thousands of their users.

If you've started to think of yourself as a hapless peasant in a *Game of Thrones* power struggle, you're more right than you may realize. These are not traditional companies, and we are not traditional customers. These are feudal lords, and we are their vassals, peasants, and serfs.

Power has shifted in IT, in favor of both cloud-service providers and closed-platform vendors. This power shift affects many things, and it profoundly affects security.

Traditionally, computer security was the user's responsibility. Users purchased their own antivirus software and firewalls, and any breaches were blamed on their inattentiveness. It's kind of a crazy business model. Normally we expect the products and services we buy to be safe and secure, but in IT we tolerated lousy products and supported an enormous aftermarket for security.

Now that the IT industry has matured, we expect more security "out of the box." This has become possible largely because of two technology trends: cloud computing and vendor-controlled platforms. The first means that most of our data resides on other networks: Google Docs, Salesforce.com, Facebook, Gmail. The second means that our new Internet devices are both closed and controlled by the vendors, giving us limited configuration control: iPhones, ChromeBooks, Kindles, Blackberries. Meanwhile, our relationship with IT has changed. We used to use our computers to do things. We now use our vendor-controlled computing devices to go places. All of these places are owned by someone.

The new security model is that someone else takes care of it—without telling us any of the details. I have no control over the security of my Gmail or my photos on Flickr. I can't demand greater security for my presentations on Prezi or my task list on Trello, no matter how confidential they are. I can't audit any of these cloud services. I can't delete cookies on my iPad or ensure that files are securely erased. Updates on my Kindle happen automatically, without my knowledge or consent. I have so little visibility into the security of Facebook that I have no idea what operating system they're using.

There are a lot of good reasons why we're all flocking to these cloud services and vendor-controlled platforms. The benefits are enormous, from cost to convenience to reliability to security itself. But it is inherently a feudal relationship. We cede control of our data and computing platforms to these companies and trust that they will treat us well and protect us from harm. And if we pledge complete allegiance to them—if we let them control our email and calendar and address book and photos and everything—we get even more benefits. We become their vassals; or, on a bad day, their serfs.

There are a lot of feudal lords out there. Google and Apple are the obvious ones, but Microsoft is trying to control both user data and the end-user platform as well. Facebook is another lord, controlling much of the socializing we do on the Internet. Other feudal lords are smaller and more specialized— Amazon, Yahoo, Verizon, and so on—but the model is the same.

To be sure, feudal security has its advantages. These companies are much better at security than the average user. Automatic backup has saved a lot of data after hardware failures, user mistakes, and malware infections. Automatic updates have increased security dramatically. This is also true for small organizations; they are more secure than they would be if they tried to do it themselves. For large corporations with dedicated IT security departments, the benefits are less clear. Sure, even large companies outsource critical functions like tax preparation and cleaning services, but large companies have specific requirements for security, data retention, audit, and so on—and that's just not possible with most of these feudal lords.

Feudal security also has its risks. Vendors can, and do, make security mistakes affecting hundreds of thousands of people. Vendors can lock people into relationships, making it hard for them to take their data and leave. Vendors can act arbitrarily, against our interests; Facebook regularly does this when it changes peoples' defaults, implements new features, or modifies its privacy policy. Many vendors give our data to the government without notice, consent, or a warrant; almost all sell it for profit. This isn't surprising, really; companies should be expected to act in their own self-interest and not in their users' best interest.

The feudal relationship is inherently based on power. In Medieval Europe, people would pledge their allegiance to a feudal lord in exchange for that lord's protection. This arrangement changed as the lords realized that they had all the power and could do whatever they wanted. Vassals were used and abused; peasants were tied to their land and became serfs.

It's the Internet lords' popularity and ubiquity that enable them to profit; laws and government relationships make it easier for them to hold onto power. These lords are vying with each other for profits and power. By spending time on their sites and giving them our personal information—whether through search queries, e-mails, status updates, likes, or simply our behavioral characteristics—we are providing the raw material for that struggle. In this way we are like serfs, toiling the land for our feudal lords. If you don't believe me, try to take your data with you when you leave Facebook. And when war breaks out among the giants, we become collateral damage.

So how do we survive? Increasingly, we have little alternative but to trust *someone*, so we need to decide who we trust—and who we don't—and then act accordingly. This isn't easy; our feudal lords go out of their way not to be transparent about their actions, their security, or much of anything. Use whatever power you have—as individuals, none; as large corporations, more—to negotiate with your lords. And, finally, don't be extreme in any way: politically, socially, culturally. Yes, you can be shut down without recourse, but it's usually those on the edges that are affected. Not much solace, I agree, but it's something.

On the policy side, we have an action plan. In the short term, we need to keep circumvention—the ability to modify our hardware, software, and data files—legal and preserve net neutrality. Both of these things limit how much the lords can take advantage of us, and they increase the possibility that the market will force them to be more benevolent. The last thing we want is the government—that's us—spending resources to enforce one particular business model over another and stifling competition.

In the longer term, we all need to work to reduce the power imbalance. Medieval feudalism evolved into a more balanced relationship in which lords had responsibilities as well as rights. Today's Internet feudalism is both ad-hoc and one-sided. We have no choice but to trust the lords, but we receive very few assurances in return. The lords have a lot of rights, but few responsibilities or limits. We need to balance this relationship, and government intervention is the only way we're going to get it. In medieval Europe, the rise of the centralized state and the rule of law provided the stability that feudalism lacked. The Magna Carta first forced responsibilities on governments and put humans on the long road toward government by the people and for the people.

We need a similar process to rein in our Internet lords, and it's not something that market forces are likely to provide. The very definition of power is changing, and the issues are far bigger than the Internet and our relationships with our IT providers.

2

Crime, Terrorism, Spying, and War

America's Dilemma: Close Security Holes, or Exploit Them Ourselves

Originally published in Wired News, *May 1, 2008*

On April 27, 2007, Estonia was attacked in cyberspace. Following a diplomatic incident with Russia about the relocation of a Soviet World War II memorial, the networks of many Estonian organizations, including the Estonian parliament, banks, ministries, newspapers and broadcasters, were attacked and—in many cases—shut down. Estonia was quick to blame Russia, which was equally quick to deny any involvement.

It was hyped as the first cyberwar: Russia attacking Estonia in cyberspace. But nearly a year later, evidence that the Russian government was involved in the denial-of-service attacks still hasn't emerged. Though Russian hackers were indisputably the major instigators of the attack, the only individuals positively identified have been young ethnic Russians living inside Estonia, who were pissed off over the statue incident.

You know you've got a problem when you can't tell a hostile attack by another nation from bored kids with an axe to grind.

Separating cyberwar, cyberterrorism and cybercrime isn't easy; these days you need a scorecard to tell the difference. It's not just that it's hard to trace people in cyberspace, it's that military and civilian attacks—and defenses—look the same.

The traditional term for technology the military shares with civilians is "dual use." Unlike hand grenades and tanks and missile targeting systems, dual-use technologies have both military and civilian applications. Dual-use technologies used to be exceptions; even things you'd expect to be dual use, like radar systems and toilets, were designed differently for the military. But today, almost all information technology is dual use. We both use the same operating systems, the same networking protocols, the same applications, and even the same security software.

And attack technologies are the same. The recent spurt of targeted hacks against US military networks, commonly attributed to China, exploit the same vulnerabilities and use the same techniques as criminal attacks against corporate networks. Internet worms make the jump to classified military networks in less than 24 hours, even if those networks are physically separate. The Navy Cyber Defense Operations Command uses the same tools against the same threats as any large corporation.

Because attackers and defenders use the same IT technology, there is a fundamental tension between cyberattack and cyberdefense. The National Security Agency has referred to this as the "equities issue," and it can be summarized as follows: When a military discovers a vulnerability in a dual-use technology, they can do one of two things. They can alert the manufacturer and fix the vulnerability, thereby protecting both the good guys and the bad guys. Or they can keep quiet about the vulnerability and not tell anyone, thereby leaving the good guys insecure but also leaving the bad guys insecure.

The equities issue has long been hotly debated inside the NSA. Basically, the NSA has two roles: eavesdrop on their stuff, and protect our stuff. When both sides use the same stuff, the agency has to decide whether to exploit vulnerabilities to eavesdrop on their stuff or close the same vulnerabilities to protect our stuff.

In the 1980s and before, the tendency of the NSA was to keep vulnerabilities to themselves. In the 1990s, the tide shifted, and the NSA was starting to open up and help us all improve our security defense. But after the attacks of 9/11, the NSA shifted back to the attack: vulnerabilities were to be hoarded in secret. Slowly, things in the US are shifting back again.

So now we're seeing the NSA help secure Windows Vista and releasing their own version of Linux. The DHS, meanwhile, is funding a project to secure popular open source software packages, and across the Atlantic the UK's GCHQ is finding bugs in PGPDisk and reporting them back to the company. (NSA is rumored to be doing the same thing with BitLocker.)

I'm in favor of this trend, because my security improves for free. Whenever the NSA finds a security problem and gets the vendor to fix it, our security gets better. It's a side-benefit of dual-use technologies.

But I want governments to do more. I want them to use their buying power to improve my security. I want them to offer countrywide contracts for software, both security and non-security, that have explicit security requirements. If these contracts are big enough, companies will work to modify their products to meet those requirements. And again, we all benefit from the security improvements.

The only example of this model I know about is a US government-wide procurement competition for full-disk encryption, but this can certainly be done with firewalls, intrusion detection systems, databases, networking hardware, even operating systems.

When it comes to IT technologies, the equities issue should be a no-brainer. The good uses of our common hardware, software, operating systems, network protocols, and everything else vastly outweigh the bad uses. It's time that the government used its immense knowledge and experience, as well as its buying power, to improve cybersecurity for all of us.

Are Photographers Really a Threat?

Originally published in the Guardian, *June 4, 2008*

What is it with photographers these days? Are they really all terrorists, or does everyone just think they are?

Since 9/11, there has been an increasing war on photography. Photographers have been harassed, questioned, detained, arrested or worse, and declared to be unwelcome. We've been repeatedly told to watch out for photographers, especially suspicious ones. Clearly any terrorist is going to first photograph his target, so vigilance is required.

Except that it's nonsense. The 9/11 terrorists didn't photograph anything. Nor did the London transport bombers, the Madrid subway bombers, or the liquid bombers arrested in 2006. Timothy McVeigh didn't photograph the Oklahoma City Federal Building. The Unabomber didn't photograph anything; neither did shoe-bomber Richard Reid. Photographs aren't being found amongst the papers of Palestinian suicide bombers. The IRA wasn't known for its photography. Even those manufactured terrorist plots that the US government likes to talk about—the Ft. Dix terrorists, the JFK airport bombers, the Miami 7, the Lackawanna 6—no photography.

Given that real terrorists, and even wannabe terrorists, don't seem to photograph anything, why is it such pervasive conventional wisdom that terrorists photograph their targets? Why are our fears so great that we have no choice but to be suspicious of any photographer?

Because it's a movie-plot threat.

A movie-plot threat is a specific threat, vivid in our minds like the plot of a movie. You remember them from the months after the 9/11 attacks: anthrax spread from crop dusters, a contaminated milk supply, terrorist scuba divers armed with almanacs. Our imaginations run wild with detailed and specific threats, from the news, and from actual movies and television shows. These movie plots resonate in our minds and in the minds of others we talk to. And many of us get scared.

Terrorists taking pictures is a quintessential detail in any good movie. Of course it makes sense that terrorists will take pictures of their targets. They have to do reconnaissance, don't they? We need 45 minutes of television action before the actual terrorist attack—90 minutes if it's a movie—and a photography scene is just perfect. It's our movie-plot terrorists that are photographers, even if the real-world ones are not.

The problem with movie-plot security is it only works if we guess the plot correctly. If we spend a zillion dollars defending Wimbledon and terrorists blow up a different sporting event, that's money wasted. If we post guards all over the Underground and terrorists bomb a crowded shopping area, that's also a waste. If we teach everyone to be alert for photographers, and terrorists don't take photographs, we've wasted money and effort, and taught people to fear something they shouldn't.

And even if terrorists did photograph their targets, the math doesn't make sense. Billions of photographs are taken by honest people every year, 50 billion by amateurs alone in the US. And the national monuments you imagine terrorists taking photographs of are the same ones tourists like to take pictures of. If you see someone taking one of those photographs, the odds are infinitesimal that he's a terrorist.

Of course, it's far easier to explain the problem than it is to fix it. Because we're a species of storytellers, we find movie-plot threats uniquely compelling. A single vivid scenario will do more to convince people that photographers might be terrorists than all the data I can muster to demonstrate that they're not.

Fear aside, there aren't many legal restrictions on what you can photograph from a public place that's already in public view. If you're harassed, it's almost certainly a law enforcement official, public or private, acting way beyond his authority. There's nothing in any post-9/11 law that restricts your right to photograph.

This is worth fighting. Search "photographer rights" on Google and download one of the several wallet documents that can help you if you get harassed; I found one for the UK, US, and Australia. Don't cede your right to photograph in public. Don't propagate the terrorist photographer story. Remind them that prohibiting photography was something we used to ridicule about the USSR. Eventually sanity will be restored, but it may take a while.

CCTV Doesn't Keep Us Safe, Yet the Cameras Are Everywhere

Originally published in the Guardian, *June 26, 2008*

Pervasive security cameras don't substantially reduce crime. There are exceptions, of course, and that's what gets the press. Most famously, CCTV cameras helped catch James Bulger's murderers in 1993. And earlier this year, they helped convict Steve Wright of murdering five women in the Ipswich area. But these are the well-publicized exceptions. Overall, CCTV cameras aren't very effective.

This fact has been demonstrated again and again: by a comprehensive study for the Home Office in 2005, by several studies in the US, and again with new data announced last month by New Scotland Yard. They actually solve very few crimes, and their deterrent effect is minimal.

Conventional wisdom predicts the opposite. But if that were true, then camera-happy London, with something like 500,000, would be the safest city on the planet. It isn't, of course, because of technological limitations of cameras, organizational limitations of police and the adaptive abilities of criminals.

To some, it's comforting to imagine vigilant police monitoring every camera, but the truth is very different. Most CCTV footage is never looked at until well after a crime is committed. When it is examined, it's very common for the viewers not to identify suspects. Lighting is bad and images are grainy, and criminals tend not to stare helpfully at the lens. Cameras break far too often. The best camera systems can still be thwarted by sunglasses or hats. Even when they afford quick identification—think of the 2005 London transport bombers and the 9/11 terrorists—police are often able to identify suspects without the cameras. Cameras afford a false sense of security, encouraging laziness when we need police to be vigilant.

The solution isn't for police to watch the cameras. Unlike an officer walking the street, cameras only look in particular directions at particular locations. Criminals know this, and can easily adapt by moving their crimes to someplace not watched by a camera—and there will always be such places. Additionally, while a police officer on the street can respond to a crime in progress, the same officer in front of a CCTV screen can only dispatch another officer to arrive much later. By their very nature, cameras result in underused and misallocated police resources.

Cameras aren't completely ineffective, of course. In certain circumstances, they're effective in reducing crime in enclosed areas with minimal foot traffic. Combined with adequate lighting, they substantially reduce both personal attacks and auto-related crime in car parks. And from some perspectives, simply moving crime around is good enough. If a local Tesco installs cameras in its store, and a robber targets the store next door as a result, that's money well spent by Tesco. But it doesn't reduce the overall crime rate, so is a waste of money to the township.

But the question really isn't whether cameras reduce crime; the question is whether they're worth it. And given their cost (£500 m in the past 10 years), their limited effectiveness, the potential for abuse (spying on naked women in their own homes, sharing nude images, selling best-of videos, and even spying on national politicians) and their Orwellian effects on privacy and civil liberties, most of the time they're not. The funds spent on CCTV cameras would be far better spent on hiring experienced police officers.

We live in a unique time in our society: the cameras are everywhere, and we can still see them. Ten years ago, cameras were much rarer than they are today. And in 10 years, they'll be so small you won't even notice them. Already, companies like L-1 Security Solutions are developing police-state CCTV surveillance technologies like facial recognition for China, technology that will find their way into countries like the UK. The time to address appropriate limits on this technology is before the cameras fade from notice.

Chinese Cyberattacks: Myth or Menace?

Originally published in Information Security, *July 2008*

This essay appeared as the second half of a point/counterpoint with Marcus Ranum.

The popular media narrative is that there is a coordinated attempt by the Chinese government to hack into US computers—military, government, corporate—and steal secrets. The truth is a lot more complicated.

There certainly is a lot of hacking coming out of China. Any company that does security monitoring sees it all the time. Of course, they can't prove that it comes out of China. But the majority of servers used in the attacks are located in China, using DNS bouncers that can only be registered by people literate in Chinese. The hacker websites where different hackers and hacker groups brag about their exploits and sell hacker tools and how-to videos are written in Chinese. Technically, it's possible all the attackers are from, say, Canada and trying to disguise themselves, but it seems pretty unlikely.

These hacker groups seem not to be working for the Chinese government. They don't seem to be coordinated by the Chinese military. They're basically young, male, patriotic Chinese citizens, demonstrating they're as good as everyone else. Besides the American networks the media likes to talk about, their targets also include pro-Tibet, pro-Taiwan, Falun Gong and pro-Uyghur sites.

The hackers are in this for two reasons: fame and glory, and an attempt to make a living. The fame and glory comes from their nationalistic goals. Some of these hackers are heroes in China. They're upholding the country's honor against both anti-Chinese forces like the pro-Tibet movement and larger forces like the United States. And the money comes from several sources. The groups sell owned computers, malware services and data they steal on the black market. They sell hacker tools and videos to others wanting to pay. They even sell t-shirts, hats and other merchandise on their websites.

This is not to say the Chinese military ignores the hacker groups within their country. The People's Liberation Army has long had a doctrine of "informationization." It considers cyberwarfare a leapfrog technology, one that will allow it to achieve military parity with the West without having to engage in an expensive missile-for-missile arms race like the one that bankrupted the Soviet Union. Certainly the Chinese government knows the leaders of the hacker movement and chooses to look the other way. It probably buys good stuff, and probably recruits for its organizations from this self-selecting pool of experienced hacking experts. It certainly learns from the hackers.

And some of the hackers are good. Scott Henderson has been tracking Chinese hacker groups for years and writes about them in his blog, www.thedarkvisitor.com, and his book of the same name. He's watched the hackers become more sophisticated in tools and techniques. They're stealthy. They do good network reconnaissance. My guess is what the Pentagon thinks is the problem is only a small percentage of the actual problem.

And they discover their own vulnerabilities. Earlier this year, F-Secure found an attack against a pro-Tibet network that used an unpatched zero-day vulnerability to install a backdoor. That same attack was used two weeks earlier against a large multinational defense contractor. They also hoard vulnerabilities. During the 1999 conflict over the two-states theory, in a heated exchange with a group of Taiwanese hackers, one Chinese group threatened to unleash multiple stockpiled worms at once. There was no reason to disbelieve this threat.

If anything, the fact that these groups aren't being run by the Chinese government makes the problem worse. Without central political coordination, they're likely to take more risks, do stupider things and generally ignore the political fallout of their actions. In this regard, they're more like a non-state actor. So while I'm perfectly happy that the US government is using the threat of Chinese hacking as an impetus to get its cybersecurity in order, and I hope it succeeds, I also hope the US government recognizes that these groups are not acting under the direction of the Chinese military and doesn't treat their actions as officially approved by the Chinese government.

How a Classic Man-in-the-Middle Attack Saved Colombian Hostages

Originally published in Wired News, *July 10, 2008*

Last week's dramatic rescue of 15 hostages held by the guerrilla organization FARC was the result of months of intricate deception on the part of the Colombian government. At the center was a classic man-in-the-middle attack.

In a man-in-the-middle attack, the attacker inserts himself between two communicating parties. Both believe they're talking to each other, and the attacker can delete or modify the communications at will.

The *Wall Street Journal* reported how this gambit played out in Colombia: "The plan had a chance of working because, for months, in an operation one army officer likened to a "broken telephone," military intelligence had been able to convince Ms. Betancourt's captor, Gerardo Aguilar, a guerrilla known as "Cesar," that he was communicating with his top bosses in the guerrillas' seven-man secretariat. Army intelligence convinced top guerrilla leaders that they were talking to Cesar. In reality, both were talking to army intelligence."

This ploy worked because Cesar and his guerrilla bosses didn't know one another well. They didn't recognize one another's voices, and didn't have a friendship or shared history that could have tipped them off about the ruse. Man-in-the-middle is defeated by context, and the FARC guerrillas didn't have any.

And that's why man-in-the-middle, abbreviated MITM in the computer-security community, is such a problem online: Internet communication is often stripped of any context. There's no way to recognize someone's face. There's no way to recognize someone's voice. When you receive an e-mail purporting to come from a person or organization, you have no idea who actually sent it. When you visit a website, you have no idea if you're really visiting that website. We all like to pretend that we know who we're communicating with—and for the most part, of course, there isn't any attacker inserting himself into our communications—but in reality, we don't. And there are lots of hacker tools that exploit this unjustified trust, and implement MITM attacks.

Even with context, it's still possible for MITM to fool both sides—because electronic communications are often intermittent. Imagine that one of the FARC guerrillas became suspicious about who he was talking to. So he asks a question about their shared history as a test: "What did we have for dinner that time last year?" or something like that. On the telephone, the attacker wouldn't be able to answer quickly, so his ruse would be discovered. But e-mail conversation isn't synchronous. The attacker could simply pass that question through to the other end of the communications, and when he got the answer back, he would be able to reply.

This is the way MITM attacks work against web-based financial systems. A bank demands authentication from the user: a password, a one-time code from a token or whatever. The attacker sitting in the middle receives the request from the bank and passes it to the user. The user responds to the attacker, who passes that response to the bank. Now the bank assumes it is talking to the legitimate user, and the attacker is free to send transactions directly to the bank. This kind of attack completely bypasses any two-factor authentication mechanisms, and is becoming a more popular identity-theft tactic.

There are cryptographic solutions to MITM attacks, and there are secure web protocols that implement them. Many of them require shared secrets, though, making them useful only in situations where people already know and trust one another.

The NSA-designed STU-III and STE secure telephones solve the MITM problem by embedding the identity of each phone together with its key. (The NSA creates all keys and is trusted by everyone, so this works.) When two phones talk to each other securely, they exchange keys and display the other phone's identity on a screen. Because the phone is in a secure location, the user now knows who he is talking to, and if the phone displays another organization—as it would if there were a MITM attack in progress—he should hang up.

Zfone, a secure VoIP system, protects against MITM attacks with a short authentication string. After two Zfone terminals exchange keys, both computers display a four-character string. The users are supposed to manually verify that both strings are the same—"my screen says 5C19; what does yours say?"—to ensure that the phones are communicating directly with each other and not with an MITM. The AT&T TSD-3600 worked similarly.

This sort of protection is embedded in SSL, although no one uses it. As it is normally used, SSL provides an encrypted communications link to whoever is at the other end: bank and phishing site alike. And the better phishing sites create valid SSL connections, so as to more effectively fool users. But if the user wanted to, he could manually check the SSL certificate to see if it was issued to "National Bank of Trustworthiness" or "Two Guys With a Computer in Nigeria."

No one does, though, because you have to both remember and be willing to do the work. (The browsers could make this easier if they wanted to, but they don't seem to want to.) In the real world, you can easily tell a branch of your bank from a money changer on a street corner. But on the Internet, a phishing site can be easily made to look like your bank's legitimate website. Any method of telling the two apart takes work. And that's the first step to fooling you with a MITM attack.

Man-in-the-middle isn't new, and it doesn't have to be technological. But the Internet makes the attacks easier and more powerful, and that's not going to change anytime soon.

How to Create the Perfect Fake Identity

Originally published in Wired News, *September 4, 2008*

Let me start off by saying that I'm making this whole thing up.

Imagine you're in charge of infiltrating sleeper agents into the United States. The year is 1983, and the proliferation of identity databases is making it increasingly difficult to create fake credentials. Ten years ago, someone could have just shown up in the country and gotten a driver's license, Social Security card and bank account—possibly using the identity of someone roughly the same age who died as a young child—but it's getting harder. And you know that trend will only continue. So you decide to grow your own identities.

Call it "identity farming." You invent a handful of infants. You apply for Social Security numbers for them. Eventually, you open bank accounts for them, file tax returns for them, register them to vote, and apply for credit cards in their name. And now, 25 years later, you have a handful of identities ready and waiting for some real people to step into them.

There are some complications, of course. Maybe you need people to sign their name as parents—or, at least, mothers. Maybe you need doctors to fill out birth certificates. Maybe you need to fill out paperwork certifying that you're home-schooling these children. You'll certainly want to exercise their financial identity: depositing money into their bank accounts and withdrawing it from ATMs, using their credit cards and paying the bills, and so on. And you'll need to establish some sort of addresses for them, even if it is just a mail drop.

You won't be able to get driver's licenses or photo IDs in their name. That isn't critical, though; in the US, more than 20 million adult citizens don't have photo IDs. But other than that, I can't think of any reason why identity farming wouldn't work.

Here's the real question: Do you actually have to show up for any part of your life?

Again, I made this all up. I have no evidence that anyone is actually doing this. It's not something a criminal organization is likely to do; twenty-five years is too distant a payoff horizon. The same logic holds true for terrorist organizations; it's not worth it. It might have been worth it to the KGB—although perhaps harder to justify after the Soviet Union broke up in 1991—and might be an attractive option for existing intelligence adversaries like China.

Immortals could also use this trick to self-perpetuate themselves, inventing their own children and gradually assuming their identity, then killing their parents off. They could even show up for their own driver's license photos, wearing a beard as the father and blue spiked hair as the son. I'm told this is a common idea in *Highlander* fan fiction.

The point isn't to create another movie plot threat, but to point out the central role that data has taken on in our lives. Previously, I've said that we all have a data shadow that follows us around, and that more and more institutions interact with our data shadows instead of with us. We only intersect with our data shadows once in a while—when we apply for a driver's license or passport, for example—and those interactions are authenticated by older, less-secure interactions. The rest of the world assumes that our photo IDs glue us to our data shadows, ignoring the rather flimsy connection between us and our plastic cards. (And, no, REAL-ID won't help.)

It seems to me that our data shadows are becoming increasingly distinct from us, almost with a life of their own. What's important now is our shadows; we're secondary. And as our society relies more and more on these shadows, we might even become unnecessary.

Our data shadows can live a perfectly normal life without us.

A Fetishistic Approach to Security Is a Perverse Way to Keep Us Safe

Originally published in the Guardian, *September 4, 2008*

We spend far more effort defending our countries against specific movie-plot threats, rather than the real, broad threats. In the US during the months after the 9/11 attacks, we feared terrorists with scuba gear, terrorists with crop dusters and terrorists contaminating our milk supply. Both the UK and the US fear terrorists with small bottles of liquid. Our imaginations run wild with vivid specific threats. Before long, we're envisioning an entire movie plot, without Bruce Willis saving the day. And we're scared.

It's not just terrorism; it's any rare risk in the news. The big fear in Canada right now, following a particularly gruesome incident, is random decapitations on intercity buses. In the US, fears of school shootings are much greater than the actual risks. In the UK, it's child predators. And people all over the world mistakenly fear flying more than driving. But the very definition of news is something that hardly ever happens. If an incident is in the news, we shouldn't worry about it. It's when something is so common that it's no longer news—car crashes, domestic violence—that we should worry. But that's not the way people think.

Psychologically, this makes sense. We are a species of storytellers. We have good imaginations and we respond more emotionally to stories than to data. We also judge the probability of something by how easy it is to imagine, so stories that are in the news feel more probable—and ominous—than stories that are not. As a result, we overreact to the rare risks we hear stories about, and fear specific plots more than general threats.

The problem with building security around specific targets and tactics is that it's only effective if we happen to guess the plot correctly. If we spend billions defending the Underground and terrorists bomb a school instead, we've wasted our money. If we focus on the World Cup and terrorists attack Wimbledon, we've wasted our money.

It's this fetish-like focus on tactics that results in the security follies at airports. We ban guns and knives, and terrorists use box-cutters. We take away box-cutters and corkscrews, so they put explosives in their shoes. We screen shoes, so they use liquids. We take away liquids, and they're going to do something else. Or they'll ignore airplanes entirely and attack a school, church, theatre, stadium, shopping mall, airport terminal outside the security area, or any of the other places where people pack together tightly.

These are stupid games, so let's stop playing. Some high-profile targets deserve special attention and some tactics are worse than others. Airplanes are particularly important targets because they are national symbols and because a small bomb can kill everyone aboard. Seats of government are also symbolic, and therefore attractive, targets. But targets and tactics are interchangeable.

The following three things are true about terrorism. One, the number of potential terrorist targets is infinite. Two, the odds of the terrorists going after any one target is zero. And three, the cost to the terrorist of switching targets is zero.

We need to defend against the broad threat of terrorism, not against specific movie plots. Security is most effective when it doesn't require us to guess. We need to focus resources on intelligence and investigation: identifying terrorists, cutting off their funding and stopping them regardless of what their plans are. We need to focus resources on emergency response: lessening the impact of a terrorist attack, regardless of what it is. And we need to face the geopolitical consequences of our foreign policy.

In 2006, UK police arrested the liquid bombers not through diligent airport security, but through intelligence and investigation. It didn't matter what the bombers' target was. It didn't matter what their tactic was. They would have been arrested regardless. That's smart security. Now we confiscate liquids at airports, just in case another group happens to attack the exact same target in exactly the same way. That's just illogical.

The Seven Habits of Highly Ineffective Terrorists

Originally published in Wired News, *October 1, 2008*

Most counterterrorism policies fail, not because of tactical problems, but because of a fundamental misunderstanding of what motivates terrorists in the first place. If we're ever going to defeat terrorism, we need to understand what drives people to become terrorists in the first place.

Conventional wisdom holds that terrorism is inherently political, and that people become terrorists for political reasons. This is the "strategic" model of terrorism, and it's basically an economic model. It posits that people resort to terrorism when they believe—rightly or wrongly—that terrorism is worth it; that is, when they believe the political gains of terrorism minus the political costs are greater than if they engaged in some other, more peaceful form of protest. It's assumed, for example, that people join Hamas to achieve a Palestinian state; that people join the PKK to attain a Kurdish national homeland; and that people join al-Qaida to, among other things, get the United States out of the Persian Gulf.

If you believe this model, the way to fight terrorism is to change that equation, and that's what most experts advocate. Governments tend to minimize the political gains of terrorism through a no-concessions policy; the international community tends to recommend reducing the political grievances of terrorists via appeasement, in hopes of getting them to renounce violence. Both advocate policies to provide effective nonviolent alternatives, like free elections.

Historically, none of these solutions has worked with any regularity. Max Abrahms, a predoctoral fellow at Stanford University's Center for International Security and Cooperation, has studied dozens of terrorist groups from all over the world. He argues that the model is wrong. In a paper published this year in *International Security* that—sadly—doesn't have the title "Seven Habits of Highly Ineffective Terrorists," he discusses, well, seven habits of highly ineffective terrorists. These seven tendencies are seen in terrorist organizations all over the world, and they directly contradict the theory that terrorists are political maximizers.

Terrorists, he writes, (1) attack civilians, a policy that has a lousy track record of convincing those civilians to give the terrorists what they want; (2) treat terrorism as a first resort, not a last resort, failing to embrace nonviolent alternatives like elections; (3) don't compromise with their target country, even when those compromises are in their best interest politically; (4) have protean political platforms, which regularly, and sometimes radically, change; (5) often engage in anonymous attacks, which precludes the target countries making political concessions to them; (6) regularly attack other terrorist groups with the same political platform; and (7) resist disbanding, even when they consistently fail to achieve their political objectives or when their stated political objectives have been achieved.

Abrahms has an alternative model to explain all this: People turn to terrorism for social solidarity. He theorizes that people join terrorist organizations worldwide in order to be part of a community, much like the reason inner-city youths join gangs in the United States.

The evidence supports this. Individual terrorists often have no prior involvement with a group's political agenda, and often join multiple terrorist groups with incompatible platforms. Individuals who join terrorist groups are frequently not oppressed in any way, and often can't describe the political goals of their organizations. People who join terrorist groups most often have friends or relatives who are members of the group, and the great majority of terrorists are socially isolated: unmarried young men or widowed women who weren't working prior to joining. These things are true for members of terrorist groups as diverse as the IRA and al-Qaida.

For example, several of the 9/11 hijackers planned to fight in Chechnya, but they didn't have the right paperwork so they attacked America instead.

The mujahedeen had no idea whom they would attack after the Soviets withdrew from Afghanistan, so they sat around until they came up with a new enemy: America. Pakistani terrorists regularly defect to another terrorist group with a totally different political platform. Many new al-Qaida members say, unconvincingly, that they decided to become a jihadist after reading an extreme, anti-American blog, or after converting to Islam, sometimes just a few weeks before. These people know little about politics or Islam, and they frankly don't even seem to care much about learning more. The blogs they turn to don't have a lot of substance in these areas, even though more informative blogs do exist.

All of this explains the seven habits. It's not that they're ineffective; it's that they have a different goal. They might not be effective politically, but they are effective socially: They all help preserve the group's existence and cohesion.

This kind of analysis isn't just theoretical; it has practical implications for counterterrorism. Not only can we now better understand who is likely to become a terrorist, we can engage in strategies specifically designed to weaken the social bonds within terrorist organizations. Driving a wedge between group members—commuting prison sentences in exchange for actionable intelligence, planting more double agents within terrorist groups—will go a long way to weakening the social bonds within those groups.

We also need to pay more attention to the socially marginalized than to the politically downtrodden, like unassimilated communities in Western countries. We need to support vibrant, benign communities and organizations as alternative ways for potential terrorists to get the social cohesion they need. And finally, we need to minimize collateral damage in our counterterrorism operations, as well as clamping down on bigotry and hate crimes, which just creates more dislocation and social isolation, and the inevitable calls for revenge.

Why Society Should Pay the True Costs of Security

Originally published in the Guardian, *October 2, 2008*

It's not true that no one worries about terrorists attacking chemical plants. It's just that our politics seem to leave us unable to deal with the threat. Toxins such as ammonia, chlorine, propane and flammable mixtures are being produced or stored as a result of legitimate industrial processes. Chlorine gas is particularly toxic; in addition to bombing a plant, someone could hijack a chlorine truck or blow up a railcar. Phosgene is even more dangerous. And many chemical plants are located in places where an act of sabotage—or an accident—could threaten thousands of people.

The problem of securing chemical plants is simple once you understand the underlying economics. Normally, we leave the security of something up to its owner. The basic idea is that the owner of each chemical plant 1) best understands the risks, and 2) is the one who loses out if security fails. Any outsider—i.e., regulatory agency—is just going to get it wrong. It's the basic free-market argument, and in most instances it makes a lot of sense.

And chemical plants have security. They have cameras, fences, guards. They have built-in fail-safe mechanisms. For example, many large chemical companies use hazardous substances like phosgene, methyl isocyanate and ethylene oxide in their plants, but don't ship them between locations. They minimize the amounts that are stored.

This is all good and right, and what free-market capitalism dictates. The problem is, that isn't enough. Any rational owner of a chemical plant will only secure the plant up to its value to him or her. That is, if the plant is worth $100m (£55m), then it makes no sense to spend $200m on securing it. If the odds of it being attacked are less than 1%, it doesn't even make sense to spend $1m on securing it. The mathematics are more complicated than this, because you have to factor in such things as the reputational cost of having your name splashed all over the media after an incident, but that's the basic idea.

But to society, the cost of an attack can be much, much greater. If a terrorist blows up a particularly toxic plant in the middle of a densely populated area, deaths could be in the tens of thousands and damage could be in the hundreds of millions. Indirect economic damage could be in the billions. The owner of the chlorine plant would pay none of these potential costs.

Sure, the owner could be sued. But they're not at risk for more than the value of the company—and, in any case, they'd probably be smarter to take the chance. Expensive lawyers can work wonders, courts can be fickle and the government could step in and bail the company out. And a smart company can often protect itself by spinning off the risky asset in a subsidiary company, or selling it off completely. The overall result is that chemical plants are secured to a much smaller degree than the risk warrants.

If we—the community living near the chemical plant, or the nation as a whole—expect the owner of that plant to spend money for increased security to account for those externalities, we're going to have to pay for it.

We have three ways of doing that. One, we can do it ourselves, stationing government police or military or contractors around the chemical plants. Two, we can pay the owners to do it, subsidizing some sort of security standard. Or three, we could regulate security and force the companies to pay for it themselves.

There's no free lunch, of course. "We," as in society, still pay for it in increased prices for whatever the chemical plants are producing, but the cost is paid for by the consumers rather than by taxpayers. Asking nicely just isn't going to work.

Why Technology Won't Prevent Identity Theft

Originally published in the Wall Street Journal, *January 9, 2009*

Impersonation isn't new. In 1556, a Frenchman was executed for impersonating Martin Guerre and this week hackers impersonated Barack Obama on Twitter. It's not even unique to humans: mockingbirds, Viceroy butterflies, and the brown octopus all use impersonation as a survival strategy. For people, detecting impersonation is a hard problem for three reasons: we need to verify the identity of people we don't know, we interact with people through "narrow" communications channels like the telephone and Internet, and we want computerized systems to do the verification for us.

Traditional impersonation involves people fooling people. It's still done today: impersonating garbage men to collect tips, impersonating parking lot attendants to collect fees, or impersonating the French president to fool Sarah Palin. Impersonating people like policemen, security guards, and meter readers is a common criminal tactic.

These tricks work because we all regularly interact with people we don't know. No one could successfully impersonate your brother, your best friend, or your boss, because you know them intimately. But a policeman or a parking lot attendant? That's just someone with a badge or a uniform. But badges and ID cards only help if you know how to verify one. Do you know what a valid police ID looks like? Or how to tell a real telephone repairman's badge from a forged one?

Still, it's human nature to trust these credentials. We naturally trust uniforms, even though we know that anyone can wear one. When we visit a Web site, we use the professionalism of the page to judge whether or not it's really legitimate—never mind that anyone can cut and paste graphics. Watch the next time someone other than law enforcement verifies your ID; most people barely look at it.

Impersonation is even easier over limited communications channels. On the telephone, how can you distinguish someone working at your credit card company from someone trying to steal your account details and login information? On e-mail, how can you distinguish someone from your company's tech support from a hacker trying to break into your network—or the mayor of Paris from an impersonator? Once in a while someone frees himself from jail by faxing a forged release order to his warden. This is social engineering: impersonating someone convincingly enough to fool the victim.

These days, a lot of identity verification happens with computers. Computers are fast at computation but not very good at judgment, and can be tricked. So people can fool speed cameras by taping a fake license plate over the real one, fingerprint readers with a piece of tape, or automatic face scanners with—and I'm not making this up—a photograph of a face held in front of their own. Even the most bored policeman wouldn't fall for any of those tricks.

This is why identity theft is such a big problem today. So much authentication happens online, with only a small amount of information: user ID, password, birth date, Social Security number, and so on. Anyone who gets that information can impersonate you to a computer, which doesn't know any better.

Despite all of these problems, most authentication systems work most of the time. Even something as ridiculous as faxed signatures work, and can be legally binding. But no authentication system is perfect, and impersonation is always possible.

This lack of perfection is okay, though. Security is a trade-off, and any well-designed authentication system balances security with ease of use, customer acceptance, cost, and so on. More authentication isn't always better. Banks make this trade-off when they don't bother authenticating signatures on checks under amounts like $25,000; it's cheaper to deal with fraud after the fact. Web sites make this trade-off when they use simple passwords instead of something more secure, and merchants make this trade-off when they don't bother verifying your signature against your credit card. We make this trade-off when we accept police badges, Best Buy uniforms, and faxed signatures with only a cursory amount of verification.

Good authentication systems also balance false positives against false negatives. Impersonation is just one way these systems can fail; they can also fail to authenticate the real person. An ATM is better off allowing occasional fraud than preventing legitimate account holders access to their money. On the other hand, a false positive in a nuclear launch system is much more dangerous; better to not launch the missiles.

Decentralized authentication systems work better than centralized ones. Open your wallet, and you'll see a variety of physical tokens used to identify you to different people and organizations: your bank, your credit card company, the library, your health club, and your employer, as well as a catch-all driver's license used to identify you in a variety of circumstances. That assortment is actually more secure than a single centralized identity card: each system must be broken individually, and breaking one doesn't give the attacker access to everything. This is one of the reasons that centralized systems like REAL-ID make us less secure.

Finally, any good authentication system uses defense in depth. Since no authentication system is perfect, there need to be other security measures in place if authentication fails. That's why all of a corporation's assets and information isn't available to anyone who can bluff his way into the corporate offices. That is why credit card companies have expert systems analyzing suspicious spending patterns. And it's why identity theft won't be solved by making personal information harder to steal.

We can reduce the risk of impersonation, but it will always be with us; technology cannot "solve" it in any absolute sense. Like any security, the trick is to balance the trade-offs. Too little security, and criminals withdraw money from all our bank accounts. Too much security and when Barack Obama calls to congratulate you on your reelection, you won't believe it's him.

Terrorists May Use Google Earth, but Fear Is No Reason to Ban It

Originally published in the Guardian, *January 29, 2009*

It regularly comes as a surprise to people that our own infrastructure can be used against us. And in the wake of terrorist attacks or plots, there are fear-induced calls to ban, disrupt or control that infrastructure. According to officials investigating the Mumbai attacks, the terrorists used images from Google Earth to help learn their way around. This isn't the first time Google

Earth has been charged with helping terrorists: in 2007, Google Earth images of British military bases were found in the homes of Iraqi insurgents. Incidents such as these have led many governments to demand that Google remove or blur images of sensitive locations: military bases, nuclear reactors, government buildings, and so on. An Indian court has been asked to ban Google Earth entirely.

This isn't the only way our information technology helps terrorists. Last year, a US army intelligence report worried that terrorists could plan their attacks using Twitter, and there are unconfirmed reports that the Mumbai terrorists read the Twitter feeds about their attacks to get real-time information they could use. British intelligence is worried that terrorists might use voice over IP services such as Skype to communicate. Terrorists may train on Second Life and World of Warcraft. We already know they use websites to spread their message and possibly even to recruit.

Of course, all of this is exacerbated by open-wireless access, which has been repeatedly labeled a terrorist tool and which has been the object of attempted bans.

Mobile phone networks help terrorists, too. The Mumbai terrorists used them to communicate with each other. This has led some cities, including London, to propose turning off mobile phone coverage in the event of a terrorist attack.

Let's all stop and take a deep breath. By its very nature, communications infrastructure is general. It can be used to plan both legal and illegal activities, and it's generally impossible to tell which is which. When I send and receive email, it looks exactly the same as a terrorist doing the same thing. To the mobile phone network, a call from one terrorist to another looks exactly the same as a mobile phone call from one victim to another. Any attempt to ban or limit infrastructure affects everybody. If India bans Google Earth, a future terrorist won't be able to use it to plan; nor will anybody else. Open Wi-Fi networks are useful for many reasons, the large majority of them positive, and closing them down affects all those reasons. Terrorist attacks are very rare, and it is almost always a bad trade-off to deny society the benefits of a communications technology just because the bad guys might use it too.

Communications infrastructure is especially valuable during a terrorist attack. Twitter was the best way for people to get real-time information about the attacks in Mumbai. If the Indian government shut Twitter down—or London blocked mobile phone coverage—during a terrorist attack, the lack of communications for everyone, not just the terrorists, would increase the level of terror and could even increase the body count. Information lessens fear and makes people safer.

None of this is new. Criminals have used telephones and mobile phones since they were invented. Drug smugglers use airplanes and boats, radios and satellite phones. Bank robbers have long used cars and motorcycles as getaway vehicles, and horses before then. I haven't seen it talked about yet, but the Mumbai terrorists used boats as well. They also wore boots. They ate lunch at restaurants, drank bottled water, and breathed the air. Society survives all of this because the good uses of infrastructure far outweigh the bad uses, even though the good uses are—by and large—small and pedestrian and the bad uses are rare and spectacular. And while terrorism turns society's very infrastructure against itself, we only harm ourselves by dismantling that infrastructure in response— just as we would if we banned cars because bank robbers used them too.

Thwarting an Internal Hacker

Originally published in the Wall Street Journal, *February 16, 2009*

Rajendrasinh Makwana was a UNIX contractor for Fannie Mae. On October 24, he was fired. Before he left, he slipped a logic bomb into the organization's network. The bomb would have "detonated" on January 31. It was programmed to disable access to the server on which it was running, block any network monitoring software, systematically and irretrievably erase everything—and then replicate itself on all 4,000 Fannie Mae servers. Court papers claim the damage would have been in the millions of dollars, a number that seems low. Fannie Mae would have been shut down for at least a week.

Luckily—and it does seem it was pure luck—another programmer discovered the script a week later, and disabled it.

Insiders are a perennial problem. They have access, and they're known by the system. They know how the system and its security works, and its weak points. They have opportunity. Bank heists, casino thefts, large-scale corporate fraud, train robberies: many of the most impressive criminal attacks involve insiders. And, like Makwana's attempt at revenge, these insiders can have pretty intense motives—motives that can only intensify as the economy continues to suffer and layoffs increase.

Insiders are especially pernicious attackers because they're trusted. They have access because they're *supposed* to have access. They have opportunity, and an understanding of the system, because they use it—or they designed, built, or installed it. They're already inside the security system, making them much harder to defend against.

It's not possible to design a system without trusted people. They're everywhere. In offices, employees are trusted people given access to facilities and resources, and allowed to act—sometimes broadly, sometimes narrowly—in the company's name. In stores, employees are allowed access to the back room and the cash register; and customers are trusted to walk into the store and touch the merchandise. IRS employees are trusted with personal tax information; hospital employees are trusted with personal health information. Banks, airports, and prisons couldn't operate without trusted people.

Replacing trusted people with computers doesn't make the problem go away; it just moves it around and makes it even more complex. The computer, software, and network designers, implementers, coders, installers, maintainers, etc. are all trusted people. See any analysis of the security of electronic voting machines, or some of the frauds perpetrated against computerized gambling machines, for some graphic examples of the risks inherent in replacing people with computers.

Of course, this problem is much, much older than computers. And the solutions haven't changed much throughout history, either. There are five basic techniques to deal with trusted people:

1. Limit the number of trusted people. This one is obvious. The fewer people who have root access to the computer system, know the combination to the safe, or have the authority to sign checks, the more secure the system is.

2. Ensure that trusted people are also trustworthy. This is the idea behind background checks, lie detector tests, personality profiling, prohibiting convicted felons from getting certain jobs, limiting other jobs to citizens, the TSA's no-fly list, and so on, as well as behind bonding employees, which means there are deep pockets standing behind them if they turn out not to be trustworthy.

3. Limit the amount of trust each person has. This is compartmentalization; the idea here is to limit the amount of damage a person can do if he ends up not being trustworthy. This is the concept behind giving people keys that only unlock their office or passwords that only unlock their account, as well as "need to know" and other levels of security clearance.

4. Give people overlapping spheres of trust. This is what security professionals call defense in depth. It's why it takes two people with two separate keys to launch nuclear missiles, and two signatures on corporate checks over a certain value. It's the idea behind bank tellers requiring management overrides for high-value transactions, double-entry bookkeeping, and all those guards and cameras at casinos. It's why, when you go to a movie theater, one person sells you a ticket and another person standing a few yards away tears it in half: It makes it much harder for one employee to defraud the system. It's why key bank employees need to take their two-week vacations all at once—so their replacements have a chance to uncover any fraud.

5. Detect breaches of trust after the fact and prosecute the guilty. In the end, the four previous techniques can only do so well. Trusted people can subvert a system. Most of the time, we discover the security breach after the fact and then punish the perpetrator through the legal system: publicly, so as to provide a deterrence effect and increase the overall level of security in society. This is why audit is so vital.

These security techniques don't only protect against fraud or sabotage; they protect against the more common problem: mistakes. Trusted people aren't perfect; they can inadvertently cause damage. They can make a mistake, or they can be tricked into making a mistake through social engineering.

Good security systems use multiple measures, all working together. Fannie Mae certainly limits the number of people who have the ability to slip malicious scripts into their computer systems, and certainly limits the access that most of these people have. It probably has a hiring process that makes it less likely that malicious people come to work at Fannie Mae. It obviously doesn't have an audit process by which a change one person makes on the servers is checked by someone else; I'm sure that would be prohibitively expensive. Certainly the company's IT department should have terminated Makwana's network access as soon as he was fired, and not at the end of the day.

In the end, systems will always have trusted people who can subvert them. It's important to keep in mind that incidents like this don't happen very often; that most people are honest and honorable. Security is very much designed to protect against the dishonest minority. And often little things—like disabling access immediately upon termination—can go a long way.

An Enterprising Criminal Has Spotted a Gap in the Market

Originally published in the Guardian, *April 2, 2009*

Before his arrest, Tom Berge stole lead roof tiles from several buildings in south-east England, including the Honeywood Museum in Carshalton, the Croydon parish church, and the Sutton high school for girls. He then sold those tiles to scrap metal dealers.

As a security expert, I find this story interesting for two reasons. First, among attempts to ban, or at least censor, Google Earth, lest it help the terrorists, here is an actual crime that relied on the service: Berge needed Google Earth for reconnaissance.

But more interesting is the discrepancy between the value of the lead tiles to the original owner and to the thief. The Sutton school had to spend £10,000 to buy new lead tiles; the Croydon Church had to repair extensive water damage after the theft. But Berge only received £700 a tonne from London scrap metal dealers.

This isn't an isolated story; the same dynamic is in play with other commodities as well.

There is an epidemic of copper wiring thefts worldwide; copper is being stolen out of telephone and power stations—and off poles in the streets—and thieves have died because they didn't understand the dangers of high voltage. Homeowners are returning from holiday to find the copper pipes stolen from their houses. In 2001, scrap copper was worth 70c (50p) a pound in the US. In April 2008, it was worth $4.

Gasoline siphoning became more common as pump prices rose. And used restaurant grease, formerly either given away or sold for pennies to farmers, is being stolen from restaurant carparks and turned into biofuels. Newspapers and other recyclables are stolen from pavements, and trees are stolen and resold as Christmas trees.

Iron fences have been stolen from buildings and houses, manhole covers have been stolen from the middle of streets, and aluminum guard rails have been stolen from roadways. Steel is being stolen for scrap, too. In 2004 in Ukraine, thieves stole an entire steel bridge.

These crimes are particularly expensive to society because the replacement cost is much higher than the thief's profit. A manhole is worth $5–$10 as scrap, but it costs $500 to replace, including labor. A thief may take $20 worth of copper from a construction site, but do $10,000 in damage in the process. And the increased threat means more money being spent on security to protect those commodities in the first place.

Security can be viewed as a tax on the honest, and these thefts demonstrate that our taxes are going up. And unlike many taxes, we don't benefit from their collection. The cost to society of retrofitting manhole covers with locks, or replacing them with less resalable alternatives, is high; but there is no benefit other than reducing theft.

These crimes are a harbinger of the future: evolutionary pressure on our society, if you will. Criminals are often referred to as social parasites, but they are an early warning system of societal changes. Unfettered by laws or moral restrictions, they can be the first to respond to changes that the rest of society will be slower to pick up on. In fact, currently there's a reprieve. Scrap metal prices are all down from last year—copper is currently $1.62 per pound, and lead is half what Berge got—and thefts are down too.

We've designed much of our infrastructure around the assumptions that commodities are cheap and theft is rare. We don't protect transmission lines, manhole covers, iron fences, or lead flashing on roofs. But if commodity prices really are headed for new higher stable points, society will eventually react and find alternatives for these items—or find ways to protect them. Criminals were the first to point this out, and will continue to exploit the system until it destabilizes.

We Shouldn't Poison Our Minds with Fear of Bioterrorism

Originally published in the Guardian, *May 14, 2009*

Terrorists attacking our food supply is a nightmare scenario that has been given new life during the recent swine flu outbreak. Although it seems easy to do, understanding why it hasn't happened is important. GR Dalziel, at the Nanyang Technological University in Singapore, has written a report chronicling every confirmed case of malicious food contamination in the world since

1950: 365 cases in all, plus 126 additional unconfirmed cases. What he found demonstrates the reality of terrorist food attacks.

It turns out 72% of the food poisonings occurred at the end of the food supply chain—at home—typically by a friend, relative, neighbor, or co-worker trying to kill or injure a specific person. A characteristic example is Heather Mook of York, who in 2007 tried to kill her husband by putting rat poison in his spaghetti.

Most of these cases resulted in fewer than five casualties—Mook only injured her husband in this incident—although 16% resulted in five or more. Of the 19 cases that claimed 10 or more lives, four involved serial killers operating over several years.

Another 23% of cases occurred at the retail or food service level. A 1998 incident in Japan, where someone put arsenic in a curry sold at a summer festival, killing four and hospitalizing 63, is a typical example. Only 11% of these incidents resulted in 100 or more casualties, while 44% resulted in none.

There are very few incidents of people contaminating the actual food supply. People deliberately contaminated a water supply seven times, resulting in three deaths. There is only one example of someone deliberately contaminating a crop before harvest—in Australia in 2006—and the crops were recalled before they could be sold. And in the three cases of someone deliberately contaminating food during packaging and distribution, including a 2005 case in the UK where glass and needles were baked into loaves of bread, no one died or was injured.

This isn't the stuff of bioterrorism. The closest example occurred in 1984 in the US, where members of a religious group known as the Rajneeshees contaminated several restaurant salad bars with *Salmonella enterica typhimurium*, sickening 751, hospitalizing 45, but killing no one. In fact, no one knew this was malicious until a year later, when one of the perpetrators admitted it.

Almost all of the food contaminations used conventional poisons such as cyanide, drain cleaner, mercury, or weed killer. There were nine incidents of biological agents, including salmonella, ricin, and fecal matter, and eight cases of radiological matter. The 2006 London poisoning of the former KGB agent Alexander Litvinenko with polonium-210 in his tea is an example of the latter.

And that assassination illustrates the real risk of malicious food poisonings. What is discussed in terrorist training manuals, and what the CIA is worried about, is the use of contaminated food in targeted assassinations. The quantities involved for mass poisonings are too great, the nature of the food supply too vast and the details of any plot too complicated and unpredictable to be a real threat. That becomes crystal clear as you read the details of the different incidents: it's hard to kill one person, and very hard to kill dozens. Hundreds, thousands: it's just not going to happen any time soon. The fear of bioterror is much greater, and the panic from any bioterror scare will injure more people, than bioterrorism itself.

Far more dangerous are accidental contaminations due to negligent industry practices, such as the 2006 spinach E coli and, more recently, peanut salmonella contaminations in the US, the 2008 milk contaminations in China, and the BSE-infected beef from earlier this decade. And the systems we have in place to deal with these accidental contaminations also work to mitigate any intentional ones.

In 2004, the then US secretary of health and human services, Tommy Thompson, said on Fox News: "I cannot understand why terrorists have not attacked our food supply. Because it is so easy to do."

Guess what? It's not at all easy to do.

Raising the Cost of Paperwork Errors Will Improve Accuracy

Originally published in the Guardian, *June 24, 2009*

It's a sad, horrific story. Homeowner returns to find his house demolished. The demolition company was hired legitimately but there was a mistake and it demolished the wrong house. The demolition company relied on GPS co-ordinates, but requiring street addresses isn't a solution. A typo in the address is just as likely, and it would have demolished the house just as quickly. The problem is less how the demolishers knew which house to knock down, and more how they confirmed that knowledge. They trusted the paperwork, and the paperwork was wrong. Informality works when everybody knows everybody else. When merchants and customers know each other, government officials and citizens know each other, and people know their neighbors, people know what's going on. In that sort of milieu, if something goes wrong, people notice.

In our modern anonymous world, paperwork is how things get done. Traditionally, signatures, forms, and watermarks all made paperwork official.

Forgeries were possible but difficult. Today, there's still paperwork, but for the most part it only exists until the information makes its way into a computer database. Meanwhile, modern technology—computers, fax machines and desktop publishing software—has made it easy to forge paperwork. Every case of identity theft has, at its core, a paperwork failure. Fake work orders, purchase orders, and other documents are used to steal computers, equipment, and stock. Occasionally, fake faxes result in people being sprung from prison. Fake boarding passes can get you through airport security. This month hackers officially changed the name of a Swedish man.

A reporter even changed the ownership of the Empire State Building. Sure, it was a stunt, but this is a growing form of crime. Someone pretends to be you—preferably when you're away on holiday—and sells your home to someone else, forging your name on the paperwork. You return to find someone else living in your house, someone who thinks he legitimately bought it. In some senses, this isn't new. Paperwork mistakes and fraud have happened ever since there was paperwork. And the problem hasn't been fixed yet for several reasons.

One, our sloppy systems generally work fine, and it's how we get things done with minimum hassle. Most people's houses don't get demolished and most people's names don't get maliciously changed. As common as identity theft is, it doesn't happen to most of us. These stories are news because they are so rare. And in many cases, it's cheaper to pay for the occasional blunder than ensure it never happens.

Two, sometimes the incentives aren't in place for paperwork to be properly authenticated. The people who demolished that family home were just trying to get a job done. The same is true for government officials processing title and name changes. Banks get paid when money is transferred from one account to another, not when they find a paperwork problem. We're all irritated by forms stamped 17 times, and other mysterious bureaucratic processes, but these are actually designed to detect problems.

And three, there's a psychological mismatch: it is easy to fake paperwork, yet for the most part we act as if it has magical properties of authenticity. What's changed is scale. Fraud can be perpetrated against hundreds of thousands, automatically. Mistakes can affect that many people, too. What we need are laws that penalize people or companies—criminally or civilly—who make paperwork errors. This raises the cost of mistakes, making authenticating paperwork more attractive, which changes the incentives of those on the receiving end of the paperwork. And that will cause the market to devise technologies to verify the provenance, accuracy, and integrity of information: telephone verification, addresses and GPS co-ordinates, cryptographic authentication, systems that double- and triple-check, and so on.

We can't reduce society's reliance on paperwork, and we can't eliminate errors based on it. But we can put economic incentives in place for people and companies to authenticate paperwork more.

So-Called Cyberattack Was Overblown

Originally published in MPR News Q, *July 13, 2009*

To hear the media tell it, the United States suffered a major cyberattack last week. Stories were everywhere. "Cyber Blitz hits US, Korea" was the headline in Thursday's Wall Street Journal. North Korea was blamed.

Where were you when North Korea attacked America? Did you feel the fury of North Korea's armies? Were you fearful for your country? Or did your resolve strengthen, knowing that we would defend our homeland bravely and valiantly?

My guess is that you didn't even notice, that—if you didn't open a newspaper or read a news website—you had no idea anything was happening. Sure, a few government websites were knocked out, but that's not alarming or even uncommon. Other government websites were attacked but defended themselves, the sort of thing that happens all the time. If this is what an international cyberattack looks like, it hardly seems worth worrying about at all.

Politically motivated cyberattacks are nothing new. We've seen UK vs. Ireland. Israel vs. the Arab states. Russia vs. several former Soviet Republics. India vs. Pakistan, especially after the nuclear bomb tests in 1998. China vs. the United States, especially in 2001 when a US spy plane collided with a Chinese fighter jet. And so on and so on.

The big one happened in 2007, when the government of Estonia was attacked in cyberspace following a diplomatic incident with Russia about the relocation of a Soviet World War II memorial. The networks of many Estonian organizations, including the Estonian parliament, banks, ministries, newspapers and broadcasters, were attacked and—in many cases—shut down. Estonia was quick to blame Russia, which was equally quick to deny any involvement.

It was hyped as the first cyberwar, but after two years there is still no evidence that the Russian government was involved. Though Russian hackers were indisputably the major instigators of the attack, the only individuals positively identified have been young ethnic Russians living inside Estonia, who were angry over the statue incident.

Poke at any of these international incidents, and what you find are kids playing politics. Last Wednesday, South Korea's National Intelligence Service admitted that it didn't actually know that North Korea was behind the attacks: "North Korea or North Korean sympathizers in the South" was what it said. Once again, it'll be kids playing politics.

This isn't to say that cyberattacks by governments aren't an issue, or that cyberwar is something to be ignored. The constant attacks by Chinese nationals against US networks may not be government-sponsored, but it's pretty clear that they're tacitly government-approved. Criminals, from lone hackers to organized crime syndicates, attack networks all the time. And war expands to fill every possible theater: land, sea, air, space, and now cyberspace. But cyberterrorism is nothing more than a media invention designed to scare people. And for there to be a cyberwar, there first needs to be a war.

Israel is currently considering attacking Iran in cyberspace, for example. If it tries, it'll discover that attacking computer networks is an inconvenience to the nuclear facilities it's targeting, but doesn't begin to substitute for bombing them.

In May, President Obama gave a major speech on cybersecurity. He was right when he said that cybersecurity is a national security issue, and that the government needs to step up and do more to prevent cyberattacks. But he couldn't resist hyping the threat with scare stories: "In one of the most serious cyber incidents to date against our military networks, several thousand computers were infected last year by malicious software—malware," he said. What he didn't add was that those infections occurred because the Air Force couldn't be bothered to keep its patches up to date.

This is the face of cyberwar: easily preventable attacks that, even when they succeed, only a few people notice. Even this current incident is turning out to be a sloppily modified five-year-old worm that no modern network should still be vulnerable to.

Securing our networks doesn't require some secret advanced NSA technology. It's the boring network security administration stuff we already know how to do: keep your patches up to date, install good anti-malware software, correctly configure your firewalls and intrusion-detection systems, monitor your networks. And while some government and corporate networks do a pretty good job at this, others fail again and again.

Enough of the hype and the bluster. The news isn't the attacks, but that some networks had security lousy enough to be vulnerable to them.

Why Framing Your Enemies Is Now Virtually Child's Play

Originally published in the Guardian, *October 15, 2009*

A few years ago, a company began to sell a liquid with identification codes suspended in it. The idea was that you would paint it on your stuff as proof of ownership. I commented that I would paint it on someone else's stuff, then call the police.

I was reminded of this recently when a group of Israeli scientists demonstrated that it's possible to fabricate DNA evidence. So now, instead of leaving your own DNA at a crime scene, you can leave fabricated DNA. And it isn't even necessary to fabricate. In Charlie Stross's novel *Halting State*, the bad guys foul a crime scene by blowing around the contents of a vacuum cleaner bag, containing the DNA of dozens, if not hundreds, of people.

This kind of thing has been going on forever. It's an arms race, and when technology changes, the balance between attacker and defender changes. But when automated systems do the detecting, the results are different. Face recognition software can be fooled by cosmetic surgery, or sometimes even just a photograph. And when fooling them becomes harder, the bad guys fool them on a different level. Computer-based detection gives the defender economies of scale, but the attacker can use those same economies of scale to defeat the detection system.

Google, for example, has anti-fraud systems that detect—and shut down—advertisers who try to inflate their revenue by repeatedly clicking on their own AdSense ads. So people built bots to repeatedly click on the AdSense ads of their competitors, trying to convince Google to kick them out of the system.

Similarly, when Google started penalizing a site's search engine rankings for having "bad neighbors"—backlinks from link farms, adult or gambling sites, or blog spam—people engaged in sabotage: they built link farms and left blog comment spam linking to their competitors' sites.

The same sort of thing is happening on Yahoo Answers. Initially, companies would leave answers pushing their products, but Yahoo started policing this.

So people have written bots to report abuse on all their competitors. There are Facebook bots doing the same sort of thing.

Last month, Google introduced Sidewiki, a browser feature that lets you read and post comments on virtually any webpage. People and industries are worried about the effects unrestrained commentary might have on their businesses, and how they might control the comments. I'm sure Google has sophisticated systems ready to detect commercial interests that try to take advantage of the system, but are they ready to deal with commercial interests that try to frame their competitors? And do we want to give one company the power to decide which comments should rise to the top and which get deleted?

Whenever you build a security system that relies on detection and identification, you invite the bad guys to subvert the system so it detects and identifies someone else. Sometimes this is hard—leaving someone else's fingerprints on a crime scene is hard, as is using a mask of someone else's face to fool a guard watching a security camera—and sometimes it's easy. But when automated systems are involved, it's often very easy. It's not just hardened criminals that try to frame each other, it's mainstream commercial interests.

With systems that police Internet comments and links, there's money involved in commercial messages—so you can be sure some will take advantage of it. This is the arms race. Build a detection system, and the bad guys try to frame someone else. Build a detection system to detect framing, and the bad guys try to frame someone else framing someone else. Build a detection system to detect framing of framing, and well, there's no end, really. Commercial speech is on the Internet to stay; we can only hope that they don't pollute the social systems we use so badly that they're no longer useful.

Beyond Security Theater

Originally published in New Internationalist, *n. 427, November 2009, pp. 10–13*

Terrorism is rare, far rarer than many people think. It's rare because very few people want to commit acts of terrorism, and executing a terrorist plot is much harder than television makes it appear. The best defenses against terrorism are largely invisible: investigation, intelligence, and emergency response. But even these are less effective at keeping us safe than our social and political policies, both at home and abroad. However, our elected leaders don't think this way: they are far more likely to implement security theater against movie-plot threats.

A movie-plot threat is an overly specific attack scenario. Whether it's terrorists with crop dusters, terrorists contaminating the milk supply, or terrorists attacking the Olympics, specific stories affect our emotions more intensely than mere data does. Stories are what we fear. It's not just hypothetical stories: terrorists flying planes into buildings, terrorists with bombs in their shoes or in their water bottles, and terrorists with guns and bombs waging a coordinated attack against a city are even scarier movie-plot threats because they actually happened.

Security theater refers to security measures that make people feel more secure without doing anything to actually improve their security. An example: the photo ID checks that have sprung up in office buildings. No-one has ever explained why verifying that someone has a photo ID provides any actual security, but it looks like security to have a uniformed guard-for-hire looking at ID cards. Airport-security examples include the National Guard troops stationed at US airports in the months after 9/11—their guns had no bullets. The US color-coded system of threat levels, the pervasive harassment of photographers, and the metal detectors that are increasingly common in hotels and office buildings since the Mumbai terrorist attacks, are additional examples.

To be sure, reasonable arguments can be made that some terrorist targets are more attractive than others: airplanes because a small bomb can result in the death of everyone aboard, monuments because of their national significance, national events because of television coverage, and transportation because of the numbers of people who commute daily. But there are literally millions of potential targets in any large country (there are five million commercial buildings alone in the US), and hundreds of potential terrorist tactics; it's impossible to defend every place against everything, and it's impossible to predict which tactic and target terrorists will try next.

Feeling and Reality

Security is both a feeling and a reality. The propensity for security theater comes from the interplay between the public and its leaders. When people are scared, they need something done that will make them feel safe, even if it doesn't truly make them safer. Politicians naturally want to do something in response to crisis, even if that something doesn't make any sense.

Often, this "something" is directly related to the details of a recent event: we confiscate liquids, screen shoes, and ban box cutters on airplanes. But it's not the target and tactics of the last attack that are important, but the next attack. These measures are only effective if we happen to guess what the next terrorists are planning. If we spend billions defending our rail systems, and the terrorists bomb a shopping mall instead, we've wasted our money. If we concentrate airport security on screening shoes and confiscating liquids, and the terrorists hide explosives in their brassieres and use solids, we've wasted our money. Terrorists don't care what they blow up and it shouldn't be our goal merely to force the terrorists to make a minor change in their tactics or targets.

Our penchant for movie plots blinds us to the broader threats. And security theater consumes resources that could better be spent elsewhere.

Any terrorist attack is a series of events: something like planning, recruiting, funding, practicing, executing, aftermath. Our most effective defenses are at the beginning and end of that process—intelligence, investigation, and emergency response—and least effective when they require us to guess the plot correctly. By intelligence and investigation, I don't mean the broad data-mining or eavesdropping systems that have been proposed and in some cases implemented—those are also movie-plot stories without much basis in actual effectiveness—but instead the traditional "follow the evidence" type of investigation that has worked for decades.

Unfortunately for politicians, the security measures that work are largely invisible. Such measures include enhancing the intelligence-gathering abilities of the secret services, hiring cultural experts and Arabic translators, building bridges with Islamic communities both nationally and internationally, funding police capabilities—both investigative arms to prevent terrorist attacks, and emergency communications systems for after attacks occur—and arresting terrorist plotters without media fanfare. They do not include expansive new police or spying laws. Our police don't need any new laws to deal with terrorism; rather, they need apolitical funding. These security measures don't make good television, and they don't help, come re-election time. But they work, addressing the reality of security instead of the feeling.

The arrest of the "liquid bombers" in London is an example: they were caught through old-fashioned intelligence and police work. Their choice of target (airplanes) and tactic (liquid explosives) didn't matter; they would have been arrested regardless.

But even as we do all of this we cannot neglect the feeling of security, because it's how we collectively overcome the psychological damage that terrorism causes. It's not security theater we need, it's direct appeals to our feelings. The best way to help people feel secure is by acting secure around them. Instead of reacting to terrorism with fear, we—and our leaders—need to react with indomitability.

Refuse to Be Terrorized

By not overreacting, by not responding to movie-plot threats, and by not becoming defensive, we demonstrate the resilience of our society, in our laws, our culture, our freedoms. There is a difference between indomitability and arrogant "bring 'em on" rhetoric. There's a difference between accepting the inherent risk that comes with a free and open society, and hyping the threats.

We should treat terrorists like common criminals and give them all the benefits of true and open justice—not merely because it demonstrates our indomitability, but because it makes us all safer. Once a society starts circumventing its own laws, the risks to its future stability are much greater than terrorism.

Supporting real security even though it's invisible, and demonstrating indomitability even though fear is more politically expedient, requires real courage. Demagoguery is easy. What we need is leaders willing both to do what's right and to speak the truth.

Despite fearful rhetoric to the contrary, terrorism is not a transcendent threat. A terrorist attack cannot possibly destroy a country's way of life; it's only our reaction to that attack that can do that kind of damage. The more we undermine our own laws, the more we convert our buildings into fortresses, the more we reduce the freedoms and liberties at the foundation of our societies, the more we're doing the terrorists' job for them.

We saw some of this in the Londoners' reaction to the 2005 transport bombings. Among the political and media hype and fearmongering, there was a thread of firm resolve. People didn't fall victim to fear. They rode the trains and buses the next day and continued their lives. Terrorism's goal isn't murder; terrorism attacks the mind, using victims as a prop. By refusing to be terrorized, we deny the terrorists their primary weapon: our own fear.

Today, we can project indomitability by rolling back all the fear-based post-9/11 security measures. Our leaders have lost credibility; getting it back requires a decrease in hyperbole. Ditch the invasive mass surveillance systems and new police state-like powers. Return airport security to pre-9/11 levels. Remove swagger from our foreign policies. Show the world that our legal system is up to the challenge of terrorism. Stop telling people to report all suspicious activity; it does little but make us suspicious of each other, increasing both fear and helplessness.

Terrorism has always been rare, and for all we've heard about 9/11 changing the world, it's still rare. Even 9/11 failed to kill as many people as automobiles do in the US every single month. But there's a pervasive myth that terrorism is easy. It's easy to imagine terrorist plots, both large-scale "poison the food supply" and small-scale "10 guys with guns and cars." Movies and television bolster this myth, so many people are surprised that there have been so few attacks in Western cities since 9/11. Certainly intelligence and investigation successes have made it harder, but mostly it's because terrorist attacks are actually hard. It's hard to find willing recruits, to co-ordinate plans, and to execute those plans—and it's easy to make mistakes.

Counterterrorism is also hard, especially when we're psychologically prone to muck it up. Since 9/11, we've embarked on strategies of defending specific targets against specific tactics, overreacting to every terrorist video, stoking fear, demonizing ethnic groups, and treating the terrorists as if they were legitimate military opponents who could actually destroy a country or a way of life—all of this plays into the hands of terrorists. We'd do much better by leveraging the inherent strengths of our modern democracies and the natural advantages we have over the terrorists: our adaptability and survivability, our international network of laws and law enforcement, and the freedoms and liberties that make our society so enviable. The way we live is open enough to make terrorists rare; we are observant enough to prevent most of the terrorist plots that exist, and indomitable enough to survive the even fewer terrorist plots that actually succeed. We don't need to pretend otherwise.

Cold War Encryption Is Unrealistic in Today's Trenches

Originally published in the Japan Times, *December 23, 2009*

Sometimes mediocre encryption is better than strong encryption, and sometimes no encryption is better still.

The *Wall Street Journal* reported this week that Iraqi, and possibly also Afghan, militants are using commercial software to eavesdrop on US Predators, other unmanned aerial vehicles, or UAVs, and even piloted planes. The systems weren't "hacked"—the insurgents can't control them—but because the downlink is unencrypted, they can watch the same video stream as the coalition troops on the ground.

The naive reaction is to ridicule the military. Encryption is so easy that HDTVs do it—just a software routine and you're done—and the Pentagon has known about this flaw since Bosnia in the 1990s. But encrypting the data is the easiest part; key management is the hard part. Each UAV needs to share a key with the ground station. These keys have to be produced, guarded, transported, used and then destroyed. And the equipment, both the Predators and the ground terminals, needs to be classified and controlled, and all the users need security clearance.

The command and control channel is, and always has been, encrypted—because that's both more important and easier to manage. UAVs are flown by airmen sitting at comfortable desks on US military bases, where key management is simpler. But the video feed is different. It needs to be available to all sorts of people, of varying nationalities and security clearances, on a variety of field terminals, in a variety of geographical areas, in all sorts of conditions—with everything constantly changing. Key management in this environment would be a nightmare.

Additionally, how valuable is this video downlink to the enemy? The primary fear seems to be that the militants watch the video, notice their compound being surveilled and flee before the missiles hit. Or notice a bunch of Marines walking through a recognizable area and attack them. This might make a great movie scene, but it's not very realistic. Without context, and just by peeking at random video streams, the risk caused by eavesdropping is low.

Contrast this with the additional risks if you encrypt: A soldier in the field doesn't have access to the real-time video because of a key management failure; a UAV can't be quickly deployed to a new area because the keys aren't in place; we can't share the video information with our allies because we can't give them the keys; most soldiers can't use this technology because they don't have the right clearances. Given this risk analysis, not encrypting the video is almost certainly the right decision.

There is another option, though. During the Cold War, the NSA's primary adversary was Soviet intelligence, and it developed its crypto solutions accordingly. Even though that level of security makes no sense in Bosnia, and certainly not in Iraq and Afghanistan, it is what the NSA had to offer. If you encrypt, they said, you have to do it "right."

The problem is, the world has changed. Today's insurgent adversaries don't have KGB-level intelligence gathering or cryptanalytic capabilities. At the same time, computer and network data gathering has become much cheaper and easier, so they have technical capabilities the Soviets could only dream of. Defending against these sorts of adversaries doesn't require military-grade encryption only where it counts; it requires commercial-grade encryption everywhere possible.

This sort of solution would require the NSA to develop a whole new level of lightweight commercial-grade security systems for military applications—not just office-data "Sensitive but Unclassified" or "For Official Use Only" classifications. It would require the NSA to allow keys to be handed to uncleared UAV operators, and perhaps read over insecure phone lines and stored in people's back pockets. It would require the sort of ad hoc key management systems you find in Internet protocols, or in DRM systems. It wouldn't be anywhere near perfect, but it would be more commensurate with the actual threats.

And it would help defend against a completely different threat facing the Pentagon: The PR threat. Regardless of whether the people responsible made the right security decision when they rushed the Predator into production, or when they convinced themselves that local adversaries wouldn't know how to exploit it, or when they forgot to update their Bosnia-era threat analysis to account for advances in technology, the story is now being played out in the press. The Pentagon is getting beaten up because it's not protecting against the threat—because it's easy to make a sound bite where the threat sounds really dire. And now it has to defend against the perceived threat to the troops, regardless of whether the defense actually protects the troops or not. Reminds me of the TSA, actually.

So the military is now committed to encrypting the video. . . eventually. The next generation Predators, called Reapers—Who names this stuff? Second-grade boys?—will have the same weakness. Maybe we'll have encrypted video by 2010, or 2014, but I don't think that's even remotely possible unless the NSA relaxes its key management and classification requirements and embraces a lightweight, less secure encryption solution for these sorts of situations. The real failure here is the failure of the Cold War security model to deal with today's threats.

Profiling Makes Us Less Safe

Originally published in New York Times Room for Debate *blog, January 4, 2010*

There are two kinds of profiling. There's behavioral profiling based on how someone acts, and there's automatic profiling based on name, nationality, method of ticket purchase, and so on. The first one can be effective, but is very hard to do right. The second one makes us all less safe. The problem with automatic profiling is that it doesn't work.

Terrorists don't fit a profile and cannot be plucked out of crowds by computers. They're European, Asian, African, Hispanic, and Middle Eastern, male and female, young and old. Umar Farouk Abdul Mutallab was Nigerian. Richard Reid, the shoe bomber, was British with a Jamaican father. Germaine Lindsay, one of the 7/7 London bombers, was Afro-Caribbean. Dirty bomb suspect Jose Padilla was Hispanic-American. The 2002 Bali terrorists were Indonesian. Timothy McVeigh was a white American. So was the Unabomber. The Chechen terrorists who blew up two Russian planes in 2004 were female. Palestinian terrorists routinely recruit "clean" suicide bombers, and have used unsuspecting Westerners as bomb carriers.

Without an accurate profile, the system can be statistically demonstrated to be no more effective than random screening.

And, even worse, profiling creates two paths through security: one with less scrutiny and one with more. And once you do that, you invite the terrorists to take the path with less scrutiny. That is, a terrorist group can safely probe any profiling system and figure out how to beat the profile. And once they do, they're going to get through airport security with the minimum level of screening every time.

As counterintuitive as it may seem, we're all more secure when we randomly select people for secondary screening—even if it means occasionally screening wheelchair-bound grandmothers and innocent looking children. And, as an added bonus, it doesn't needlessly anger the ethnic groups we need on our side if we're going to be more secure against terrorism.

Fixing Intelligence Failures

Originally published in San Francisco Chronicle, *January 15, 2010*

President Obama in his speech last week rightly focused on fixing the intelligence failures that resulted in Umar Farouk Abdulmutallab being ignored, rather than on technologies targeted at the details of his underwear-bomb plot. But while Obama's instincts are right, reforming intelligence for this new century and its new threats is a more difficult task than he might like.

We don't need new technologies, new laws, new bureaucratic overlords, or—for heaven's sake—new agencies. What prevents information sharing among intelligence organizations is the culture of the generation that built those organizations.

The US intelligence system is a sprawling apparatus, spanning the FBI and the State Department, the CIA and the National Security Agency, and the Department of Homeland Security—itself an amalgamation of two dozen different organizations—designed and optimized to fight the Cold War. The single, enormous adversary then was the Soviet Union: as bureaucratic as they come, with a huge budget, and capable of very sophisticated espionage operations. We needed to defend against technologically advanced electronic eavesdropping operations, their agents trying to bribe or seduce our agents, and a worldwide intelligence gathering capability that hung on our every word.

In that environment, secrecy was paramount. Information had to be protected by armed guards and double fences, shared only among those with appropriate security clearances and a legitimate "need to know," and it was better not to transmit information at all than to transmit it insecurely.

Today's adversaries are different. There are still governments, like China, that are after our secrets. But the secrets they're after are more often corporate than military, and most of the other organizations of interest are like al Qaeda: decentralized, poorly funded and incapable of the intricate spy versus spy operations the Soviet Union could pull off.

Against these adversaries, sharing is far more important than secrecy. Our intelligence organizations need to trade techniques and expertise with industry, and they need to share information among the different parts of themselves. Today's terrorist plots are loosely organized ad hoc affairs, and those dots that are so important for us to connect beforehand might be on different desks, in different buildings, owned by different organizations.

Critics have pointed to laws that prohibited inter-agency sharing but, as the 9/11 commission found, the law allows for far more sharing than goes on. It doesn't happen because of inter-agency rivalries, a reliance on outdated information systems, and a culture of secrecy. What we need is an intelligence community that shares ideas and hunches and facts on their versions of Facebook, Twitter and wikis. We need the bottom-up organization that has made the Internet the greatest collection of human knowledge and ideas ever assembled.

The problem is far more social than technological. Teaching your mom to "text" and your dad to Twitter doesn't make them part of the Internet generation, and giving all those cold warriors blogging lessons won't change their mentality—or the culture. The reason this continues to be a problem, the reason President George W. Bush couldn't change things even after the 9/11 commission came to much the same conclusions as President Obama's recent review did, is generational.

The Internet is the greatest generation gap since rock "n" roll, and it's just as true inside government as out. We might have to wait for the elders inside these agencies to retire and be replaced by people who grew up with the Internet.

Spy Cameras Won't Make Us Safer

Originally published in CNN, February 25, 2010

On January 19, a team of at least 15 people assassinated Hamas leader Mahmoud al-Mabhouh. The Dubai police released video footage of 11 of them. While it was obviously a very professional operation, the 27 minutes of video is fascinating in its banality. Team members walk through the airport, check in and out of hotels, get in and out of taxis. They make no effort to hide themselves from the cameras, sometimes seeming to stare directly into them. They obviously don't care that they're being recorded, and—in fact—the cameras didn't prevent the assassination, nor as far as we know have they helped as yet in identifying the killers.

Pervasive security cameras don't substantially reduce crime. This fact has been demonstrated repeatedly: in San Francisco public housing, in a New York apartment complex, in Philadelphia, in Washington, DC, in study after study in both the US and the UK. Nor are they instrumental in solving many crimes after the fact.

There are exceptions, of course, and proponents of cameras can always cherry-pick examples to bolster their argument. These success stories are what convince us; our brains are wired to respond more strongly to anecdotes than to data. But the data is clear: CCTV cameras have minimal value in the fight against crime.

While it's comforting to imagine vigilant police monitoring every camera, the truth is very different, for a variety of reasons: technological limitations of cameras, organizational limitations of police, and the adaptive abilities of criminals. No one looks at most CCTV footage until well after a crime is committed. And when the police do look at the recordings, it's very common for them to be unable to identify suspects. Criminals don't often stare helpfully at the lens, and—unlike the Dubai assassins—tend to wear sunglasses and hats. Cameras break far too often. Even when they afford quick identification—think of the footage of the 9/11 terrorists going through airport security, or the 7/7 London transport bombers just before the bombs exploded—police are often able to identify those suspects even without the cameras. Cameras afford a false sense of security, encouraging laziness when we need police to be vigilant.

The solution isn't for police to watch the cameras more diligently. Unlike an officer walking the street, cameras only look in particular directions at particular locations. Criminals know this, and can easily adapt by moving their crimes to places not watched by a camera—and there will always be such places. And while a police officer on the street can respond to a crime in progress, someone watching a CCTV screen can only dispatch an officer to arrive much later. By their very nature, cameras result in underused and misallocated police resources.

Cameras aren't completely ineffective, of course. Used properly, they're effective in reducing crime in enclosed areas with minimal foot traffic. Combined with adequate lighting, they substantially reduce both personal attacks and auto-related crime in multi-story parking garages. And sometimes it is cost-effective for a store to install cameras to catch shoplifters, or a casino to install cameras to detect cheaters. But these are instances where there is a specific risk at a specific location.

But the important question isn't whether cameras solve past crime or deter future crime; it's whether they're a good use of resources. They're expensive, both in money and their Orwellian effects on privacy and civil liberties. Their inevitable misuse is another cost: police have already spied on naked women in their own homes, shared nude images, sold best-of videos, and spied on national politicians. While we might be willing to accept these downsides for a real increase in security, cameras don't provide that. Despite our predilection for preferring technological solutions over human ones, the funds now spent on CCTV cameras would be far better spent on hiring and training police officers.

We live in a unique time in our society: cameras are everywhere, but we can still see them. Ten years ago, cameras were much rarer than they are today. Ten years from now, they'll be so small you won't even notice them. Already, people can buy surveillance cameras in household objects to spy on their spouses and baby sitters—I particularly like the one hidden in a shower mirror—cameras in pens to spy on their colleagues, and remotely turn on laptop cameras to spy on anyone. Companies are developing police state–type CCTV surveillance technologies for China, technology that will find its way into countries like the US

If universal surveillance were the answer, lots of us would have moved to former East Germany. If surveillance cameras were the answer, camera-happy London, with something like 500,000 of them at a cost of $700 million, would be the safest city on the planet. We didn't and it isn't, because surveillance and surveillance cameras don't make us safer. The money spent on cameras in London, and in cities across America, could be much better spent on actual policing.

Scanners, Sensors Are Wrong Way to Secure the Subway

Originally published in Daily News, *April 7, 2010*

People intent on preventing a Moscow-style terrorist attack against the New York subway system are proposing a range of expensive new underground security measures, some temporary and some permanent.

They should save their money—and instead invest every penny they're considering pouring into new technologies into intelligence and old-fashioned policing.

Intensifying security at specific stations only works against terrorists who aren't smart enough to move to another station. Cameras are useful only if all the stars align: The terrorists happen to walk into the frame, the video feeds are being watched in real time and the police can respond quickly enough to be effective. They're much more useful *after* an attack, to figure out who pulled it off.

Installing biological and chemical detectors requires similarly implausible luck—plus a terrorist plot that includes the specific biological or chemical agent that is being detected.

What all these misguided reactions have in common is that they're based on "movie-plot threats": overly specific attack scenarios. They fill our imagination vividly, in full color with rich detail. Before long, we're envisioning an entire story line, with or without Bruce Willis saving the day. And we're scared.

It's not that movie-plot threats are not worth worrying about. It's that each one—Moscow's subway attack, the bombing of the Oklahoma City federal building, etc.—is too specific. These threats are infinite, and the bad guys can easily switch among them.

New York has thousands of possible targets, and there are dozens of possible tactics. Implementing security against movie-plot threats is only effective if we correctly guess which specific threat to protect against. That's unlikely.

A far better strategy is to spend our limited counterterrorism resources on investigation and intelligence—and on emergency response. These measures don't hinge on any specific threat; they don't require us to guess the tactic or target correctly. They're effective in a variety of circumstances, even nonterrorist ones.

The result may not be flashy or outwardly reassuring—as are pricey new scanners in airports. But the strategy will save more lives.

The 2006 arrest of the liquid bombers—who wanted to detonate liquid explosives to be brought onboard airliners traveling from England to North America—serves as an excellent example. The plotters were arrested in their London apartments, and their attack was foiled before they ever got to the airport.

It didn't matter if they were using liquids or solids or gases. It didn't even matter if they were targeting airports or shopping malls or theaters. It was a straightforward, although hardly simple, matter of following leads.

Gimmicky security measures are tempting—but they're distractions we can't afford. The Christmas Day bomber chose his tactic because it would circumvent last year's security measures, and the next attacker will choose his tactic—and target—according to similar criteria. Spend money on cameras and guards in the subways, and the terrorists will simply modify their plot to render those countermeasures ineffective.

Humans are a species of storytellers, and the Moscow story has obvious parallels in New York. When we read the word "subway," we can't help but think about the system we use every day. This is a natural response, but it doesn't make for good public policy. We'd all be safer if we rose above the simple parallels and the need to calm our fears with expensive and seductive new technologies—and countered the threat the smart way.

Preventing Terrorist Attacks in Crowded Areas

Originally published in New York Times Room for Debate *blog,*
May 3, 2010

In the wake of Saturday's failed Times Square car bombing, it's natural to ask how we can prevent this sort of thing from happening again. The answer is stop focusing on the specifics of what actually happened, and instead think about the threat in general.

Think about the security measures commonly proposed. Cameras won't help. They don't prevent terrorist attacks, and their forensic value after the fact is minimal. In the Times Square case, surely there's enough other evidence—the car's identification number, the auto body shop the stolen license plates came from, the name of the fertilizer store—to identify the guy. We will almost certainly not need the camera footage. The images released so far, like the images in so many other terrorist attacks, may make for exciting television, but their value to law enforcement officers is limited.

Check points won't help, either. You can't check everybody and everything. There are too many people to check, and too many train stations, buses, theaters, department stores and other places where people congregate. Patrolling guards, bomb-sniffing dogs, chemical and biological weapons detectors: they all suffer from similar problems. In general, focusing on specific tactics or defending specific targets doesn't make sense. They're inflexible; possibly effective if you guess the plot correctly, but completely ineffective if you don't. At best, the countermeasures just force the terrorists to make minor changes in their tactic and target.

It's much smarter to spend our limited counterterrorism resources on measures that don't focus on the specific. It's more efficient to spend money on investigating and stopping terrorist attacks before they happen, and responding effectively to any that occur. This approach works because it's flexible and adaptive; it's effective regardless of what the bad guys are planning for next time.

After the Christmas Day airplane bombing attempt, I was asked how we can better protect our airplanes from terrorist attacks. I pointed out that the event was a security success—the plane landed safely, nobody was hurt, a terrorist was in custody—and that the next attack would probably have nothing to do with explosive underwear. After the Moscow subway bombing, I wrote that overly specific security countermeasures like subway cameras and sensors were a waste of money.

Now we have a failed car bombing in Times Square. We can't protect against the next imagined movie-plot threat. Isn't it time to recognize that the bad guys are flexible and adaptive, and that we need the same quality in our countermeasures?

Where Are All the Terrorist Attacks?

Originally published in AOL News, *May 4, 2010*

As the details of the Times Square car bomb attempt emerge in the wake of Faisal Shahzad's arrest Monday night, one thing has already been made clear: Terrorism is fairly easy. All you need is a gun or a bomb, and a crowded target. Guns are easy to buy. Bombs are easy to make. Crowded targets—not only in New York, but all over the country—are easy to come by. If you're willing to die in the aftermath of your attack, you could launch a pretty effective terrorist attack with a few days of planning, maybe less.

But if it's so easy, why aren't there more terrorist attacks like the failed car bomb in New York's Times Square? Or the terrorist shootings in Mumbai? Or the Moscow subway bombings? After the enormous horror and tragedy of 9/11, why have the past eight years been so safe in the US?

There are actually several answers to this question. One, terrorist attacks are harder to pull off than popular imagination—and the movies—lead everyone to believe. Two, there are far fewer terrorists than the political rhetoric of the past eight years leads everyone to believe. And three, random minor terrorist attacks don't serve Islamic terrorists' interests right now.

Hard to Pull Off

Terrorism sounds easy, but the actual attack is the easiest part.

Putting together the people, the plot and the materials is hard. It's hard to sneak terrorists into the US It's hard to grow your own inside the US It's hard to operate; the general population, even the Muslim population, is against you.

Movies and television make terrorist plots look easier than they are. It's hard to hold conspiracies together. It's easy to make a mistake. Even 9/11, which was planned before the climate of fear that event engendered, just barely succeeded. Today, it's much harder to pull something like that off without slipping up and getting arrested.

Few Terrorists

But even more important than the difficulty of executing a terrorist attack, there aren't a lot of terrorists out there.

Al-Qaida isn't a well-organized global organization with movie-plot-villain capabilities; it's a loose collection of people using the same name. Despite the post-9/11 rhetoric, there isn't a terrorist cell in every major city. If you think about the major terrorist plots we've foiled in the US—the JFK bombers, the Fort Dix plotters—they were mostly amateur terrorist wannabes with no connection to any sort of al-Qaida central command, and mostly no ability to effectively carry out the attacks they planned.

The successful terrorist attacks—the Fort Hood shooter, the guy who flew his plane into the Austin IRS office, the anthrax mailer—were largely nut cases operating alone. Even the unsuccessful shoe bomber, and the equally unsuccessful Christmas Day underwear bomber, had minimal organized help—and that help originated outside the US.

Terrorism doesn't occur without terrorists, and they are far rarer than popular opinion would have it.

Small Attacks Aren't Enough

Lastly, and perhaps most subtly, there's not a lot of value in unspectacular terrorism anymore.

If you think about it, terrorism is essentially a PR stunt. The death of innocents and the destruction of property isn't the goal of terrorism; it's just the tactic used. And acts of terrorism are intended for two audiences: for the victims, who are supposed to be terrorized as a result, and for the allies and potential allies of the terrorists, who are supposed to give them more funding and generally support their efforts.

An act of terrorism that doesn't instill terror in the target population is a failure, even if people die. And an act of terrorism that doesn't impress the terrorists' allies is not very effective, either.

Fortunately for us and unfortunately for the terrorists, 9/11 upped the stakes. It's no longer enough to blow up something like the Oklahoma City Federal Building. Terrorists need to blow up airplanes or the Brooklyn Bridge or the Sears Tower or JFK airport—something big to impress the folks back home. Small no-name targets just don't cut it anymore.

Note that this is very different than terrorism by an occupied population: the IRA in Northern Ireland, Iraqis in Iraq, Palestinians in Israel. Setting aside the actual politics, all of these terrorists believe they are repelling foreign invaders. That's not the situation here in the US

So, to sum up: If you're just a loner wannabe who wants to go out with a bang, terrorism is easy. You're more likely to get caught if you take a long time to plan or involve a bunch of people, but you might succeed. If you're a representative of al-Qaida trying to make a statement in the US, it's much harder. You just don't have the people, and you're probably going to slip up and get caught.

Worst-Case Thinking Makes Us Nuts, Not Safe

Originally published in CNN, May 12, 2010

At a security conference recently, the moderator asked the panel of distinguished cybersecurity leaders what their nightmare scenario was. The answers were the predictable array of large-scale attacks: against our communications infrastructure, against the power grid, against the financial system, in combination with a physical attack.

I didn't get to give my answer until the afternoon, which was: "My nightmare scenario is that people keep talking about their nightmare scenarios."

There's a certain blindness that comes from worst-case thinking. An extension of the precautionary principle, it involves imagining the worst possible outcome and then acting as if it were a certainty. It substitutes imagination for thinking, speculation for risk analysis and fear for reason. It fosters powerlessness and vulnerability and magnifies social paralysis. And it makes us more vulnerable to the effects of terrorism.

Worst-case thinking means generally bad decision making for several reasons. First, it's only half of the cost-benefit equation. Every decision has costs and benefits, risks and rewards. By speculating about what can possibly go wrong, and then acting as if that is likely to happen, worst-case thinking focuses only on the extreme but improbable risks and does a poor job at assessing outcomes.

Second, it's based on flawed logic. It begs the question by assuming that a proponent of an action must prove that the nightmare scenario is impossible.

Third, it can be used to support any position or its opposite. If we build a nuclear power plant, it could melt down. If we don't build it, we will run short of power and society will collapse into anarchy. If we allow flights near Iceland's volcanic ash, planes will crash and people will die. If we don't, organs won't arrive in time for transplant operations and people will die. If we don't invade Iraq, Saddam Hussein might use the nuclear weapons he might have. If we do, we might destabilize the Middle East, leading to widespread violence and death.

Of course, not all fears are equal. Those that we tend to exaggerate are more easily justified by worst-case thinking. So terrorism fears trump privacy fears, and almost everything else; technology is hard to understand and therefore scary; nuclear weapons are worse than conventional weapons; our children need to be protected at all costs; and annihilating the planet is bad. Basically, any fear that would make a good movie plot is amenable to worst-case thinking.

Fourth and finally, worst-case thinking validates ignorance. Instead of focusing on what we know, it focuses on what we don't know—and what we can imagine.

Remember Defense Secretary Donald Rumsfeld's quote? "Reports that say that something hasn't happened are always interesting to me, because as we know, there are known knowns; there are things we know we know. We also know there are known unknowns; that is to say we know there are some things we do not know. But there are also unknown unknowns—the ones we don't know we don't know." And this: "the absence of evidence is not evidence of absence." Ignorance isn't a cause for doubt; when you can fill that ignorance with imagination, it can be a call to action.

Even worse, it can lead to hasty and dangerous acts. You can't wait for a smoking gun, so you act as if the gun is about to go off. Rather than making us safer, worst-case thinking has the potential to cause dangerous escalation.

The new undercurrent in this is that our society no longer has the ability to calculate probabilities. Risk assessment is devalued. Probabilistic thinking is repudiated in favor of "possibilistic thinking": Since we can't know what's likely to go wrong, let's speculate about what can possibly go wrong.

Worst-case thinking leads to bad decisions, bad systems design, and bad security. And we all have direct experience with its effects: airline security and the TSA, which we make fun of when we're not appalled that they're harassing 93-year-old women or keeping first-graders off airplanes. You can't be too careful!

Actually, you can. You can refuse to fly because of the possibility of plane crashes. You can lock your children in the house because of the possibility of child predators. You can eschew all contact with people because of the possibility of hurt. Steven Hawking wants to avoid trying to communicate with aliens because they might be hostile; does he want to turn off all the planet's television broadcasts because they're radiating into space? It isn't hard to parody worst-case thinking, and at its extreme it's a psychological condition.

Frank Furedi, a sociology professor at the University of Kent, writes: "Worst-case thinking encourages society to adopt fear as one of the dominant principles around which the public, the government and institutions should organize their life. It institutionalizes insecurity and fosters a mood of confusion and powerlessness. Through popularizing the belief that worst cases are normal, it incites people to feel defenseless and vulnerable to a wide range of future threats."

Even worse, it plays directly into the hands of terrorists, creating a population that is easily terrorized—even by failed terrorist attacks like the Christmas Day underwear bomber and the Times Square SUV bomber.

When someone is proposing a change, the onus should be on them to justify it over the status quo. But worst case thinking is a way of looking at the world that exaggerates the rare and unusual and gives the rare much more credence than it deserves.

It isn't really a principle; it's a cheap trick to justify what you already believe. It lets lazy or biased people make what seem to be cogent arguments without understanding the whole issue. And when people don't need to refute counterarguments, there's no point in listening to them.

Threat of "Cyberwar" Has Been Hugely Hyped

Originally published in CNN, *July 7, 2010*

There's a power struggle going on in the US government right now.

It's about who is in charge of cyber security, and how much control the government will exert over civilian networks. And by beating the drums of war, the military is coming out on top.

"The United States is fighting a cyberwar today, and we are losing," said former NSA director—and current cyberwar contractor—Mike McConnell. "Cyber 9/11 has happened over the last ten years, but it happened slowly so we don't see it," said former National Cyber Security Division director Amit Yoran. Richard Clarke, whom Yoran replaced, wrote an entire book hyping the threat of cyberwar.

General Keith Alexander, the current commander of the US Cyber Command, hypes it every chance he gets. This isn't just rhetoric of a few overeager government officials and headline writers; the entire national debate on cyberwar is plagued with exaggerations and hyperbole.

Googling those names and terms—as well as "cyber Pearl Harbor," "cyber Katrina," and even "cyber Armageddon"—gives some idea how pervasive these memes are. Prefix "cyber" to something scary, and you end up with something really scary.

Cyberspace has all sorts of threats, day in and day out. Cybercrime is by far the largest: fraud, through identity theft and other means, extortion, and so on. Cyber-espionage is another, both government- and corporate-sponsored. Traditional hacking, without a profit motive, is still a threat. So is cyber-activism: people, most often kids, playing politics by attacking government and corporate websites and networks.

These threats cover a wide variety of perpetrators, motivations, tactics, and goals. You can see this variety in what the media has mislabeled as "cyberwar." The attacks against Estonian websites in 2007 were simple hacking attacks by ethnic Russians angry at anti-Russian policies; these were denial-of-service attacks, a normal risk in cyberspace and hardly unprecedented.

A real-world comparison might be if an army invaded a country, then all got in line in front of people at the DMV so they couldn't renew their licenses. If that's what war looks like in the 21st century, we have little to fear.

Similar attacks against Georgia, which accompanied an actual Russian invasion, were also probably the responsibility of citizen activists or organized crime. A series of power blackouts in Brazil was caused by criminal extortionists—or was it sooty insulators? China is engaging in espionage, not war, in cyberspace. And so on.

One problem is that there's no clear definition of "cyberwar." What does it look like? How does it start? When is it over? Even cybersecurity experts don't know the answers to these questions, and it's dangerous to broadly apply the term "war" unless we know a war is going on.

Yet recent news articles have claimed that China declared cyberwar on Google, that Germany attacked China, and that a group of young hackers declared cyberwar on Australia. (Yes, cyberwar is so easy that even kids can do it.) Clearly we're not talking about real war here, but a rhetorical war: like the war on terror.

We have a variety of institutions that can defend us when attacked: the police, the military, the Department of Homeland Security, various commercial products and services, and our own personal or corporate lawyers. The legal framework for any particular attack depends on two things: the attacker and the motive. Those are precisely the two things you don't know when you're being attacked on the Internet. We saw this on July 4 last year, when US and South Korean websites were attacked by unknown perpetrators from North Korea—or perhaps England. Or was it Florida?

We surely need to improve our cybersecurity. But words have meaning, and metaphors matter. There's a power struggle going on for control of our nation's cybersecurity strategy, and the NSA and DoD are winning. If we frame the debate in terms of war, if we accept the military's expansive cyberspace definition of "war," we feed our fears.

We reinforce the notion that we're helpless—what person or organization can defend itself in a war?—and others need to protect us. We invite the military to take over security, and to ignore the limits on power that often get jettisoned during wartime.

If, on the other hand, we use the more measured language of cybercrime, we change the debate. Crime fighting requires both resolve and resources, but it's done within the context of normal life. We willingly give our police extraordinary powers of investigation and arrest, but we temper these powers with a judicial system and legal protections for citizens.

We need to be prepared for war, and a Cyber Command is just as vital as an Army or a Strategic Air Command. And because kid hackers and cyber-warriors use the same tactics, the defenses we build against crime and espionage will also protect us from more concerted attacks. But we're not fighting a cyberwar now, and the risks of a cyberwar are no greater than the risks of a ground invasion. We need peacetime cyber-security, administered within the myriad structure of public and private security institutions we already have.

Cyberwar and the Future of Cyber Conflict

Originally published in Financial Times, *December 2, 2010*

The world is gearing up for cyberwar. The US Cyber Command became operational in November. NATO has enshrined cyber security among its new strategic priorities. The head of Britain's armed forces said recently that boosting cyber capability is now a huge priority for the UK. And we know China is already engaged in broad cyber espionage attacks against the west. So how can we control a burgeoning cyber arms race?

We may already have seen early versions of cyberwars in Estonia and Georgia, possibly perpetrated by Russia. It's hard to know for certain, not only because such attacks are often impossible to trace, but because we have no clear definitions of what a cyberwar actually is.

Does the 2007 attacks against Estonia, traced to a young Russian man living in Tallinn and no one else, count? What about a virus from an unknown origin, possibly targeted at an Iranian nuclear complex? Or espionage from within China, but not specifically directed by its government? To such questions one must add even more basic issues, like when a cyberwar is understood to have begun, and how it ends. When even cyber security experts can't answer these questions, it's hard to expect much from policymakers.

We can set parameters. It is obviously not an act of war just to develop digital weapons targeting another country. Using cyberattacks to spy on another nation is a grey area, which gets greyer still when a country penetrates information networks, just to see if it can do so. Penetrating such networks and leaving a backdoor open, or even leaving logic bombs behind to be used later, is a harder case—yet the US and China are doing this to each other right now.

And what about when one country deliberately damages the economy of another, as one of the WikiLeaks cables shows that a member of China's politburo did against Google in January 2010? Definitions and rules are hard not just because the tools of war have changed, but because cyberspace puts them into the hands of a broader group of people. Previously only the military had weapons. Now anyone with sufficient computer skills can take matters into their own hands.

There are more basic problems too. When a nation is attacked in a regular conflict, a variety of military and civil institutions respond. The legal framework for this depends on two things: the attacker and the motive. But when you're attacked on the Internet, those are precisely the two things you don't know. We don't know if Georgia was attacked by the Russian government, or just some hackers living in Russia. In spite of much speculation, we don't know the origin, or target, of Stuxnet. We don't even know if last July 4's attacks against US and South Korean computers originated in North Korea, China, England, or Florida.

When you don't know, it's easy to get it wrong; and to retaliate against the wrong target, or for the wrong reason. That means it is easy for things to get out of hand. So while it is legitimate for nations to build offensive and defensive cyberwar capabilities we also need to think now about what can be done to limit the risk of cyberwar.

A first step would be a hotline between the world's cyber commands, modeled after similar hotlines among nuclear commands. This would at least allow governments to talk to each other, rather than guess where an attack came from. More difficult, but more important, are new cyberwar treaties. These could stipulate a no first use policy, outlaw unaimed weapons, or mandate weapons that self-destruct at the end of hostilities. The Geneva Conventions need to be updated too.

Cyber weapons beg to be used, so limits on stockpiles, and restrictions on tactics, are a logical end point. International banking, for instance, could be declared off-limits. Whatever the specifics, such agreements are badly needed. Enforcement will be difficult, but that's not a reason not to try. It's not too late to reverse the cyber arms race currently under way. Otherwise, it is only a matter of time before something big happens: perhaps by the rash actions of a low level military officer, perhaps by a non-state actor, perhaps by accident. And if the target nation retaliates, we could actually find ourselves in a cyberwar.

Why Terror Alert Codes Never Made Sense

Originally published in CNN, *January 28, 2011*

The Department of Homeland Security is getting rid of the color-coded threat level system. It was introduced after 9/11, and was supposed to tell you how likely a terrorist attack might be. Except that it never did.

Attacks happened more often when the level was yellow ("significant risk") than when it was orange ("high risk"). And the one time it was red ("severe risk"), nothing happened. It's never been blue or green, the two least dangerous levels.

The system has been at yellow for the past four years, and before then the changes seemed more timed to political events than actual terrorist threats. Not that any of this matters. We all ignored the levels because they didn't tell us anything useful.

The problem is that the color-coded threat levels were vague and long-term, and didn't correspond to useful actions people can take. Compare the color-coded threat levels with the US military's DEFCON system. At each DEFCON level, there are specific actions people have to take: The real details of those actions are secret, but at DEFCON 3—I'm making this up—you might call everyone back from leave, at another you fuel all the bombers, at another you arm the bombs, and so on.

Knowing the current DEFCON level is important for those in the military, because it dictates what actions you should be taking. What am I supposed to do when the terrorist threat level is yellow? Or orange? I have no idea.

And no one else did, either. Were there plane trips you delayed when the level was orange that you made when it was yellow? Did any company base business decisions on it? Do we think the president consulted the level every morning?

Consider hurricane warnings. Hurricanes are short-term events, and it's obvious when the danger is imminent and when it's over.

People can do useful things in response to a hurricane warning—board up their windows, stay in the basement, evacuate—and there is a discrete period when their lives are markedly different; there is utility in the higher alert mode, even if nothing comes of it.

Compare people's reactions to hurricane threats with their reactions to earthquake threats.

According to scientists, California could experience a huge earthquake sometime in the next 200 years. Even though the magnitude of the disaster will be enormous, people can't stay alert for two centuries.

The news seems to have generated the same levels of short-term fear and long-term apathy in Californians that the terrorist threat level system does. It's human nature; people simply can't be vigilant indefinitely, and if a stimulus is constant, people learn to ignore it.

Any alert system that instills a vague feeling of dread or panic, without giving people anything to do in response, is ineffective. And a terrorist threat level that warns of a "significant risk of terrorist attacks"—that's what yellow is—for years is ignored.

The DHS could have lowered the level to something more reasonable, but that would have been politically impossible. If there was a terrorist attack and the threat level had been blue or green, the DHS would have been blamed for not warning us. Keeping the level high might increase the general dread among some people and cause sniggering among others, but it helps protect the jobs of those charged with keeping us safe from terrorism.

So good riddance to the color-coded terrorist alert system, that relic of our immediate post-9/11 panic. It never did serve any security purpose. And it will be much easier for us to accept that we are, and have been for a while, at a "low risk of terrorist attacks"—threat level green—when no politician has to risk his job by formally admitting it.

Debate Club: An International Cyberwar Treaty Is the Only Way to Stem the Threat

Originally published in US News, *June 8, 2012*

We're in the early years of a cyberwar arms race. It's expensive, it's destabilizing, and it threatens the very fabric of the Internet we use every day. Cyberwar treaties, as imperfect as they might be, are the only way to contain the threat.

If you read the press and listen to government leaders, we're already in the middle of a cyberwar. By any normal definition of the word "war," this is ridiculous.

But the definition of cyberwar has been expanded to include government-sponsored espionage, potential terrorist attacks in cyberspace, large-scale criminal fraud, and even hacker kids attacking government networks and critical infrastructure. This definition is being pushed both by the military and by government contractors, who are gaining power and making money on cyberwar fear.

The danger is that military problems beg for military solutions. We're starting to see a power grab in cyberspace by the world's militaries: large-scale monitoring of networks, military control of Internet standards, even military takeover of cyberspace. Last year's debate over an "Internet kill switch" is an example of this; it's the sort of measure that might be deployed in wartime but makes no sense in peacetime. At the same time, countries are engaging in offensive actions in cyberspace, with tools like Stuxnet and Flame.

Arms races stem from ignorance and fear: ignorance of the other side's capabilities, and fear that their capabilities are greater than yours. Once cyberweapons exist, there will be an impetus to use them. Both Stuxnet and Flame damaged networks other than their intended targets. Any military-inserted backdoors in Internet systems make us more vulnerable to criminals and hackers. And it is only a matter of time before something big happens, perhaps by the rash actions of a low-level military officer, perhaps by a non-state actor, perhaps by accident. And if the target nation retaliates, we could find ourselves in a real cyberwar.

The cyberwar arms race is destabilizing.

International cooperation and treaties are the only way to reverse this. Banning cyberweapons entirely is a good goal, but almost certainly unachievable. More likely are treaties that stipulate a no-first-use policy, outlaw unaimed or broadly targeted weapons, and mandate weapons that self-destruct at the end of hostilities. Treaties that restrict tactics and limit stockpiles could be a next step. We could prohibit cyberattacks against civilian infrastructure; international banking, for example, could be declared off-limits.

Yes, enforcement will be difficult. Remember how easy it was to hide a chemical weapons facility? Hiding a cyberweapons facility will be even easier. But we've learned a lot from our Cold War experience in negotiating nuclear, chemical, and biological treaties. The very act of negotiating limits the arms race and paves the way to peace. And even if they're breached, the world is safer because the treaties exist.

There's a common belief within the US military that cyberweapons treaties are not in our best interest: that we currently have a military advantage in cyberspace that we should not squander. That's not true. We might have an offensive advantage—although that's debatable—but we certainly don't have a defensive advantage. More importantly, as a heavily networked country, we are inherently vulnerable in cyberspace.

Cyberspace threats are real. Military threats might get the publicity, but the criminal threats are both more dangerous and more damaging. Militarizing cyberspace will do more harm than good. The value of a free and open Internet is enormous.

Stop cyberwar fear mongering. Ratchet down cyberspace saber rattling. Start negotiations on limiting the militarization of cyberspace and increasing international police cooperation. This won't magically make us safe, but it will make us safer.

Overreaction and Overly Specific Reactions to Rare Risks

Originally published in CNN, July 31, 2012

Horrific events, such as the massacre in Aurora, can be catalysts for social and political change. Sometimes it seems that they're the only catalyst; recall how drastically our policies toward terrorism changed after 9/11 despite how moribund they were before.

The problem is that fear can cloud our reasoning, causing us to overreact and to overly focus on the specifics. And the key is to steer our desire for change in that time of fear.

Our brains aren't very good at probability and risk analysis. We tend to exaggerate spectacular, strange and rare events, and downplay ordinary, familiar and common ones. We think rare risks are more common than they are. We fear them more than probability indicates we should.

There is a lot of psychological research that tries to explain this, but one of the key findings is this: People tend to base risk analysis more on stories than on data. Stories engage us at a much more visceral level, especially stories that are vivid, exciting or personally involving.

If a friend tells you about getting mugged in a foreign country, that story is more likely to affect how safe you feel traveling to that country than reading a page of abstract crime statistics will.

Novelty plus dread plus a good story equals overreaction.

And who are the major storytellers these days? Television and the Internet. So when news programs and sites endlessly repeat the story from Aurora, with interviews with those in the theater, interviews with the families and commentary by anyone who has a point to make, we start to think this is something to fear, rather than a rare event that almost never happens and isn't worth worrying about. In other words, reading five stories about the same event feels somewhat like five separate events, and that skews our perceptions.

We see the effects of this all the time.

It's strangers by whom we fear being murdered, kidnapped, raped and assaulted, when it's far more likely that any perpetrator of such offenses is a relative or a friend. We worry about airplane crashes and rampaging shooters instead of automobile crashes and domestic violence—both of which are far more common and far, far more deadly.

Our greatest recent overreaction to a rare event was our response to the terrorist attacks of 9/11. I remember then-Attorney General John Ashcroft giving a speech in Minnesota—where I live—in 2003 in which he claimed that the fact there were no new terrorist attacks since 9/11 was proof that his policies were working. I remember thinking: "There were no terrorist attacks in the two years preceding 9/11, and you didn't have any policies. What does that prove?"

What it proves is that terrorist attacks are very rare, and perhaps our national response wasn't worth the enormous expense, loss of liberty, attacks on our Constitution and damage to our credibility on the world stage. Still, overreacting was the natural thing for us to do. Yes, it was security theater and not real security, but it made many of us feel safer.

The rarity of events such as the Aurora massacre doesn't mean we should ignore any lessons it might teach us. Because people overreact to rare events, they're useful catalysts for social introspection and policy change. The key here is to focus not on the details of the particular event but on the broader issues common to all similar events.

Installing metal detectors at movie theaters doesn't make sense—there's no reason to think the next crazy gunman will choose a movie theater as his venue, and how effectively would a metal detector deter a lone gunman anyway?—but understanding the reasons why the United States has so many gun deaths compared with other countries does. The particular motivations of alleged killer James Holmes aren't relevant—the next gunman will have different motivations—but the general state of mental health care in the United States is.

Even with this, the most important lesson of the Aurora massacre is how rare these events actually are. Our brains are primed to believe that movie theaters are more dangerous than they used to be, but they're not. The riskiest part of the evening is still the car ride to and from the movie theater, and even that's very safe.

But wear a seat belt all the same.

Militarizing Cyberspace Will Do More Harm Than Good

Originally published in the Irish Times, *November 29, 2012*

We're in the early years of a cyberwar arms race. It's expensive, it's destabilizing and it threatens the very fabric of the Internet we use every day. Cyberwar treaties, as imperfect as they might be, are the only way to contain the threat.

If you read the press and listen to government leaders, we're already in the middle of a cyberwar. By any normal definition of the word "war," this is ridiculous. But the definition of cyberwar has been expanded to include government-sponsored espionage, potential terrorist attacks in cyberspace, large-scale criminal fraud and even hacker kids attacking government networks and critical infrastructure. This definition is being pushed by the military and government contractors, both of which are gaining power and making money from cyberwar fears.

The main problem is that there are no good definitions of war in cyberspace. Also, we are increasingly seeing war-like tactics used in broader cyber conflicts. Technology is spreading capability, and the same "weaponry" is being used by everyone, from hackers to criminals to national militaries. It used to be that you could figure out whether you were at war by the weaponry deployed—but that is no longer the case.

This is important. When you're being attacked, there are a variety of organizations you can call on to defend yourself: the police, the military, whoever does anti-terrorism security in your country, your corporate lawyers.

The legal regime in which that defense operates depends on two things: who's attacking you, and why. Unfortunately, when you're being attacked in cyberspace, the two things you don't know are who's attacking you, and why. That makes defense, and national cyber defense policy, difficult.

The easy reaction is to lump all of these unknown attacks into "cyberwar." The corresponding danger is that military problems beg for military solutions.

We're starting to see a power grab in cyberspace by the world's militaries: large-scale monitoring of networks, military control of Internet standards, even military takeover of cyberspace.

The debate in the US over an "Internet kill switch" is another example; it's the sort of measure that might be deployed in wartime but makes no sense in peacetime. At the same time, countries are increasingly engaging in offensive actions in cyberspace, with tools such as Ghostnet (China), Stuxnet (US and Israel) and Flame (origin unknown).

A lot of what is being called cyberwar is little more than hacktivism—what I think of as kids playing politics—or criminal activity. Yes, it causes damage. Yes, we need to more effectively police cyberspace. But "police" is the operative word here. These are not threats that require a military response.

Arms races stem from ignorance and fear: ignorance of the other side's capabilities and fear that its capabilities are greater than one's own. Once cyberweapons exist, there will be an impetus to use them. Both Stuxnet and Flame damaged networks other than their intended targets. Any military-inserted backdoors in Internet systems make us more vulnerable to criminals and hackers.

It is only a matter of time before something big happens, perhaps by the rash actions of a low-level military officer, perhaps by a non-state actor, perhaps by accident. If the target nation retaliates, we could find ourselves in a real cyberwar.

The cyberwar arms race is destabilizing. International co-operation and treaties are the only way to reverse this. Banning cyberweapons entirely is a good goal, but almost certainly unachievable.

More likely are treaties that stipulate a no-first-use policy, outlaw unaimed or broadly targeted weapons, and mandate weapons that self-destruct at the end of hostilities. Treaties that restrict tactics and limit stockpiles could be a next step. We could also prohibit cyberattacks against civilian infrastructure; international banking, for example, could be declared off-limits.

Yes, enforcement will be difficult. Remember how easy it was to hide a chemical weapons facility? Hiding a cyberweapons facility will be even easier. But we have learnt a lot from our cold war experience in negotiating nuclear, chemical and biological treaties. The very act of negotiating limits the arms race and paves the way to peace. Even if they're breached, the world is safer because the treaties exist.

There's a common belief within the US military that cyberweapons treaties are not in the nation's best interest: that Americans have a military advantage in cyberspace that it should not squander. That's not true.

The US might have an offensive advantage—although that's debatable—but it certainly doesn't have a defensive advantage. More importantly, any heavily networked country such as the US is inherently vulnerable in cyberspace.

Cyberspace threats are real but militarizing cyberspace will do more harm than good. The value of a free and open Internet is enormous.

Rhetoric of Cyber War Breeds Fear—and More Cyber War

Originally published in the Irish Times, *March 14, 2013*

Americans have a weird relationship with the word "war." We hate using it to describe actual wars but we love using it in a rhetorical context. We had the war on poverty, the war on crime, the war on drugs and the war on terror.

One of the big "wars" we're talking about now is cyber war and, in this case, the word is dangerous. It is both a rhetorical war as well as something with elements of actual combat. The word also confuses the political debate about how to deal with cyber security.

The danger is that words frame the debate. If we use the rhetoric of war, we invoke feelings of fear and helplessness. We understand that this is something nations do to each other and that it's not "normal" time when we're at war.

We accept a different set of security solutions, one that more easily ignores freedoms and liberties.

We are more willing to let the military take over our Internet infrastructure and spy on our citizens.

On the other hand, if we use the rhetoric of peacetime espionage we think more about the rule of law and allow a much more limited role for the military.

Attacks from China

If you have been paying attention to the press recently, you might think China just started a cyberwar, attacking everyone in cyberspace.

First the *New York Times* announced it was the victim of a sophisticated cyberattack from China, one intended to obtain the names of Chinese nationals co-operating with the press.

Then the security firm Mandiant released a report naming a particular Chinese military unit as the source of a large number of cyberattacks against targets around the world.

Meanwhile, US president Barack Obama has signed a new cyber-security directive, citing threats from China as one of the motivations behind this action.

First, we need to understand that there is no cyber war going on. We are not nations at war and claiming otherwise is destabilizing. This is all espionage, something that has been going on between nations ever since nations were invented—and the US is giving as good as it's getting.

Seymour Hersh has written in the *New Yorker* magazine about US military operations in China.

Meanwhile, the US Cyber Command recently announced that it is expanding from 900 people to almost 5,000, while the National Security Agency is building a massive new data center in Utah. I'm sure China is just as fearful of the US as the US is of China.

While there are certainly a lot of state-sponsored cyberattacks emanating from China, it is not really news.

We in the security industry have been writing about Chinese cyberattacks for years, in earnest since the mid-2000s. Certainly, Internet-enabled espionage has been going on ever since there was an Internet.

GhostNet

In 2010, Google announced it was the victim of a sophisticated series of cyber-attacks from China.

As with the attacks against the *New York Times*, the hackers were looking for particular people—in this case, human rights activists. Like the others, this attack was directed at more than one company.

At least 20 other large companies were targeted as well: Internet and technological companies, media companies and traditional companies.

In 2009, security researchers discovered a very sophisticated surveillance network they called GhostNet. They found it during an audit of the Dalai Lama's computers.

When they unraveled the command and control network, they found it was operating against high-value political, economic and media targets in 103 countries.

While there is no direct evidence that the Chinese were behind this, the list of targets read like a Who's Who of targets on whom China wants to spy.

The Chinese may deny particular incidents but they make no secret about their general policies.

They have been writing about their doctrine of domination in cyberspace for even longer. From our perspective there is not much new in the revelations of the past month. Still, the increasingly hostile war rhetoric and saber-rattling is worrisome.

We are in the early years of a cyberwar arms race. Arms races are fuelled by two things: ignorance and fear.

We don't know about the enemy's capabilities and we're afraid they're greater than our own.

So we spend more on weaponry, then even more. The other side does the same and the result is both dangerous and destabilizing.

Profitable

On the other hand, it's very profitable—for some.

There is an enormous amount of money and power that results from escalating a cyberwar arms race: power for the military, power for law enforcement and power for the large government contractors that support these organizations.

These are the people pounding the drums of cyber war and making news headlines warning us of a cyber 9/11, a cyber Pearl Harbor or—my favorite —a cyber Armageddon.

As long as "cyber" remains a prefix that scares, it will continue to be used as a tool to influence policy.

The Boston Marathon Bombing: Keep Calm and Carry On

Originally published in the Atlantic, *April 15, 2013*

As the details about the bombings in Boston unfold, it'd be easy to be scared. It'd be easy to feel powerless and demand that our elected leaders do something—anything—to keep us safe.

It'd be easy, but it'd be wrong. We need to be angry and empathize with the victims without being scared. Our fears would play right into the perpetrators' hands—and magnify the power of their victory for whichever goals whatever group behind this, still to be uncovered, has. We don't have to be scared, and we're not powerless. We actually have all the power here, and there's one thing we can do to render terrorism ineffective: Refuse to be terrorized.

It's hard to do, because terrorism is designed precisely to scare people—far out of proportion to its actual danger. A huge amount of research on fear and the brain teaches us that we exaggerate threats that are rare, spectacular, immediate, random—in this case involving an innocent child—senseless, horrific and graphic. Terrorism pushes all of our fear buttons, really hard, and we overreact.

But our brains are fooling us. Even though this will be in the news for weeks, we should recognize this for what it is: a rare event. That's the very definition of news: something that is unusual—in this case, something that almost never happens.

Remember after 9/11 when people predicted we'd see these sorts of attacks every few months? That never happened, and it wasn't because the TSA confiscated knives and snow globes at airports. Give the FBI credit for rolling up terrorist networks and interdicting terrorist funding, but we also exaggerated the threat. We get our ideas about how easy it is to blow things up from television and the movies. It turns out that terrorism is much harder than most people think. It's hard to find willing terrorists, it's hard to put a plot together, it's hard to get materials, and it's hard to execute a workable plan. As a collective group, terrorists are dumb, and they make dumb mistakes; criminal masterminds are another myth from movies and comic books.

Even the 9/11 terrorists got lucky.

If it's hard for us to keep this in perspective, it will be even harder for our leaders. They'll be afraid that by speaking honestly about the impossibility of attaining absolute security or the inevitability of terrorism—or that some American ideals are worth maintaining even in the face of adversity—they will be branded as "soft on terror." And they'll be afraid that Americans might vote them out of office. Perhaps they're right, but where are the leaders who aren't afraid? What has happened to "the only thing we have to fear is fear itself"?

Terrorism, even the terrorism of radical Islamists and right-wing extremists and lone actors all put together, is not an "existential threat" against our nation. Even the events of 9/11, as horrific as they were, didn't do existential damage to our nation. Our society is more robust than it might seem from watching the news. We need to start acting that way.

There are things we can do to make us safer, mostly around investigation, intelligence, and emergency response, but we will never be 100-percent safe from terrorism; we need to accept that.

How well this attack succeeds depends much less on what happened in Boston than by our reactions in the coming weeks and months. Terrorism isn't primarily a crime against people or property. It's a crime against our minds, using the deaths of innocents and destruction of property as accomplices. When we react from fear, when we change our laws and policies to make our country less open, the terrorists succeed, even if their attacks fail. But when we refuse to be terrorized, when we're indomitable in the face of terror, the terrorists fail, even if their attacks succeed.

Don't glorify the terrorists and their actions by calling this part of a "war on terror." Wars involve two legitimate sides. There's only one legitimate side here; those on the other are criminals. They should be found, arrested, and punished. But we need to be vigilant not to weaken the very freedoms and liberties that make this country great, meanwhile, just because we're scared.

Empathize, but refuse to be terrorized. Instead, be indomitable—and support leaders who are as well. That's how to defeat terrorists.

Why FBI and CIA Didn't Connect the Dots

Originally published in CNN, *May 2, 2013*

The FBI and the CIA are being criticized for not keeping better track of Tamerlan Tsarnaev in the months before the Boston Marathon bombings. How could they have ignored such a dangerous person? How do we reform the intelligence community to ensure this kind of failure doesn't happen again?

It's an old song by now, one we heard after the 9/11 attacks in 2001 and after the Underwear Bomber's failed attack in 2009. The problem is that connecting the dots is a bad metaphor, and focusing on it makes us more likely to implement useless reforms.

Connecting the dots in a coloring book is easy and fun. They're right there on the page, and they're all numbered. All you have to do is move your pencil from one dot to the next, and when you're done, you've drawn a sailboat. Or a tiger. It's so simple that 5-year-olds can do it.

But in real life, the dots can only be numbered after the fact. With the benefit of hindsight, it's easy to draw lines from a Russian request for information to a foreign visit to some other piece of information that might have been collected.

In hindsight, we know who the bad guys are. Before the fact, there are an enormous number of potential bad guys.

How many? We don't know. But we know that the no-fly list had 21,000 people on it last year. The Terrorist Identities Datamart Environment, also known as the watch list, has 700,000 names on it.

We have no idea how many potential "dots" the FBI, CIA, NSA and other agencies collect, but it's easily in the millions. It's easy to work backwards through the data and see all the obvious warning signs. But before a terrorist attack, when there are millions of dots—some important but the vast majority unimportant—uncovering plots is a lot harder.

Rather than thinking of intelligence as a simple connect-the-dots picture, think of it as a million unnumbered pictures superimposed on top of each other. Or a random-dot stereogram. Is it a sailboat, a puppy, two guys with pressure-cooker bombs or just an unintelligible mess of dots? You try to figure it out.

It's not a matter of not enough data, either.

Piling more data onto the mix makes it harder, not easier. The best way to think of it is a needle-in-a-haystack problem; the last thing you want to do is increase the amount of hay you have to search through.

The television show "Person of Interest" is fiction, not fact.

There's a name for this sort of logical fallacy: hindsight bias.

First explained by psychologists Daniel Kahneman and Amos Tversky, it's surprisingly common. Since what actually happened is so obvious once it happens, we overestimate how obvious it was before it happened.

We actually misremember what we once thought, believing that we knew all along that what happened would happen. It's a surprisingly strong tendency, one that has been observed in countless laboratory experiments and real-world examples of behavior. And it's what all the post-Boston-Marathon bombing dot-connectors are doing.

Before we start blaming agencies for failing to stop the Boston bombers, and before we push "intelligence reforms" that will shred civil liberties without making us any safer, we need to stop seeing the past as a bunch of obvious dots that need connecting.

Kahneman, a Nobel prize winner, wisely noted: "Actions that seemed prudent in foresight can look irresponsibly negligent in hindsight." Kahneman calls it "the illusion of understanding," explaining that the past is only so understandable because we have cast it as simple inevitable stories and leave out the rest.

Nassim Taleb, an expert on risk engineering, calls this tendency the "narrative fallacy." We humans are natural storytellers, and the world of stories is much more tidy, predictable and coherent than the real world.

Millions of people behave strangely enough to warrant the FBI's notice, and almost all of them are harmless. It is simply not possible to find every plot beforehand, especially when the perpetrators act alone and on impulse.

We have to accept that there always will be a risk of terrorism, and that when the occasional plot succeeds, it's not necessarily because our law enforcement systems have failed.

The FBI's New Wiretapping Plan Is Great News for Criminals

Originally published in Foreign Policy, *May 29, 2013*

The FBI wants a new law that will make it easier to wiretap the Internet. Although its claim is that the new law will only maintain the status quo, it's really much worse than that. This law will result in less-secure Internet products and create a foreign industry in more-secure alternatives. It will impose costly burdens on affected companies. It will assist totalitarian governments in spying on their own citizens. And it won't do much to hinder actual criminals and terrorists.

As the FBI sees it, the problem is that people are moving away from traditional communication systems like telephones onto computer systems like Skype. Eavesdropping on telephones used to be easy. The FBI would call the phone company, which would bring agents into a switching room and allow them to literally tap the wires with a pair of alligator clips and a tape recorder. In the 1990s, the government forced phone companies to provide an analogous capability on digital switches; but today, more and more communications happens over the Internet.

What the FBI wants is the ability to eavesdrop on *everything*. Depending on the system, this ranges from easy to impossible. E-mail systems like Gmail are easy. The mail resides in Google's servers, and the company has an office full of people who respond to requests for lawful access to individual accounts from governments all over the world. Encrypted voice systems like Silent Circle are impossible to eavesdrop on—the calls are encrypted from one computer to the other, and there's no central node to eavesdrop from. In those cases, the only way to make the system eavesdroppable is to add a backdoor to the user software. This is precisely the FBI's proposal. Companies that refuse to comply would be fined $25,000 a day.

The FBI believes it can have it both ways: that it can open systems to its eavesdropping, but keep them secure from anyone else's eavesdropping. That's just not possible. It's impossible to build a communications system that allows the FBI surreptitious access but doesn't allow similar access by others. When it comes to security, we have two options: We can build our systems to be as secure as possible from eavesdropping, or we can deliberately weaken their security. We have to choose one or the other.

This is an old debate, and one we've been through many times. The NSA even has a name for it: the equities issue. In the 1980s, the equities debate was about export control of cryptography. The government deliberately weakened US cryptography products because it didn't want foreign groups to have access to secure systems. Two things resulted: fewer Internet products with cryptography, to the insecurity of everybody, and a vibrant foreign security industry based on the unofficial slogan "Don't buy the US stuff—it's lousy."

In 1993, the debate was about the Clipper Chip. This was another deliberately weakened security product, an encrypted telephone. The FBI convinced AT&T to add a backdoor that allowed for surreptitious wiretapping. The product was a complete failure. Again, why would anyone buy a deliberately weakened security system?

In 1994, the Communications Assistance for Law Enforcement Act mandated that US companies build eavesdropping capabilities into phone switches. These were sold internationally; some countries liked having the ability to spy on their citizens. Of course, so did criminals, and there were public scandals in Greece (2005) and Italy (2006) as a result.

In 2012, we learned that every phone switch sold to the Department of Defense had security vulnerabilities in its surveillance system. And just this May, we learned that Chinese hackers breached Google's system for providing surveillance data for the FBI.

The new FBI proposal will fail in all these ways and more. The bad guys will be able to get around the eavesdropping capability, either by building their own security systems—not very difficult—or buying the more-secure foreign products that will inevitably be made available. Most of the good guys, who don't understand the risks or the technology, will not know enough to bother and will be less secure. The eavesdropping functions will 1) result in more obscure—and less secure—product designs, and 2) be vulnerable to exploitation by criminals, spies, and everyone else. US companies will be forced to compete at a disadvantage; smart customers won't buy the substandard stuff when there are more-secure foreign alternatives. Even worse, there are lots of foreign governments who want to use these sorts of systems to spy on their own citizens. Do we really want to be exporting surveillance technology to the likes of China, Syria, and Saudi Arabia?

The FBI's short-sighted agenda also works against the parts of the government that are still working to secure the Internet for everyone. Initiatives within the NSA, the DOD, and DHS to do everything from securing computer operating systems to enabling anonymous web browsing will all be harmed by this.

What to do, then? The FBI claims that the Internet is "going dark," and that it's simply trying to maintain the status quo of being able to eavesdrop. This characterization is disingenuous at best. We are entering a golden age of surveillance; there's more electronic communications available for eavesdropping than ever before, including whole new classes of information: location tracking, financial tracking, and vast databases of historical communications such as e-mails and text messages. The FBI's surveillance department has it better than ever. With regard to voice communications, yes, software phone calls will be harder to eavesdrop upon. (Although there are questions about Skype's security.) That's just part of the evolution of technology, and one that on balance is a positive thing.

Think of it this way: We don't hand the government copies of our house keys and safe combinations. If agents want access, they get a warrant and then pick the locks or bust open the doors, just as a criminal would do. A similar system would work on computers. The FBI, with its increasingly non-transparent procedures and systems, has failed to make the case that this isn't good enough.

Finally there's a general principle at work that's worth explicitly stating. All tools can be used by the good guys and the bad guys. Cars have enormous societal value, even though bank robbers can use them as getaway cars. Cash is no different. Both good guys and bad guys send e-mails, use Skype, and eat at all-night restaurants. But because society consists overwhelmingly of good guys, the good uses of these dual-use technologies greatly outweigh the bad uses. Strong Internet security makes us all safer, even though it helps the bad guys as well. And it makes no sense to harm all of us in an attempt to harm a small subset of us.

US Offensive Cyberwar Policy

Originally published in CNN, *June 18, 2013*

Today, the United States is conducting offensive cyberwar actions around the world.

More than passively eavesdropping, we're penetrating and damaging foreign networks for both espionage and to ready them for attack. We're creating custom-designed Internet weapons, pre-targeted and ready to be "fired" against some piece of another country's electronic infrastructure on a moment's notice.

This is much worse than what we're accusing China of doing to us. We're pursuing policies that are both expensive and destabilizing and aren't making the Internet any safer. We're reacting from fear, and causing other countries to counter-react from fear. We're ignoring resilience in favor of offense.

Welcome to the cyberwar arms race, an arms race that will define the Internet in the 21st century.

Presidential Policy Directive 20, issued last October and released by Edward Snowden, outlines US cyberwar policy. Most of it isn't very interesting, but there are two paragraphs about "Offensive Cyber Effect Operations," or OCEO, that are intriguing:

OECO can offer unique and unconventional capabilities to advance US national objectives around the world with little or no warning to the adversary or target and with potential effects ranging from subtle to severely damaging. The development and sustainment of OCEO capabilities, however, may require considerable time and effort if access and tools for a specific target do not already exist.

The United States Government shall identify potential targets of national importance where OCEO can offer a favorable balance of effectiveness and risk as compared with other instruments of national power, establish and maintain OCEO capabilities integrated as appropriate with other US offensive capabilities, and execute those capabilities in a manner consistent with the provisions of this directive.

These two paragraphs, and another paragraph about OCEO, are the only parts of the document classified "top secret." And that's because what they're saying is very dangerous.

Cyberattacks have the potential to be both immediate and devastating. They can disrupt communications systems, disable national infrastructure, or, as in the case of Stuxnet, destroy nuclear reactors; but only if they've been created and targeted beforehand. Before launching cyberattacks against another country, we have to go through several steps.

We have to study the details of the computer systems they're running and determine the vulnerabilities of those systems. If we can't find exploitable vulnerabilities, we need to create them: leaving "backdoors" in hacker speak. Then we have to build new cyberweapons designed specifically to attack those systems.

Sometimes we have to embed the hostile code in those networks—these are called "logic bombs"—to be unleashed in the future. And we have to keep penetrating those foreign networks, because computer systems always change and we need to ensure that the cyberweapons are still effective.

Like our nuclear arsenal during the Cold War, our cyberweapons arsenal must be pretargeted and ready to launch.

That's what Obama directed the US Cyber Command to do. We can see glimpses of how effective we are in Snowden's allegations that the NSA is currently penetrating foreign networks around the world: "We hack network backbones—like huge Internet routers, basically—that give us access to the communications of hundreds of thousands of computers without having to hack every single one."

The NSA and the US Cyber Command are basically the same thing. They're both at Fort Meade in Maryland, and they're both led by Gen. Keith Alexander. The same people who hack network backbones are also building weapons to destroy those backbones. At a March Senate briefing, Alexander boasted of creating more than a dozen offensive cyber units.

Longtime NSA watcher James Bamford reached the same conclusion in his recent profile of Alexander and the US Cyber Command (written before the Snowden revelations). He discussed some of the many cyberweapons the US purchases:

*According to Defense News' C4ISR Journal and Bloomberg
Businessweek, Endgame also offers its intelligence clients—agencies
like Cyber Command, the NSA, the CIA, and British intelligence—a
unique map showing them exactly where their targets are located.
Dubbed Bonesaw, the map displays the geolocation and digital
address of basically every device connected to the Internet around the
world, providing what's called network situational awareness. The
client locates a region on the password-protected web-based map, then
picks a country and city—say, Beijing, China. Next the client types
in the name of the target organization, such as the Ministry of Public
Security's No. 3 Research Institute, which is responsible for computer
security—or simply enters its address, 6 Zhengyi Road. The map
will then display what software is running on the computers inside
the facility, what types of malware some may contain, and a menu
of custom-designed exploits that can be used to secretly gain entry.
It can also pinpoint those devices infected with malware, such as the
Conficker worm, as well as networks turned into botnets and zom-
bies—the equivalent of a back door left open. . .*

*The buying and using of such a subscription by nation-states could
be seen as an act of war. "If you are engaged in reconnaissance on
an adversary's systems, you are laying the electronic battlefield and
preparing to use it" wrote Mike Jacobs, a former NSA director for
information assurance, in a McAfee report on cyberwarfare. "In my
opinion, these activities constitute acts of war, or at least a prelude
to future acts of war." The question is, who else is on the secretive
company's client list? Because there is as of yet no oversight or regulation of the cyberweapons trade, companies in the cyber-industrial
complex are free to sell to whomever they wish. "It should be illegal,"
said the former senior intelligence official involved in cyberwarfare.
"I knew about Endgame when I was in intelligence. The intelligence
community didn't like it, but they're the largest consumer of that
business."*

That's the key question: How much of what the United States is currently
doing is an act of war by international definitions? Already we're accusing
China of penetrating our systems in order to map "military capabilities that

could be exploited during a crisis." What PPD-20 and Snowden describe is much worse, and certainly China, and other countries, are doing the same.

All of this mapping of vulnerabilities and keeping them secret for offensive use makes the Internet less secure, and these pre-targeted, ready-to-unleash cyberweapons are destabilizing forces on international relationships. Rooting around other countries' networks, analyzing vulnerabilities, creating backdoors, and leaving logic bombs could easily be construed as an act of war. And all it takes is one over-achieving national leader for this all to tumble into actual war.

It's time to stop the madness. Yes, our military needs to invest in cyberwar capabilities, but we also need international rules of cyberwar, more transparency from our own government on what we are and are not doing, international cooperation between governments and viable cyberweapons treaties. Yes, these are difficult. Yes, it's a long slow process. Yes, there won't be international consensus, certainly not in the beginning. But even with all of those problems, it's a better path to go down than the one we're on now.

We can start by taking most of the money we're investing in offensive cyberwar capabilities and spend them on national cyberspace resilience. MAD, mutually assured destruction, made sense because there were two superpowers opposing each other. On the Internet there are all sorts of different powers, from nation-states to much less organized groups. An arsenal of cyberweapons begs to be used, and, as we learned from Stuxnet, there's always collateral damage to innocents when they are. We're much safer with a strong defense than with a counterbalancing offense.

3 Human Aspects of Security

Secret Questions Blow a Hole in Security

Originally published in ComputerWeekly, *April 4, 2008*

It's a mystery to me why websites think "secret questions" are a good idea. We sign up for an online service, choose a hard-to-guess (and equally hard-to-remember) password, and are then presented with a "secret question" to answer.

Twenty years ago, there was just one secret question: What's your mother's maiden name? Today, there are several: What street did you grow up on? What's the name of your favorite teacher? What's your favorite color? Often, you get to choose.

The idea is to give customers a backup password. If you forget your password, then the secret question is a way to verify your identity. It's a great idea from a customer service perspective—users are less likely to forget their first pet's name than some random password—but terrible for security.

The answer to the secret question is much easier to guess than a good password, and the information is much more public. I'll bet my childhood address is in some database somewhere. And worse, everybody seems to use the same series of secret questions.

The result is that the normal security protocol (passwords) falls back to a much less secure protocol (secret questions). The security of the entire system suffers. I'm sure the designers of the system thought the fallback system would only be used rarely, when a user forgot their password. But any good security engineer realizes that bad guys can force the failure whenever they want, and that the whole security of the system rests on the security of the weaker of the two subsystems.

What can be done? As a customer, my usual technique is to type a completely random answer for the security question. I madly slap at my keyboard for a few seconds, and then forget about it. This ensures that an attacker has little chance of bypassing the password protection by successfully guessing the answer to my secret question, but it is pretty unpleasant if I forget my password. The one time this happened to me, I had to call the company to get my password and question reset. Yes, it was a right pain.

Which is maybe what should happen in the first place. I like to think that if I forget my password, it is really hard to gain access to my account. I want it to be so hard that an attacker can't possibly do it. I know this is a customer service issue, but it's a security issue, too. And if the password is controlling access to something important—like my bank account—then the bypass mechanism should be harder, not easier.

Passwords have reached the end of their useful life. Today, they only work for low-security applications. The secret question is just one manifestation of that fact.

When You Lose a Piece of Kit, the Real Loss Is the Data It Contains

Originally published in the Guardian, *December 4, 2008*

These days, losing electronic devices is less about the hardware and more about the data. Hardly a week goes by without another newsworthy data loss. People leave thumb drives, memory sticks, mobile phones and even computers everywhere. And some of that data isn't easily replaceable. Sure, you can blame it on personal or organizational sloppiness, but part of the problem is that more and more information fits on smaller and smaller devices.

My primary computer is an ultraportable laptop. It contains every email I've sent and received over the past 12 years—I think of it as my backup brain—as well as an enormous amount of personal and work-related documents.

I have several USB thumb drives, including an 8GB drive that serves as my primary backup while travelling. It contains a complete copy of the past 12 months of my life. A larger USB portable drive serves as my primary storage device for photographs; I carry that around regularly, too, as I like to edit my photos on flights.

My mobile phone is a Palm Treo smartphone. It holds not only my frequently called phone numbers, but my entire address book—including any personal notes I've made—my calendar for the past 10 years, hundreds of emails, all my text messages and a log of every phone call I've made and received. At least, it would if I didn't take specific pains to clean that information out once in a while.

Backup DVDs. iPods with calendars and address books. USB drives with portable desktops. I could go on. The upside to this is that so much of our information is at our fingertips. I travel so extensively that I need my office anywhere I am, so I want everything with me everywhere. The downside is that it's now amazingly easy to lose an enormous amount of information. And there are two problems with that. One, you've lost the information. And two, that perhaps someone else has found it.

The first problem is easily solvable with backup. Everything you own should be backed up regularly. Not just your computer, but your PDA and mobile phone and anything else with personal data. Backups should be tested regularly. There's nothing worse than losing something and having the backups fail when you try to restore to a replacement device.

The second problem is solvable several ways. The best way is encryption. On your computer, hard-disk encryption programs like PGPDisk or TrueCrypt allow you to encrypt files, folders or entire disk partitions. Several manufacturers market USB thumb drives with built-in encryption. Some PDA manufacturers are starting to add password protection—not as good as encryption, but at least it's something—to their devices, and there are a few aftermarket PDA encryption programs. I use these wherever possible, and I strongly recommend that everyone else do the same.

Where encryption isn't possible, pay attention and erase unneeded data. Delete old emails from your BlackBerry, texts from your cellphone and old data from your address books regularly. It can be difficult to know exactly what your PDA is storing, and how to erase it. Manufacturers could help with this by introducing better functionality and thereby making the devices easier to use.

Another thing manufacturers can do is to provide the option to delete the data remotely if the device is lost. This is still a new idea, but it's gaining traction in the corporate market. These systems frequently allow for remote backup of the data, solving both problems at once. One last piece of advice:

for work-related equipment, you should follow your company's backup and security policies.

The goal here is peace of mind. When people lose computers or phones or USB drives, the real loss isn't the physical object, but the data contained within it. And while we won't be able to make these devices harder to lose, especially as they continue to shrink in physical size and grow in data capacity, we can make their loss cost merely money, not information or privacy.

The Kindness of Strangers

Originally published in the Wall Street Journal, *March 12, 2009*

When I was growing up, children were commonly taught: "don't talk to strangers." Strangers might be bad, we were told, so it's prudent to steer clear of them.

And yet most people are honest, kind, and generous, especially when someone asks them for help. If a small child is in trouble, the smartest thing he can do is find a nice-looking stranger and talk to him.

These two pieces of advice may seem to contradict each other, but they don't. The difference is that in the second instance, the child is choosing which stranger to talk to. Given that the overwhelming majority of people will help, the child is likely to get help if he chooses a random stranger. But if a stranger comes up to a child and talks to him or her, it's not a random choice. It's more likely, although still unlikely, that the stranger is up to no good.

As a species, we tend to help each other, and a surprising amount of our security and safety comes from the kindness of strangers. During disasters: floods, earthquakes, hurricanes, bridge collapses. In times of personal tragedy. And even in normal times.

If you're sitting in a café working on your laptop and need to get up for a minute, ask the person sitting next to you to watch your stuff. He's very unlikely to steal anything. Or, if you're nervous about that, ask the three people sitting around you. Those three people don't know each other, and will not only watch your stuff, but they'll also watch each other to make sure no one steals anything.

Again, this works because you're selecting the people. If three people walk up to you in the café and offer to watch your computer while you go to the bathroom, don't take them up on that offer. Your odds of getting three honest people are much lower.

Some computer systems rely on the kindness of strangers, too. The Internet works because nodes benevolently forward packets to each other without any recompense from either the sender or receiver of those packets. Wikipedia works because strangers are willing to write for, and edit, an encyclopedia—with no recompense.

Collaborative spam filtering is another example. Basically, once someone notices a particular e-mail is spam, he marks it, and everyone else in the network is alerted that it's spam. Marking the e-mail is a completely altruistic task; the person doing it gets no benefit from the action. But he receives benefit from everyone else doing it for other e-mails.

Tor is a system for anonymous Web browsing. The details are complicated, but basically, a network of Tor servers passes Web traffic among each other in such a way as to anonymize where it came from. Think of it as a giant shell game. As a Web surfer, I put my Web query inside a shell and send it to a random Tor server. That server knows who I am but not what I am doing. It passes that shell to another Tor server, which passes it to a third. That third server—which knows what I am doing but not who I am—processes the Web query. When the Web page comes back to that third server, the process reverses itself and I get my Web page. Assuming enough Web surfers are sending enough shells through the system, even someone eavesdropping on the entire network can't figure out what I'm doing.

It's a very clever system, and it protects a lot of people, including journalists, human rights activists, whistleblowers, and ordinary people living in repressive regimes around the world. But it only works because of the kindness of strangers. No one gets any benefit from being a Tor server; it uses up bandwidth to forward other people's packets around. It's more efficient to be a Tor client and use the forwarding capabilities of others. But if there are no Tor servers, then there's no Tor. Tor works because people are willing to set themselves up as servers, at no benefit to them.

Alibi clubs work along similar lines. You can find them on the Internet, and they're loose collections of people willing to help each other out with alibis. Sign up, and you're in. You can ask someone to pretend to be your doctor and call your boss. Or someone to pretend to be your boss and call your spouse. Or maybe someone to pretend to be your spouse and call your boss. Whatever you want, just ask and some anonymous stranger will come to your rescue. And because your accomplice is an anonymous stranger, it's safer than asking a friend to participate in your ruse.

There are risks in these sorts of systems. Regularly, marketers and other people with agendas try to manipulate Wikipedia entries to suit their interests. Intelligence agencies can, and almost certainly have, set themselves up as Tor servers to better eavesdrop on traffic. And a do-gooder could join an alibi club just to expose other members. But for the most part, strangers are willing to help each other, and systems that harvest this kindness work very well on the Internet.

Blaming the User Is Easy—But It's Better to Bypass Them Altogether

Originally published in the Guardian, *March 12, 2009*

Blaming the victim is common in IT: users are to blame because they don't patch their systems, choose lousy passwords, fall for phishing attacks, and so on. But, while users are, and will continue to be, a major source of security problems, focusing on them is an unhelpful way to think.

People regularly don't do things they are supposed to: changing the oil in their cars, going to the dentist, replacing the batteries in their smoke detectors. Why? Because people learn from experience. If something is immediately harmful, such as touching a hot stove or petting a live tiger, they quickly learn not to do it. But if someone skips an oil change, ignores a computer patch, or chooses a lousy password, it's unlikely to matter. No feedback, no learning.

We've tried to solve this in several ways. We give people rules of thumb: oil change every 5,000 miles; secure password guidelines. Or we send notifications: smoke alarms beep at us, dentists send postcards, Google warns us if we are about to visit a website suspected of hosting malware. But, again, the effects of ignoring these aren't generally felt immediately.

This makes security primarily a hindrance to the user. It's a recurring obstacle: something that interferes with the seamless performance of the user's task. And it's human nature, wired into our reasoning skills, to remove recurring obstacles. So, if the consequences of bypassing security aren't obvious, then people will naturally do it.

This is the problem with Microsoft's User Account Control (UAC). Introduced in Vista, the idea is to improve security by limiting the privileges applications have when they're running. But the security prompts pop up too frequently, and there's rarely any ill-effect from ignoring them. So people do ignore them.

This doesn't mean user education is worthless. On the contrary, user education is an important part of any corporate security program. And at home, the more users understand security threats and hacker tactics, the more secure their systems are likely to be. But we should also recognize the limitations of education.

The solution is to better design security systems that assume uneducated users: to prevent them from changing security settings that would leave them exposed to undue risk, or—even better—to take security out of their hands entirely.

For example, we all know that backups are a good thing. But if you forget to do a backup this week, nothing terrible happens. In fact, nothing terrible happens for years on end when you forget. So, despite what you know, you start believing that backups aren't really that important. Apple got the solution right with its backup utility Time Machine. Install it, plug in an external hard drive, and you are automatically backed up against hardware failure and human error. It's easier to use it than not.

For its part, Microsoft has made great strides in securing its operating system, providing default security settings in Windows XP and even more in Windows Vista to ensure that, when a naive user plugs a computer in, it's not defenseless.

Unfortunately, blaming the user can be good business. Mobile phone companies save money if they can bill their customers when a calling card number is stolen and used fraudulently. British banks save money by blaming users when they are victims of chip-and-pin fraud. This is continuing, with some banks going so far as to accuse the victim of perpetrating the fraud, despite evidence of large-scale fraud by organized crime syndicates.

The legal system needs to fix the business problems, but system designers need to work on the technical problems. They must accept that security systems that require the user to do the right thing are doomed to fail. And then they must design resilient security nevertheless.

The Value of Self-Enforcing Protocols

Originally published in Threatpost, *August 10, 2009*

There are several ways two people can divide a piece of cake in half. One way is to find someone impartial to do it for them. This works, but it requires another person. Another way is for one person to divide the piece, and the other person to complain (to the police, a judge, or his parents) if he doesn't think it's fair. This also works, but still requires another person—at least to resolve disputes. A third way is for one person to do the dividing, and for the other person to choose the half he wants.

That third way, known by kids, pot smokers, and everyone else who needs to divide something up quickly and fairly, is called cut-and-choose. People use it because it's a self-enforcing protocol: a protocol designed so that neither party can cheat.

Self-enforcing protocols are useful because they don't require trusted third parties. Modern systems for transferring money—checks, credit cards, PayPal—require trusted intermediaries like banks and credit card companies to facilitate the transfer. Even cash transfers require a trusted government to issue currency, and they take a cut in the form of seigniorage. Modern contract protocols require a legal system to resolve disputes. Modern commerce wasn't possible until those systems were in place and generally trusted, and complex business contracts still aren't possible in areas where there is no fair judicial system. Barter is a self-enforcing protocol: nobody needs to facilitate the transaction or resolve disputes. It just works.

Self-enforcing protocols are safer than other types because participants don't gain an advantage from cheating. Modern voting systems are rife with the potential for cheating, but an open show of hands in a room—one that everyone in the room can count for himself—is self-enforcing. On the other hand, there's no secret ballot, late voters are potentially subjected to coercion, and it doesn't scale well to large elections. But there are mathematical election protocols that have self-enforcing properties, and some cryptographers have suggested their use in elections.

Here's a self-enforcing protocol for determining property tax: the homeowner decides the value of the property and calculates the resultant tax, and the government can either accept the tax or buy the home for that price. Sounds unrealistic, but the Greek government implemented exactly that system for the taxation of antiquities. It was the easiest way to motivate people to accurately report the value of antiquities.

A VAT, or value-added tax, is a self-enforcing alternative to sales tax. Sales tax is collected on the entire value of the thing at the point of retail sale; both the customer and the store owner want to cheat the government. But VAT is collected at every step between raw materials and that final customer; it's the difference between the price of the materials sold and the materials bought.

Buyers want official receipts with as high a purchase price as possible, so each buyer along the chain keeps each seller honest. Yes, there's still an incentive to cheat on the final sale to the customer, but the amount of tax collected at that point is much lower.

Of course, self-enforcing protocols aren't perfect. For example, someone in a cut-and-choose can punch the other guy and run away with the entire piece of cake. But perfection isn't the goal here; the goal is to reduce cheating by taking away potential avenues of cheating. Self-enforcing protocols improve security not by implementing countermeasures that prevent cheating, but by leveraging economic incentives so that the parties don't want to cheat.

One more self-enforcing protocol. Imagine a pirate ship that encounters a storm. The pirates are all worried about their gold, so they put their personal bags of gold in the safe. During the storm, the safe cracks open, and all the gold mixes up and spills out on the floor. How do the pirates determine who owns what? They each announce to the group how much gold they had. If the total of all the announcements matches what's in the pile, it's divided as people announced. If it's different, then the captain keeps it all. I can think of all kinds of ways this can go wrong—the captain and one pirate can collude to throw off the total, for example—but it is self-enforcing against individual misreporting.

Reputation Is Everything in IT Security

Originally published in the Guardian, *November 11, 2009*

In the past, our relationship with our computers was technical. We cared what CPU they had and what software they ran. We understood our networks and how they worked. We were experts, or we depended on someone else for expertise. And security was part of that expertise.

This is changing. We access our email via the web, from any computer or from our phones. We use Facebook, Google Docs, even our corporate networks, regardless of hardware or network. We, especially the younger of us, no longer care about the technical details. Computing is infrastructure; it's a commodity. It's less about products and more about services; we simply expect it to work, like telephone service or electricity or a transportation network.

Infrastructures can be spread on a broad continuum, ranging from generic to highly specialized. Power and water are generic; who supplies them doesn't really matter. Mobile phone services, credit cards, ISPs, and airlines are mostly generic. More specialized infrastructure services are restaurant meals, haircuts, and social networking sites. Highly specialized services include tax preparation for complex businesses, management consulting, legal services, and medical services.

Sales for these services are driven by two things: price and trust. The more generic the service is, the more price dominates. The more specialized it is, the more trust dominates. IT is something of a special case because so much of it is free. So, for both specialized IT services where price is less important and for generic IT services—think Facebook—where there is no price, trust will grow in importance. IT is becoming a reputation-based economy, and this has interesting ramifications for security.

Some years ago, the major credit card companies became concerned about the plethora of credit-card-number thefts from sellers' databases. They worried that these might undermine the public's trust in credit cards as a secure payment system for the Internet. They knew the sellers would only protect these databases up to the level of the threat to the seller, and not to the greater level of threat to the industry as a whole. So they banded together and produced a security standard called PCI. It's wholly industry-enforced—by an industry that realized its reputation was more valuable than the sellers' databases.

A reputation-based economy means that infrastructure providers care more about security than their customers do. I realized this 10 years ago with my own company. We provided network-monitoring services to large corporations, and our internal network security was much more extensive than our customers'. Our customers secured their networks—that's why they hired us, after all—but only up to the value of their networks. If we mishandled any of our customers' data, we would have lost the trust of all of our customers.

I heard the same story at an ENISA conference in London last June, when an IT consultant explained that he had begun encrypting his laptop years before his customers did. While his customers might decide that the risk of losing their data wasn't worth the hassle of dealing with encryption, he knew that if he lost data from one customer, he risked losing all of his customers.

As IT becomes more like infrastructure, more like a commodity, expect service providers to improve security to levels greater than their customers would have done themselves.

In IT, customers learn about company reputation from many sources: magazine articles, analyst reviews, recommendations from colleagues, awards, certifications, and so on. Of course, this only works if customers have accurate information. In a reputation economy, companies have a motivation to hide their security problems.

You've all experienced a reputation economy: restaurants. Some restaurants have a good reputation, and are filled with regulars. When restaurants get a bad reputation, people stop coming and they close. Tourist restaurants—whose main attraction is their location, and whose customers frequently don't know anything about their reputation—can thrive even if they aren't any good. And sometimes a restaurant can keep its reputation—an award in a magazine, a special occasion restaurant that "everyone knows" is the place to go—long after its food and service have declined.

The reputation economy is far from perfect.

When to Change Passwords

Originally published in Dark Reading, *November 10, 2010*

How often should you change your password? I get asked that question a lot, usually by people annoyed at their employer's or bank's password expiration policy—people who finally memorized their current password and are realizing they'll have to write down their new one. How could that possibly be more secure, they want to know.

The answer depends on what the password is used for.

The downside of changing passwords is that it makes them harder to remember. And if you force people to change their passwords regularly, they're more likely to choose easy-to-remember—and easy-to-guess—passwords than they are if they can use the same passwords for many years. So any password-changing policy needs to be chosen with that consideration in mind.

The primary reason to give an authentication credential—not just a password, but any authentication credential—an expiration date is to limit the amount of time a lost, stolen, or forged credential can be used by someone else. If a membership card expires after a year, then if someone steals that card he can at most get a year's worth of benefit out of it. After that, it's useless.

This becomes less important when the credential contains a biometric—even a photograph—or is verified online. It's much less important for a credit card or passport to have an expiration date now that they're not so much bearer documents as just pointers to a database. If, for example, the credit card database knows when a card is no longer valid, there's no reason to put an expiration date on the card. But the expiration date does mean that a forgery is only good for a limited length of time.

Passwords are no different. If a hacker gets your password either by guessing or stealing it, he can access your network as long as your password is valid. If you have to update your password every quarter, that significantly limits the utility of that password to the attacker.

At least, that's the traditional theory. It assumes a passive attacker, one who will eavesdrop over time without alerting you that he's there. In many cases today, though, that assumption no longer holds. An attacker who gets the password to your bank account by guessing or stealing it isn't going to eavesdrop. He's going to transfer money out of your account—and then you're going to notice. In this case, it doesn't make a lot of sense to change your password regularly—but it's vital to change it immediately after the fraud occurs.

Someone committing espionage in a private network is more likely to be stealthy. But he's also not likely to rely on the user credential he guessed and stole; he's going to install backdoor access or create his own account. Here again, forcing network users to regularly change their passwords is less important than forcing everyone to change their passwords immediately after the spy is detected and removed—you don't want him getting in again.

Social networking sites are somewhere in the middle. Most of the criminal attacks against Facebook users use the accounts for fraud. "Help! I'm in London and my wallet was stolen. Please wire money to this account. Thank you." Changing passwords periodically doesn't help against this attack, although—of course—change your password as soon as you regain control of your account. But if your kid sister has your password—or the tabloid press, if you're that kind of celebrity—they're going to listen in until you change it. And you might not find out about it for months.

So in general: you don't need to regularly change the password to your computer or online financial accounts (including the accounts at retail sites); definitely not for low-security accounts. You should change your corporate login password occasionally, and you need to take a good hard look at your friends, relatives, and paparazzi before deciding how often to change your Facebook password. But if you break up with someone you've shared a computer with, change them all.

Two final points. One, this advice is for login passwords. There's no reason to change any password that is a key to an encrypted file. Just keep the same password as long as you keep the file, unless you suspect it's been compromised.

And two, it's far more important to choose a good password for the sites that matter—don't worry about sites you don't care about that nonetheless demand that you register and choose a password—in the first place than it is to change it. So if you have to worry about something, worry about that. And write your passwords down, or use a program like Password Safe.

The Big Idea: Bruce Schneier

Originally published in Whatever, *February 16, 2012*

My big idea is a big question. Every cooperative system contains parasites. How do we ensure that society's parasites don't destroy society's systems?

It's all about trust, really. Not the intimate trust we have in our close friends and relatives, but the more impersonal trust we have in the various people and systems we interact with in society. I trust airline pilots, hotel clerks, ATMs, restaurant kitchens, and the company that built the computer I'm writing this short essay on. I trust that they have acted and will act in the ways I expect them to. This type of trust is more a matter of consistency or predictability than of intimacy.

Of course, all of these systems contain parasites. Most people are naturally trustworthy, but some are not. There are hotel clerks who will steal your credit card information. There are ATMs that have been hacked by criminals. Some restaurant kitchens serve tainted food. There was even an airline pilot who deliberately crashed his Boeing 767 into the Atlantic Ocean in 1999.

My central metaphor is the Prisoner's Dilemma, which nicely exposes the tension between group interest and self-interest. And the dilemma even gives us a terminology to use: cooperators act in the group interest, and defectors act in their own selfish interest, to the detriment of the group. Too many defectors, and everyone suffers—often catastrophically.

The Prisoner's Dilemma is not only useful in describing the problem, but also serves as a way to organize solutions. We humans have developed four basic mechanisms for ways to limit defectors: what I call societal pressure. We use morals, reputation, laws, and security systems. It's all coercion, really, although we don't call it that. I'll spare you the details; it would require a book to explain. And it did.

This book marks another chapter in my career's endless series of generalizations. From mathematical security—cryptography—to computer and network security; from there to security technology in general; then to the economics of security and the psychology of security; and now to—I suppose—the sociology of security. The more I try to understand how security works, the more of the world I need to encompass within my model.

When I started out writing this book, I thought I'd be talking a lot about the global financial crisis of 2008. It's an excellent example of group interest vs. self-interest, and how a small minority of parasites almost destroyed the planet's financial system. I even had a great quote by former Federal Reserve Chairman Alan Greenspan, where he admitted a "flaw" in his worldview. The exchange, which took place when he was being questioned by Congressman Henry Waxman at a 2008 Congressional hearing, was once the opening paragraphs of my book. I called the defectors "the dishonest minority," which was my original title.

That unifying example eventually faded into the background, to be replaced by a lot of separate examples. I talk about overfishing, childhood immunizations, paying taxes, voting, stealing, airplane security, gay marriage, and a whole lot of other things. I dumped the phrase "dishonest minority" entirely, partly because I didn't need it and partly because a vocal few early readers were reading it not as "the small percentage of us that are dishonest" but as "the minority group that is dishonest"—not at all the meaning I was trying to convey.

I didn't even realize I was talking about trust until most of the way through. It was a couple of early readers who—coincidentally, on the same day—told me my book wasn't about security, it was about trust. More specifically, it was about how different societal pressures, security included, induce trust. This interplay between cooperators and defectors, trust and security, compliance and coercion, affects everything having to do with people.

In the book, I wander through a dizzying array of academic disciplines: experimental psychology, evolutionary psychology, sociology, economics, behavioral economics, evolutionary biology, neuroscience, game theory, systems dynamics, anthropology, archeology, history, political science, law, philosophy, theology, cognitive science, and computer security. It sometimes felt as if I were blundering through a university, kicking down doors and demanding answers. "You anthropologists: what can you tell me about early human transgressions and punishments?" "Okay neuroscientists, what's the brain chemistry of cooperation? And you evolutionary psychologists, how can you explain that?" "Hey philosophers, what have you got?" I downloaded thousands—literally—of academic papers. In pre-Internet days I would have had to move into an academic library.

What's really interesting to me is what this all means for the future. We've never been able to eliminate defections. No matter how much societal pressure we bring to bear, we can't bring the murder rate in society to zero. We'll never see the end of bad corporate behavior, or embezzlement, or rude people who make cell phone calls in movie theaters. That's fine, but it starts getting interesting when technology makes each individual defection more dangerous. That is, fishermen will survive even if a few of them defect and overfish—until defectors can deploy driftnets and single-handedly collapse the fishing stock. The occasional terrorist with a machine gun isn't a problem for society in the overall scheme of things; but a terrorist with a nuclear weapon could be.

Also—and this is the final kicker—not all defectors are bad. If you think about the notions of cooperating and defecting, they're defined in terms of the societal norm. Cooperators are people who follow the formal or informal rules of society. Defectors are people who, for whatever reason, break the rules. That definition says nothing about the absolute morality of the society or its rules. When society is in the wrong, it's defectors who are in the vanguard for change. So it was defectors who helped escaped slaves in the antebellum American South. It's defectors who are agitating to overthrow repressive regimes in the Middle East. And it's defectors who are fueling the Occupy Wall Street movement. Without defectors, society stagnates.

We simultaneously need more societal pressure to deal with the effects of technology, and less societal pressure to ensure an open, free, and evolving society. This is our big challenge for the coming decade.

High-Tech Cheats in a World of Trust

Originally published in New Scientist, *February 27, 2012*

I can put my cash card into an ATM anywhere in the world and take out a fistful of local currency, while the corresponding amount is debited from my bank account at home. I don't even think twice: regardless of the country, I trust that the system will work.

The whole world runs on trust. We trust that people on the street won't rob us, that the bank we deposited money in last month returns it this month, that the justice system punishes the guilty and exonerates the innocent. We trust the food we buy won't poison us, and the people we let in to fix our boiler won't murder us.

My career has taken me from cryptography to information security, general security technology to the economics and psychology of security. Most recently, I have become interested in how we induce trustworthy behavior.

Society is, after all, an interdependent system that requires widespread cooperation to function. People need to act in ways that are expected of them, to be consistent and compliant. And not just individuals, but organizations and systems.

But in any cooperative system, there is an alternative, parasitic, strategy available—cheating. A parasite obtains the benefits of widespread cooperation while at the same time taking advantage of it. There are—and always will be—robbers, crooked banks and judges who take bribes. So how do we ensure that the parasites are kept to a small enough minority to not ruin everything for everyone?

Remember the variations on the Prisoner's Dilemma, the game theory scenarios framed by Merrill Flood and Melvin Dresher at the US RAND Corporation think tank in 1950 that show why two individuals might not cooperate, even if it looks to be in their best interest to do so. The paradox is that it is in our collective interest to be trustworthy and cooperate, while it is in our individual self-interest to be parasitic and defect, or cheat. If too many defect, society stops functioning, the crime rate soars, international banking collapses and judicial rulings become available for sale to the highest bidder. No one would trust anyone, because there wouldn't be enough trust to go around.

The way to solve this is to put our thumb on the scales. If we can increase the benefits of cooperation or the costs of defection, we can induce people to act in the group interest—because it is also in their self-interest. In my book *Liars and Outliers*, I call such mechanisms societal pressures. A bank's reputation in the community is a societal pressure. So is the lock on the ATM that keeps criminals out.

This problem isn't new, nor unique to us. Since all complex systems must deal with the problems resulting from parasites it is not surprising that we have a complex interplay of societal pressures. The most basic are moral systems regulating our own behavior, and reputational systems we use to regulate each other's behavior. Most of us try not to treat others unfairly because it makes us feel bad and we know they will treat us badly in return. Most don't steal because we feel guilty—and there are consequences when we are caught. We recognize it is in our long-term self-interest not to act in our immediate self-interest.

Morals and reputation worked well enough for primitive lifestyles, but these began to fail as society grew too large. Trust is personal and intimate among people who know each other, and morals and reputation are easily limited to an in-group. Institutional systems—laws—formalized reputational systems, and security technologies allowed societal pressure to scale up as we expanded into ever-larger groups.

So my naive trust in ATMs turns out to be based on many complex things: the moral inclinations of most of the people involved in building and operating transfer systems; the fact that a financial institution with a reputation for cheating would probably lose its customers; the myriad banking laws and regulations that exist to punish fraudsters; and knowing that the very different security measures underpinning ATMs, bank transfers and banking will work properly even if some of those involved would prefer to cheat me.

This trust isn't absolute, of course. Not every societal pressure affects everyone equally. Some care more about their reputations, others are naturally law-abiding and still others are better at picking locks. But the goal isn't total compliance, just to limit the scope for defection. Criminals still target ATMs, and the occasional rogue bank employee steals money from accounts. But for the most part, societal pressures keep defector damage small enough to keep the system intact.

But sometimes the scope is too great and underlying systems come crashing down. Overfishing has destroyed breeding stocks in many places. Crime and corruption have devastated some countries. The international banking system almost collapsed in 2008. But in general, societal pressures work as a delicate balance between cooperation and defection: too little societal pressure and the scope of defection becomes too great; too much and security is too costly.

This balance isn't static—technological changes disrupt it all the time. The changes can be related to defecting, so ATM-based "card skimmers" make it easier for criminals to steal my codes and empty my bank account. Or they may be related to security, with computerized auditing technology making it more difficult for fraudulent transactions to go through the system unnoticed. Or they could be unrelated to either: cheap telecoms make it easier to interconnect bank networks globally. Like societal pressures, these things change the Prisoner's Dilemma calculations.

Life becomes dangerously insecure when new technologies, innovations and ideas increase the scope of defection. Defectors innovate. New attacks become possible. Existing attacks become easier, cheaper, more reliable or more devastating. More people may defect, simply because it's easier to. In response, society must also innovate, to reduce the scope of defection and restore the balance. This dynamic is as old as civilization.

Global banking, terrorists with nuclear weapons, genetic engineering, bio-weapons, pandemics: we now have such dangerous systems that a few defectors can wreak havoc so great that reactive rebalancing might not be enough. Worse still, by the time that society realizes that the scope of defection has increased and societal pressures need to be increased, irreversible damage may already have been done.

To add to the complexity, not all defectors are bad. Neither cooperation nor defection relate to any absolute standard of morality. It is defectors who are in the vanguard for change, such as those who helped escaped slaves in the US south before the civil war. It is defectors who agitate to overthrow repressive regimes in the Middle East—and defectors who fuel the Occupy movement. Without them, society stagnates.

How to achieve this balance is at the core of many of our policy debates about the Internet. Anonymity is essential to freedom and liberty and saves the lives of dissidents everywhere. Yet it also protects criminals. Copyright both protects and stifles innovation. And balance is central to debates about air security, terrorism in general, and protecting economies against financial fraud. The big challenge will be to understand how to simultaneously provide both more societal pressure to deal with the threats of technology, and less pressure to ensure an open, free and evolving society.

Detecting Cheaters

Originally published in IEEE Security & Privacy, *March/April 2011*

Our brains are specially designed to deal with cheating in social exchanges. The evolutionary psychology explanation is that we evolved brain heuristics for the social problems that our prehistoric ancestors had to deal with. Once humans became good at cheating, they then had to become good at detecting cheating—otherwise, the social group would fall apart.

Perhaps the most vivid demonstration of this can be seen with variations on what's known as the Wason selection task, named after the psychologist who first studied it. Back in the 1960s, it was a test of logical reasoning; today, it's used more as a demonstration of evolutionary psychology. But before we get to the experiment, let's get into the mathematical background.

Propositional calculus is a system for deducing conclusions from true premises. It uses variables for statements because the logic works regardless of what the statements are. College courses on the subject are taught by either the mathematics or the philosophy department, and they're not generally considered to be easy classes. Two particular rules of inference are relevant here: *modus ponens* and *modus tollens*. Both allow you to reason from a statement of the form, "if P, then Q." (If Socrates was a man, then Socrates was mortal. If you are to eat dessert, then you must first eat your vegetables. If it is raining, then Gwendolyn had Crunchy Wunchies for breakfast. That sort of thing.) *Modus ponens* goes like this:

> *If P, then Q. P. Therefore, Q.*

In other words, if you assume the conditional rule is true, and if you assume the antecedent of that rule is true, then the consequent is true. So,

> *If Socrates was a man, then Socrates was mortal. Socrates was a man. Therefore, Socrates was mortal.*

Modus tollens is more complicated:

> *If P, then Q. Not Q. Therefore, not P.*

> *If Socrates was a man, then Socrates was mortal. Socrates was not mortal. Therefore, Socrates was not a man.*

This makes sense: if Socrates was not mortal, then he was a demigod or a stone statue or something.

Both are valid forms of logical reasoning. If you know "if P, then Q" and "P," then you know "Q." If you know "if P, then Q" and "not Q," then you know "not P." (The other two similar forms don't work. If you know "if P, then Q" and "Q," you don't know anything about "P." And if you know "if P, then Q" and "not P," then you don't know anything about "Q.")

If I explained this in front of an audience full of normal people, not mathematicians or philosophers, most of them would be lost. Unsurprisingly, they would have trouble either explaining the rules or using them properly. Just ask any grad student who has had to teach a formal logic class; people have trouble with this.

Consider the Wason selection task. Subjects are presented with four cards next to each other on a table. Each card represents a person, with each side listing some statement about that person. The subject is then given a general rule and asked which cards he would have to turn over to ensure that the four people satisfied that rule. For example, the general rule might be, "If a person travels to Boston, then he or she takes a plane." The four cards might correspond to travelers and have a destination on one side and a mode of transport on the other. On the side facing the subject, they read: "went to Boston," "went to New York," "took a plane," and "took a car." Formal logic states that the rule is violated if someone goes to Boston without taking a plane. Translating into propositional calculus, there's the general rule: if P, then Q. The four cards are "P," "not P," "Q," and "not Q." To verify that "if P, then Q" is a valid rule, you have to verify *modus ponens* by turning over the "P" card and making sure that the reverse says "Q." To verify *modus tollens*, you turn over the "not Q" card and make sure that the reverse doesn't say "P."

Shifting back to the example, you need to turn over the "went to Boston" card to make sure that person took a plane, and you need to turn over the "took a car" card to make sure that person didn't go to Boston. You don't—as many people think—need to turn over the "took a plane" card to see if it says "went to Boston" because you don't care. The person might have been flying to Boston, New York, San Francisco, or London. The rule only says that people going to Boston fly; it doesn't break the rule if someone flies elsewhere.

If you're confused, you aren't alone. When Wason first did this study, fewer than 10 percent of his subjects got it right. Others replicated the study and got similar results. The best result I've seen is "fewer than 25 percent." Training in formal logic doesn't seem to help very much. Neither does ensuring that the example is drawn from events and topics with which the subjects are familiar. People are just bad at the Wason selection task. They also tend to only take college logic classes upon requirement.

This isn't just another "math is hard" story. There's a point to this. The one variation of this task that people are surprisingly good at getting right is when the rule has to do with cheating and privilege. For example, change the four cards to children in a family—"gets dessert," "doesn't get dessert," "ate vegetables," and "didn't eat vegetables"—and change the rule to "If a child gets dessert, he or she ate his or her vegetables." Many people—65 to 80 percent—get it right immediately. They turn over the "ate dessert" card, making sure the child ate his vegetables, and they turn over the "didn't eat vegetables" card, making sure the child didn't get dessert. Another way of saying this is that they turn over the "benefit received" card to make sure the cost was paid. And they turn over the "cost not paid" card to make sure no benefit was received. They look for cheaters.

The difference is startling. Subjects don't need formal logic training. They don't need math or philosophy. When asked to explain their reasoning, they say things like the answer "popped out at them."

Researchers, particularly evolutionary psychologists Leda Cosmides and John Tooby, have run this experiment with a variety of wordings and settings and on a variety of subjects: adults in the US, UK, Germany, Italy, France, and Hong Kong; Ecuadorian schoolchildren; and Shiriar tribesmen in Ecuador. The results are the same: people are bad at the Wason selection task, except when the wording involves cheating.

In the world of propositional calculus, there's absolutely no difference between a rule about traveling to Boston by plane and a rule about eating vegetables to get dessert. But in our brains, there's an enormous difference: the first is an arbitrary rule about the world, and the second is a rule of social exchange. It's of the form "If you take Benefit B, you must first satisfy Requirement R."

Our brains are optimized to detect cheaters in a social exchange. We're good at it. Even as children, we intuitively notice when someone gets a benefit he didn't pay the cost for. Those of us who grew up with a sibling have experienced how the one child not only knew that the other cheated, but felt compelled to announce it to the rest of the family. As adults, we might have learned that life isn't fair, but we still know who among our friends cheats in social exchanges. We know who doesn't pay his or her fair share of a group meal. At an airport, we might not notice the rule "If a plane is flying internationally, then it boards 15 minutes earlier than domestic flights." But we'll certainly notice who breaks the "If you board first, then you must be a first-class passenger" rule.

Lance Armstrong and the Prisoner's Dilemma of Doping in Professional Sports

Originally published in Wired, *October 26, 2012*

Doping in professional sports is back in the news, as the overwhelming evidence against Lance Armstrong led to his being stripped of his seven Tour de France titles and more. But instead of focusing on the issues of performance-enhancing drugs and whether professional athletes be allowed to take them, I'd like to talk about the security and economic aspects of the issue.

Because drug testing is a *security* issue. Various sports federations around the world do their best to detect illegal doping, and players do their best to evade the tests. It's a classic security arms race: Improvements in detection technologies lead to improvements in drug detection evasion, which in turn spur the development of better detection capabilities. Right now, it seems drugs are winning; in some places, these drug tests are described as "intelligence tests"—if you can't get around them, you don't deserve to play.

But unlike other security arms races, the detectors have the *ability to look into the past*. A laboratory tested Lance Armstrong's urine in 2005 and found traces of the banned substance erythropoietin (EPO). What's interesting is that the urine sample tested was from 1999. Back then, there weren't any good tests for EPO in urine. Today there are, and the lab took a frozen urine sample—who knew that labs save urine samples from athletes?—and tested it. Armstrong was later cleared (the lab procedures were sloppy), but I don't think people understood the real ramifications of the episode: Testing can go back in time.

The ability to test backward has two major effects:

1. While those who develop new performance-enhancing drugs know exactly what sorts of tests anti-doping laboratories are going to run, and can test their drugs' ability to evade detection beforehand—they don't know what sorts of tests will be developed in the future. Athletes can't assume that just because a drug is undetectable today it will remain so years later.

2. Athletes accused of doping based on years-old urine samples have no way of defending themselves. They can't resubmit to testing; it's too late. (Though if I were an athlete worried about this I would regularly deposit urine "in escrow" to gain some ability to contest accusations.)

The Doping Arms Race as Prisoner's Dilemma

The doping arms race will continue because of the incentives: It's a classic Prisoner's Dilemma. Consider for example competing athletes Alice and Bob, who are individually deciding whether to take drugs or not. Alice thinks:

If Bob doesn't take any drugs, then it will be in my best interest to take them. They will give me a performance edge against Bob. I have a better chance of winning.

Similarly, if Bob takes drugs, it's also in my interest to agree to take them. At least that way Bob won't have an advantage over me.

So even though I have no control over what Bob chooses to do, taking drugs gives me the better outcome, regardless of his action.

Unfortunately, Bob goes through exactly the same analysis. As a result, they both take performance-enhancing drugs and neither has the advantage over the other. If they could just trust each other, they could refrain from taking the drugs and maintain the same non-advantage status, without any legal or physical danger.

But competing athletes can't trust each other, and everyone feels he or she has to dope—continuing to search out newer and increasingly undetectable drugs so they can compete. And the arms race continues.

The Ever-Evolving Problem

It's been this way in bicycle racing for decades. In the 1970s, cyclists used corticosteroids and psychostimulants such as Ritalin, and newly developed norepinephrine-dopamine re-uptake inhibitors such as Pemoline. They were banned, and by the end of the decade assays were developed to detect those substances. In the 1980s, athletes turned to newly developed analogs of endogenous substances made possible through recombinant DNA technology, including human growth hormone, testosterone, anabolic steroids, and synthetic human EPO.

Because EPO is a glycoprotein hormone that controls red blood cell production, it acts to increase oxygenation—an effect valued as highly by endurance athletes as it was by people suffering from anemia. EPO use became rampant in cycling and other sports, and continues to be rampant in spite of bans since the early 1990s and the development in the late 1990s of carbon-isotope ratio tests. Such tests are capable of determining whether substances are made naturally by the body, or come from performance-enhancing drugs.

Next came analogs of analogs, such as darbepoetin alfa (Aranesp), a variation on EPO that became commercially available in 2001. It swiftly gained a following among bike racers and other endurance athletes, and a test to detect it soon followed in 2003. Yet another EPO replacement, Mircera, found its way to both the medical and sports markets in 2007, and assays to detect it were developed by 2008.

Norbolethone, first developed in 1966, was resurrected in the late 1990s and marketed as the first designer steroid by an entrepreneurial bodybuilder-turned-chemist intent on evading detection by the doping police. Its fingerprint was traceable by 2002. This scenario was replayed with tetrahydrogestrinone and madol, with assays developed within two years of their introduction into sports. The mid-to-late 2000s have seen an increase in blood doping through blood transfusions used to increase blood oxygen concentrations. This was soon followed by the development of flow cytometry tests to detect it.

The as-yet-unrealized prospect of gene doping has led some regulatory bodies to preemptively ban any non-therapeutic uses of genetic technology in sports. Presumably tests to detect athletes using them will follow.

Testing and Enforcing

Some sports are more vigilant about drug detection than others. European bicycle racing is particularly vigilant; so are the Olympics. This can lead to some perverse outcomes. In at least two instances, positive tests for norandrosterone, a steroid of which traces are found naturally in human urine, have been traced to adulterated supplements consumed by unsuspecting bicycle racers. Another athlete tested positive for benzodiazepine after consuming a Chinese herbal product. The most widely used urine test for EPO has been found to result in false positives in urine collected after strenuous physical exercise, though this conclusion has been hotly contested by the test's developer and others.

The most widely used tests—rapid-screen immunoassays—all too frequently yield false positives in individuals taking routine over-the-counter and prescription pain relievers, and allergy and acid reflux medications. Two days after winning the first British medal in Alpine skiing at the 2002 Winter Games in Salt Lake City, Alain Baxter was forced to return the bronze medal due to a positive test for methamphetamine... resulting from a Vicks Vapor Inhaler.

American professional sports are far more lenient, often trying to give the appearance of vigilance while still allowing athletes to use performance-enhancing drugs. They know that fans want to see beefy linebackers, powerful sluggers, and lightning-fast sprinters. So, with a wink and a nod, American enforcers only test for the easy stuff.

In the end, doping is all about economics. Athletes will continue to dope because the Prisoner's Dilemma forces them to do so. Sports authorities will either improve their detection capabilities or continue to pretend to do so, because they depend on fans and associated revenues. And as technology continues to improve, professional athletes will become more like deliberately designed racing cars.

Trust and Society

Originally published in the Montréal Review, *February 2013*

This morning, I flew from Boston to New York. Before that, I woke up in a hotel, trusting everyone on the staff who has a master key. I took a Boston taxi to the airport, trusting not just the taxi driver, but everyone else on the road. At Boston's Logan Airport, I had to trust everyone who worked for the airline, everyone who worked at the airport, and the thousands of other passengers. I also had to trust everyone who came in contact with the food I bought and ate before boarding my plane. In New York, I similarly had to trust everyone at LaGuardia Airport, my New York taxi driver, and the staff at my new hotel—where I am right now, writing this.

If I had to count, I'd guess I easily had to trust a hundred thousand people—and that was all before 10:30 this morning.

Humans are a trusting species. There were 120 people on my plane, almost all of them strangers to each other, and at no point did anyone jump up and attack the person sitting next to them. It's absurd for me to even say it, but if we had been a planeload of chimpanzees, that would have been impossible. Trust is essential for society to function—our civilization would collapse completely without it—and the fact that we don't think about it is a measure of how well that trust works.

Liars and Outliers is a book about trust and society. It's a way of thinking about society, and it's a way of conceptualizing society's problems. It's not a book about why trust is important; lots of people write about that. It's a book about how we induce trust: about how security enables trust. There were a lot of complicated mechanisms in play this morning to ensure that no one mugged me on the street, my taxi driver didn't rob me on the way to the airport, and the plane was staffed with a competent pilot. *Liars and Outliers* is a book about those mechanisms.

Trust is a complicated concept, and the word is overloaded with many meanings. There's a personal and intimate type of trust. When I say that I trust a friend, or a spouse, I'm talking less about their specific actions and more about them as a person. I have a general reliance that they will behave in a trustworthy manner. In other words, I know their intentions and I trust their actions will be informed by those intentions.

There's also a less intimate, less personal form of trust. When I got into the taxicab this morning, I didn't know the driver's intentions. For all I knew, he could have been a bank robber by night. But I did trust that, for the specific interaction of taxi driver and passenger, he would behave in a trustworthy manner. And he trusted me to do the same. This is a much more limited form of trust. Maybe it's more "confidence" than trust, and maybe the driver's actions are more like "compliance" than trustworthiness, but it's the type of trust that makes society function. I like to call this sort of trust "cooperation."

In today's society, we need to trust not only people, but institutions and systems. It's not so much that I trusted the particular pilot who flew my plane this morning, but the airline that produces well-trained and well-rested pilots according to some schedule. And it's not so much that I trusted the particular taxi driver, but instead the taxi licensing system and overall police system that produced him. Similarly, when I used an ATM this morning—another interesting exercise in trust—it's less that I trusted that particular machine, bank, and service company—but instead that I trusted the national banking system to debit the proper amount from my bank account back home.

Here's how I like to look at it. All complex ecosystems require cooperation. This is true for biological ecosystems, social systems, and sociotechnical systems. Also, in any cooperative system, there also exists an alternative parasitical strategy. Examples include tapeworms in your digestive tract, thieves in a market, spammers on e-mail, and people who refuse to pay their taxes. These parasites can only survive if they're not too successful. That is, if their number gets too large or too powerful, the underlying system collapses. If there are too many tapeworms in your digestive tract, you die and then they die. Too many thieves in a market, and no one visits the market anymore and the thieves starve. Too many people stop paying their taxes, and you get Greece.

This means there is a fundamental tension between cooperation and what I call defection. (Students of game theory will immediately recognize these terms.) It's a tension between us as individuals and us collectively as society. We might individually want each other's stuff, but we're all better off living in a theft-free society. We might individually not want to pay our taxes, but we're all better off if everyone does. And so on. More to the point, we're individually better off if everyone cooperates *except us*. If I can both 1) live in a theft-free society, and 2) steal your stuff, I personally have the best of both worlds. But if everyone acts that way, society collapses.

Most of us recognize this: that it's not in our long-term best interest to act in our short-term self-interest. But not everyone does. That's why we need mechanisms to induce trust. That's why we need security. And that's what *Liars and Outliers* is about.

How Secure Is the Papal Election?

Originally published in CNN, *February 21, 2013*

As the College of Cardinals prepares to elect a new pope, security people like me wonder about the process. How does it work, and just how hard would it be to hack the vote?

The rules for papal elections are steeped in tradition. John Paul II last codified them in 1996, and Benedict XVI left the rules largely untouched. The "Universi Dominici Gregis on the Vacancy of the Apostolic See and the Election of the Roman Pontiff" is surprisingly detailed.

Every cardinal younger than 80 is eligible to vote. We expect 117 to be voting. The election takes place in the Sistine Chapel, directed by the church chamberlain. The ballot is entirely paper-based, and all ballot counting is done by hand. Votes are secret, but everything else is open.

First, there's the "pre-scrutiny" phase.

"At least two or three" paper ballots are given to each cardinal, presumably so that a cardinal has extras in case he makes a mistake. Then nine election officials are randomly selected from the cardinals: three "scrutineers," who count the votes; three "revisers," who verify the results of the scrutineers; and three "infirmarii," who collect the votes from those too sick to be in the chapel. Different sets of officials are chosen randomly for each ballot.

Each cardinal, including the nine officials, writes his selection for pope on a rectangular ballot paper "as far as possible in handwriting that cannot be identified as his." He then folds the paper lengthwise and holds it aloft for everyone to see.

When everyone has written his vote, the "scrutiny" phase of the election begins. The cardinals proceed to the altar one by one. On the altar is a large chalice with a paten—the shallow metal plate used to hold communion wafers during Mass—resting on top of it. Each cardinal places his folded ballot on the paten. Then he picks up the paten and slides his ballot into the chalice.

If a cardinal cannot walk to the altar, one of the scrutineers—in full view of everyone—does this for him.

If any cardinals are too sick to be in the chapel, the scrutineers give the infirmarii a locked empty box with a slot, and the three infirmarii together collect those votes. If a cardinal is too sick to write, he asks one of the infirmarii to do it for him. The box is opened, and the ballots are placed onto the paten and into the chalice, one at a time.

When all the ballots are in the chalice, the first scrutineer shakes it several times to mix them. Then the third scrutineer transfers the ballots, one by one, from one chalice to another, counting them in the process. If the total number of ballots is not correct, the ballots are burned and everyone votes again.

To count the votes, each ballot is opened, and the vote is read by each scrutineer in turn, the third one aloud. Each scrutineer writes the vote on a tally sheet. This is all done in full view of the cardinals.

The total number of votes cast for each person is written on a separate sheet of paper. Ballots with more than one name (overvotes) are void, and I assume the same is true for ballots with no name written on them (undervotes). Illegible or ambiguous ballots are much more likely, and I presume they are discarded as well.

Then there's the "post-scrutiny" phase. The scrutineers tally the votes and determine whether there's a winner. We're not done yet, though.

The revisers verify the entire process: ballots, tallies, everything. And then the ballots are burned. That's where the smoke comes from: white if a pope has been elected, black if not—the black smoke is created by adding water or a special chemical to the ballots.

Being elected pope requires a two-thirds plus one vote majority. This is where Pope Benedict made a change. Traditionally a two-thirds majority had been required for election. Pope John Paul II changed the rules so that after roughly 12 days of fruitless votes, a simple majority was enough to elect a pope. Benedict reversed this rule.

How hard would this be to hack?

First, the system is entirely manual, making it immune to the sorts of technological attacks that make modern voting systems so risky.

Second, the small group of voters—all of whom know each other—makes it impossible for an outsider to affect the voting in any way. The chapel is cleared and locked before voting. No one is going to dress up as a cardinal and sneak into the Sistine Chapel. In short, the voter verification process is about as good as you're ever going to find.

A cardinal can't stuff ballots when he votes. The complicated paten-and-chalice ritual ensures that each cardinal votes once—his ballot is visible—and also keeps his hand out of the chalice holding the other votes. Not that they haven't thought about this: The cardinals are in "choir dress" during the voting, which has translucent lace sleeves under a short red cape, making sleight-of-hand tricks much harder. Additionally, the total would be wrong.

The rules anticipate this in another way: "If during the opening of the ballots the scrutineers should discover two ballots folded in such a way that they appear to have been completed by one elector, if these ballots bear the same name, they are counted as one vote; if however they bear two different names, neither vote will be valid; however, in neither of the two cases is the voting session annulled." This surprises me, as if it seems more likely to happen by accident and result in two cardinals' votes not being counted.

Ballots from previous votes are burned, which makes it harder to use one to stuff the ballot box. But there's one wrinkle: "If however a second vote is to take place immediately, the ballots from the first vote will be burned only at the end, together with those from the second vote." I assume that's done so there's only one plume of smoke for the two elections, but it would be more secure to burn each set of ballots before the next round of voting.

The scrutineers are in the best position to modify votes, but it's difficult. The counting is conducted in public, and there are multiple people checking every step. It'd be possible for the first scrutineer, if he were good at sleight of hand, to swap one ballot paper for another before recording it. Or for the third scrutineer to swap ballots during the counting process. Making the ballots large would make these attacks harder. So would controlling the blank ballots better, and only distributing one to each cardinal per vote. Presumably cardinals change their mind more often during the voting process, so distributing extra blank ballots makes sense.

There's so much checking and rechecking that it's just not possible for a scrutineer to misrecord the votes. And since they're chosen randomly for each ballot, the probability of a cabal being selected is extremely low. More interesting would be to try to attack the system of selecting scrutineers, which isn't well-defined in the document. Influencing the selection of scrutineers and revisers seems a necessary first step toward influencing the election.

If there's a weak step, it's the counting of the ballots.

There's no real reason to do a precount, and it gives the scrutineer doing the transfer a chance to swap legitimate ballots with others he previously stuffed up his sleeve. Shaking the chalice to randomize the ballots is smart, but putting the ballots in a wire cage and spinning it around would be more secure—albeit less reverent.

I would also add some kind of white-glove treatment to prevent a scrutineer from hiding a pencil lead or pen tip under his fingernails. Although the requirement to write out the candidate's name in full provides some resistance against this sort of attack.

Probably the biggest risk is complacency. What might seem beautiful in its tradition and ritual during the first ballot could easily become cumbersome and annoying after the twentieth ballot, and there will be a temptation to cut corners to save time. If the Cardinals do that, the election process becomes more vulnerable.

A 1996 change in the process lets the cardinals go back and forth from the chapel to their dorm rooms, instead of being locked in the chapel the whole time, as was done previously. This makes the process slightly less secure but a lot more comfortable.

Of course, one of the infirmarii could do what he wanted when transcribing the vote of an infirm cardinal. There's no way to prevent that. If the infirm cardinal were concerned about that but not privacy, he could ask all three infirmarii to witness the ballot.

There are also enormous social—religious, actually—disincentives to hacking the vote. The election takes place in a chapel and at an altar. The cardinals swear an oath as they are casting their ballot—further discouragement. The chalice and paten are the implements used to celebrate the Eucharist, the holiest act of the Catholic Church. And the scrutineers are explicitly exhorted not to form any sort of cabal or make any plans to sway the election, under pain of excommunication.

The other major security risk in the process is eavesdropping from the outside world. The election is supposed to be a completely closed process, with nothing communicated to the world except a winner. In today's high-tech world, this is very difficult. The rules explicitly state that the chapel is to be checked for recording and transmission devices "with the help of trustworthy individuals of proven technical ability." That was a lot easier in 2005 than it will be in 2013.

What are the lessons here?

First, open systems conducted within a known group make voting fraud much harder. Every step of the election process is observed by everyone, and everyone knows everyone, which makes it harder for someone to get away with anything.

Second, small and simple elections are easier to secure. This kind of process works to elect a pope or a club president, but quickly becomes unwieldy for a large-scale election. The only way manual systems could work for a larger group would be through a pyramid-like mechanism, with small groups reporting their manually obtained results up the chain to more central tabulating authorities.

And third: When an election process is left to develop over the course of a couple of thousand years, you end up with something surprisingly good.

The Court of Public Opinion

Originally published in Wired, *February 26, 2013*

Recently, Elon Musk and the *New York Times* took to Twitter and the Internet to argue the data—and their grievances—over a failed road test and car review. Meanwhile, an Applebee's server is part of a Change.org petition to get her job back after posting a pastor's no-tip receipt comment online. And when he wasn't paid quickly enough, a local Fitness SF web developer rewrote the company's webpage to air his complaint.

All of these "cases" are seeking their judgments in the court of public opinion. The court of public opinion has a full docket; even brick-and-mortar establishments aren't immune.

More and more individuals—and companies—are augmenting, even bypassing entirely, traditional legal process hoping to get a more favorable hearing in public.

Every day we have to interact with thousands of strangers, from people we pass on the street to people who touch our food to people we enter short-term business relationships with. Even though most of us don't have the ability to protect our interests with physical force, we can all be confident when dealing with these strangers because—at least in part—we trust that the legal system will intervene on our behalf in case of a problem. Sometimes that problem involves people who break the rules of society, and the criminal courts deal with them; when the problem is a disagreement between two parties, the civil courts will. Courts are an ancient system of justice, and modern society cannot function without them.

What matters in this system are the facts and the laws. Courts are intended to be impartial and fair in doling out their justice, and societies flourish based on the extent to which we approach this ideal. When courts are unfair—when judges can be bribed, when the powerful are treated better, when more expensive lawyers produce more favorable outcomes—society is harmed. We become more fearful and less able to trust each other. We are less willing to enter into agreement with strangers, and we spend more effort protecting our own because we don't believe the system is there to back us up.

The court of public opinion is an alternative system of justice. It's very different from the traditional court system: This court is based on reputation, revenge, public shaming, and the whims of the crowd. Having a good story is more important than having the law on your side. Being a sympathetic underdog is more important than being fair. Facts matter, but there are no standards of accuracy. The speed of the Internet exacerbates this; a good story spreads faster than a bunch of facts.

This court delivers *reputational* justice. Arguments are measured in relation to reputation. If one party makes a claim against another that seems plausible, based on both of their reputations, then that claim is likely to be received favorably. If someone makes a claim that clashes with the reputations of the parties, then it's likely to be disbelieved. Reputation is, of course, a commodity, and loss of reputation is the penalty this court imposes. In that respect, it less often recompenses the injured party and more often exacts revenge or retribution. And while those losses may be brutal, the effects are usually short-lived.

The court of public opinion has significant limitations. It works better for revenge and justice than for dispute resolution. It can punish a company for unfairly firing one of its employees or lying in an automobile test drive, but it's less effective at unraveling a complicated patent litigation or navigating a bankruptcy proceeding.

In many ways, this is a return to a medieval notion of "fama," or reputation. In other ways, it's like mob justice: sometimes benign and beneficial, sometimes terrible (think French Revolution). Trial by public opinion isn't new; remember Rodney King and O.J. Simpson?

Mass media has enabled this system for centuries. But the Internet, and social media in particular, has changed how it's being used.

Now it's being used more deliberately, more often, by more and more powerful entities as a redress mechanism. Perhaps because it's perceived to be more efficient or perhaps because one of the parties feels they can get a more favorable hearing in this new court, but it's being used instead of lawsuits. Instead of a sideshow to actual legal proceedings, it is turning into an alternate system of dispute resolution and justice.

Part of this trend is because the Internet makes taking a case in front of the court of public opinion so much easier. It used to be that the injured party had to convince a traditional media outlet to make his case public; now he can take his case directly to the people. And while it's still a surprise when some cases go viral while others languish in obscurity, it's simply more effective to present your case on Facebook or Twitter.

Another reason is that the traditional court system is increasingly viewed as unfair. Today, money *can* buy justice: not by directly bribing judges, but by hiring better lawyers and forcing the other side to spend more money than they are able to. We know that the courts treat the rich and the poor differently, that corporations can get away with crimes individuals cannot, and that the powerful can lobby to get the specific laws and regulations they want—irrespective of any notions of fairness.

Smart companies have already prepared for battles in the court of public opinion. They've hired policy experts. They've hired firms to monitor Facebook, Twitter, and other Internet venues where these battles originate. They have response strategies and communications plans in place. They've recognized that while this court is very different from the traditional legal system, money and power does count and that there are ways to tip the outcomes in their favor: For example, fake grassroots movements can be just as effective on the Internet as they can in the offline world.

It's time we recognize the court of public opinion for what it is—an alternative crowd-enabled system of justice. We need to start discussing its merits and flaws; we need to understand when it results in justice, and how it can be manipulated by the powerful. We also need to have a frank conversation about the failings of the traditional justice scheme, and why people are motivated to take their grievances to the public. Despite 24-hour PR firms and incident-response plans, this is a court where corporations and governments are at an inherent disadvantage. And because the weak will continue to run ahead of the powerful, those in power will prefer to use the more traditional mechanisms of government: police, courts, and laws.

Social-media researcher Danah Boyd had it right when she wrote here in *Wired*: "In a networked society, who among us gets to decide where the moral boundaries lie? This isn't an easy question and it's at the root of how we, as a society, conceptualize justice." It's not an easy question, but it's the key question. The moral and ethical issues surrounding the court of public opinion are the real ones, and ones that society will have to tackle in the decades to come.

On Security Awareness Training

Originally published in Dark Reading, *March 19, 2013*

Should companies spend money on security awareness training for their employees? It's a contentious topic, with respected experts on both sides of the debate. I personally believe that training users in security is generally a waste of time, and that the money can be spent better elsewhere. Moreover, I believe that our industry's focus on training serves to obscure greater failings in security design.

In order to understand my argument, it's useful to look at training's successes and failures. One area where it doesn't work very well is health. We are forever trying to train people to have healthier lifestyles: eat better, exercise more, whatever. And people are forever ignoring the lessons. One basic reason is psychological: we just aren't very good at trading off immediate gratification for long-term benefit. A healthier you is an abstract eventually; sitting in front of the television all afternoon with a McDonald's Super Monster Meal sounds really good *right now*. Similarly, computer security is an abstract benefit that gets in the way of enjoying the Internet. Good practices might protect me from a theoretical attack at some time in the future, but they're a lot of bother right now and I have more fun things to think about. This is the same trick Facebook uses to get people to give away their privacy; no one reads through new privacy policies; it's much easier to just click "OK" and start chatting with your friends. In short: security is never salient.

Another reason health training works poorly is that it's hard to link behaviors with benefits. We can train anyone—even laboratory rats—with a simple reward mechanism: push the button, get a food pellet. But with health, the connection is more abstract. If you're unhealthy, what caused it? It might have been something you did or didn't do years ago, it might have been one of the dozen things you have been doing and not doing for months, or it might have been the genes you were born with. Computer security is a lot like this, too.

Training laypeople in pharmacology also isn't very effective. We expect people to make all sorts of medical decisions at the drugstore, and they're not very good at it. Turns out that it's hard to teach expertise. We can't expect every mother to have the knowledge of a doctor or pharmacist or RN, and we certainly can't expect her to become an expert when most of the advice she's exposed to comes from manufacturers' advertising. In computer security, too, a lot of advice comes from companies with products and services to sell.

One area of health that is a training success is HIV prevention. HIV may be very complicated, but the rules for preventing it are pretty simple. And aside from certain sub-Saharan countries, we have taught people a new model of their health, and have dramatically changed their behavior. This is important: most lay medical expertise stems from folk models of health. Similarly, people have folk models of computer security. Maybe they're right and maybe they're wrong, but they're how people organize their thinking. This points to a possible way that computer security training can succeed. We should stop trying to teach expertise, and pick a few simple metaphors of security and train people to make decisions using those metaphors.

On the other hand, we still have trouble teaching people to wash their hands—even though it's easy, fairly effective, and simple to explain. Notice the difference, though. The risks of catching HIV are huge, and the cause of the security failure is obvious. The risks of not washing your hands are low, and it's not easy to tie the resultant disease to a particular not-washing decision. Computer security is more like hand washing than HIV.

Another area where training works is driving. We trained, either through formal courses or one-on-one tutoring, and passed a government test, to be allowed to drive a car. One reason that works is because driving is a near-term, really cool, obtainable goal. Another reason is even though the technology of driving has changed dramatically over the past century, that complexity has been largely hidden behind a fairly static interface. You might have learned to drive thirty years ago, but that knowledge is still relevant today. On the other hand, password advice from ten years ago isn't relevant today. Can I bank from my browser? Are PDFs safe? Are untrusted networks okay? Is JavaScript good or bad? Are my photos more secure in the cloud or on my own hard drive? The 'interface' we use to interact with computers and the Internet changes all the time, along with best practices for computer security. This makes training a lot harder.

Food safety is my final example. We have a bunch of simple rules—cooking temperatures for meat, expiration dates on refrigerated goods, the three-second rule for food being dropped on the floor—that are mostly right, but often ignored. If we can't get people to follow these rules, what hope do we have for computer security training?

To those who think that training users in security is a good idea, I want to ask: "Have you ever met an actual user?" They're not experts, and we can't expect them to become experts. The threats change constantly, the likelihood of failure is low, and there is enough complexity that it's hard for people to understand how to connect their behavior to eventual outcomes. So they turn to folk remedies that, while simple, don't really address the threats.

Even if we could invent an effective computer security training program, there's one last problem. HIV prevention training works because affecting what the average person does is valuable. Even if only half the population practices safe sex, those actions dramatically reduce the spread of HIV. But computer security is often only as strong as the weakest link. If four-fifths of company employees learn to choose better passwords, or not to click on dodgy links, one-fifth still get it wrong and the bad guys still get in. As long as we build systems that are vulnerable to the worst case, raising the average case won't make them more secure.

The whole concept of security awareness training demonstrates how the computer industry has failed. We should be designing systems that won't let users choose lousy passwords and don't care what links a user clicks on. We should be designing systems that conform to their folk beliefs of security, rather than forcing them to learn new ones. Microsoft has a great rule about system messages that require the user to make a decision. They should be NEAT: necessary, explained, actionable, and tested. That's how we should be designing security interfaces. And we should be spending money on security training for developers. These are people who can be taught expertise in a fast-changing environment, and this is a situation where raising the average behavior increases the security of the overall system.

If we security engineers do our job right, users will get their awareness training informally and organically, from their colleagues and friends. People will learn the correct folk models of security, and be able to make decisions using them. Then maybe an organization can spend an hour a year reminding their employees what good security means at that organization, both on the computer and off. That makes a whole lot more sense.

Our New Regimes of Trust

Originally published in the SciTech Lawyer, *Winter/Spring 2013*

Society runs on trust. Over the millennia, we've developed a variety of mechanisms to induce trustworthy behavior in society. These range from a sense of guilt when we cheat, to societal disapproval when we lie, to laws that arrest fraudsters, to door locks and burglar alarms that keep thieves out of our homes. They're complicated and interrelated, but they tend to keep society humming along.

The information age is transforming our society. We're shifting from evolved social systems to deliberately created socio-technical systems. Instead of having conversations in offices, we use Facebook. Instead of meeting friends, we IM. We shop online. We let various companies and governments collect comprehensive dossiers on our movements, our friendships, and our interests. We let others censor what we see and read. I could go on for pages.

None of this is news to anyone. But what's important, and much harder to predict, are the social changes resulting from these technological changes. With the rapid proliferation of computers—both fixed and mobile—computing devices and in-the-cloud processing, new ways of socialization have emerged. Facebook friends are fundamentally different than in-person friends. IM conversations are fundamentally different than voice conversations. Twitter has no pre-Internet analog. More social changes are coming. These social changes affect trust, and trust affects everything.

This isn't just academic. There has always been a balance in society between the honest and the dishonest, and technology continually upsets that balance. Online banking results in new types of cyberfraud. Facebook posts become evidence in employment and legal disputes. Cell phone location tracking can be used to round up political dissidents. Random blogs and websites become trusted sources, abetting propaganda. Crime has changed: easier impersonation, action at a greater distance, automation, and so on. The more our nation's infrastructure relies on cyberspace, the more vulnerable we are to cyberattack.

Think of this as a *security gap*: the time lag between when the bad guys figure out how to exploit a new technology and when the good guys figure out how to restore society's balance.

Critically, the security gap is larger when there's more technology, and especially in times of rapid technological change. More importantly, it's larger in times of rapid social change due to the increased use of technology. This is our world today. We don't know *how* the proliferation of networked, mobile devices will affect the systems we have in place to enable trust, but we do know it *will* affect them.

Trust is as old as our species. It's something we do naturally, and informally. We don't trust doctors because we've vetted their credentials, but because they sound learned. We don't trust politicians because we've analyzed their positions, but because we generally agree with their political philosophy—or the buzzwords they use. We trust many things because our friends trust them.

It's the same with corporations, government organizations, strangers on the street: this thing that's critical to society's smooth functioning occurs largely through intuition and relationship. Unfortunately, these traditional and low-tech mechanisms are increasingly failing us. Understanding how trust is being, and will be, affected—probably not by predicting, but rather by recognizing effects as quickly as possible—and then deliberately creating mechanisms to induce trustworthiness and enable trust, is the only thing that will enable society to adapt.

If there's anything I've learned in all my years working at the intersection of security and technology, it's that technology is rarely more than a small piece of the solution. People are always the issue and we need to think as broadly as possible about solutions. So while laws are important, they don't work in isolation. Much of our security comes from the informal mechanisms we've evolved over the millennia: systems of morals and reputation.

There will exist new regimes of trust in the information age. They simply must evolve, or society will suffer unpredictably. We have already begun fleshing out such regimes, albeit in an ad hoc manner. It's time for us to deliberately think about how trust works in the information age, and use legal, social, and technological tools to enable this trust. We might get it right by accident, but it'll be a long and ugly iterative process getting there if we do.

4 Privacy and Surveillance

The Myth of the "Transparent Society"

Originally published in Wired News, *March 6, 2008*

When I write and speak about privacy, I am regularly confronted with the mutual disclosure argument. Explained in books like David Brin's *The Transparent Society*, the argument goes something like this: In a world of ubiquitous surveillance, you'll know all about me, but I will also know all about you. The government will be watching us, but we'll also be watching the government. This is different than before, but it's not automatically worse. And because I know your secrets, you can't use my secrets as a weapon against me.

This might not be everybody's idea of utopia—and it certainly doesn't address the inherent value of privacy—but this theory has a glossy appeal, and could easily be mistaken for a way out of the problem of technology's continuing erosion of privacy. Except it doesn't work, because it ignores the crucial dissimilarity of power.

You cannot evaluate the value of privacy and disclosure unless you account for the relative power levels of the discloser and the disclosee.

If I disclose information to you, your power with respect to me increases. One way to address this power imbalance is for you to similarly disclose information to me. We both have less privacy, but the balance of power is maintained. But this mechanism fails utterly if you and I have different power levels to begin with.

An example will make this clearer. You're stopped by a police officer, who demands to see identification. Divulging your identity will give the officer enormous power over you: He or she can search police databases using the information on your ID; he or she can create a police record attached to your name; he or she can put you on this or that secret terrorist watch list. Asking to see the officer's ID in return gives you no comparable power over him or her. The power imbalance is too great, and mutual disclosure does not make it OK.

You can think of your existing power as the exponent in an equation that determines the value, to you, of more information. The more power you have, the more additional power you derive from the new data.

Another example: When your doctor says "take off your clothes," it makes no sense for you to say, "You first, doc." The two of you are not engaging in an interaction of equals.

This is the principle that should guide decision-makers when they consider installing surveillance cameras or launching data-mining programs. It's not enough to open the efforts to public scrutiny. All aspects of government work best when the relative power between the governors and the governed remains as small as possible—when liberty is high and control is low. Forced openness in government reduces the relative power differential between the two, and is generally good. Forced openness in laypeople increases the relative power, and is generally bad.

Seventeen-year-old Erik Crespo was arrested in 2005 in connection with a shooting in a New York City elevator. There's no question that he committed the shooting; it was captured on surveillance-camera videotape. But he claimed that while being interrogated, Detective Christopher Perino tried to talk him out of getting a lawyer, and told him that he had to sign a confession before he could see a judge.

Perino denied, under oath, that he ever questioned Crespo. But Crespo had received an MP3 player as a Christmas gift, and surreptitiously recorded the questioning. The defense brought a transcript and CD into evidence. Shortly thereafter, the prosecution offered Crespo a better deal than originally proffered (seven years rather than 15). Crespo took the deal, and Perino was separately indicted on charges of perjury.

Without that recording, it was the detective's word against Crespo's. And who would believe a murder suspect over a New York City detective? That power imbalance was reduced only because Crespo was smart enough to press the "record" button on his MP3 player. Why aren't all interrogations recorded? Why don't defendants have the right to those recordings, just as they have the right to an attorney? Police routinely record traffic stops from their squad cars for their own protection; that video record shouldn't stop once the suspect is no longer a threat.

Cameras make sense when trained on police, and in offices where lawmakers meet with lobbyists, and wherever government officials wield power over the people. Open-government laws, giving the public access to government records and meetings of governmental bodies, also make sense. These all foster liberty.

Ubiquitous surveillance programs that affect everyone without probable cause or warrant, like the National Security Agency's warrantless eavesdropping programs or various proposals to monitor everything on the Internet, foster control. And no one is safer in a political system of control.

Our Data, Ourselves

Originally published in Wired News, *May 15, 2008*

In the information age, we all have a data shadow.

We leave data everywhere we go. It's not just our bank accounts and stock portfolios, or our itemized bills, listing every credit card purchase and telephone call we make. It's automatic road-toll collection systems, supermarket affinity cards, ATMs and so on.

It's also our lives. Our love letters and friendly chat. Our personal e-mails and SMS messages. Our business plans, strategies and offhand conversations. Our political leanings and positions. And this is just the data we interact with. We all have shadow selves living in the data banks of hundreds of corporations' information brokers—information about us that is both surprisingly personal and uncannily complete—except for the errors that you can neither see nor correct.

What happens to our data happens to ourselves.

This shadow self doesn't just sit there: It's constantly touched. It's examined and judged. When we apply for a bank loan, it's our data that determines whether or not we get it. When we try to board an airplane, it's our data that determines how thoroughly we get searched—or whether we get to board at all. If the government wants to investigate us, they're more likely to go through our data than they are to search our homes; for a lot of that data, they don't even need a warrant.

Who controls our data controls our lives.

It's true. Whoever controls our data can decide whether we can get a bank loan, on an airplane or into a country. Or what sort of discount we get from a merchant, or even how we're treated by customer support. A potential employer can, illegally in the US, examine our medical data and decide whether or not to offer us a job. The police can mine our data and decide whether or not we're a terrorist risk. If a criminal can get hold of enough of our data, he can open credit cards in our names, siphon money out of our investment accounts, even sell our property. Identity theft is the ultimate proof that control of our data means control of our life.

We need to take back our data.

Our data is a part of us. It's intimate and personal, and we have basic rights to it. It should be protected from unwanted touch.

We need a comprehensive data privacy law. This law should protect all information about us, and not be limited merely to financial or health information. It should limit others' ability to buy and sell our information without our knowledge and consent. It should allow us to see information about us held by others, and correct any inaccuracies we find. It should prevent the government from going after our information without judicial oversight. It should enforce data deletion, and limit data collection, where necessary. And we need more than token penalties for deliberate violations.

This is a tall order, and it will take years for us to get there. It's easy to do nothing and let the market take over. But as we see with things like grocery store club cards and click-through privacy policies on websites, most people either don't realize the extent their privacy is being violated or don't have any real choice. And businesses, of course, are more than happy to collect, buy, and sell our most intimate information. But the long-term effects of this on society are toxic; we give up control of ourselves.

The Future of Ephemeral Conversation

Originally published in the Wall Street Journal, *November 21, 2008*

When he becomes president, Barack Obama will have to give up his BlackBerry. Aides are concerned that his unofficial conversations would become part of the presidential record, subject to subpoena and eventually made public as part of the country's historical record.

This reality of the information age might be particularly stark for the president, but it's no less true for all of us. Conversation used to be ephemeral.

Whether face-to-face or by phone, we could be reasonably sure that what we said disappeared as soon as we said it. Organized crime bosses worried about phone taps and room bugs, but that was the exception. Privacy was just assumed.

This has changed. We chat in e-mail, over SMS and IM, and on social networking websites like Facebook, MySpace, and LiveJournal. We blog and we Twitter. These conversations—with friends, lovers, colleagues, members of our cabinet—are not ephemeral; they leave their own electronic trails.

We know this intellectually, but we haven't truly internalized it. We type on, engrossed in conversation, forgetting we're being recorded and those recordings might come back to haunt us later.

Oliver North learned this, way back in 1987, when messages he thought he had deleted were saved by the White House PROFS system, and then subpoenaed in the Iran-Contra affair. Bill Gates learned this in 1998 when his conversational e-mails were provided to opposing counsel as part of the antitrust litigation discovery process. Mark Foley learned this in 2006 when his instant messages were saved and made public by the underage men he talked to. Paris Hilton learned this in 2005 when her cell phone account was hacked, and Sarah Palin learned it earlier this year when her Yahoo e-mail account was hacked. Someone in George W. Bush's administration learned this, and millions of e-mails went mysteriously and conveniently missing.

Ephemeral conversation is dying.

Cardinal Richelieu famously said, "If one would give me six lines written by the hand of the most honest man, I would find something in them to have him hanged." When all our ephemeral conversations can be saved for later examination, different rules have to apply. Conversation is not the same thing as correspondence. Words uttered in haste over morning coffee, whether spoken in a coffee shop or thumbed on a Blackberry, are not official pronouncements. Discussions in a meeting, whether held in a boardroom or a chat room, are not the same as answers at a press conference. And privacy isn't just about having something to hide; it has enormous value to democracy, liberty, and our basic humanity.

We can't turn back technology; electronic communications are here to stay and even our voice conversations are threatened. But as technology makes our conversations less ephemeral, we need laws to step in and safeguard ephemeral conversation. We need a comprehensive data privacy law, protecting our data and communications regardless of where it is stored or how it is processed. We need laws forcing companies to keep it private and delete it as soon as it is no longer needed. Laws requiring ISPs to store e-mails and other personal communications are exactly what we don't need.

Rules pertaining to government need to be different, because of the power differential. Subjecting the president's communications to eventual public review increases liberty because it reduces the government's power with respect to the people. Subjecting our communications to government review decreases liberty because it reduces our power with respect to the government. The president, as well as other members of government, need some ability to converse ephemerally—just as they're allowed to have unrecorded meetings and phone calls—but more of their actions need to be subject to public scrutiny.

But laws can only go so far. Law or no law, when something is made public it's too late. And many of us like having complete records of all our e-mail at our fingertips; it's like our offline brains.

In the end, this is cultural.

The Internet is the greatest generation gap since rock and roll. We're now witnessing one aspect of that generation gap: the younger generation chats digitally, and the older generation treats those chats as written correspondence. Until our CEOs blog, our Congressmen Twitter, and our world leaders send each other LOLcats—until we have a Presidential election where both candidates have a complete history on social networking sites from before they were teenagers– we aren't fully an information age society.

When everyone leaves a public digital trail of their personal thoughts since birth, no one will think twice about it being there. Obama might be on the younger side of the generation gap, but the rules he's operating under were written by the older side. It will take another generation before society's tolerance for digital ephemera changes.

How to Prevent Digital Snooping

Originally published in the Wall Street Journal, *December 9, 2008*

As the first digital president, Barack Obama is learning the hard way how difficult it can be to maintain privacy in the information age. Earlier this year, his passport file was snooped by contract workers in the State Department. In October, someone at Immigration and Customs Enforcement leaked information about his aunt's immigration status. And in November, Verizon employees peeked at his cell phone records.

What these three incidents illustrate is not that computerized databases are vulnerable to hacking—we already knew that, and anyway the perpetrators all had legitimate access to the systems they used—but how important audit is as a security measure.

When we think about security, we commonly think about preventive measures: locks to keep burglars out of our homes, bank safes to keep thieves from our money, and airport screeners to keep guns and bombs off airplanes. We might also think of detection and response measures: alarms that go off when burglars pick our locks or dynamite open bank safes, sky marshals on airplanes who respond when a hijacker manages to sneak a gun through airport security. But audit, figuring out who did what after the fact, is often far more important than any of those other three.

Most security against crime comes from audit. Of course we use locks and alarms, but we don't wear bulletproof vests. The police provide for our safety by investigating crimes after the fact and prosecuting the guilty: that's audit.

Audit helps ensure that people don't abuse positions of trust. The cash register, for example, is basically an audit system. Cashiers have to handle the store's money. To ensure they don't skim from the till, the cash register keeps an audit trail of every transaction. The store owner can look at the register totals at the end of the day and make sure the amount of money in the register is the amount that should be there.

The same idea secures us from police abuse, too. The police have enormous power, including the ability to intrude into very intimate aspects of our life in order to solve crimes and keep the peace. This is generally a good thing, but to ensure that the police don't abuse this power, we put in place systems of audit like the warrant process.

The whole NSA warrantless eavesdropping scandal was about this. Some misleadingly painted it as allowing the government to eavesdrop on foreign terrorists, but the government always had that authority. What the government wanted was to not have to submit a warrant, even after the fact, to a secret FISA court. What they wanted was to not be subject to audit.

That would be an incredibly bad idea. Law enforcement systems that don't have good audit features designed in, or are exempt from this sort of audit-based oversight, are much more prone to abuse by those in power—because they can abuse the system without the risk of getting caught. Audit is essential as the NSA increases its domestic spying. And large police databases, like the FBI Next Generation Identification System, need to have strong audit features built in.

For computerized database systems like that—systems entrusted with other people's information—audit is a very important security mechanism. Hospitals need to keep databases of very personal health information, and doctors and nurses need to be able to access that information quickly and easily. A good audit record of who accessed what when is the best way to ensure that those trusted with our medical information don't abuse that trust. It's the same with IRS records, credit reports, police databases, telephone records—anything personal that someone might want to peek at during the course of his job.

Which brings us back to President Obama. In each of those three examples, someone in a position of trust inappropriately accessed personal information. The difference between how they played out is due to differences in audit. The State Department's audit worked best; they had alarm systems in place that alerted superiors when Obama's passport files were accessed and who accessed them. Verizon's audit mechanisms worked less well; they discovered the inappropriate account access and have narrowed the culprits down to a few people. Audit at Immigration and Customs Enforcement was far less effective; they still don't know who accessed the information.

Large databases filled with personal information, whether managed by governments or corporations, are an essential aspect of the information age. And they each need to be accessed, for legitimate purposes, by thousands or tens of thousands of people. The only way to ensure those people don't abuse the power they're entrusted with is through audit. Without it, we will simply never know who's peeking at what.

Architecture of Privacy

Originally published in IEEE Security & Privacy,
January/February 2009

The Internet isn't really for us. We're here at the beginning, stumbling around, just figuring out what it's good for and how to use it. The Internet is for those born into it, those who have woven it into their lives from the beginning. The Internet is the greatest generation gap since rock and roll, and only our children can hope to understand it.

Larry Lessig famously said that, on the Internet, code is law. Facebook's architecture limits what we can do there, just as gravity limits what we can do on Earth. The 140-character limit on SMSs is as effective as a legal ban on grammar, spelling, and long-winded sentences: KTHXBYE.

As architects of the Internet, we have a special responsibility to our children to build an Internet that future generations will be proud of, one that encompasses basic human rights and values. We do this when we build systems that offer universal access support, open interfaces, and net neutrality, bypass censorship, limit surveillance, fight repression, give people control over their digital presence and digital personas, and foster individual liberty and privacy—especially privacy.

This would all be easier if the choices we made were temporary. But if history is any guide, they're not. Architecture, both physical and virtual, stays around far longer than we intend it to. College campuses built in the 1970s to limit student protests are still standing, as are buildings designed to defend against medieval siege engines. ASCII and TCP/IP aren't going anywhere anytime soon; neither are domain names, email addresses, or HTML. It's been many years, and we still haven't managed to get either DNSSEC or IPV6 deployed. A "just for now" decision can easily remain for decades.

Business and political realities make privacy harder. Some business models depend on walled gardens or invasive digital rights management controls. Other business models depend on collecting and selling personal data. Some countries depend on censorship to enforce morality or keep ideas out, while others depend on surveillance to control their citizens.

The natural tendencies of the Internet make privacy harder. Technology is the friend of intrusive tools. Digital sensors become smaller and more plentiful. More data is collected and stored every year. Privacy isn't something that occurs naturally online, it must be deliberately architected.

Companies that retain personal information put their customers at risk. Security breaches, court orders, and disgruntled employees are just a few of the ways to lose control of data. Good architectures that minimize data collection reduce these risks, just like guardrails on highways prevent more serious accidents when drivers lose control of their vehicles.

We need to be more deliberate. A lot of information-age architecture is about data: what is collected, who controls it, and how it is used. Data is the lifeblood of the information age, but much of it is very personal. We need to design systems that limit unnecessary data collection, give individuals control over their data, and limit the ability of those in power to use that data for mass surveillance.

Data is the pollution of the information age. It's a byproduct of every computer-mediated interaction; all processes produce it. It stays around forever, unless it's disposed of. It can be recycled, but it has to be done carefully. And, like physical pollution during the early decades of the industrial age, most people completely ignore the problem.

Just as we look back at the beginning of the previous century and shake our heads at how the titans of the industrial age could ignore the pollution they caused, future generations will look back at us—in the early decades of the information age—and judge our architecture, and what we did to foster freedom, liberty, and democracy. Did we build information technologies that protected people's freedoms even during times when society tried to subvert them? Or did we build technologies that could easily be modified to watch and control? History will record our choices.

Privacy in the Age of Persistence

Originally published in BBC News, *February 26, 2009*

Welcome to the future, where everything about you is saved. A future where your actions are recorded, your movements are tracked, and your conversations are no longer ephemeral. A future brought to you not by some 1984-like dystopia, but by the natural tendencies of computers to produce data.

Data is the pollution of the information age. It's a natural by-product of every computer-mediated interaction. It stays around forever, unless it's disposed of. It is valuable when reused, but it must be done carefully. Otherwise, its after-effects are toxic.

And just as 100 years ago people ignored pollution in our rush to build the Industrial Age, today we're ignoring data in our rush to build the Information Age.

Increasingly, you leave a trail of digital footprints throughout your day. Once you walked into a bookstore and bought a book with cash. Now you visit Amazon, and all of your browsing and purchases are recorded. You used to buy a train ticket with coins; now your electronic fare card is tied to your bank account. Your store affinity cards give you discounts; merchants use the data on them to reveal detailed purchasing patterns.

Data about you is collected when you make a phone call, send an e-mail message, use a credit card, or visit a website. A national ID card will only exacerbate this.

More computerized systems are watching you. Cameras are ubiquitous in some cities, and eventually face recognition technology will be able to identify individuals. Automatic license plate scanners track vehicles in parking lots and cities. Color printers, digital cameras, and some photocopy machines have embedded identification codes. Aerial surveillance is used by cities to find building permit violators and by marketers to learn about home and garden size.

As RFID chips become more common, they'll be tracked, too. Already you can be followed by your cell phone, even if you never make a call. This is wholesale surveillance; not "follow that car," but "follow every car."

Computers are mediating conversation as well. Face-to-face conversations are ephemeral. Years ago, telephone companies might have known who you called and how long you talked, but not what you said. Today you chat in e-mail, by text message, and on social networking sites. You blog and you Twitter. These conversations—with family, friends, and colleagues—can be recorded and stored.

It used to be too expensive to save this data, but computer memory is now cheaper. Computer processing power is cheaper, too; more data is cross-indexed and correlated, and then used for secondary purposes. What was once ephemeral is now permanent.

Who collects and uses this data depends on local laws. In the US, corporations collect, then buy and sell, much of this information for marketing purposes. In Europe, governments collect more of it than corporations. On both continents, law enforcement wants access to as much of it as possible for both investigation and data mining.

Regardless of country, more organizations are collecting, storing, and sharing more of it.

More is coming. Keyboard logging programs and devices can already record everything you type; recording everything you say on your cell phone is only a few years away.

A "life recorder" you can clip to your lapel that'll record everything you see and hear isn't far behind. It'll be sold as a security device, so that no-one can attack you without being recorded. When that happens, will not wearing a life recorder be used as evidence that someone is up to no good, just as prosecutors today use the fact that someone left his cell phone at home as evidence that he didn't want to be tracked?

You're living in a unique time in history: the technology is here, but it's not yet seamless. Identification checks are common, but you still have to show your ID. Soon it'll happen automatically, either by remotely querying a chip in your wallets or by recognizing your face on camera.

And all those cameras, now visible, will shrink to the point where you won't even see them. Ephemeral conversation will all but disappear, and you'll think it normal. Already your children live much more of their lives in public than you do. Your future has no privacy, not because of some police-state governmental tendencies or corporate malfeasance, but because computers naturally produce data.

Cardinal Richelieu famously said: "If one would give me six lines written by the hand of the most honest man, I would find something in them to have him hanged." When all your words and actions can be saved for later examination, different rules have to apply.

Society works precisely because conversation is ephemeral; because people forget, and because people don't have to justify every word they utter.

Conversation is not the same thing as correspondence. Words uttered in haste over morning coffee, whether spoken in a coffee shop or thumbed on a BlackBerry, are not official correspondence. A data pattern indicating "terrorist tendencies" is no substitute for a real investigation. Being constantly scrutinized undermines our social norms; furthermore, it's creepy. Privacy isn't just about having something to hide; it's a basic right that has enormous value to democracy, liberty, and our humanity.

We're not going to stop the march of technology, just as we cannot un-invent the automobile or the coal furnace. We spent the industrial age relying on fossil fuels that polluted our air and transformed our climate. Now we are working to address the consequences. (While still using said fossil fuels, of course.) This time around, maybe we can be a little more proactive.

Just as we look back at the beginning of the previous century and shake our heads at how people could ignore the pollution they caused, future generations will look back at us—living in the early decades of the information age—and judge our solutions to the proliferation of data.

We must, all of us together, start discussing this major societal change and what it means. And we must work out a way to create a future that our grandchildren will be proud of.

Should We Have an Expectation of Online Privacy?

Originally published in Information Security, *May 2009*

This essay appeared as the second half of a point/counterpoint with Marcus Ranum.

If your data is online, it is not private. Oh, maybe it seems private. Certainly, only you have access to your e-mail. Well, you and your ISP. And the sender's ISP. And any backbone provider who happens to route that mail from the sender to you. And, if you read your personal mail from work, your company. And, if they have taps at the correct points, the NSA and any other sufficiently well-funded government intelligence organization—domestic and international.

You could encrypt your mail, of course, but few of us do that. Most of us now use webmail. The general problem is that, for the most part, your online data is not under your control. Cloud computing and software as a service exacerbate this problem even more.

Your webmail is less under your control than it would be if you downloaded your mail to your computer. If you use Salesforce.com, you're relying on that company to keep your data private. If you use Google Docs, you're relying on Google. This is why the Electronic Privacy Information Center recently filed a complaint with the Federal Trade Commission: many of us are relying on Google's security, but we don't know what it is.

This is new. Twenty years ago, if someone wanted to look through your correspondence, he had to break into your house. Now, he can just break into your ISP. Ten years ago, your voicemail was on an answering machine in your office; now it's on a computer owned by a telephone company. Your financial accounts are on remote websites protected only by passwords; your credit history is collected, stored, and sold by companies you don't even know exist.

And more data is being generated. Lists of books you buy, as well as the books you look at, are stored in the computers of online booksellers. Your affinity card tells your supermarket what foods you like. What were cash transactions are now credit card transactions. What used to be an anonymous coin tossed into a toll booth is now an EZ Pass record of which highway you were on, and when. What used to be a face-to-face chat is now an e-mail, IM, or SMS conversation—or maybe a conversation inside Facebook.

Remember when Facebook recently changed its terms of service to take further control over your data? They can do that whenever they want, you know. We have no choice but to trust these companies with our security and privacy, even though they have little incentive to protect them. Neither ChoicePoint, Lexis Nexis, Bank of America, nor T-Mobile bears the costs of privacy violations or any resultant identity theft.

This loss of control over our data has other effects, too. Our protections against police abuse have been severely watered down. The courts have ruled that the police can search your data without a warrant, as long as others hold that data. If the police want to read the e-mail on your computer, they need a warrant; but they don't need one to read it from the backup tapes at your ISP.

This isn't a technological problem; it's a legal problem. The courts need to recognize that in the information age, virtual privacy and physical privacy don't have the same boundaries. We should be able to control our own data, regardless of where it is stored. We should be able to make decisions about the security and privacy of that data, and have legal recourse should companies fail to honor those decisions. And just as the Supreme Court eventually ruled that tapping a telephone was a Fourth Amendment search, requiring a warrant—even though it occurred at the phone company switching office and not in the target's home or office—the Supreme Court must recognize that reading personal e-mail at an ISP is no different.

Offhand but On Record

Originally published in the Japan Times, *August 19, 2009*

Facebook recently made changes to its service agreement in order to make members' data more accessible to other computer users. Amuse, Inc. announced last week that hackers stole credit-card information from about 150,000 clients. Hackers broke into the social network Twitter's system and stole documents.

Your online data is not private. It may seem private, but it's not. Take e-mail, for example. You might be the only person who knows your e-mail password, but you're not the only person who can read your e-mail. Your e-mail provider can read it too—along with anyone he gives access to. That can include any backbone provider who happened to route that mail from the sender to you. In addition, if you read your e-mail from work, various people at your company have access to it, too. And, if they have taps at the correct points, so can the police, the US National Security Agency, and any other well-funded national intelligence organization—along with any hackers or criminals sufficiently skilled to break into one of these sites.

Think about your Mixi or Facebook site. You're the only one with your password, but lots of other people can read your updates and look at your pictures. Your friends can see a lot of information about you—that's the whole point of these sites—and you don't really know who they share their information with. A lot of your stuff is public by default, and you probably keep it that way. You might respond to quizzes, and who knows where that data goes or who can see it. Workers at Mixi and Facebook can see everything, of course. They also grant access to portions of your data to third parties who want to sell their products to you.

You could set every privacy setting on your Mixi or Facebook site to maximum, but few of us do that—most of us don't even know how. You could encrypt your e-mail, but almost no one does that—and, anyway, that doesn't work with Webmail very easily. Maintaining your privacy is hard, even if you're an expert.

Cloud computing exacerbates this problem. If your company uses software-as-a-service providers such as Salesforce.com, contact management, or MessageLabs e-mail filtering, those companies have access to your data. If you use Google Docs, Google has access to your data. But even if you leave your data in your computer at home, you have to worry about your family or roommates, burglars, police with warrants, and Internet hackers and other criminals as well.

It's not just your online data that is at risk. It's your cell phone data—both the phone numbers you call and who call you, and the SMS messages you send and receive. It's your buying history, sitting in some credit card company's database. It's your medical records. It's the itemized list of everything you buy when you use a card that identifies you.

These risks are new. Twenty years ago, if someone wanted to look through your correspondence, they had to break into your house. Now, they can just break into your ISP. Ten years ago, your voicemail was on an answering machine in your office; now it's on a computer owned by a telephone company. Your financial accounts are on remote Web sites protected only by passwords; your credit history is collected, stored and sold by companies whose names you probably don't even know. Your digital data is no longer under your control.

And more data is being generated. Lists of everything you buy, and everything you look at but choose not to buy, are stored by online merchants both in Japan and abroad. A record of everything you browse can be stored by your ISP if they choose to. What were cash transactions are now credit card transactions. What used to be a face-to-face chat is now an e-mail, instant message, or SMS conversation—or maybe a conversation within Mixi or Facebook.

Think of the number of people and companies that can know your location. Your cell phone knows where you are. Your air-travel history is stored in various airline databases, and unless you buy your tickets anonymously, your rail travel history is stored in JR's and other databases. Even your credit card company can reconstruct your whereabouts from your purchases.

All these systems are ostensibly private and secure, but many people have legitimate access and even more—such as hackers and criminals—can get illegitimate access. Japan's Personal Information Protection Act provides only some protections and may not apply if the computers that store your information are located in some other country.

Anonymity doesn't help much. Mixi might not know your real name and address, but there are many ways to link your identity to your account. Maybe your e-mail address identifies you or your ISP knows who you are. Your cell phone identifies you and your computer might, too. Use a credit card from your account and that identifies you. True anonymity is very difficult; we regularly identify ourselves online even if we think we do not.

The lesson in all of this is that little we do is ephemeral anymore. We leave electronic audit trails everywhere we go, with everything we do. This won't change: We can't turn back technology. But as technology makes our conversations less ephemeral, we need laws to step in and safeguard our privacy. We need comprehensive data privacy laws, protecting our data and communications regardless of where it is stored or how it is processed. We need laws forcing companies to keep it private and delete it as soon as it is no longer needed, and laws giving us the right to delete our data from third-party sites. And we need international cooperation to ensure that companies cannot flaunt data privacy laws simply by moving themselves offshore.

Laws can only go so far, though. Law or no law, when something is made public, it's too late. And many of us like having complete records of all our e-mail at our fingertips; it's like our offline memory.

In the end, this is a cultural issue.

The Internet is creating the greatest generation gap since rock 'n' roll. We're now witnessing one aspect of that generation gap: The younger generation chats digitally, and the older generation treats those chats as written correspondence. Until our CEOs blog, our Diet members all Twitter, and our world leaders send each other LOLcats—until we have a national election where all the candidates have a complete history on social networking sites from before they were teenagers—we aren't fully an information age society.

When everyone leaves a public digital trail of their personal thoughts since birth, no one will think twice about it being there. Some of us might be on the younger side of the generation gap, but the rules we're operating under were written by the older side. It will take another generation before our privacy laws catch up with the death of the ephemeral conversation. Until then, we're just going to have to live with this loss of privacy.

Google's and Facebook's Privacy Illusion

Originally published in Forbes, *April 6, 2010*

In January, Facebook CEO, Mark Zuckerberg, declared the age of privacy to be over. A month earlier, Google Chief Eric Schmidt expressed a similar sentiment. Add Scott McNealy's and Larry Ellison's comments from a few years earlier, and you've got a whole lot of tech CEOs proclaiming the death of privacy—especially when it comes to young people.

It's just not true. People, including the younger generation, still care about privacy. Yes, they're far more public on the Internet than their parents: writing personal details on Facebook, posting embarrassing photos on Flickr and having intimate conversations on Twitter. But they take steps to protect their privacy and vociferously complain when they feel it violated. They're not technically sophisticated about privacy and make mistakes all the time, but that's mostly the fault of companies and Web sites that try to manipulate them for financial gain.

To the older generation, privacy is about secrecy. And, as the Supreme Court said, once something is no longer secret, it's no longer private. But that's not how privacy works, and it's not how the younger generation thinks about it. Privacy is about control. When your health records are sold to a pharmaceutical company without your permission; when a social-networking site changes your privacy settings to make what used to be visible only to your friends visible to everyone; when the NSA eavesdrops on everyone's e-mail conversations—your loss of control over that information is the issue. We may not mind sharing our personal lives and thoughts, but we want to control how, where and with whom. A privacy failure is a control failure.

People's relationship with privacy is socially complicated. Salience matters: People are more likely to protect their privacy if they're thinking about it, and less likely to if they're thinking about something else. Social-networking sites know this, constantly reminding people about how much fun it is to share photos and comments and conversations while downplaying the privacy risks. Some sites go even further, deliberately hiding information about how little control—and privacy—users have over their data. We all give up our privacy when we're not thinking about it.

Group behavior matters; we're more likely to expose personal information when our peers are doing it. We object more to losing privacy than we value its return once it's gone. Even if we don't have control over our data, an illusion of control reassures us. And we are poor judges of risk. All sorts of academic research backs up these findings.

Here's the problem: The very companies whose CEOs eulogize privacy make their money by controlling vast amounts of their users' information. Whether through targeted advertising, cross-selling or simply convincing their users to spend more time on their site and sign up their friends, more information shared in more ways, more publicly means more profits. This means these companies are motivated to continually ratchet down the privacy of their services, while at the same time pronouncing privacy erosions as inevitable and giving users the illusion of control.

You can see these forces in play with Google's launch of Buzz. Buzz is a Twitter-like chatting service, and when Google launched it in February, the defaults were set so people would follow the people they corresponded with frequently in Gmail, with the list publicly available. Yes, users could change these options, but—and Google knew this—changing options is hard and most people accept the defaults, especially when they're trying out something new. People were upset that their previously private e-mail contacts list was suddenly public. A Federal Trade Commission commissioner even threatened penalties. And though Google changed its defaults, resentment remained.

Facebook tried a similar control grab when it changed people's default privacy settings last December to make them more public. While users could, in theory, keep their previous settings, it took an effort. Many people just wanted to chat with their friends and clicked through the new defaults without realizing it.

Facebook has a history of this sort of thing. In 2006, it introduced News Feeds, which changed the way people viewed information about their friends.

There was no true privacy change in that users could not see more information than before; the change was in control—or arguably, just in the illusion of control. Still, there was a large uproar. And Facebook is doing it again; last month, the company announced new privacy changes that will make it easier for it to collect location data on users and sell that data to third parties.

With all this privacy erosion, those CEOs may actually be right—but only because they're working to kill privacy. On the Internet, our privacy options are limited to the options those companies give us and how easy they are to find. We have Gmail and Facebook accounts because that's where we socialize these days, and it's hard—especially for the younger generation—to opt out. As long as privacy isn't salient, and as long as these companies are allowed to forcibly change social norms by limiting options, people will increasingly get used to less and less privacy. There's no malice on anyone's part here; it's just market forces in action. If we believe privacy is a social good, something necessary for democracy, liberty and human dignity, then we can't rely on market forces to maintain it. Broad legislation protecting personal privacy by giving people control over their personal data is the only solution.

The Internet: Anonymous Forever

Originally published in Forbes, *May 12, 2010*

Universal identification is portrayed by some as the holy grail of Internet security. Anonymity is bad, the argument goes; and if we abolish it, we can ensure only the proper people have access to their own information. We'll know who is sending us spam and who is trying to hack into corporate networks. And when there are massive denial-of-service attacks, such as those against Estonia or Georgia or South Korea, we'll know who was responsible and take action accordingly.

The problem is that it won't work. Any design of the Internet must allow for anonymity. Universal identification is impossible. Even attribution—knowing who is responsible for particular Internet packets—is impossible. Attempting to build such a system is futile, and will only give criminals and hackers new ways to hide.

Imagine a magic world in which every Internet packet could be traced to its origin. Even in this world, our Internet security problems wouldn't be solved.

There's a huge gap between proving that a packet came from a particular computer and that a packet was directed by a particular person. This is the exact problem we have with botnets, or pedophiles storing child porn on innocents' computers. In these cases, we know the origins of the DDoS packets and the spam; they're from legitimate machines that have been hacked. Attribution isn't as valuable as you might think.

Implementing an Internet without anonymity is very difficult, and causes its own problems. In order to have perfect attribution, we'd need agencies—real-world organizations—to provide Internet identity credentials based on other identification systems: passports, national identity cards, driver's licenses, whatever. Sloppier identification systems, based on things such as credit cards, are simply too easy to subvert. We have nothing that comes close to this global identification infrastructure. Moreover, centralizing information like this actually hurts security because it makes identity theft that much more profitable a crime.

And realistically, any theoretical ideal Internet would need to allow people access even without their magic credentials. People would still use the Internet at public kiosks and at friends' houses. People would lose their magic Internet tokens just like they lose their driver's licenses and passports today. The legitimate bypass mechanisms would allow even more ways for criminals and hackers to subvert the system.

On top of all this, the magic attribution technology doesn't exist. Bits are bits; they don't come with identity information attached to them. Every software system we've ever invented has been successfully hacked, repeatedly. We simply don't have anywhere near the expertise to build an airtight attribution system.

Not that it really matters. Even if everyone could trace all packets perfectly, to the person or origin and not just the computer, anonymity would still be possible. It would just take one person to set up an anonymity server. If I wanted to send a packet anonymously to someone else, I'd just route it through that server. For even greater anonymity, I could route it through multiple servers. This is called onion routing and, with appropriate cryptography and enough users, it adds anonymity back to any communications system that prohibits it.

Attempts to banish anonymity from the Internet won't affect those savvy enough to bypass it, would cost billions, and would have only a negligible effect on security. What such attempts would do is affect the average user's access to free speech, including those who use the Internet's anonymity to survive: dissidents in Iran, China, and elsewhere.

Mandating universal identity and attribution is the wrong goal. Accept that there will always be anonymous speech on the Internet. Accept that you'll never truly know where a packet came from. Work on the problems you can solve: software that's secure in the face of whatever packet it receives, identification systems that are secure enough in the face of the risks. We can do far better at these things than we're doing, and they'll do more to improve security than trying to fix insoluble problems.

The whole attribution problem is very similar to the copy-protection/digital-rights-management problem. Just as it's impossible to make specific bits not copyable, it's impossible to know where specific bits came from. Bits are bits. They don't naturally come with restrictions on their use attached to them, and they don't naturally come with author information attached to them. Any attempts to circumvent this limitation will fail, and will increasingly need to be backed up by the sort of real-world police-state measures that the entertainment industry is demanding in order to make copy-protection work. That's how China does it: police, informants, and fear.

Just as the music industry needs to learn that the world of bits requires a different business model, law enforcement and others need to understand that the old ideas of identification don't work on the Internet. For good or for bad, whether you like it or not, there's always going to be anonymity on the Internet.

A Taxonomy of Social Networking Data

Originally published in IEEE Security & Privacy, *July/August 2010*

Lately I've been reading about user security and privacy—control, really—on social networking sites. The issues are hard and the solutions harder, but I'm seeing a lot of confusion in even forming the questions. Social networking sites deal with several different types of user data, and it's essential to separate them.

Below is my taxonomy of social networking data, which I first presented at the Internet Governance Forum meeting last November, and again—revised—at an OECD workshop on the role of Internet intermediaries in June.

- Service data is the data you give to a social networking site in order to use it. Such data might include your legal name, your age, and your credit-card number.
- Disclosed data is what you post on your own pages: blog entries, photographs, messages, comments, and so on.

- Entrusted data is what you post on other people's pages. It's basically the same stuff as disclosed data, but the difference is that you don't have control over the data once you post it—another user does.

- Incidental data is what other people post about you: a paragraph about you that someone else writes, a picture of you that someone else takes and posts. Again, it's basically the same stuff as disclosed data, but the difference is that you don't have control over it, and you didn't create it in the first place.

- Behavioral data is data the site collects about your habits by recording what you do and who you do it with. It might include games you play, topics you write about, news articles you access (and what that says about your political leanings), and so on.

- Derived data is data about you that is derived from all the other data. For example, if 80 percent of your friends self-identify as gay, you're likely gay yourself.

There are other ways to look at user data. Some of it you give to the social networking site in confidence, expecting the site to safeguard the data. Some of it you publish openly and others use it to find you. And some of it you share only within an enumerated circle of other users. At the receiving end, social networking sites can monetize all of it: generally by selling targeted advertising.

Different social networking sites give users different rights for each data type. Some are always private, some can be made private, and some are always public. Some can be edited or deleted—I know one site that allows entrusted data to be edited or deleted within a 24-hour period—and some cannot. Some can be viewed and some cannot.

It's also clear that users should have different rights with respect to each data type. We should be allowed to export, change, and delete disclosed data, even if the social networking sites don't want us to. It's less clear what rights we have for entrusted data—and far less clear for incidental data. If you post pictures from a party with me in them, can I demand you remove those pictures—or at least blur out my face? (Go look up the conviction of three Google executives in Italian court over a YouTube video.) And what about behavioral data? It's frequently a critical part of a social networking site's business model. We often don't mind if a site uses it to target advertisements, but are less sanguine when it sells data to third parties.

As we continue our conversations about what sorts of fundamental rights people have with respect to their data, and more countries contemplate regulation on social networking sites and user data, it will be important to keep this taxonomy in mind. The sorts of things that would be suitable for one type of data might be completely unworkable and inappropriate for another.

The Difficulty of Surveillance Crowdsourcing

Originally published in Threatpost, *November 8, 2010*

Internet Eyes is a UK startup designed to crowdsource digital surveillance. People pay a small fee to become a "Viewer." Once they do, they can log onto the site and view live anonymous feeds from surveillance cameras at retail stores. If they notice someone shoplifting, they can alert the store owner. Viewers get rated on their ability to differentiate real shoplifting from false alarms, can win 1,000 pounds if they detect the most shoplifting in some time interval, and otherwise get paid a wage that most likely won't cover their initial fee.

Although the system has some nod towards privacy, groups like Privacy International oppose the system for fostering a culture of citizen spies. More fundamentally, though, I don't think the system will work. Internet Eyes is primarily relying on voyeurism to compensate its Viewers. But most of what goes on in a retail store is incredibly boring. Some of it is actually voyeuristic, and very little of it is criminal. The incentives just aren't there for Viewers to do more than peek, and there's no obvious way to discouraging them from siding with the shoplifter and just watch the scenario unfold.

This isn't the first time groups have tried to crowdsource surveillance camera monitoring. Texas's Virtual Border Patrol tried the same thing: deputizing the general public to monitor the Texas-Mexico border. It ran out of money last year, and was widely criticized as a joke.

This system suffered the same problems as Internet Eyes—not enough incentive to do a good job, boredom because crime is the rare exception—as well as the fact that false alarms were very expensive to deal with.

Both of these systems remind me of the one time this idea was conceptualized correctly. Invented in 2003 by my friend and colleague Jay Walker, US HomeGuard also tried to crowdsource surveillance camera monitoring. But this system focused on one very specific security concern: people in no-man's areas. These are areas between fences at nuclear power plants or oil refineries, border zones, areas around dams and reservoirs, and so on: areas where there should never be anyone.

The idea is that people would register to become "spotters." They would get paid a decent wage (that and patriotism was the incentive), receive a stream of still photos, and be asked a very simple question: "Is there a person or a vehicle in this picture?" If a monitor clicked "yes," the photo—and the camera—would be referred to whatever professional response the camera owner had set up.

HomeGuard would monitor the monitors in two ways. One, by sending stored, known, photos to people regularly to verify that they were paying attention. And two, by sending live photos to multiple spotters and correlating the results, to many more monitors if a spotter claimed to have spotted a person or vehicle.

Just knowing that there's a person or a vehicle in a no-man's area is only the first step in a useful response, and HomeGuard envisioned a bunch of enhancements to the rest of that system. Flagged photos could be sent to the digital phones of patrolling guards, cameras could be controlled remotely by those guards, and speakers in the cameras could issue warnings. Remote citizen spotters were only useful for that first step, looking for a person or a vehicle in a photo that shouldn't contain any. Only real guards at the site itself could tell an intruder from the occasional maintenance person.

Of course the system isn't perfect. A would-be infiltrator could sneak past the spotters by holding a bush in front of him, or disguising himself as a vending machine. But it does fill in a gap in what fully automated systems can do, at least until image processing and artificial intelligence get significantly better.

HomeGuard never got off the ground. There was never any good data about whether spotters were more effective than motion sensors as a first level of defense. But more importantly, Walker says that the politics surrounding homeland security money post-9/11 was just too great to penetrate, and that as an outsider he couldn't get his ideas heard. Today, probably, the patriotic fervor that gripped so many people post-9/11 has dampened, and he'd probably have to pay his spotters more than he envisioned seven years ago. Still, I thought it was a clever idea then and I still think it's a clever idea—and it's an example of how to do surveillance crowdsourcing correctly.

Making the system more general runs into all sorts of problems. An amateur can spot a person or vehicle pretty easily, but is much harder pressed to notice a shoplifter. The privacy implications of showing random people pictures of no-man's lands is minimal, while a busy store is another matter—stores have enough individuality to be identifiable, as do people. Public photo tagging will even allow the process to be automated. And, of course, the normalization of a spy-on-your-neighbor surveillance society where it's perfectly reasonable to watch each other on cameras just in case one of us does something wrong.

The Internet Is a Surveillance State

Originally published in CNN, March 16, 2013

I'm going to start with three data points.

One: Some of the Chinese military hackers who were implicated in a broad set of attacks against the US government and corporations were identified because they accessed Facebook from the same network infrastructure they used to carry out their attacks.

Two: Hector Monsegur, one of the leaders of the LulzSec hacker movement, was identified and arrested last year by the FBI. Although he practiced good computer security and used an anonymous relay service to protect his identity, he slipped up.

And three: Paula Broadwell, who had an affair with CIA director David Petraeus, similarly took extensive precautions to hide her identity. She never logged in to her anonymous e-mail service from her home network. Instead, she used hotel and other public networks when she e-mailed him. The FBI correlated hotel registration data from several different hotels—and hers was the common name.

The Internet is a surveillance state. Whether we admit it to ourselves or not, and whether we like it or not, we're being tracked all the time. Google tracks us, both on its pages and on other pages it has access to. Facebook does the same; it even tracks non-Facebook users. Apple tracks us on our iPhones and iPads. One reporter used a tool called Collusion to track who was tracking him; 105 companies tracked his Internet use during one 36-hour period.

Increasingly, what we do on the Internet is being combined with other data about us. Unmasking Broadwell's identity involved correlating her Internet activity with her hotel stays. Everything we do now involves computers, and computers produce data as a natural by-product. Everything is now being saved and correlated, and many big-data companies make money by building up intimate profiles of our lives from a variety of sources.

Facebook, for example, correlates your online behavior with your purchasing habits offline. And there's more. There's location data from your cell phone, there's a record of your movements from closed-circuit TVs.

This is ubiquitous surveillance: All of us being watched, all the time, and that data being stored forever. This is what a surveillance state looks like, and it's efficient beyond the wildest dreams of George Orwell.

Sure, we can take measures to prevent this. We can limit what we search on Google from our iPhones, and instead use computer web browsers that allow us to delete cookies. We can use an alias on Facebook. We can turn our cell phones off and spend cash. But increasingly, none of it matters.

There are simply too many ways to be tracked. The Internet, e-mail, cell phones, web browsers, social networking sites, search engines: these have become necessities, and it's fanciful to expect people to simply refuse to use them just because they don't like the spying, especially since the full extent of such spying is deliberately hidden from us and there are few alternatives being marketed by companies that don't spy.

This isn't something the free market can fix. We consumers have no choice in the matter. All the major companies that provide us with Internet services are interested in tracking us. Visit a website and it will almost certainly know who you are; there are lots of ways to be tracked without cookies. Cell phone companies routinely undo the web's privacy protection. One experiment at Carnegie Mellon took real-time videos of students on campus and was able to identify one-third of them by comparing their photos with publicly available tagged Facebook photos.

Maintaining privacy on the Internet is nearly impossible. If you forget even once to enable your protections, or click on the wrong link, or type the wrong thing, you've permanently attached your name to whatever anonymous service you're using. Monsegur slipped up once, and the FBI got him. If the director of the CIA can't maintain his privacy on the Internet, we've got no hope.

In today's world, governments and corporations are working together to keep things that way. Governments are happy to use the data corporations collect—occasionally demanding that they collect more and save it longer—to spy on us. And corporations are happy to buy data from governments. Together the powerful spy on the powerless, and they're not going to give up their positions of power, despite what the people want.

Fixing this requires strong government will, but they're just as punch-drunk on data as the corporations. Slap-on-the-wrist fines notwithstanding, no one is agitating for better privacy laws.

So, we're done. Welcome to a world where Google knows exactly what sort of porn you all like, and more about your interests than your spouse does. Welcome to a world where your cell phone company knows exactly where you are all the time. Welcome to the end of private conversations, because increasingly your conversations are conducted by e-mail, text, or social networking sites.

And welcome to a world where all of this, and everything else that you do or is done on a computer, is saved, correlated, studied, passed around from company to company without your knowledge or consent; and where the government accesses it at will without a warrant.

Welcome to an Internet without privacy, and we've ended up here with hardly a fight.

Surveillance and the Internet of Things

Originally published in the Guardian, *May 16, 2013*

The Internet has turned into a massive surveillance tool. We're constantly monitored on the Internet by hundreds of companies—both familiar and unfamiliar. Everything we do there is recorded, collected, and collated—sometimes by corporations wanting to sell us stuff and sometimes by governments wanting to keep an eye on us.

Ephemeral conversation is over. Wholesale surveillance is the norm. Maintaining privacy from these powerful entities is basically impossible, and any illusion of privacy we maintain is based either on ignorance or on our unwillingness to accept what's really going on.

It's about to get worse, though. Companies such as Google may know more about your personal interests than your spouse, but so far it's been limited by the fact that these companies only see computer data. And even though your computer habits are increasingly being linked to your offline behavior, it's still only behavior that involves computers.

The Internet of Things refers to a world where much more than our computers and cell phones is Internet-enabled. Soon there will be Internet-connected modules on our cars and home appliances. Internet-enabled medical devices will collect real-time health data about us. There'll be Internet-connected tags on our clothing. In its extreme, *everything* can be connected to the Internet. It's really just a matter of time, as these self-powered wireless-enabled computers become smaller and cheaper.

Lots has been written about the "Internet of Things" and how it will change society for the better. It's true that it will make a lot of wonderful things possible, but the "Internet of Things" will also allow for an even greater amount of surveillance than there is today. The Internet of Things gives the governments and corporations that follow our every move something they don't yet have: eyes and ears.

Soon everything we do, both online and offline, will be recorded and stored forever. The only question remaining is who will have access to all of this information, and under what rules.

We're seeing an initial glimmer of this from how location sensors on your mobile phone are being used to track you. Of course your cell provider needs to know where you are; it can't route your phone calls to your phone otherwise. But most of us broadcast our location information to many other companies whose apps we've installed on our phone. Google Maps certainly, but also a surprising number of app vendors who collect that information. It can be used to determine where you live, where you work, and who you spend time with.

Another early adopter was Nike, whose Nike+ shoes communicate with your iPod or iPhone and track your exercising. More generally, medical devices are starting to be Internet-enabled, collecting and reporting a variety of health data. Wiring appliances to the Internet is one of the pillars of the smart electric grid. Yes, there are huge potential savings associated with the smart grid, but it will also allow power companies—and anyone they decide to sell the data to—to monitor how people move about their house and how they spend their time.

Drones are another "thing" moving onto the Internet. As their price continues to drop and their capabilities increase, they will become a very powerful surveillance tool. Their cameras are powerful enough to see faces clearly, and there are enough tagged photographs on the Internet to identify many of us. We're not yet up to a real-time Google Earth equivalent, but it's not more than a few years away. And drones are just a specific application of CCTV cameras, which have been monitoring us for years, and will increasingly be networked.

Google's Internet-enabled glasses—Google Glass—are another major step down this path of surveillance. Their ability to record both audio and video will bring ubiquitous surveillance to the next level. Once they're common, you might never know when you're being recorded in both audio and video. You might as well assume that everything you do and say will be recorded and saved forever.

In the near term, at least, the sheer volume of data will limit the sorts of conclusions that can be drawn. The invasiveness of these technologies depends on asking the right questions. For example, if a private investigator is watching you in the physical world, she or he might observe odd behavior and investigate further based on that. Such serendipitous observations are harder to achieve when you're filtering databases based on pre-programmed queries. In other words, it's easier to ask questions about what you purchased and where you were than to ask what you did with your purchases and why you went where you did. These analytical limitations also mean that companies like Google and Facebook will benefit more from the Internet of Things than individuals—not only because they have access to more data, but also because they have more sophisticated query technology. And as technology continues to improve, the ability to automatically analyze this massive data stream will improve.

In the longer term, the Internet of Things means ubiquitous surveillance. If an object "knows" you have purchased it, and communicates via either Wi-Fi or the mobile network, then whoever or whatever it is communicating with will know where you are. Your car will know who is in it, who is driving, and what traffic laws that driver is following or ignoring. No need to show ID; your identity will already be known. Store clerks could know your name, address, and income level as soon as you walk through the door. Billboards will tailor ads to you, and record how you respond to them. Fast food restaurants will know what you usually order, and exactly how to entice you to order more. Lots of companies will know whom you spend your days—and nights—with. Facebook will know about any new relationship status before you bother to change it on your profile. And all of this information will all be saved, correlated, and studied. Even now, it feels a lot like science fiction.

Will *you* know any of this? Will your friends? It depends. Lots of these devices have, and will have, privacy settings. But these settings are remarkable not in how much privacy they afford, but in how much they deny. Access will likely be similar to your browsing habits, your files stored on Dropbox, your searches on Google, and your text messages from your phone. All of your data is saved by those companies—and many others—correlated, and then bought and sold without your knowledge or consent. You'd think that your privacy settings would keep random strangers from learning everything about you, but it only keeps random strangers who *don't pay for the privilege*—or don't work for the government and have the ability to demand the data. Power is what matters here: you'll be able to keep the powerless from invading your privacy, but you'll have no ability to prevent the powerful from doing it again and again.

Government Secrets and the Need for Whistleblowers

Originally published in the Guardian, *June 6, 2013*

Yesterday, we learned that the NSA received all calling records from Verizon customers for a three-month period starting in April. That's everything except the voice content: who called who, where they were, how long the call lasted—for millions of people, both Americans and foreigners. This "metadata" allows the government to track the movements of everyone during that period, and build a detailed picture of who talks to whom. It's exactly the same data the Justice Department collected about AP journalists.

The *Guardian* delivered this revelation after receiving a copy of a secret memo about this—presumably from a whistleblower. We don't know if the other phone companies handed data to the NSA too. We don't know if this was a one-off demand or a continuously renewed demand; the order started a few days after the Boston bombers were captured by police.

We don't know a lot about how the government spies on us, but we know some things. We know the FBI has issued tens of thousands of ultra-secret National Security Letters to collect all sorts of data on people—we believe on millions of people—and has been abusing them to spy on cloud-computer users. We know it can collect a wide array of personal data from the Internet without a warrant. We also know that the FBI has been intercepting cell-phone data, all but voice content, for the past 20 years without a warrant, and can use the microphone on some powered-off cell phones as a room bug—presumably only with a warrant.

We know that the NSA has many domestic-surveillance and data-mining programs with codenames like Trailblazer, Stellar Wind, and Ragtime—deliberately using different codenames for similar programs to stymie oversight and conceal what's really going on. We know that the NSA is building an enormous computer facility in Utah to store all this data, as well as faster computer networks to process it all. We know the US Cyber Command employs 4,000 people.

We know that the DHS is also collecting a massive amount of data on people, and that local police departments are running "fusion centers" to collect and analyze this data, and covering up its failures. This is all part of the militarization of the police.

Remember in 2003, when Congress defunded the decidedly creepy Total Information Awareness program? It didn't die; it just changed names and split into many smaller programs. We know that corporations are doing an enormous amount of spying on behalf of the government: all parts.

We know all of this not because the government is honest and forthcoming, but mostly through three backchannels—inadvertent hints or outright admissions by government officials in hearings and court cases, information gleaned from government documents received under FOIA, and government whistleblowers.

There's much more we don't know, and often what we know is obsolete. We know quite a bit about the NSA's ECHELON program from a 2000 European investigation, and about the DHS's plans for Total Information Awareness from 2002, but much less about how these programs have evolved. We can make inferences about the NSA's Utah facility based on the theoretical amount of data from various sources, the cost of computation, and the power requirements from the facility, but those are rough guesses at best. For a lot of this, we're completely in the dark.

And that's wrong.

The US government is on a secrecy binge. It overclassifies more information than ever. And we learn, again and again, that our government regularly classifies things not because they need to be secret, but because their release would be embarrassing.

Knowing how the government spies on us is important. Not only because so much of it is illegal—or, to be as charitable as possible, based on novel interpretations of the law—but because we have a right to know. Democracy requires an informed citizenry in order to function properly, and transparency and accountability are essential parts of that. That means knowing what our government is doing to us, in our name. That means knowing that the government is operating within the constraints of the law. Otherwise, we're living in a police state.

We need whistleblowers.

Leaking information without getting caught is difficult. It's almost impossible to maintain privacy in the Internet Age. The WikiLeaks platform seems to have been secure—Bradley Manning was caught not because of a technological flaw, but because someone he trusted betrayed him—but the US government seems to have successfully destroyed it as a platform. None of the spin-offs have risen to become viable yet. The *New Yorker* recently unveiled its Strongbox platform for leaking material, which is still new but looks good. This link contains the best advice on how to leak information to the press via phone, email, or the post office. The National Whistleblowers Center has a page on national-security whistleblowers and their rights.

Leaking information is also very dangerous. The Obama administration has embarked on a war on whistleblowers, pursuing them—both legally and through intimidation—further than any previous administration has done. Mark Klein, Thomas Drake, and William Binney have all been persecuted for exposing technical details of our surveillance state. Bradley Manning has been treated cruelly and inhumanly—and possibly tortured—for his more-indiscriminate leaking of State Department secrets.

The Obama administration's actions against the Associated Press, its persecution of Julian Assange, and its unprecedented prosecution of Manning on charges of "aiding the enemy" demonstrate how far it's willing to go to intimidate whistleblowers—as well as the journalists who talk to them.

But whistleblowing is vital, even more broadly than in government spying. It's necessary for good government, and to protect us from abuse of power.

We need details on the full extent of the FBI's spying capabilities. We don't know what information it routinely collects on American citizens, what extra information it collects on those on various watch lists, and what legal justifications it invokes for its actions. We don't know its plans for future data collection. We don't know what scandals and illegal actions—either past or present—are currently being covered up.

We also need information about what data the NSA gathers, either domestically or internationally. We don't know how much it collects surreptitiously, and how much it relies on arrangements with various companies. We don't know how much it uses password cracking to get at encrypted data, and how much it exploits existing system vulnerabilities. We don't know whether it deliberately inserts backdoors into systems it wants to monitor, either with or without the permission of the communications-system vendors.

And we need details about the sorts of analysis the organizations perform. We don't know what they quickly cull at the point of collection, and what they store for later analysis—and how long they store it. We don't know what sort of database profiling they do, how extensive their CCTV and surveillance-drone analysis is, how much they perform behavioral analysis, or how extensively they trace friends of people on their watch lists.

We don't know how big the US surveillance apparatus is today, either in terms of money and people or in terms of how many people are monitored or how much data is collected. Modern technology makes it possible to monitor vastly more people—yesterday's NSA revelations demonstrate that they could easily surveil *everyone*—than could ever be done manually.

Whistleblowing is the moral response to immoral activity by those in power. What's important here are government programs and methods, not data about individuals. I understand I am asking for people to engage in illegal and dangerous behavior. Do it carefully and do it safely, but—and I am talking directly to you, person working on one of these secret and probably illegal programs—do it.

If you see something, say something. There are many people in the US that will appreciate and admire you.

For the rest of us, we can help by protesting this war on whistleblowers. We need to force our politicians not to punish them—to investigate the abuses and not the messengers—and to ensure that those unjustly persecuted can obtain redress.

Our government is putting its own self-interest ahead of the interests of the country. That needs to change.

Before Prosecuting, Investigate the Government

Originally published in New York Times Room for Debate *blog,*
June 11, 2013

Edward Snowden broke the law by releasing classified information. This isn't under debate; it's something everyone with a security clearance knows. It's written in plain English on the documents you have to sign when you get a security clearance, and it's part of the culture. The law is there for a good reason, and secrecy has an important role in military defense.

But before the Justice Department prosecutes Snowden, there are some other investigations that ought to happen.

We need to determine whether these National Security Agency programs are themselves legal. The administration has successfully barred anyone from bringing a lawsuit challenging these laws, on the grounds of national secrecy. Now that we know those arguments are without merit, it's time for those court challenges.

It's clear that some of the NSA programs exposed by Snowden violate the Constitution and others violate existing laws. Other people have an opposite view. The courts need to decide.

We need to determine whether classifying these programs is legal. Keeping things secret from the people is a very dangerous practice in a democracy, and the government is permitted to do so only under very specific circumstances. Reading the documents leaked so far, I don't see anything that needs to be kept secret. The argument that exposing these documents helps the terrorists doesn't even pass the laugh test; there's nothing here that changes anything any potential terrorist would do or not do. But in any case, now that the documents are public, the courts need to rule on the legality of their secrecy.

And we need to determine how we treat whistleblowers in this country. We have whistleblower protection laws that apply in some cases, particularly when exposing fraud, and other illegal behavior. NSA officials have repeatedly lied about the existence, and details, of these programs to Congress.

Only after all of these legal issues have been resolved should any prosecution of Snowden move forward. Because only then will we know the full extent of what he did, and how much of it is justified.

I believe that history will hail Snowden as a hero—his whistleblowing exposed a surveillance state and a secrecy machine run amok. I'm less optimistic of how the present day will treat him, and hope that the debate right now is less about the man and more about the government he exposed.

5 Psychology of Security

The Security Mindset

Originally published in Wired News, *March 20, 2008*

Uncle Milton Industries has been selling ant farms to children since 1956. Some years ago, I remember opening one up with a friend. There were no actual ants included in the box. Instead, there was a card that you filled in with your address, and the company would mail you some ants. My friend expressed surprise that you could get ants sent to you in the mail.

I replied: "What's really interesting is that these people will send a tube of live ants to anyone you tell them to."

Security requires a particular mindset. Security professionals—at least the good ones—see the world differently. They can't walk into a store without noticing how they might shoplift. They can't use a computer without wondering about the security vulnerabilities. They can't vote without trying to figure out how to vote twice. They just can't help it.

SmartWater is a liquid with a unique identifier linked to a particular owner. "The idea is for me to paint this stuff on my valuables as proof of ownership," I wrote when I first learned about the idea. "I think a better idea would be for me to paint it on *your* valuables, and then call the police."

Really, we can't help it.

This kind of thinking is not natural for most people. It's not natural for engineers. Good engineering involves thinking about how things can be made to work; the security mindset involves thinking about how things can be made to fail. It involves thinking like an attacker, an adversary or a criminal. You don't have to exploit the vulnerabilities you find, but if you don't see the world that way, you'll never notice most security problems.

I've often speculated about how much of this is innate, and how much is teachable. In general, I think it's a particular way of looking at the world, and that it's far easier to teach someone domain expertise—cryptography or software security or safecracking or document forgery—than it is to teach someone a security mindset.

Which is why CSE 484, an undergraduate computer-security course taught this quarter at the University of Washington, is so interesting to watch. Professor Tadayoshi Kohno is trying to teach a security mindset.

You can see the results in the blog the students are keeping. They're encouraged to post security reviews about random things: smart pill boxes, Quiet Care Elder Care monitors, Apple's Time Capsule, GM's OnStar, traffic lights, safe deposit boxes, and dorm-room security.

The most recent one is about an automobile dealership. The poster described how she was able to retrieve her car after service just by giving the attendant her last name. Now any normal car owner would be happy about how easy it was to get her car back, but someone with a security mindset immediately thinks: "Can I really get a car just by knowing the last name of someone whose car is being serviced?"

The rest of the blog post speculates on how someone could steal a car by exploiting this security vulnerability, and whether it makes sense for the dealership to have this lax security. You can quibble with the analysis—I'm curious about the liability that the dealership has, and whether their insurance would cover any losses—but that's all domain expertise. The important point is to notice, and then question, the security in the first place.

The lack of a security mindset explains a lot of bad security out there: voting machines, electronic payment cards, medical devices, ID cards, Internet protocols. The designers are so busy making these systems work that they don't stop to notice how they might fail or be made to fail, and then how those failures might be exploited. Teaching designers a security mindset will go a long way toward making future technological systems more secure.

That part's obvious, but I think the security mindset is beneficial in many more ways. If people can learn how to think outside their narrow focus and see a bigger picture, whether in technology or politics or their everyday lives, they'll be more sophisticated consumers, more skeptical citizens, less gullible people.

If more people had a security mindset, services that compromise privacy wouldn't have such a sizable market share—and Facebook would be totally different. Laptops wouldn't be lost with millions of unencrypted Social Security numbers on them, and we'd all learn a lot fewer security lessons the hard way. The power grid would be more secure. Identity theft would go way down. Medical records would be more private. If people had the security mindset, they wouldn't have tried to look at since they would have realized that they would be caught.

There's nothing magical about this particular university class; anyone can exercise his security mindset simply by trying to look at the world from an attacker's perspective. If I wanted to evade this particular security device, how would I do it? Could I follow the letter of this law but get around the spirit? If the person who wrote this advertisement, essay, article or television documentary were unscrupulous, what could he have done? And then, how can I protect myself from these attacks?

The security mindset is a valuable skill that everyone can benefit from, regardless of career path.

The Difference between Feeling and Reality in Security

Originally published in Wired News, *April 3, 2008*

Security is both a feeling and a reality, and they're different. You can feel secure even though you're not, and you can be secure even though you don't feel it. There are two different concepts mapped onto the same word—the English language isn't working very well for us here—and it can be hard to know which one we're talking about when we use the word.

There is considerable value in separating out the two concepts: in explaining how the two are different, and understanding when we're referring to one and when the other. There is value as well in recognizing when the two converge, understanding why they diverge, and knowing how they can be made to converge again.

Some fundamentals first. Viewed from the perspective of economics, security is a trade-off. There's no such thing as absolute security, and any security you get has some cost: in money, in convenience, in capabilities, in insecurities somewhere else, whatever. Every time someone makes a decision about security—computer security, community security, national security—he makes a trade-off.

People make these trade-offs as individuals. We all get to decide, individually, if the expense and inconvenience of having a home burglar alarm is worth the security. We all get to decide if wearing a bulletproof vest is worth the cost and tacky appearance. We all get to decide if we're getting our money's worth from the billions of dollars we're spending combating terrorism, and if invading Iraq was the best use of our counterterrorism resources. We might not have the power to *implement* our opinion, but we get to decide if we think it's worth it.

Now we may or may not have the expertise to make those trade-offs intelligently, but we make them anyway. All of us. People have a natural intuition about security trade-offs, and we make them, large and small, dozens of times throughout the day. We can't help it: It's part of being alive.

Imagine a rabbit, sitting in a field eating grass. And he sees a fox. He's going to make a security trade-off: Should he stay or should he flee? Over time, the rabbits that are good at making that trade-off will tend to reproduce, while the rabbits that are bad at it will tend to get eaten or starve.

So, as a successful species on the planet, you'd expect that human beings would be really good at making security trade-offs. Yet, at the same time, we can be hopelessly bad at it. We spend more money on terrorism than the data warrants. We fear flying and choose to drive instead. Why?

The short answer is that people make most trade-offs based on the *feeling* of security and not the reality.

I've written a lot about how people get security trade-offs wrong, and the cognitive biases that cause us to make mistakes. Humans have developed these biases because they make evolutionary sense. And most of the time, they work.

Most of the time—and this is important—our feeling of security matches the reality of security. Certainly, this is true of prehistory. Modern times are harder. Blame technology, blame the media, blame whatever. Our brains are much better optimized for the security trade-offs endemic to living in small family groups in the East African highlands in 100,000 B.C. than to those endemic to living in 2008 New York.

If we make security trade-offs based on the feeling of security rather than the reality, we choose security that makes us *feel* more secure over security that actually makes us more secure. And that's what governments, companies, family members and everyone else provide. Of course, there are two ways to make people feel more secure. The first is to make people actually more secure and hope they notice. The second is to make people feel more secure without making them actually more secure, and hope they don't notice.

The key here is whether we notice. The feeling and reality of security tend to converge when we take notice, and diverge when we don't. People notice when 1) there are enough positive and negative examples to draw a conclusion, and 2) there isn't too much emotion clouding the issue.

Both elements are important. If someone tries to convince us to spend money on a new type of home burglar alarm, we as society will know pretty quickly if he's got a clever security device or if he's a charlatan; we can monitor crime rates. But if that same person advocates a new national antiterrorism system, and there weren't any terrorist attacks before it was implemented, and there weren't any after it was implemented, how do we know if his system was effective?

People are more likely to realistically assess these incidents if they don't contradict preconceived notions about how the world works. For example: It's obvious that a wall keeps people out, so arguing against building a wall across America's southern border to keep illegal immigrants out is harder to do.

The other thing that matters is agenda. There are lots of people, politicians, companies and so on who deliberately try to manipulate your feeling of security for their own gain. They try to cause fear. They invent threats. They take minor threats and make them major. And when they talk about rare risks with only a few incidents to base an assessment on—terrorism is the big example here—they are more likely to succeed.

Unfortunately, there's no obvious antidote. Information is important. We can't understand security unless we understand it. But that's not enough: Few of us really understand cancer, yet we regularly make security decisions based on its risk. What we do is accept that there are experts who understand the risks of cancer, and trust them to make the security trade-offs for us.

There are some complex feedback loops going on here, between emotion and reason, between reality and our knowledge of it, between feeling and familiarity, and between the understanding of how we reason and feel about security and our analyses and feelings. We're never going to stop making security trade-offs based on the feeling of security, and we're never going to completely prevent those with specific agendas from trying to take care of us. But the more we know, the better trade-offs we'll make.

How the Human Brain Buys Security

Originally published in IEEE Security & Privacy,
July/August 2008

People tend to be risk-averse when it comes to gains, and risk-seeking when it comes to losses. If you give people a choice between a $500 sure gain and a coin-flip chance of a $1,000 gain, about 75 percent will pick the sure gain. But give people a choice between a $500 sure loss and a coin-flip chance of a $1,000 loss, about 75 percent will pick the coin flip.

People don't have a standard mathematical model of risk in their heads. Their trade-offs are more subtle, and result from how our brains have developed. A computer might not see the difference between the two choices—it's simply a measure of how risk-averse you are—but humans do.

This fact might not seem like a big deal, but it overturned standard economic theory when it was first proposed in 1979. It's called "prospect theory," and was developed by Daniel Kahneman and Amos Tversky to explain how people make trade-offs that involve risk.

Evolutionarily, it makes sense. It's a better survival strategy to accept sure small gains rather than risk them for larger ones, and risk larger losses rather than accept smaller ones. Lions, for example, chase young or wounded wildebeest because the investment needed to kill them is lower. Mature and healthy prey would probably be more nutritious, but there's a risk of missing lunch entirely if it gets away. Because animals tend to live on the razor's edge between starvation and reproduction, any loss of food can result in death, and the best option is to risk everything for the chance of no loss at all.

This cognitive bias, demonstrated again and again by many researchers—across ages, genders, cultures, and even species—is so powerful that it can lead to logically inconsistent results. Google "Asian disease experiment" for an almost surreal example. Describing the same policy in two different ways, either as "200 lives saved out of 600" or "400 lives lost out of 600," yields wildly different risk reactions.

Prospect theory explains one of the biggest problems our industry has with selling security: no one actually wants to buy it. Salespeople have long known there are basically two motivations to get people to buy: greed and fear. Either buyers want something—and thus spend to get it—or don't want something, and spend to help prevent it. It's much easier to sell greed than fear.

Security is a fear sell. It's a choice between a small sure loss—the cost of the security product—and a large risky loss—the potential results of an attack on a network. Of course, there's a lot more to the sale. Buyers must be convinced that the product works, and they must understand the threats and the risk that something bad will happen. But all things being equal, buyers would rather take the chance than buy the security.

Sellers know this, even if they don't understand why, and are continually trying to frame security products in positive terms: slogans like "We take care of security so you can focus on your business," or carefully crafted ROI models that demonstrate how profitable a security purchase can be.

Another option is to push the fear button really hard. Our brains might prefer risky large losses to sure smaller losses, but when we're really scared we'll do almost anything to make that feeling go away. In our industry, we call it FUD—fear, uncertainty, and doubt. We've seen fear alter the political landscape in several countries following the 9/11 terrorist attacks.

The better solution is not to sell security directly, but to include it as part of a more general product or service. Your car comes with safety and security features built in; they're not sold separately. And it should be the same with computers and networks. Vendors need to build security into the products and services that customers actually want. Security is inherently about avoiding a negative, so you can never ignore the cognitive bias embedded so deeply in the human brain. But if you understand it, you have a better chance of overcoming it.

Does Risk Management Make Sense?

Originally published in Information Security, *October 2008*

This essay appeared as the first half of a point-counterpoint with Marcus Ranum.

We engage in risk management all the time, but it only makes sense if we do it right.

"Risk management" is just a fancy term for the cost-benefit tradeoff associated with any security decision. It's what we do when we react to fear, or try to make ourselves feel secure. It's the fight-or-flight reflex that evolved in primitive fish and remains in all vertebrates. It's instinctual, intuitive and fundamental to life, and one of the brain's primary functions.

Some have hypothesized that humans have a "risk thermostat" that tries to maintain some optimal risk level. It explains why we drive our motorcycles faster when we wear a helmet, or are more likely to take up smoking during wartime. It's our natural risk management in action.

The problem is our brains are intuitively suited to the sorts of risk management decisions endemic to living in small family groups in the East African highlands in 100,000 BC, and not to living in the New York City of 2008. We make systematic risk management mistakes—miscalculating the probability of rare events, reacting more to stories than data, responding to the feeling of security rather than reality, and making decisions based on irrelevant context. And that risk cockpit of ours? It's not nearly as finely tuned as we might like it to be.

Like a rabbit that responds to an oncoming car with its default predator avoidance behavior—dart left, dart right, dart left, and at the last moment jump—instead of just getting out of the way, our Stone Age intuition doesn't serve us well in a modern technological society. So when we in the security industry use the term "risk management," we don't want you to do it by trusting your gut. We want you to do risk management consciously and intelligently, to analyze the tradeoff and make the best decision.

This means balancing the costs and benefits of any security decision—buying and installing a new technology, implementing a new procedure or forgoing a common precaution. It means allocating a security budget to mitigate different risks by different amounts. It means buying insurance to transfer some risks to others. It's what businesses do, all the time, about everything. IT security has its own risk management decisions, based on the threats and the technologies.

There's never just one risk, of course, and bad risk management decisions often carry an underlying tradeoff. Terrorism policy in the US. is based more on politics than actual security risk, but the politicians who make these decisions are concerned about the risks of not being re-elected.

Many corporate security decisions are made to mitigate the risk of lawsuits rather than address the risk of any actual security breach. And individuals make risk management decisions that consider not only the risks to the corporation, but the risks to their departments' budgets, and to their careers.

You can't completely remove emotion from risk management decisions, but the best way to keep risk management focused on the data is to formalize the methodology. That's what companies that manage risk for a living—insurance companies, financial trading firms and arbitrageurs—try to do. They try to replace intuition with models, and hunches with mathematics.

The problem in the security world is we often lack the data to do risk management well. Technological risks are complicated and subtle. We don't know how well our network security will keep the bad guys out, and we don't know the cost to the company if we don't keep them out. And the risks change all the time, making the calculations even harder. But this doesn't mean we shouldn't try.

You can't avoid risk management; it's fundamental to business just as to life. The question is whether you're going to try to use data or whether you're going to just react based on emotions, hunches and anecdotes.

How the Great Conficker Panic Hacked into Human Credulity

Originally published in the Guardian, *April 23, 2009*

Conficker's April Fool's joke—the huge, menacing build-up and then nothing—is a good case study on how we think about risks, one whose lessons are applicable far outside computer security. Generally, our brains aren't very good at probability and risk analysis. We tend to use cognitive short-cuts instead of thoughtful analysis. This worked fine for the simple risks we encountered for most of our species' existence, but it's less effective against the complex risks society forces us to face today.

We tend to judge the probability of something happening on how easily we can bring examples to mind. It's why people tend to buy earthquake insurance after an earthquake, when the risk is lowest. It's why those of us who have been the victims of a crime tend to fear crime more than those who haven't. And it's why we fear a repeat of 9/11 more than other types of terrorism.

We fear being murdered, kidnapped, raped, and assaulted by strangers, when friends and relatives are far more likely to do those things to us. We worry about plane crashes instead of car crashes, which are far more common. We tend to exaggerate spectacular, strange, and rare events, and downplay more ordinary, familiar, and common ones.

We also respond more to stories than to data. If I show you statistics on crime in New York, you'll probably shrug and continue your vacation planning. But if a close friend gets mugged there, you're more likely to cancel your trip.

And specific stories are more convincing than general ones. That is why we buy more insurance against plane accidents than against travel accidents, or accidents in general. Or why, when surveyed, we are willing to pay more for air travel insurance covering "terrorist acts" than "all possible causes. "That is why, in experiments, people judge specific scenarios more likely than more general ones, even if the general ones include the specific.

Conficker's 1 April deadline was precisely the sort of event humans tend to overreact to. It's a specific threat, which convinces us that it's credible. It's a specific date, which focuses our fear. Our natural tendency to exaggerate makes it more spectacular, which further increases our fear. Its repetition by the media makes it even easier to bring to mind. As the story becomes more vivid, it becomes more convincing.

The *New York Times* called it an "unthinkable disaster", the television news show *60 Minutes* said it could "disrupt the entire Internet," and we at the *Guardian* warned that it might be a "deadly threat." Naysayers were few and drowned out.

The first of April passed without incident, but Conficker is no less dangerous today. About 2.2m computers worldwide are still infected with Conficker.A and B, and about 1.3m more are infected with the nastier Conficker.C. It's true that on 1 April Conficker.C tried a new trick to update itself, but its authors could have updated the worm using another mechanism any day. In fact, they updated it on 8 April, and can do so again.

And Conficker is just one of many, many dangerous worms being run by criminal organizations. It came with a date and got a lot of press—that 1 April date was more hype than reality—but it's not particularly special. In short, there are many criminal organizations on the Internet using worms and other forms of malware to infect computers. They then use those computers to send spam, commit fraud, and infect more computers. The risks are real and serious. Luckily, keeping your anti-virus software up-to-date and not clicking on strange attachments can keep you pretty secure. Conficker spreads through a Windows vulnerability that was patched in October. You do have automatic update turned on, right?

But people being people, it takes a specific story for us to protect ourselves.

How Science Fiction Writers Can Help, or Hurt, Homeland Security

Originally published in Wired News, *June 18, 2009*

A couple of years ago, the Department of Homeland Security hired a bunch of science fiction writers to come in for a day and think of ways terrorists could attack America. If our inability to prevent 9/11 marked a failure of imagination, as some said at the time, then who better than science fiction writers to inject a little imagination into counterterrorism planning?

I discounted the exercise at the time, calling it "embarrassing." I never thought that 9/11 was a failure of imagination. I thought, and still think, that 9/11 was primarily a confluence of three things: the dual failure of centralized coordination and local control within the FBI, and some lucky breaks on the part of the attackers. More imagination leads to more movie-plot threats—which contributes to overall fear and overestimation of the risks. And that doesn't help keep us safe at all.

Recently, I read a paper by Magne Jørgensen that provides some insight into why this is so. Titled More Risk Analysis Can Lead to Increased Over-Optimism and Over-Confidence, the paper isn't about terrorism at all. It's about software projects.

Most software development project plans are overly optimistic, and most planners are overconfident about their overoptimistic plans. Jørgensen studied how risk analysis affected this. He conducted four separate experiments on software engineers, and concluded (though there are lots of caveats in the paper, and more research needs to be done) that performing more risk analysis can make engineers more overoptimistic instead of more realistic.

Potential explanations all come from behavioral economics: cognitive biases that affect how we think and make decisions. (I've written about some of these biases and how they affect security decisions, and there's a great book on the topic as well.)

First, there's a control bias. We tend to underestimate risks in situations where we are in control, and overestimate risks in situations when we are not in control. Driving versus flying is a common example. This bias becomes stronger with familiarity, involvement and a desire to experience control, all of which increase with increased risk analysis. So the more risk analysis, the greater the control bias, and the greater the underestimation of risk.

The second explanation is the availability heuristic. Basically, we judge the importance or likelihood of something happening by the ease of bringing instances of that thing to mind. So we tend to overestimate the probability of a rare risk that is seen in a news headline, because it is so easy to imagine. Likewise, we underestimate the probability of things occurring that don't happen to be in the news. A corollary of this phenomenon is that, if we're asked to think about a series of things, we overestimate the probability of the last thing thought about because it's more easily remembered.

According to Jørgensen's reasoning, people tend to do software risk analysis by thinking of the severe risks first, and then the more manageable risks. So the more risk analysis that's done, the less severe the last risk imagined, and thus the greater the underestimation of the total risk.

The third explanation is similar: the peak end rule. When thinking about a total experience, people tend to place too much weight on the last part of the experience. In one experiment, people had to hold their hands under cold water for one minute. Then, they had to hold their hands under cold water for one minute again, then keep their hands in the water for an additional 30 seconds while the temperature was gradually raised. When asked about it afterwards, most people preferred the second option to the first, even though the second had more total discomfort. (An intrusive medical device was redesigned along these lines, resulting in a longer period of discomfort but a relatively comfortable final few seconds. People liked it a lot better.) This means, like the second explanation, that the least severe last risk imagined gets greater weight than it deserves.

Fascinating stuff. But the biases produce the reverse effect when it comes to movie-plot threats. The more you think about far-fetched terrorism possibilities, the more outlandish and scary they become, and the less control you think you have. This causes us to overestimate the risks.

Think about this in the context of terrorism. If you're asked to come up with threats, you'll think of the significant ones first. If you're pushed to find more, if you hire science-fiction writers to dream them up, you'll quickly get into the low-probability movie plot threats. But since they're the last ones generated, they're more available. (They're also more vivid—science fiction writers are good at that—which also leads us to overestimate their probability.) They also suggest we're even less in control of the situation than we believed. Spending too much time imagining disaster scenarios leads people to overestimate the risks of disaster.

I'm sure there's also an anchoring effect in operation. This is another cognitive bias, where people's numerical estimates of things are affected by numbers they've most recently thought about, even random ones. People who are given a list of three risks will think the total number of risks are lower than people who are given a list of 12 risks. So if the science fiction writers come up with 137 risks, people will believe that the number of risks is higher than they otherwise would—even if they recognize the 137 number is absurd.

Jørgensen does not believe risk analysis is useless in software projects, and I don't believe scenario brainstorming is useless in counterterrorism. Both can lead to new insights and, as a result, a more intelligent analysis of both specific risks and general risk. But an over-reliance on either can be detrimental.

Last month, at the 2009 Homeland Security Science & Technology Stakeholders Conference in Washington D.C., science fiction writers helped the attendees think differently about security. This seems like a far better use of their talents than imagining some of the zillions of ways terrorists can attack America.

Privacy Salience and Social Networking Sites

Originally published in the Guardian, *July 15, 2009*

Reassuring people about privacy makes them more, not less, concerned. It's called "privacy salience," and Leslie John, Alessandro Acquisti, and George Loewenstein—all at Carnegie Mellon University—demonstrated this in a series of clever experiments. In one, subjects completed an online survey consisting of a series of questions about their academic behavior—"Have you ever cheated on an exam?" for example. Half of the subjects were first required to sign a consent warning—designed to make privacy concerns more salient—while the other half did not. Also, subjects were randomly assigned to receive either a privacy confidentiality assurance, or no such assurance. When the privacy concern was made salient (through the consent warning), people reacted negatively to the subsequent confidentiality assurance and were less likely to reveal personal information.

In another experiment, subjects completed an online survey where they were asked a series of personal questions, such as "Have you ever tried cocaine?" Half of the subjects completed a frivolous-looking survey—"How BAD are U??"—with a picture of a cute devil. The other half completed the same survey with the title "Carnegie Mellon University Survey of Ethical Standards," complete with a university seal and official privacy assurances. The results showed that people who were reminded about privacy were less likely to reveal personal information than those who were not.

Privacy salience does a lot to explain social networking sites and their attitudes towards privacy. From a business perspective, social networking sites don't want their members to exercise their privacy rights very much. They want members to be comfortable disclosing a lot of data about themselves.

Joseph Bonneau and Soeren Preibusch of Cambridge University have been studying privacy on 45 popular social networking sites around the world. (You may not have realized that there *are* 45 popular social networking sites around the world.) They found that privacy settings were often confusing and hard to access; Facebook, with its 61 privacy settings, is the worst. To understand some of the settings, they had to create accounts with different settings so they could compare the results. Privacy tends to increase with the age and popularity of a site. General-use sites tend to have more privacy features than niche sites.

But their most interesting finding was that sites consistently hide any mentions of privacy. Their splash pages talk about connecting with friends, meeting new people, sharing pictures: the benefits of disclosing personal data.

These sites do talk about privacy, but only on hard-to-find privacy policy pages. There, the sites give strong reassurances about their privacy controls and the safety of data members choose to disclose on the site. There, the sites display third-party privacy seals and other icons designed to assuage any fears members have.

It's the Carnegie Mellon experimental result in the real world. Users care about privacy, but don't really think about it day to day. The social networking sites don't want to remind users about privacy, even if they talk about it positively, because any reminder will result in users remembering their privacy fears and becoming more cautious about sharing personal data. But the sites also need to reassure those "privacy fundamentalists" for whom privacy is always salient, so they have very strong pro-privacy rhetoric for those who take the time to search them out. The two different marketing messages are for two different audiences.

Social networking sites are improving their privacy controls as a result of public pressure. At the same time, there is a counterbalancing business pressure to decrease privacy; watch what's going on right now on Facebook, for example. Naively, we should expect companies to make their privacy policies clear to allow customers to make an informed choice. But the marketing need to reduce privacy salience will frustrate market solutions to improve privacy; sites would much rather obfuscate the issue than compete on it as a feature.

Security, Group Size, and the Human Brain

Originally published in IEEE Security & Privacy,
July/August 2009

If the size of your company grows past 150 people, it's time to get name badges. It's not that larger groups are somehow less secure, it's just that 150 is the cognitive limit to the number of people a human brain can maintain a coherent social relationship with.

Primatologist Robin Dunbar derived this number by comparing neocortex —the "thinking" part of the mammalian brain—volume with the size of primate social groups. By analyzing data from 38 primate genera and extrapolating to the human neocortex size, he predicted a human "mean group size" of roughly 150.

This number appears regularly in human society; it's the estimated size of a Neolithic farming village, the size at which Hittite settlements split, and the basic unit in professional armies from Roman times to the present day. Larger group sizes aren't as stable because their members don't know each other well enough. Instead of thinking of the members as people, we think of them as groups of people. For such groups to function well, they need externally imposed structure, such as name badges.

Of course, badges aren't the only way to determine in-group/out-group status. Other markers include insignia, uniforms, and secret handshakes. They have different security properties and some make more sense than others at different levels of technology, but once a group reaches 150 people, it has to do something.

More generally, there are several layers of natural human group size that increase with a ratio of approximately three: 5, 15, 50, 150, 500, and 1500—although, really, the numbers aren't as precise as all that, and groups that are less focused on survival tend to be smaller. The layers relate to both the intensity and intimacy of relationship and the frequency of contact.

The smallest, three to five, is a "clique": the number of people from whom you would seek help in times of severe emotional distress. The twelve to 20 group is the "sympathy group": people with which you have special ties. After that, 30 to 50 is the typical size of hunter-gatherer overnight camps, generally drawn from the same pool of 150 people. No matter what size company you work for, there are only about 150 people you consider to be "co-workers." (In small companies, Alice and Bob handle accounting. In larger companies, it's the accounting department—and maybe you know someone there personally.) The 500-person group is the "megaband," and the 1,500-person group is the "tribe." Fifteen hundred is roughly the number of faces we can put names to, and the typical size of a hunter-gatherer society.

These numbers are reflected in military organization throughout history: squads of 10 to 15 organized into platoons of three to four squads, organized into companies of three to four platoons, organized into battalions of three to four companies, organized into regiments of three to four battalions, organized into divisions of two to three regiments, and organized into corps of two to three divisions.

Coherence can become a real problem once organizations get above about 150 in size. So as group sizes grow across these boundaries, they have more externally imposed infrastructure—and more formalized security systems. In intimate groups, pretty much all security is ad hoc. Companies smaller than 150 don't bother with name badges; companies greater than 500 hire a guard to sit in the lobby and check badges. The military have had centuries of experience with this under rather trying circumstances, but even there the real commitment and bonding invariably occurs at the company level. Above that you need to have rank imposed by discipline.

The whole brain-size comparison might be bunk, and a lot of evolutionary psychologists disagree with it. But certainly security systems become more formalized as groups grow larger and their members less known to each other. When do more formal dispute resolution systems arise: town elders, magistrates, judges? At what size boundary are formal authentication schemes required? Small companies can get by without the internal forms, memos, and procedures that large companies require; when does what tend to appear? How does punishment formalize as group size increases? And how do all these things affect group coherence? People act differently on social networking sites like Facebook when their list of "friends" grows larger and less intimate. Local merchants sometimes let known regulars run up tabs. I lend books to friends with much less formality than a public library. What examples have you seen?

People Understand Risks—But Do Security Staff Understand People?

Originally published in the Guardian, *August 5, 2009*

People have a natural intuition about risk, and in many ways it's very good. It fails at times due to a variety of cognitive biases, but for normal risks that people regularly encounter, it works surprisingly well: often better than we give it credit for.

This struck me as I listened to yet another conference presenter complaining about security awareness training. He was talking about the difficulty of getting employees at his company to actually follow his security policies: encrypting data on memory sticks, not sharing passwords, not logging in from untrusted wireless networks. "We have to make people understand the risks," he said.

It seems to me that his co-workers understand the risks better than he does. They know what the real risks are at work, and that they all revolve around not getting the job done. Those risks are real and tangible, and employees feel them all the time. The risks of not following security procedures are much less real. Maybe the employee will get caught, but probably not. And even if he does get caught, the penalties aren't serious.

Given this accurate risk analysis, any rational employee will regularly circumvent security to get his or her job done. That's what the company rewards, and that's what the company actually wants.

"Fire someone who breaks security procedure, quickly and publicly," I suggested to the presenter. "That'll increase security awareness faster than any of your posters or lectures or newsletters." If the risks are real, people will get it.

You see the same sort of risk intuition on motorways. People are less careful about posted speed limits than they are about the actual speeds police issue tickets for. It's also true on the streets: people respond to real crime rates, not public officials proclaiming that a neighborhood is safe.

The warning stickers on ladders might make you think the things are considerably riskier than they are, but people have a good intuition about ladders and ignore most of the warnings. (This isn't to say that some people don't do stupid things around ladders, but for the most part they're safe. The warnings are more about the risk of lawsuits to ladder manufacturers than risks to people who climb ladders.)

As a species, we are naturally tuned in to the risks inherent in our environment. Throughout our evolution, our survival depended on making reasonably accurate risk management decisions intuitively, and we're so good at it, we don't even realize we're doing it.

Parents know this. Children have surprisingly perceptive risk intuition. They know when parents are serious about a threat and when their threats are empty. And they respond to the real risks of parental punishment, not the inflated risks based on parental rhetoric. Again, awareness training lectures don't work; there have to be real consequences.

It gets even weirder. The University College London professor John Adams popularized the metaphor of a mental risk thermostat. We tend to seek some natural level of risk, and if something becomes less risky, we tend to make it more risky. Motorcycle riders who wear helmets drive faster than riders who don't.

Our risk thermostats aren't perfect (that newly helmeted motorcycle rider will still decrease his overall risk) and will tend to remain within the same domain (he might drive faster, but he won't increase his risk by taking up smoking), but in general, people demonstrate an innate and finely tuned ability to understand and respond to risks.

Of course, our risk intuition fails spectacularly and often, with regards to rare risks, unknown risks, voluntary risks, and so on. But when it comes to the common risks we face every day—the kinds of risks our evolutionary survival depended on—we're pretty good.

So whenever you see someone in a situation who you think doesn't understand the risks, stop first and make sure you understand the risks. You might be surprised.

Nature's Fears Extend to Online Behavior

Originally published in the Japan Times, *November 3, 2009*

It's hard work being prey. Watch the birds at a feeder. They're constantly on alert, and will fly away from food—from easy nutrition—at the slightest movement or sound. Given that I've never, ever seen a bird plucked from a feeder by a predator, it seems like a whole lot of wasted effort against a small threat.

Assessing and reacting to risk is one of the most important things a living creature has to deal with. The amygdala, an ancient part of the brain that first evolved in primitive fishes, has that job. It's what's responsible for the fight-or-flight reflex. Adrenaline in the bloodstream, increased heart rate, increased muscle tension, sweaty palms; that's the amygdala in action. You notice it when you fear a dark alley, have vague fears of terrorism, or worry about predators stalking your children on the Internet. And it works fast, faster than consciousnesses: show someone a snake and their amygdala will react before their conscious brain registers that they're looking at a snake.

Fear motivates all sorts of animal behaviors. Schooling, flocking, and herding are all security measures. Not only is it less likely that any member of the group will be eaten, but each member of the group has to spend less time watching out for predators. Animals as diverse as bumblebees and monkeys both avoid food in areas where predators are common. Different prey species have developed various alarm calls, some surprisingly specific. And some prey species have even evolved to react to the alarms given off by other species.

Evolutionary biologist Randolph Nesse has studied animal defenses, particularly those that seem to be overreactions. These defenses are mostly all-or-nothing; a creature can't do them halfway. Birds flying off, sea cucumbers expelling their stomachs, and vomiting are examples. Using signal-detection theory, Nesse showed that all-or-nothing defenses are expected to have many false alarms. "The smoke detector principle shows that the overresponsiveness of many defenses is an illusion. The defenses appear overresponsive because they are 'inexpensive' compared to the harms they protect against and because errors of too little defense are often more costly than errors of too much defense." So, according to the theory, if flight costs 100 calories, both in flying and lost eating time, and there's a 1 in 100 chance of being eaten if you don't fly away, it's smarter for survival to use up 10,000 calories repeatedly flying at the slightest movement even though there's a 99 percent false-alarm rate. Whatever the numbers happen to be for a particular species, it has evolved to get the trade-off right.

This makes sense, until the conditions that the species evolved under change quicker than evolution can react to. Even though there are far fewer predators in the city, birds at my feeder react as if they were in the primeval forest. Even birds safe in a zoo's aviary don't realize that the situation has changed.

Humans are both no different and very different. We, too, feel fear and react with our amygdala, but we also have a conscious brain that can override those reactions. And we too live in a world very different from the one we evolved in. Our reflexive defenses might be optimized for the risks endemic to living in small family groups in the East African highlands in 100,000 B.C.—not Tokyo in 2009. But we can go beyond fear, and actually think sensibly about security.

Far too often, we don't. We tend to be poor judges of risk. We overreact to rare risks, we ignore long-term risks, we magnify risks that are also morally offensive. We get risks wrong—threats, probabilities and costs—all the time. When we're afraid, really afraid, we'll do almost anything to make that fear go away. Politicians and marketers, both, have learned to push that fear button to get us to do what they want.

One night last month, I was woken from my hotel-room sleep by a loud, piercing alarm. There was no way I could ignore it, but I weighed the risks and did what any reasonable person would do under the circumstances: I stayed in bed and waited for the alarm to be turned off. No point getting dressed, walking down 10 flights of stairs, and going outside into the cold for what invariably would be a false alarm—serious hotel fires are very rare. Unlike the bird in an aviary, I knew better.

You can disagree with my risk calculus, and I'm sure many hotel guests walked downstairs and outside to the designated assembly point. But it's important to recognize that the ability to have this sort of discussion is uniquely human. And we need to have the discussion repeatedly, whether the topic is the monitoring of our children's Web-surfing habits, outsourcing our corporate IT infrastructure, or even the potential military invasion of another country. These things aren't part of our evolutionary history; we have no natural sense of how to respond to them. Our fears are often calibrated wrong, and reason is the only way we can override them.

6 Security and Technology

The Ethics of Vulnerability Research

Originally published in Information Security, *May 2008*

This was originally published as the first half of a point/counterpoint with Marcus Ranum.

The standard way to take control of someone else's computer is by exploiting a vulnerability in a software program on it. This was true in the 1960s when buffer overflows were first exploited to attack computers. It was true in 1988 when the Morris worm exploited a Unix vulnerability to attack computers on the Internet, and it's still how most modern malware works.

Vulnerabilities are software mistakes—mistakes in specification and design, but mostly mistakes in programming. Any large software package will have thousands of mistakes. These vulnerabilities lie dormant in our software systems, waiting to be discovered. Once discovered, they can be used to attack systems. This is the point of security patching: eliminating known vulnerabilities. But many systems don't get patched, so the Internet is filled with known, exploitable vulnerabilities.

New vulnerabilities are hot commodities. A hacker who discovers one can sell it on the black market, blackmail the vendor with disclosure, or simply publish it without regard to the consequences. Even if he does none of these, the mere fact the vulnerability is known by someone increases the risk to every user of that software. Given that, is it ethical to research new vulnerabilities?

Unequivocally, yes. Despite the risks, vulnerability research is enormously valuable. Security is a mindset, and looking for vulnerabilities nurtures that mindset. Deny practitioners this vital learning tool, and security suffers accordingly.

Security engineers see the world differently than other engineers. Instead of focusing on how systems work, they focus on how systems fail, how they can be made to fail, and how to prevent—or protect against—those failures. Most software vulnerabilities don't ever appear in normal operations, only when an attacker deliberately exploits them. So security engineers need to think like attackers.

People without the mindset sometimes think they can design security products, but they can't. And you see the results all over society—in snake-oil cryptography, software, Internet protocols, voting machines, and fare card and other payment systems. Many of these systems had someone in charge of "security" on their teams, but it wasn't someone who thought like an attacker.

This mindset is difficult to teach, and may be something you're born with or not. But in order to train people possessing the mindset, they need to search for and find security vulnerabilities—again and again and again. And this is true regardless of the domain. Good cryptographers discover vulnerabilities in others' algorithms and protocols. Good software security experts find vulnerabilities in others' code. Good airport security designers figure out new ways to subvert airport security. And so on.

This is so important that when someone shows me a security design by someone I don't know, my first question is, "What has the designer broken?" Anyone can design a security system that he cannot break. So when someone announces, "Here's my security system, and I can't break it," your first reaction should be, "Who are you?" If he's someone who has broken dozens of similar systems, his system is worth looking at. If he's never broken anything, the chance is zero that it will be any good.

Vulnerability research is vital because it trains our next generation of computer security experts. Yes, newly discovered vulnerabilities in software and airports put us at risk, but they also give us more realistic information about how good the security actually is. And yes, there are more and less responsible—and more and less legal—ways to handle a new vulnerability. But the bad guys are constantly searching for new vulnerabilities, and if we have any hope of securing our systems, we need the good guys to be at least as competent. To me, the question isn't whether it's ethical to do vulnerability research. If someone has the skill to analyze and provide better insights into the problem, the question is whether it is ethical for him not to do vulnerability research.

I've Seen the Future, and It Has a Kill Switch

Originally published in Wired News, *June 26, 2008*

It used to be that just the entertainment industries wanted to control your computers—and televisions and iPods and everything else—to ensure that you didn't violate any copyright rules. But now everyone else wants to get their hooks into your gear.

OnStar will soon include the ability for the police to shut off your engine remotely. Buses are getting the same capability, in case terrorists want to re-enact the movie *Speed*. The Pentagon wants a kill switch installed on airplanes, and is worried about potential enemies installing kill switches on their own equipment.

Microsoft is doing some of the most creative thinking along these lines, with something it's calling "Digital Manners Policies." According to its patent application, DMP-enabled devices would accept broadcast "orders" limiting their capabilities. Cellphones could be remotely set to vibrate mode in restaurants and concert halls, and be turned off on airplanes and in hospitals. Cameras could be prohibited from taking pictures in locker rooms and museums, and recording equipment could be disabled in theaters. Professors finally could prevent students from texting one another during class.

The possibilities are endless, and very dangerous. Making this work involves building a nearly flawless hierarchical system of authority. That's a difficult security problem even in its simplest form. Distributing that system among a variety of different devices—computers, phones, PDAs, cameras, record-ers—with different firmware and manufacturers, is even more difficult. Not to mention delegating different levels of authority to various agencies, enterprises, industries and individuals, and then enforcing the necessary safeguards.

Once we go down this path—giving one device authority over other devices—the security problems start piling up. Who has the authority to limit functionality of my devices, and how do they get that authority? What prevents them from abusing that power? Do I get the ability to override their limitations? In what circumstances, and how? Can they override my override?

How do we prevent this from being abused? Can a burglar, for example, enforce a "no photography" rule and prevent security cameras from working? Can the police enforce the same rule to avoid another Rodney King incident?

Do the police get "superuser" devices that cannot be limited, and do they get "supercontroller" devices that can limit anything? How do we ensure that only they get them, and what do we do when the devices inevitably fall into the wrong hands?

It's comparatively easy to make this work in closed specialized systems—OnStar, airplane avionics, military hardware—but much more difficult in open-ended systems. If you think Microsoft's vision could possibly be securely designed, all you have to do is look at the dismal effectiveness of the various copy-protection and digital-rights-management systems we've seen over the years. That's a similar capabilities-enforcement mechanism, albeit simpler than these more general systems.

And that's the key to understanding this system. Don't be fooled by the scare stories of wireless devices on airplanes and in hospitals, or visions of a world where no one is yammering loudly on their cellphones in posh restaurants. This is really about media companies wanting to exert their control further over your electronics. They not only want to prevent you from surreptitiously recording movies and concerts, they want your new television to enforce good "manners" on your computer, and not allow it to record any programs. They want your iPod to politely refuse to copy music to a computer other than your own. They want to enforce *their* legislated definition of manners: to control what you do and when you do it, and to charge you repeatedly for the privilege whenever possible.

"Digital Manners Policies" is a marketing term. Let's call this what it really is: Selective Device Jamming. It's not polite, it's dangerous. It won't make anyone more secure—or more polite.

Software Makers Should Take Responsibility

Originally published in the Guardian, *July 17, 2008*

A recent study of Internet browsers worldwide discovered that over half—52%—of Internet Explorer users weren't using the current version of the software. For other browsers the numbers were better, but not much: 17% of Firefox users, 35% of Safari users, and 44% of Opera users were using an old version.

This is particularly important because browsers are an increasingly common vector for Internet attacks, and old versions of browsers don't have all their security patches up to date. They're open to attack through vulnerabilities the vendors have already fixed.

Security professionals are quick to blame users who don't use the latest update and install every patch. "Keeping up is critical for security," they say, and "if someone doesn't update their system, it's their own fault that they get hacked." This sounds a lot like blaming the victim: "He should have known not to walk down that deserted street; it's his own fault he was mugged." Of course the victim could have –and quite possibly should have—taken further precautions, but the real blame lies elsewhere.

It's not as if patching is easy. Even in a corporate setting, systems administrators have trouble keeping up with the never-ending flow of software patches. There could easily be dozens per week across all operating systems and applications, and far too often they break things. Microsoft's Automatic Update feature has automated the process, but that's the exception. Patching is triage, and administrators are constantly prioritizing it along with everything else they're doing.

It's the system that's broken. There's no other industry where shoddy products are sold to a public that expects regular problems, and where consumers are the ones who have to learn how to fix them. If an automobile manufacturer has a problem with a car and issues a recall notice, it's a rare occurrence and a big deal—and you can take your car in and get it fixed for free. Computers are the only mass-market consumer item that pushes this burden onto the consumer, requiring him to have a high level of technical sophistication just to survive.

It doesn't have to be this way. It is possible to write quality software. It is possible to sell software products that work properly, and don't need to be constantly patched. The problem is that it's expensive and time consuming. Software vendors won't do it, of course, because the marketplace won't reward it.

The key to fixing this is software liabilities. Computers are also the only mass-market consumer item where the vendors accept no liability for faults. The reason automobiles are so well designed is that manufacturers face liabilities if they screw up. A lack of software liability is effectively a vast government subsidy of the computer industry. It allows them to produce more products faster, with less concern about safety, security, and quality.

Last summer, the House of Lords Science and Technology Committee issued a report on "Personal Internet Security." I was invited to give testimony for that report, and one of my recommendations was that software vendors be held liable when they are at fault. Their final report included that recommendation. The government rejected the recommendations in that report last autumn, and last week the committee issued a report on their follow-up inquiry, which still recommends software liabilities.

Good for them.

I'm not implying that liabilities are easy, or that all the liability for security vulnerabilities should fall on the vendor. But the courts are good at partial liability. Any automobile liability suit has many potential responsible parties: the car, the driver, the road, the weather, possibly another driver and another car, and so on. Similarly, a computer failure has several parties who may be partially responsible: the software vendor, the computer vendor, the network vendor, the user, possibly another hacker, and so on. But we're never going to get there until we start. Software liability is the market force that will motivate companies to improve their software quality—and everyone's security.

Lesson from the DNS Bug: Patching Isn't Enough

Originally published in Wired News, *July 23, 2008*

Despite the best efforts of the security community, the details of a critical Internet vulnerability discovered by Dan Kaminsky about six months ago have leaked. Hackers are racing to produce exploit code, and network operators who haven't already patched the hole are scrambling to catch up. The whole mess is a good illustration of the problems with researching and disclosing flaws like this.

The details of the vulnerability aren't important, but basically it's a form of DNS cache poisoning. The DNS system is what translates domain names people understand, like www.schneier.com, to IP addresses computers understand: 204.11.246.1. There is a whole family of vulnerabilities where the DNS system on your computer is fooled into thinking that the IP address for www.badsite .com is really the IP address for www.goodsite.com—there's no way for you to tell the difference—and that allows the criminals at www.badsite.com to trick you into doing all sorts of things, like giving up your bank account details.

Kaminsky discovered a particularly nasty variant of this cache-poisoning attack.

Here's the way the timeline was supposed to work: Kaminsky discovered the vulnerability about six months ago, and quietly worked with vendors to patch it. (There's a fairly straightforward fix, although the implementation nuances are complicated.) Of course, this meant describing the vulnerability to them; why would companies like Microsoft and Cisco believe him otherwise? On July 8, he held a press conference to announce the vulnerability—but not the details—and reveal that a patch was available from a long list of vendors. We would all have a month to patch, and Kaminsky would release details of the vulnerability at the BlackHat conference early next month.

Of course, the details leaked. How isn't important; it could have leaked a zillion different ways. Too many people knew about it for it to remain secret. Others who knew the general idea were too smart not to speculate on the details. I'm kind of amazed the details remained secret for this long; undoubtedly it had leaked into the underground community before the public leak two days ago. So now everyone who back-burnered the problem is rushing to patch, while the hacker community is racing to produce working exploits.

What's the moral here? It's easy to condemn Kaminsky: If he had shut up about the problem, we wouldn't be in this mess. But that's just wrong. Kaminsky found the vulnerability by accident. There's no reason to believe he was the first one to find it, and it's ridiculous to believe he would be the last. Don't shoot the messenger. The problem is with the DNS protocol; it's insecure.

The real lesson is that the patch treadmill doesn't work, and it hasn't for years. This cycle of finding security holes and rushing to patch them before the bad guys exploit those vulnerabilities is expensive, inefficient and incomplete. We need to design security into our systems right from the beginning. We need assurance. We need security engineers involved in system design. This process won't prevent every vulnerability, but it's much more secure—and cheaper—than the patch treadmill we're all on now.

What a security engineer brings to the problem is a particular mindset. He thinks about systems from a security perspective. It's not that he discovers all possible attacks before the bad guys do; it's more that he anticipates potential types of attacks, and defends against them even if he doesn't know their details. I see this all the time in good cryptographic designs. It's over-engineering based on intuition, but if the security engineer has good intuition, it generally works.

Kaminsky's vulnerability is a perfect example of this. Years ago, cryptographer Daniel J. Bernstein looked at DNS security and decided that Source Port Randomization was a smart design choice. That's exactly the work-around being rolled out now following Kaminsky's discovery. Bernstein didn't discover Kaminsky's attack; instead, he saw a general class of attacks and realized that this enhancement could protect against them. Consequently, the DNS program he wrote in 2000, djbdns, doesn't need to be patched; it's already immune to Kaminsky's attack.

That's what a good design looks like. It's not just secure against known attacks; it's also secure against unknown attacks. We need more of this, not just on the Internet but in voting machines, ID cards, transportation payment cards... everywhere. Stop assuming that systems are secure unless demonstrated insecure; start assuming that systems are insecure unless designed securely.

Why Being Open about Security Makes Us All Safer in the Long Run

Originally published in the Guardian, *August 7, 2008*

London's Oyster card has been cracked, and the final details will become public in October. NXP Semiconductors, the Philips spin-off that makes the system, lost a court battle to prevent the researchers from publishing. People might be able to use this information to ride for free, but the sky won't be falling. And the publication of this serious vulnerability actually makes us all safer in the long run.

Here's the story. Every Oyster card has a radio-frequency identification chip that communicates with readers mounted on the ticket barrier. That chip, the "Mifare Classic" chip, is used in hundreds of other transport systems as well—Boston, Los Angeles, Brisbane, Amsterdam, Taipei, Shanghai, Rio de Janeiro—and as an access pass in thousands of companies, schools, hospitals, and government buildings around Britain and the rest of the world.

The security of Mifare Classic is terrible. This is not an exaggeration; it's kindergarten cryptography. Anyone with any security experience would be embarrassed to put his name to the design. NXP attempted to deal with this embarrassment by keeping the design secret.

The group that broke Mifare Classic is from Radboud University Nijmegen in the Netherlands. They demonstrated the attack by riding the Underground for free, and by breaking into a building. Their two papers (one is already online) will be published at two conferences this autumn.

The second paper is the one that NXP sued over. They called disclosure of the attack "irresponsible," warned that it will cause "immense damages," and claimed that it "will jeopardize the security of assets protected with systems incorporating the Mifare IC." The Dutch court would have none of it: "Damage to NXP is not the result of the publication of the article but of the production and sale of a chip that appears to have shortcomings."

Exactly right. More generally, the notion that secrecy supports security is inherently flawed. Whenever you see an organization claiming that design secrecy is necessary for security—in ID cards, in voting machines, in airport security—it invariably means that its security is lousy and it has no choice but to hide it. Any competent cryptographer would have designed Mifare's security with an open and public design.

Secrecy is fragile. Mifare's security was based on the belief that no one would discover how it worked; that's why NXP had to muzzle the Dutch researchers. But that's just wrong. Reverse-engineering isn't hard. Other researchers had already exposed Mifare's lousy security. A Chinese company even sells a compatible chip. Is there any doubt that the bad guys already know about this, or will soon enough?

Publication of this attack might be expensive for NXP and its customers, but it's good for security overall. Companies will only design security as good as their customers know to ask for. NXP's security was so bad because customers didn't know how to evaluate security: either they don't know what questions to ask, or didn't know enough to distrust the marketing answers they were given. This court ruling encourages companies to build security properly rather than relying on shoddy design and secrecy, and discourages them from promising security based on their ability to threaten researchers.

It's unclear how this break will affect Transport for London. Cloning takes only a few seconds, and the thief only has to brush up against someone carrying a legitimate Oyster card. But it requires an RFID reader and a small piece of software which, while feasible for a techie, are too complicated for the average fare dodger. The police are likely to quickly arrest anyone who tries to sell cloned cards on any scale. TfL promises to turn off any cloned cards within 24 hours, but that will hurt the innocent victim who had his card cloned more than the thief.

The vulnerability is far more serious to the companies that use Mifare Classic as an access pass. It would be very interesting to know how NXP presented the system's security to them.

And while these attacks only pertain to the Mifare Classic chip, it makes me suspicious of the entire product line. NXP sells a more secure chip and has another on the way, but given the number of basic cryptography mistakes NXP made with Mifare Classic, one has to wonder whether the "more secure" versions will be sufficiently so.

Boston Court's Meddling with "Full Disclosure" Is Unwelcome

Originally published in Wired News, *August 21, 2008*

In eerily similar cases in the Netherlands and the United States, courts have recently grappled with the computer-security norm of "full disclosure," asking whether researchers should be permitted to disclose details of a fare-card vulnerability that allows people to ride the subway for free.

The "Oyster card" used on the London Tube was at issue in the Dutch case, and a similar fare card used on the Boston "T" was the center of the US case. The Dutch court got it right, and the American court, in Boston, got it wrong from the start—despite facing an open-and-shut case of First Amendment prior restraint.

The US court has since seen the error of its ways—but the damage is done. The MIT security researchers who were prepared to discuss their Boston findings at the DefCon security conference were prevented from giving their talk.

The ethics of full disclosure are intimately familiar to those of us in the computer-security field. Before full disclosure became the norm, researchers would quietly disclose vulnerabilities to the vendors—who would routinely ignore them. Sometimes vendors would even threaten researchers with legal action if they disclosed the vulnerabilities.

Later on, researchers started disclosing the existence of a vulnerability but not the details. Vendors responded by denying the security holes' existence, or calling them just theoretical. It wasn't until full disclosure became the norm that vendors began consistently fixing vulnerabilities quickly. Now that vendors routinely patch vulnerabilities, researchers generally give them advance notice to allow them to patch their systems before the vulnerability is published. But even with this "responsible disclosure" protocol, it's the threat of disclosure that motivates them to patch their systems. Full disclosure is the mechanism by which computer security improves.

Outside of computer security, secrecy is much more the norm. Some security communities, like locksmiths, behave much like medieval guilds, divulging the secrets of their profession only to those within it. These communities hate open research, and have responded with surprising vitriol to researchers who have found serious vulnerabilities in bicycle locks, combination safes, master-key systems, and many other security devices.

Researchers have received a similar reaction from other communities more used to secrecy than openness. Researchers—sometimes young students—who discovered and published flaws in copyright-protection schemes, voting-machine security, and now wireless access cards have all suffered recriminations and sometimes lawsuits for not keeping the vulnerabilities secret. When Christopher Soghoian created a website allowing people to print fake airline boarding passes, he got several unpleasant visits from the FBI.

This preference for secrecy comes from confusing a vulnerability with information *about* that vulnerability. Using secrecy as a security measure is fundamentally fragile. It assumes that the bad guys don't do their own security research. It assumes that no one else will find the same vulnerability. It assumes that information won't leak out even if the research results are suppressed. These assumptions are all incorrect.

The problem isn't the researchers; it's the products themselves. Companies will only design security as good as what their customers know to ask for. Full disclosure helps customers evaluate the security of the products they buy, and educates them in how to ask for better security. The Dutch court got it exactly right when it wrote: "Damage to NXP is not the result of the publication of the article but of the production and sale of a chip that appears to have shortcomings."

In a world of forced secrecy, vendors make inflated claims about their products, vulnerabilities don't get fixed, and customers are no wiser. Security research is stifled, and security technology doesn't improve. The only beneficiaries are the bad guys.

If you'll forgive the analogy, the ethics of full disclosure parallel the ethics of not paying kidnapping ransoms. We all know why we don't pay kidnappers: It encourages more kidnappings. Yet in every kidnapping case, there's someone—a spouse, a parent, an employer—with a good reason why, in this one case, we should make an exception.

The reason we want researchers to publish vulnerabilities is because that's how security improves. But in every case there's someone—the Massachusetts Bay Transit Authority, the locksmiths, an election machine manufacturer—who argues that, in this one case, we should make an exception.

We shouldn't. The benefits of responsibly publishing attacks greatly outweigh the potential harm. Disclosure encourages companies to build security properly rather than relying on shoddy design and secrecy, and discourages them from promising security based on their ability to threaten researchers. It's how we learn about security, and how we improve future security.

Quantum Cryptography: As Awesome as It Is Pointless

Originally published in Wired News, *October 16, 2008*

Quantum cryptography is back in the news, and the basic idea is still unbelievably cool, in theory, and nearly useless in real life.

The idea behind quantum crypto is that two people communicating using a quantum channel can be absolutely sure no one is eavesdropping. Heisenberg's uncertainty principle requires anyone measuring a quantum system to disturb it, and that disturbance alerts legitimate users as to the eavesdropper's presence. No disturbance, no eavesdropper—period.

This month we've seen reports on a new working quantum-key distribution network in Vienna, and a new quantum-key distribution technique out of Britain. Great stuff, but headlines like the BBC's "Unbreakable" encryption unveiled" are a bit much.

The basic science behind quantum crypto was developed, and prototypes built, in the early 1980s by Charles Bennett and Giles Brassard, and there have been steady advances in engineering since then. I describe basically how it all works in *Applied Cryptography, 2nd Edition* (pages 554–7). At least one company already sells quantum-key distribution products.

Note that this is totally separate from quantum computing, which also has implications for cryptography. Several groups are working on designing and building a quantum computer, which is fundamentally different from a classical computer. If one were built—and we're talking science fiction here—then it could factor numbers and solve discrete-logarithm problems very quickly. In other words, it could break all of our commonly used public-key algorithms. For symmetric cryptography it's not that dire: A quantum computer would effectively halve the key length, so that a 256-bit key would be only as secure as a 128-bit key today. Pretty serious stuff, but years away from being practical. I think the best quantum computer today can factor the number 15.

While I like the science of quantum cryptography—my undergraduate degree was in physics—I don't see any commercial value in it. I don't believe it solves any security problem that needs solving. I don't believe that it's worth paying for, and I can't imagine anyone but a few technophiles buying and deploying it. Systems that use it don't magically become unbreakable, because the quantum part doesn't address the weak points of the system.

Security is a chain; it's as strong as the weakest link. Mathematical cryptography, as bad as it sometimes is, is the strongest link in most security chains. Our symmetric and public-key algorithms are pretty good, even though they're not based on much rigorous mathematical theory. The real problems are elsewhere: computer security, network security, user interface and so on.

Cryptography is the one area of security that we can get right. We already have good encryption algorithms, good authentication algorithms and good key-agreement protocols. Maybe quantum cryptography can make that link stronger, but why would anyone bother? There are far more serious security problems to worry about, and it makes much more sense to spend effort securing those.

As I've often said, it's like defending yourself against an approaching attacker by putting a huge stake in the ground. It's useless to argue about whether the stake should be 50 feet tall or 100 feet tall, because either way, the attacker is going to go around it. Even quantum cryptography doesn't "solve" all of cryptography: The keys are exchanged with photons, but a conventional mathematical algorithm takes over for the actual encryption.

I'm always in favor of security research, and I have enjoyed following the developments in quantum cryptography. But as a product, it has no future. It's not that quantum cryptography might be insecure; it's that cryptography is already sufficiently secure.

Passwords Are Not Broken, but How We Choose Them Sure Is

Originally published in the Guardian, *November 13, 2008*

I've been reading a lot about how passwords are no longer good security. The reality is more complicated. Passwords are still secure enough for many applications, but you have to choose a good one. And that's hard. The best way to explain how to choose a good password is to describe how they're broken. The most serious attack is called offline password guessing. There are commercial programs that do this, sold primarily to police departments. There are also hacker tools that do the same thing.

As computers have become faster, the guessers have got better, sometimes being able to test hundreds of thousands of passwords per second. These guessers might run for months on many machines simultaneously.

They guess intelligently. They don't run through every eight-letter combination from "aaaaaaaa" to "zzzzzzzz" in order. That's 200bn possible passwords, most of them very unlikely. They try the most common password first: "password1." (Don't laugh; the most common password used to be "password.")

A typical password consists of a root plus an appendage. The root isn't necessarily a dictionary word, but it's something pronounceable. An appendage is either a suffix (90% of the time) or a prefix (10% of the time). One guesser I studied starts with a dictionary of about 1,000 common passwords, things like "letmein," "temp," "123456," and so on. Then it tests them each with about 100 common suffix appendages: "1," "4u," "69," "abc," "!" and so on. It recovers about 24% of all passwords with just these 100,000 combinations.

Then the guesser tries different dictionaries: English words, names, foreign words, phonetic patterns and so on for roots; two digits, dates, single symbols and so on for appendages. It runs the dictionaries with various capitalizations and common substitutions: "$" for "s," "@" for "a," "1" for "l" and so on. With a couple of weeks to a month's worth of time, this guessing strategy breaks about two-thirds of all passwords. But that assumes no biographical data. Any smart guesser collects whatever personal information it can on the subject before beginning. Postal codes are common appendages, so they're tested.

It also tests names and addresses from the address book, meaningful dates, and any other personal information. If it can, the guesser indexes the target hard drive and creates a dictionary out of every printable string, including deleted files. If you ever kept an email with your password, or saved it in an obscure file somewhere, or if your program ever stored it in memory, this process will grab it. And it will recover your password faster.

So if you want your password to be hard to guess, you should choose something that this process will miss. My advice is to take a sentence and turn it into a password. Something like "This little piggy went to market" might become "tlpWENT2m." That nine-character password won't be in anyone's dictionary. Of course, don't use this one, because I've written about it. Choose your own sentence—something personal.

Strong passwords can still fail because people are sloppy. They write them on Post-it notes stuck to their monitors, share them with friends, or choose the same passwords for multiple applications. (I don't care about low-security passwords here, only about ones that matter: your bank accounts, your credit cards, etc.) Websites are sloppy, too, allowing people to set up easy-to-guess "secret questions" as a backup password or email them to customers.

If you can't remember your passwords, write them down and put the paper in your wallet. But just write the sentence—or better yet—a hint that will help you remember your sentence. Or use a free program like Password Safe, which I designed to help people securely store all their passwords. Don't feel this is a failure; most of us have far too many passwords to be able to remember them all.

Passwords can still provide good authentication if used properly. The rise of alternate forms of authentication is more because people don't use passwords securely, and less because they don't work anymore.

America's Next Top Hash Function Begins

Originally published in Wired News, *November 19, 2008*

You might not have realized it, but the next great battle of cryptography began this month. It's not a political battle over export laws or key escrow or NSA eavesdropping, but an academic battle over who gets to be the creator of the next hash standard.

Hash functions are the most commonly used cryptographic primitive, and the most poorly understood. You can think of them as fingerprint functions: They take an arbitrary long data stream and return a fixed length, and effectively unique, string. The security comes from the fact that while it's easy to generate the fingerprint from a file, it's infeasible to go the other way and generate a file given a fingerprint.

Originally created to make digital signatures more efficient, hashes are now used to secure the very fundamentals of our information infrastructure: in password logins, secure web connections, encryption key management, virus and malware scanning, and almost every cryptographic protocol in current use. Without cryptographic hash functions, the Internet would simply not work. At the same time, there isn't a good theory of hash functions. Unlike encryption algorithms, there are no secret keys involved; this makes it harder to mathematically define exactly what hash functions are.

The National Institute of Standards and Technology, NIST, is holding a competition to replace the SHA family of hash functions. "SHA" stands for "Secure Hash Algorithm." It was developed by the NSA in 1993 to replace the commercial MD4 and MD5 algorithms, and has been updated several times since then. All the SHA algorithms are very similar, and have been increasingly under attack, so NIST wants to replace them.

The competition is important because, unlike other technological standards, committee design—balancing the interests of diverse constituents—isn't conducive to good security. Security is best when it's designed by expert teams and then subjected to public review. And cryptography is best when it's chosen by competition.

In 1997, NIST held a competition for a block cipher to replace DES. Fifteen candidates and three-and-a-half years later, Rijndael became the new Advanced Encryption Standard—AES. NIST is doing the same thing for what it's calling SHA-3 (not, for some unexplained reason, the Advanced Hash Standard or AHS).

The deadline was October 31, and NIST received 64 submissions. This isn't surprising—I predicted 80—as most of the 15 AES submitters were professors, whose students at the time have become professors themselves, with their own students. (If NIST does a stream cipher competition in another ten years, they should expect about 256 submissions.) These submissions came from academia, from industry, and from hobbyists. *CIO* magazine recently interviewed one of the submitters, who is 15. Twenty-eight submissions have been made public by the submitters, and six of those have been broken.

NIST is going through all the submissions right now, making sure they are complete and proper. Their goal is to publish all accepted submissions by the end of November, in advance of the First Hash Function Candidate

Conference, to be held in Belgium right after the Fast Software Encryption workshop in February.

The group expects to quickly make a first cut of algorithms—hopefully to about a dozen—and give the community a year of cryptanalysis before making a second cut in 2010. After another year of cryptanalysis, NIST will choose a winner in 2011. Expect a final standard by 2012.

My advice for software developers is to let the process run its course. While it's tempting to use the new cool algorithms in your designs, it's far too soon to trust any of them. This process is likely to result in all sorts of new research results in hash function security, and some real cryptanalytic surprises. Give the community a few years to figure out which ones are good and which aren't.

I've previously called this sort of thing a cryptographic demolition derby: The last one left standing wins. But that's only partially true. Certainly all the groups will spend the next few years trying to cryptanalyze each other, but in the end there will be a bunch of unbroken algorithms. NIST will select one based on performance and features.

NIST has stated that the goal of this process is not to choose the best standard but to choose a good standard. I think that's smart; in this process, the best is the enemy of the good. While there's no rush to choose a new standard—the SHA-2 algorithms will remain secure for the foreseeable future—we don't want to analyze the candidates forever.

Personally, I was part of a group of eight cryptographers that submitted Skein to the competition. A decade ago, writing Twofish and participating in the AES process was the most fun I had ever had in cryptography. These next few years promise to be even more fun.

Tigers Use Scent, Birds Use Calls—Biometrics Are Just Animal Instinct

Originally published in the Guardian, *January 8, 2009*

Biometrics may seem new, but they're the oldest form of identification. Tigers recognize each other's scent; penguins recognize calls. Humans recognize each other by sight from across the room, voices on the phone, signatures on contracts and photographs on drivers' licenses. Fingerprints have been used to identify people at crime scenes for more than 100 years.

What is new about biometrics is that computers are now doing the recognizing: thumbprints, retinal scans, voiceprints, and typing patterns. There's a lot of technology involved here, in trying to both limit the number of false positives (someone else being mistakenly recognized as you) and false negatives (you being mistakenly not recognized). Generally, a system can choose to have less of one or the other; less of both is very hard.

Biometrics can vastly improve security, especially when paired with another form of authentication such as passwords. But it's important to understand their limitations as well as their strengths. On the strength side, biometrics are hard to forge. It's hard to affix a fake fingerprint to your finger or make your retina look like someone else's. Some people can mimic voices, and make-up artists can change people's faces, but these are specialized skills.

On the other hand, biometrics are easy to steal. You leave your fingerprints everywhere you touch, your retinal scan everywhere you look. Regularly, hackers have copied the prints of officials from objects they've touched and posted them on the Internet. We haven't yet had an example of a large biometric database being hacked into, but the possibility is there. Biometrics are unique identifiers, but they're not secrets.

And a stolen biometric can fool some systems. It can be as easy as cutting out a signature, pasting it on to a contract and then faxing the page to someone. The person on the other end doesn't know that the signature isn't valid because he didn't see it fixed on to the page. Remote logins by fingerprint fail in the same way. If there's no way to verify the print came from an actual reader, not from a stored computer file, the system is much less secure.

A more secure system is to use a fingerprint to unlock your mobile phone or computer. Because there is a trusted path from the fingerprint reader to the stored fingerprint the system uses to compare, an attacker can't inject a previously stored print as easily as he can cut and paste a signature. A photo on an ID card works the same way: the verifier can compare the face in front of him with the face on the card.

Fingerprints on ID cards are more problematic, because the attacker can try to fool the fingerprint reader. Researchers have made false fingers out of rubber or glycerin. Manufacturers have responded by building readers that also detect pores or a pulse.

The lesson is that biometrics work best if the system can verify that the biometric came from the person at the time of verification. The biometric identification system at the gates of the CIA headquarters works because there's a guard with a large gun making sure no one is trying to fool the system.

Of course, not all systems need that level of security. At Counterpane, the security company I founded, we installed hand geometry readers at the access doors to the operations center. Hand geometry is a hard biometric to copy, and the system was closed and didn't allow electronic forgeries. It worked very well.

One more problem with biometrics: they don't fail well. Passwords can be changed, but if someone copies your thumbprint, you're out of luck: you can't update your thumb. Passwords can be backed up, but if you alter your thumbprint in an accident, you're stuck. The failures don't have to be this spectacular: a voice print reader might not recognize someone with a sore throat, or a fingerprint reader might fail outside in freezing weather. Biometric systems need to be analyzed in light of these possibilities.

Biometrics are easy, convenient, and when used properly, very secure; they're just not a panacea. Understanding how they work and fail is critical to understanding when they improve security and when they don't.

The Secret Question Is: Why Do IT Systems Use Insecure Passwords?

Originally published in the Guardian, *February 19, 2009*

Since January, the Conficker.B worm has been spreading like wildfire across the Internet, infecting the French navy, hospitals in Sheffield, the court system in Houston, Texas, and millions of computers worldwide. One of the ways it spreads is by cracking administrator passwords on networks. Which leads to the important question: why are IT administrators still using easy-to-guess passwords?

Computer authentication systems have two basic requirements. They need to keep the bad guys from accessing your account, and they need to allow you to access your account. Both are important, and every system is a balancing act between the two. Too little security, and the bad guys will get in too easily. But if the authentication system is too complicated, restrictive, or hard to use, you won't be able, or won't bother, to use it.

Passwords are the most common authentication system. They're easy to implement and use, which is why they're so popular. But, as computers have become faster, password-guessing has become easier. Most people don't choose complicated enough passwords to remain secure against modern password-guessing attacks. Conficker.B is even less clever—it just tries a list of about 200 common passwords.

To combat password-guessing, many systems force users to choose harder-to-guess passwords—requiring minimum lengths, non-alpha-numeric characters, etc.—and change their passwords more frequently. The first makes guessing harder, and the second makes a guessed password less valuable. This, of course, makes the system more annoying, so users respond by writing their passwords down and taping them to their monitors, or simply forgetting them more often. Smarter users use a secure password database such as Password Safe.

Users forgetting their passwords can be expensive—customer service reps have to field phone calls and reset passwords—so some systems include a backup authentication system: a secret question. If you forget your password, you can authenticate yourself with some personal information that only you know, such as your mother's maiden name, your favorite schoolteacher, the street you grew up on, the name of your first pet and so on. This may make the system more usable, but it also makes it much less secure: answers can be easily guessed, and are often known by people close to you.

A common enhancement is a one-time password generator, such as a SecurID token. This is a small device with a screen that displays a password that changes every time the button is pressed. This is called two-factor authentication, and is much more secure, because this token—"something you have"—is combined with a password—"something you know." But it's less usable, because the tokens have to be purchased and distributed to all users, and far too often it's "something you lost or forgot." And it costs money. Tokens are more frequently used in corporate environments, but banks and some online gaming worlds have taken to using them, although sometimes only as an option, because people don't like them.

In most cases, how an authentication system works when a legitimate user tries to log on is much more important than how it works when an impostor tries to log on. No security system is perfect, and there is some level of fraud associated with any of these authentication methods. But the instances of fraud are rare compared to the number of times someone tries to log on legitimately. If a given authentication system lets the bad guys in one in a 100 times, a bank could decide to live with the problem, or try to solve it in some other way. But if the same authentication system prevented legitimate customers from logging on even one in 1,000 times, the number of complaints would be enormous and the system wouldn't survive one week.

Balancing security and usability is hard, and many organizations get it wrong. But it's also evolving; organizations need to tighten their security and continue to push more involved authentication methods; and more savvy Internet users will then be willing to accept them. And IT administrators need to be leading that evolutionary change.

The Pros and Cons of Password Masking

Originally published in Schneier on Security, *July 3, 2009*

Usability guru Jakob Nielsen opened up a can of worms when he made the case for unmasking passwords in his blog. I chimed in that I agreed. Almost 165 comments on my blog (and several articles, essays, and many other blog posts) later, the consensus is that we were wrong.

I was certainly too glib. Like any security countermeasure, password masking has value. But like any countermeasure, password masking is not a panacea. And the costs of password masking need to be balanced with the benefits.

The cost is accuracy. When users don't get visual feedback from what they're typing, they're more prone to make mistakes. This is especially true with character strings that have non-standard characters and capitalization. This has several ancillary costs:

- Users get pissed off.
- Users are more likely to choose easy-to-type passwords, reducing both mistakes and security. Removing password masking will make people more comfortable with complicated passwords: they'll become easier to memorize and easier to use.

The benefits of password masking are more obvious:

- Security from shoulder surfing. If people can't look over your shoulder and see what you're typing, they're much less likely to be able to steal your password. Yes, they can look at your fingers instead, but that's *much* harder than looking at the screen. Surveillance cameras are also an issue: it's easier to watch someone's fingers on recorded video, but reading a cleartext password off a screen is trivial.

In some situations, there is a trust dynamic involved. Do you type your password while your boss is standing over your shoulder watching? How about your spouse or partner? Your parent or child? Your teacher or students? At ATMs, there's a social convention of standing away from someone using the machine, but that convention doesn't apply to computers. You might not trust the person standing next to you enough to let him see your password, but don't feel comfortable telling him to look away. Password masking solves that social awkwardness.

■ Security from screen scraping malware. This is less of an issue; keyboard loggers are more common and unaffected by password masking. And if you have that kind of malware on your computer, you've got all sorts of problems.

■ A security "signal." Password masking alerts users, and I'm thinking users who aren't particularly security savvy, that passwords are a secret.

I believe that shoulder surfing isn't nearly the problem it's made out to be. One, lots of people use their computers in private, with no one looking over their shoulders. Two, personal handheld devices are used very close to the body, making shoulder surfing all that much harder. Three, it's hard to quickly and accurately memorize a random non-alphanumeric string that flashes on the screen for a second or so.

This is not to say that shoulder surfing isn't a threat. It is. And, as many readers pointed out, password masking is one of the reasons it isn't more of a threat. And the threat is greater for those who are not fluent computer users: slow typists and people who are likely to choose bad passwords. But I believe that the risks are overstated.

Password masking is definitely important on public terminals with short PINs. (I'm thinking of ATMs.) The value of the PIN is large, shoulder surfing is more common, and a four-digit PIN is easy to remember in any case.

And lastly, this problem largely disappears on the Internet on your personal computer. Most browsers include the ability to save and then automatically populate password fields, making the usability problem go away at the expense of another security problem (the security of the password becomes the security of the computer). There's a Firefox plugin that gets rid of password masking. And programs like my own Password Safe allow passwords to be cut and pasted into applications, also eliminating the usability problem.

One approach is to make it a configurable option. High-risk banking applications could turn password masking on by default; other applications could turn it off by default. Browsers in public locations could turn it on by default. I like this, but it complicates the user interface.

A reader mentioned BlackBerry's solution, which is to display each character briefly before masking it; that seems like an excellent compromise.

I, for one, would like the option. I cannot type complicated WEP keys into Windows—twice! what's the deal with that?—without making mistakes. I cannot type my rarely used and very complicated PGP keys without making a mistake unless I turn off password masking. That's what I was reacting to when I said "I agree."

So was I wrong? Maybe. Okay, probably. Password masking definitely improves security; many readers pointed out that they regularly use their computer in crowded environments, and rely on password masking to protect their passwords. On the other hand, password masking reduces accuracy and makes it less likely that users will choose secure and hard-to-remember passwords, I will concede that the password masking trade-off is more beneficial than I thought in my snap reaction, but also that the answer is not nearly as obvious as we have historically assumed.

Technology Shouldn't Give Big Brother a Head Start

Originally published in MPR News Q, *July 31, 2009*

China is the world's most successful Internet censor. While the Great Firewall of China isn't perfect, it effectively limits information flowing in and out of the country. But now the Chinese government is taking things one step further.

Under a requirement taking effect soon, every computer sold in China will have to contain the Green Dam Youth Escort software package. Ostensibly a pornography filter, it is government spyware that will watch every citizen on the Internet. Green Dam has many uses. It can police a list of forbidden Web sites. It can monitor a user's reading habits. It can even enlist the computer in some massive botnet attack, as part of a hypothetical future cyberwar.

China's actions may be extreme, but they're not unique. Democratic governments around the world—Sweden, Canada and the United Kingdom, for example—are rushing to pass laws giving their police new powers of Internet surveillance, in many cases requiring communications system providers to redesign products and services they sell.

Many are passing data retention laws, forcing companies to keep information on their customers. Just recently, the German government proposed giving itself the power to censor the Internet.

The United States is no exception. The 1994 CALEA law required phone companies to facilitate FBI eavesdropping, and since 2001, the NSA has built substantial eavesdropping systems in the United States. The government has repeatedly proposed Internet data retention laws, allowing surveillance into past activities as well as present.

Systems like this invite criminal appropriation and government abuse. New police powers, enacted to fight terrorism, are already used in situations of normal crime. Internet surveillance and control will be no different.

Official misuses are bad enough, but the unofficial uses worry me more. Any surveillance and control system must itself be secured. An infrastructure conducive to surveillance and control invites surveillance and control, both by the people you expect and by the people you don't.

China's government designed Green Dam for its own use, but it's already been subverted. Why does anyone think that criminals won't be able to use it to steal bank account and credit card information, use it to launch other attacks, or turn it into a massive spam-sending botnet?

Why does anyone think that only authorized law enforcement will mine collected Internet data or eavesdrop on phone and IM conversations?

These risks are not theoretical. After 9/11, the National Security Agency built a surveillance infrastructure to eavesdrop on telephone calls and e-mails within the United States.

Although procedural rules stated that only non-Americans and international phone calls were to be listened to, actual practice didn't always match those rules. NSA analysts collected more data than they were authorized to, and used the system to spy on wives, girlfriends and famous people like former President Bill Clinton.

But that's not the most serious misuse of a telecommunications surveillance infrastructure. In Greece, between June 2004 and March 2005, someone wiretapped more than 100 cell phones belonging to members of the Greek government—the prime minister and the ministers of defense, foreign affairs and justice.

Ericsson built this wiretapping capability into Vodafone's products, and enabled it only for governments that requested it. Greece wasn't one of those governments, but someone still unknown—a rival political party? organized crime?—figured out how to surreptitiously turn the feature on.

Researchers have already found security flaws in Green Dam that would allow hackers to take over the computers. Of course there are additional flaws, and criminals are looking for them.

Surveillance infrastructure can be exported, which also aids totalitarianism around the world. Western companies like Siemens, Nokia, and Secure Computing built Iran's surveillance infrastructure. US companies helped build China's electronic police state. Twitter's anonymity saved the lives of Iranian dissidents—anonymity that many governments want to eliminate.

Every year brings more Internet censorship and control—not just in countries like China and Iran, but in the United States, the United Kingdom, Canada and other free countries.

The control movement is egged on by both law enforcement, trying to catch terrorists, child pornographers and other criminals, and by media companies, trying to stop file sharers.

It's bad civic hygiene to build technologies that could someday be used to facilitate a police state. No matter what the eavesdroppers and censors say, these systems put us all at greater risk. Communications systems that have no inherent eavesdropping capabilities are more secure than systems with those capabilities built in.

Lockpicking and the Internet

Originally published in Dark Reading, *August 10, 2009*

Physical locks aren't very good. They keep the honest out, but any burglar worth his salt can pick the common door lock pretty quickly.

It used to be that most people didn't know this. Sure, we all watched television criminals and private detectives pick locks with an ease only found on television and thought it realistic, but somehow we still held onto the belief that our own locks kept us safe from intruders.

The Internet changed that.

First was the *MIT Guide to Lockpicking*, written by the late Bob ("Ted the Tool") Baldwin. Then came Matt Blaze's 2003 paper on breaking master key systems. After that, came a flood of lock picking information on the Net: opening a bicycle lock with a Bic pen, key bumping, and more. Many of these techniques were already known in both the criminal and locksmith communities. The locksmiths tried to suppress the knowledge, believing their guildlike secrecy was better than openness. But they've lost: never has there been more public information about lock picking—or safecracking, for that matter.

Lock companies have responded with more complicated locks, and more complicated disinformation campaigns.

There seems to be a limit to how secure you can make a wholly mechanical lock, as well as a limit to how large and unwieldy a key the public will accept. As a result, there is increasing interest in other lock technologies.

As a security technologist, I worry that if we don't fully understand these technologies and the new sorts of vulnerabilities they bring, we may be trading a flawed technology for an even worse one. Electronic locks are vulnerable to attack, often in new and surprising ways.

Start with keypads, more and more common on house doors. These have the benefit that you don't have to carry a physical key around, but there's the problem that you can't give someone the key for a day and then take it away when that day is over. As such, the security decays over time—the longer the keypad is in use, the more people know how to get in. More complicated electronic keypads have a variety of options for dealing with this, but electronic keypads work only when the power is on, and battery-powered locks have their own failure modes. Plus, far too many people never bother to change the default entry code.

Keypads have other security failures, as well. I regularly see keypads where four of the 10 buttons are more worn than the other six. They're worn from use, of course, and instead of 10,000 possible entry codes, I now have to try only 24.

Fingerprint readers are another technology, but there are many known security problems with those. And there are operational problems, too: They're hard to use in the cold or with sweaty hands; and leaving a key with a neighbor to let the plumber in starts having a spy-versus-spy feel.

Some companies are going even further. Earlier this year, Schlage launched a series of locks that can be opened either by a key, a four-digit code, or the Internet. That's right: The lock is online. You can send the lock SMS messages or talk to it via a website, and the lock can send you messages when someone opens it—or even when someone tries to open it and fails.

Sounds nifty, but putting a lock on the Internet opens up a whole new set of problems, none of which we fully understand. Even worse: Security is only as strong as the weakest link. Schlage's system combines the inherent "pickability" of a physical lock, the new vulnerabilities of electronic keypads, and the hacking risk of online. For most applications, that's simply too much risk.

The Battle Is On against Facebook and Co. to Regain Control of Our Files

Originally published in the Guardian, *September 9, 2009*

File deletion is all about control. This used to not be an issue. Your data was on your computer, and you decided when and how to delete a file. You could use the delete function if you didn't care about whether the file could be recovered or not, and a file erase program—I use BCWipe for Windows—if you wanted to ensure no one could ever recover the file.

As we move more of our data onto cloud computing platforms such as Gmail and Facebook, and closed proprietary platforms such as the Kindle and the iPhone deleting data is much harder.

You have to trust that these companies will delete your data when you ask them to, but they're generally not interested in doing so. Sites like these are more likely to make your data inaccessible than they are to physically delete it. Facebook is a known culprit: actually deleting your data from its servers requires a complicated procedure that may or may not work. And even if you do manage to delete your data, copies are certain to remain in the companies' backup systems. Gmail explicitly says this in its privacy notice.

Online backups, SMS messages, photos on photo sharing sites, smartphone applications that store your data in the network: you have no idea what really happens when you delete pieces of data or your entire account, because you're not in control of the computers that are storing the data.

This notion of control also explains how Amazon was able to delete a book that people had previously purchased on their Kindle e-book readers. The legalities are debatable, but Amazon had the technical ability to delete the file because it controls all Kindles. It has designed the Kindle so that it determines when to update the software, whether people are allowed to buy Kindle books, and when to turn off people's Kindles entirely.

Vanish is a research project by Roxana Geambasu and colleagues at the University of Washington. They designed a prototype system that automatically deletes data after a set time interval. So you can send an email, create a Google Doc, post an update to Facebook, or upload a photo to Flickr, all designed to disappear after a set period of time. And after it disappears, no one—not anyone who downloaded the data, not the site that hosted the data, not anyone who intercepted the data in transit, not even you—will be able to read it. If the police arrive at Facebook or Google or Flickr with a warrant, they won't be able to read it.

The details are complicated, but Vanish breaks the data's decryption key into a bunch of pieces and scatters them around the web using a peer-to-peer network. Then it uses the natural turnover in these networks—machines constantly join and leave—to make the data disappear. Unlike previous programs that supported file deletion, this one doesn't require you to trust any company, organization, or website. It just happens.

Of course, Vanish doesn't prevent the recipient of an email or the reader of a Facebook page from copying the data and pasting it into another file, just as Kindle's deletion feature doesn't prevent people from copying a book's files and saving them on their computers. Vanish is just a prototype at this point, and it only works if all the people who read your Facebook entries or view your Flickr pictures have it installed on their computers as well; but it's a good demonstration of how control affects file deletion. And while it's a step in the right direction, it's also new and therefore deserves further security analysis before being adopted on a wide scale.

We've lost the control of data on some of the computers we own, and we've lost control of our data in the cloud. We're not going to stop using Facebook and Twitter just because they're not going to delete our data when we ask them to, and we're not going to stop using Kindles and iPhones because they may delete our data when we don't want them to. But we need to take back control of data in the cloud, and projects like Vanish show us how we can.

Now we need something that will protect our data when a large corporation decides to delete it.

The Difficulty of Un-Authentication

Originally published in Threatpost, *September 28, 2009*

In computer security, a lot of effort is spent on the authentication problem. Whether it's passwords, secure tokens, secret questions, image mnemonics, or something else, engineers are continually coming up with more complicated—and hopefully more secure—ways for you to prove you are who you say you are over the Internet.

This is important stuff, as anyone with an online bank account or remote corporate network knows. But a lot less thought and work have gone into the other end of the problem: how do you tell the system on the other end of the line that you're no longer there? How do you unauthenticate yourself?

My home computer requires me to log out or turn my computer off when I want to unauthenticate. This works for me because I know enough to do it, but lots of people just leave their computer on and running when they walk away. As a result, many office computers are left logged in when people go to lunch, or when they go home for the night. This, obviously, is a security vulnerability.

The most common way to combat this is by having the system time out. I could have my computer log me out automatically after a certain period of inactivity—five minutes, for example. Getting it right requires some fine tuning, though. Log the person out too quickly, and he gets annoyed; wait too long before logging him out, and the system could be vulnerable during that time. My corporate e-mail server logs me out after 10 minutes or so, and I regularly get annoyed at my corporate e-mail system.

Some systems have experimented with a token: a USB authentication token that has to be plugged in for the computer to operate, or an RFID token that logs people out automatically when the token moves more than a certain distance from the computer. Of course, people will be prone to just leave the token plugged in to their computer all the time; but if you attach it to their car keys or the badge they have to wear at all times when walking around the office, the risk is minimized.

That's expensive, though. A research project used a Bluetooth device, like a cell phone, and measured its proximity to a computer. The system could be programmed to lock the computer if the Bluetooth device moved out of range.

Some systems log people out after every transaction. This wouldn't work for computers, but it can work for ATMs. The machine spits my card out before it gives me my cash, or just requires a card swipe, and makes sure I take it out of the machine. If I want to perform another transaction, I have to reinsert my card and enter my PIN a second time.

There's a physical analogue that everyone can explain: door locks. Does your door lock behind you when you close the door, or does it remain unlocked until you lock it? The first instance is a system that automatically logs you out, and the second requires you to log out manually. Both types of locks are sold and used, and which one you choose depends on both how you use the door and who you expect to try to break in.

Designing systems for usability is hard, especially when security is involved. Almost by definition, making something secure makes it less usable. Choosing an unauthentication method depends a lot on how the system is used as well as the threat model. You have to balance increasing security with pissing the users off, and getting that balance right takes time and testing, and is much more an art than a science.

Is Antivirus Dead?

Originally published in Information Security, *November 2009*

This essay appeared as the second half of a point/counterpoint with Marcus Ranum.

Security is never black and white. If someone asks, "for best security, should I do A or B?" the answer almost invariably is both. But security is always a trade-off. Often it's impossible to do both A and B—there's no time to do both, it's too expensive to do both, or whatever—and you have to choose. In that case, you look at A and B and you make your best choice. But it's almost always more secure to do both.

Yes, antivirus programs have been getting less effective as new viruses are more frequent and existing viruses mutate faster. Yes, antivirus companies are forever playing catch-up, trying to create signatures for new viruses. Yes, signature-based antivirus software won't protect you when a virus is new, before the signature is added to the detection program. Antivirus is by no means a panacea.

On the other hand, an antivirus program with up-to-date signatures will protect you from a lot of threats. It'll protect you against viruses, against spyware, against Trojans—against all sorts of malware. It'll run in the background, automatically, and you won't notice any performance degradation at all. And—here's the best part—it can be free. AVG won't cost you a penny. To me, this is an easy trade-off, certainly for the average computer user who clicks on attachments he probably shouldn't click on, downloads things he probably shouldn't download, and doesn't understand the finer workings of Windows Personal Firewall.

Certainly security would be improved if people used whitelisting programs such as Bit9 Parity and Savant Protection—and I personally recommend Malwarebytes' Anti-Malware—but a lot of users are going to have trouble with this. The average user will probably just swat away the "you're trying to run a program not on your whitelist" warning message or—even worse—wonder why his computer is broken when he tries to run a new piece of software. The average corporate IT department doesn't have a good idea of what software is running on all the computers within the corporation, and doesn't want the administrative overhead of managing all the change requests. And whitelists aren't a panacea, either: they don't defend against malware that attaches itself to data files (think Word macro viruses), for example.

One of the newest trends in IT is consumerization, and if you don't already know about it, you soon will. It's the idea that new technologies, the cool stuff people want, will become available for the consumer market before they become available for the business market. What it means to business is that people—employees, customers, partners—will access business networks from wherever they happen to be, with whatever hardware and software they have. Maybe it'll be the computer you gave them when you hired them. Maybe it'll be their home computer, the one their kids use. Maybe it'll be their cell phone or PDA, or a computer in a hotel's business center. Your business will have no way to know what they're using, and—more importantly—you'll have no control.

In this kind of environment, computers are going to connect to each other without a whole lot of trust between them. Untrusted computers are going to connect to untrusted networks. Trusted computers are going to connect to untrusted networks. The whole idea of "safe computing" is going to take on a whole new meaning—every man for himself. A corporate network is going to need a simple, dumb, signature-based antivirus product at the gateway of its network. And a user is going to need a similar program to protect his computer.

Bottom line: antivirus software is neither necessary nor sufficient for security, but it's still a good idea. It's not a panacea that magically makes you safe, nor is it is obsolete in the face of current threats. As countermeasures go, it's cheap, it's easy, and it's effective. I haven't dumped my antivirus program, and I have no intention of doing so anytime soon.

I don't even want an Xbox.

Virus and Protocol Scares Happen Every Day—but Don't Let Them Worry You

Originally published in the Guardian, *December 9, 2009*

Last month, researchers found a security flaw in the SSL protocol, which is used to protect sensitive web data. The protocol is used for online commerce, webmail, and social networking sites. Basically, hackers could hijack an SSL session and execute commands without the knowledge of either the client or the server. The list of affected products is enormous.

If this sounds serious to you, you're right. It is serious. Given that, what should you do now? Should you not use SSL until it's fixed, and only pay for Internet purchases over the phone? Should you download some kind of protection? Should you take some other remedial action? What?

If you read the IT press regularly, you'll see this sort of question again and again. The answer for this particular vulnerability, as for pretty much any other vulnerability you read about, is the same: do nothing. That's right, nothing. Don't panic. Don't change your behavior. Ignore the problem, and let the vendors figure it out.

There are several reasons for this. One, it's hard to figure out which vulnerabilities are serious and which are not. Vulnerabilities such as this happen multiple times a month. They affect different software, different operating systems, and different web protocols. The press either mentions them or not, somewhat randomly; just because it's in the news doesn't mean it's serious.

Two, it's hard to figure out if there's anything you can do. Many vulnerabilities affect operating systems or Internet protocols. The only sure fix would be to avoid using your computer. Some vulnerabilities have surprising consequences. The SSL vulnerability mentioned above could be used to hack Twitter. Did you expect that? I sure didn't.

Three, the odds of a particular vulnerability affecting you are small. There are a lot of fish in the Internet, and you're just one of billions.

Four, often you can't do anything. These vulnerabilities affect clients and servers, individuals and corporations. A lot of your data isn't under your direct control—it's on your web-based email servers, in some corporate database, or in a cloud computing application. If a vulnerability affects the computers running Facebook, for example, your data is at risk, whether you log in to Facebook or not.

It's much smarter to have a reasonable set of default security practices and continue doing them. This includes:

1. Install an antivirus program if you run Windows, and configure it to update daily. It doesn't matter which one you use; they're all about the same. For Windows, I like the free version of AVG Internet Security. Apple Mac and Linux users can ignore this, as virus writers target the operating system with the largest market share.

2. Configure your OS and network router properly. Microsoft's operating systems come with a lot of security enabled by default; this is good. But have someone who knows what they're doing check the configuration of your router, too.

3. Turn on automatic software updates. This is the mechanism by which your software patches itself in the background, without you having to do anything. Make sure it's turned on for your computer, OS, security software, and any applications that have the option. Yes, you have to do it for everything, as they often have separate mechanisms.

4. Show common sense regarding the Internet. This might be the hardest thing, and the most important. Know when an email is real, and when you shouldn't click on the link. Know when a website is suspicious. Know when something is amiss.

5. Perform regular backups. This is vital. If you're infected with something, you may have to reinstall your operating system and applications. Good backups ensure you don't lose your data—documents, photographs, music—if that becomes necessary.

That's basically it. I could give a longer list of safe computing practices, but this short one is likely to keep you safe. After that, trust the vendors. They spent all last month scrambling to fix the SSL vulnerability, and they'll spend all this month scrambling to fix whatever new vulnerabilities are discovered. Let that be their problem.

The Failure of Cryptography to Secure Modern Networks

Originally published in Dark Reading, *June 30, 2010*

For a while now, I've pointed out that cryptography is singularly ill-suited to solve the major network security problems of today: denial-of-service attacks, website defacement, theft of credit card numbers, identity theft, viruses and worms, DNS attacks, network penetration, and so on.

Cryptography was invented to protect communications: data in motion. This is how cryptography was used throughout most of history, and this is how the militaries of the world developed the science. Alice was the sender, Bob the receiver, and Eve the eavesdropper. Even when cryptography was used to protect stored data—data at rest—it was viewed as a form of communication. In *Applied Cryptography*, I described encrypting stored data in this way: "a stored message is a way for someone to communicate with himself through time." Data storage was just a subset of data communication.

In modern networks, the difference is much more profound. Communications are immediate and instantaneous. Encryption keys can be ephemeral, and systems like the STU-III telephone can be designed such that encryption keys are created at the beginning of a call and destroyed as soon as the call is completed. Data storage, on the other hand, occurs over time. Any encryption keys must exist as long as the encrypted data exists. And storing those keys becomes as important as storing the unencrypted data was. In a way, encryption doesn't reduce the number of secrets that must be stored securely; it just makes them much smaller.

Historically, the reason key management worked for stored data was that the key could be stored in a secure location: the human brain. People would remember keys and, barring physical and emotional attacks on the people themselves, would not divulge them. In a sense, the keys were stored in a "computer" that was not attached to any network. And there they were safe.

This whole model falls apart on the Internet. Much of the data stored on the Internet is only peripherally intended for use by people; it's primarily intended for use by other computers. And therein lies the problem. Keys can no longer be stored in people's brains. They need to be stored on the same computer, or at least the network, that the data resides on. And that is much riskier.

Let's take a concrete example: credit card databases associated with web-sites. Those databases are not encrypted because it doesn't make any sense. The whole point of storing credit card numbers on a website is so it's accessible—so each time I buy something, I don't have to type it in again. The website needs to dynamically query the database and retrieve the numbers, millions of times a day. If the database were encrypted, the website would need the key. But if the key were on the same network as the data, what would be the point of encrypting it? Access to the website equals access to the database in either case. Security is achieved by good access control on the website and database, not by encrypting the data.

The same reasoning holds true elsewhere on the Internet as well. Much of the Internet's infrastructure happens automatically, without human interven-tion. This means that any encryption keys need to reside in software on the network, making them vulnerable to attack. In many cases, the databases are queried so often that they are simply left in plaintext, because doing oth-erwise would cause significant performance degradation. Real security in these contexts comes from traditional computer security techniques, not from cryptography.

Cryptography has inherent mathematical properties that greatly favor the defender. Adding a single bit to the length of a key adds only a slight amount of work for the defender, but doubles the amount of work the attacker has to do. Doubling the key length doubles the amount of work the defender has to do (if that—I'm being approximate here), but increases the attacker's workload expo-nentially. For many years, we have exploited that mathematical imbalance.

Computer security is much more balanced. There'll be a new attack, and a new defense, and a new attack, and a new defense. It's an arms race between attacker and defender. And it's a very fast arms race. New vulnerabilities are discovered all the time. The balance can tip from defender to attacker over-night, and back again the night after. Computer security defenses are inher-ently very fragile.

Unfortunately, this is the model we're stuck with. No matter how good the cryptography is, there is some other way to break into the system. Recall how the FBI read the PGP-encrypted email of a suspected Mafia boss several years ago. They didn't try to break PGP; they simply installed a keyboard sniffer on the target's computer. Notice that SSL- and TLS-encrypted web communications are increasingly irrelevant in protecting credit card numbers; criminals prefer to steal them by the hundreds of thousands from back-end databases.

On the Internet, communications security is much less important than the security of the endpoints. And increasingly, we can't rely on cryptography to solve our security problems.

The Story behind the Stuxnet Virus

Originally published in Forbes, *October 7, 2010*

Computer security experts are often surprised at which stories get picked up by the mainstream media. Sometimes it makes no sense. Why this particular data breach, vulnerability, or worm and not others? Sometimes it's obvious. In the case of Stuxnet, there's a great story.

As the story goes, the Stuxnet worm was designed and released by a government—the US and Israel are the most common suspects—specifically to attack the Bushehr nuclear power plant in Iran. How could anyone not report that? It combines computer attacks, nuclear power, spy agencies and a country that's a pariah to much of the world. The only problem with the story is that it's almost entirely speculation.

Here's what we do know: Stuxnet is an Internet worm that infects Windows computers. It primarily spreads via USB sticks, which allows it to get into computers and networks not normally connected to the Internet. Once inside a network, it uses a variety of mechanisms to propagate to other machines within that network and gain privilege once it has infected those machines. These mechanisms include both known and patched vulnerabilities, and four "zero-day exploits": vulnerabilities that were unknown and unpatched when the worm was released. (All the infection vulnerabilities have since been patched.)

Stuxnet doesn't actually do anything on those infected Windows computers, because they're not the real target. What Stuxnet looks for is a particular model of Programmable Logic Controller (PLC) made by Siemens (the press often refers to these as SCADA systems, which is technically incorrect). These are small embedded industrial control systems that run all sorts of automated processes: on factory floors, in chemical plants, in oil refineries, at pipelines—and, yes, in nuclear power plants. These PLCs are often controlled by computers, and Stuxnet looks for Siemens SIMATIC WinCC/ Step 7 controller software.

If it doesn't find one, it does nothing. If it does, it infects it using yet another unknown and unpatched vulnerability, this one in the controller software. Then it reads and changes particular bits of data in the controlled PLCs. It's impossible to predict the effects of this without knowing what the PLC is doing and how it is programmed, and that programming can be unique based on the application. But the changes are very specific, leading many to believe that Stuxnet is targeting a specific PLC, or a specific group of PLCs, performing a specific function in a specific location—and that Stuxnet's authors knew exactly what they were targeting.

It's already infected more than 50,000 Windows computers, and Siemens has reported 14 infected control systems, many in Germany. (These numbers were certainly out of date as soon as I typed them.) We don't know of any physical damage Stuxnet has caused, although there are rumors that it was responsible for the failure of India's INSAT-4B satellite in July. We believe that it did infect the Bushehr plant.

All the anti-virus programs detect and remove Stuxnet from Windows systems.

Stuxnet was first discovered in late June, although there's speculation that it was released a year earlier. As worms go, it's very complex and got more complex over time. In addition to the multiple vulnerabilities that it exploits, it installs its own driver into Windows. These have to be signed, of course, but Stuxnet used a stolen legitimate certificate. Interestingly, the stolen certificate was revoked on July 16, and a Stuxnet variant with a different stolen certificate was discovered on July 17.

Over time the attackers swapped out modules that didn't work and replaced them with new ones—perhaps as Stuxnet made its way to its intended target. Those certificates first appeared in January. USB propagation, in March.

Stuxnet has two ways to update itself. It checks back to two control servers, one in Malaysia and the other in Denmark, but also uses a peer-to-peer update system: When two Stuxnet infections encounter each other, they compare versions and make sure they both have the most recent one. It also has a kill date of June 24, 2012. On that date, the worm will stop spreading and delete itself.

We don't know who wrote Stuxnet. We don't know why. We don't know what the target is, or if Stuxnet reached it. But you can see why there is so much speculation that it was created by a government.

Stuxnet doesn't act like a criminal worm. It doesn't spread indiscriminately. It doesn't steal credit card information or account login credentials. It doesn't herd infected computers into a botnet. It uses multiple zero-day vulnerabilities. A criminal group would be smarter to create different worm variants and use one in each. Stuxnet performs sabotage. It doesn't threaten sabotage, like a criminal organization intent on extortion might.

Stuxnet was expensive to create. Estimates are that it took 8 to 10 people six months to write. There's also the lab setup—surely any organization that goes to all this trouble would test the thing before releasing it—and the intelligence gathering to know exactly how to target it. Additionally, zero-day exploits are valuable. They're hard to find, and they can only be used once. Whoever wrote Stuxnet was willing to spend a lot of money to ensure that whatever job it was intended to do would be done.

None of this points to the Bushehr nuclear power plant in Iran, though. Best I can tell, this rumor was started by Ralph Langner, a security researcher from Germany. He labeled his theory "highly speculative," and based it primarily on the facts that Iran had an usually high number of infections (the rumor that it had the most infections of any country seems not to be true), that the Bushehr nuclear plant is a juicy target, and that some of the other countries with high infection rates—India, Indonesia, and Pakistan—are countries where the same Russian contractor involved in Bushehr is also involved. This rumor moved into the computer press and then into the mainstream press, where it became the accepted story, without any of the original caveats.

Once a theory takes hold, though, it's easy to find more evidence. The word "myrtus" appears in the worm: an artifact that the compiler left, possibly by accident. That's the myrtle plant. Of course, that doesn't mean that druids wrote Stuxnet. According to the story, it refers to Queen Esther, also known as Hadassah; she saved the Persian Jews from genocide in the 4th century B.C. "Hadassah" means "myrtle" in Hebrew.

Stuxnet also sets a registry value of "19790509" to alert new copies of Stuxnet that the computer has already been infected. It's rather obviously a date, but instead of looking at the gazillion things—large and small—that happened on that the date, the story insists it refers to the date Persian Jew Habib Elghanain was executed in Tehran for spying for Israel.

Sure, these markers could point to Israel as the author. On the other hand, Stuxnet's authors were uncommonly thorough about not leaving clues in their code; the markers could have been deliberately planted by someone who wanted to frame Israel. Or they could have been deliberately planted by Israel, who wanted us to think they were planted by someone who wanted to frame Israel. Once you start walking down this road, it's impossible to know when to stop.

Another number found in Stuxnet is 0xDEADF007. Perhaps that means "Dead Fool" or "Dead Foot," a term that refers to an airplane engine failure. Perhaps this means Stuxnet is trying to cause the targeted system to fail. Or perhaps not. Still, a targeted worm designed to cause a specific sabotage seems to be the most likely explanation.

If that's the case, why is Stuxnet so sloppily targeted? Why doesn't Stuxnet erase itself when it realizes it's not in the targeted network? When it infects a network via USB stick, it's supposed to only spread to three additional computers and to erase itself after 21 days—but it doesn't do that. A mistake in programming, or a feature in the code not enabled? Maybe we're not supposed to reverse engineer the target. By allowing Stuxnet to spread globally, its authors committed collateral damage worldwide. From a foreign policy perspective, that seems dumb. But maybe Stuxnet's authors didn't care.

My guess is that Stuxnet's authors, and its target, will forever remain a mystery.

The Dangers of a Software Monoculture

Originally published in Information Security, *November 2010*

This essay appeared as the first half of a point/counterpoint with Marcus Ranum.

In 2003, a group of security experts—myself included—published a paper saying that 1) software monocultures are dangerous and 2) Microsoft, being the largest creator of monocultures out there, is the most dangerous. Marcus Ranum responded with an essay that basically said we were full of it. Now, eight years later, Marcus and I thought it would be interesting to revisit the debate.

The basic problem with a monoculture is that it's all vulnerable to the same attack. The Irish Potato Famine of 1845–9 is perhaps the most famous monoculture-related disaster. The Irish planted only one variety of potato, and the genetically identical potatoes succumbed to a rot caused by *Phytophthora infestans*. Compare that with the diversity of potatoes traditionally grown in

South America, each one adapted to the particular soil and climate of its home, and you can see the security value in heterogeneity.

Similar risks exist in networked computer systems. If everyone is using the same operating system or the same applications software or the same networking protocol, and a security vulnerability is discovered in that OS or software or protocol, a single exploit can affect everyone. This is the problem of large-scale Internet worms: many have affected millions of computers on the Internet.

If our networking environment weren't homogeneous, a single worm couldn't do so much damage. We'd be more like South America's potato crop than Ireland's. Conclusion: monoculture is bad; embrace diversity or die along with everyone else.

This analysis makes sense as far as it goes, but suffers from three basic flaws. The first is the assumption that our IT monoculture is as simple as the potato's. When the particularly virulent Storm worm hit, it only affected from 1–10 million of its billion-plus possible victims. Why? Because some computers were running updated antivirus software, or were within locked-down networks, or whatever. Two computers might be running the same OS or applications software, but they'll be inside different networks with different firewalls and IDSs and router policies, they'll have different antivirus programs and different patch levels and different configurations, and they'll be in different parts of the Internet connected to different servers running different services. As Marcus pointed out back in 2003, they'll be a little bit different themselves. That's one of the reasons large-scale Internet worms don't infect everyone—as well as the network's ability to quickly develop and deploy patches, new antivirus signatures, new IPS signatures, and so on.

The second flaw in the monoculture analysis is that it downplays the cost of diversity. Sure, it would be great if a corporate IT department ran half Windows and half Linux, or half Apache and half Microsoft IIS, but doing so would require more expertise and cost more money. It wouldn't cost twice the expertise and money—there is some overlap—but there are significant economies of scale that result from everyone using the same software and configuration. A single operating system locked down by experts is far more secure than two operating systems configured by sysadmins who aren't so expert. Sometimes, as Mark Twain said: "Put all your eggs in one basket, and then guard that basket!"

The third flaw is that you can only get a limited amount of diversity by using two operating systems, or routers from three vendors. South American potato diversity comes from hundreds of different varieties. Genetic diversity comes from millions of different genomes. In monoculture terms, two is little better than one. Even worse, since a network's security is primarily the minimum of the security of its components, a diverse network is less secure because it is vulnerable to attacks against any of its heterogeneous components.

Some monoculture is necessary in computer networks. As long as we have to talk to each other, we're all going to have to use TCP/IP, HTML, PDF, and all sorts of other standards and protocols that guarantee interoperability. Yes, there will be different implementations of the same protocol—and this is a good thing—but that won't protect you completely. You can't be too different from everyone else on the Internet, because if you were, you couldn't be on the Internet.

Species basically have two options for propagating their genes: the lobster strategy and the avian strategy. Lobsters lay 5,000 to 40,000 eggs at a time, and essentially ignore them. Only a minuscule percentage of the hatchlings live to be four weeks old, but that's sufficient to ensure gene propagation; from every 50,000 eggs, an average of two lobsters is expected to survive to legal size. Conversely, birds produce only a few eggs at a time, then spend a lot of effort ensuring that most of the hatchlings survive. In ecology, this is known as r/K selection theory. In either case, each of those offspring varies slightly genetically, so if a new threat arises, some of them will be more likely to survive. But even so, extinctions happen regularly on our planet; neither strategy is foolproof.

Our IT infrastructure is a lot more like a bird than a lobster. Yes, monoculture is dangerous and diversity is important. But investing time and effort in ensuring our current infrastructure's survival is even more important.

How Changing Technology Affects Security

Originally published in IEEE Security & Privacy, *March/April 2012*

Security is a tradeoff, a balancing act between attacker and defender. Unfortunately, that balance is never static. Changes in technology affect both sides. Society uses new technologies to decrease what I call the *scope of defection*—what attackers can get away with—and attackers use new technologies to increase it. What's interesting is the difference between how the two groups incorporate new technologies.

Changes in security systems can be slow. Society has to implement any new security technology as a group, which implies agreement and coordination and—in some instances—a lengthy bureaucratic procurement process. Meanwhile, an attacker can just use the new technology. For example, at the end of the horse-and-buggy era, it was easier for a bank robber to use his new motorcar as a getaway vehicle than it was for a town's police department to decide it needed a police car, get the budget to buy one, choose which one to buy, buy it, and then develop training and policies for it. And if only one police department did this, the bank robber could just move to another town. Defectors are more agile and adaptable, making them much better at being early adopters of new technology.

We saw it in law enforcement's initial inability to deal with Internet crime. Criminals were simply more flexible. Traditional criminal organizations like the Mafia didn't immediately move onto the Internet; instead, new Internet-savvy criminals sprung up. They set up websites like CardersMarket and DarkMarket, and established new organized crime groups within a decade or so of the Internet's commercialization. Meanwhile, law enforcement simply didn't have the organizational fluidity to adapt as quickly. Cities couldn't fire their old-school detectives and replace them with people who understood the Internet. The detectives' natural inertia and tendency to sweep problems under the rug slowed things even more. They spent the better part of a decade playing catch-up.

There's one more problem: defenders are in what military strategist Carl von Clausewitz calls "the position of the interior." They have to defend against every possible attack, while the defector only has to find one flaw that allows one way through the defenses. As systems get more complicated due to technology, more attacks become possible. This means defectors have a first-mover advantage; they get to try the new attack first. Consequently, society is constantly responding: shoe scanners in response to the shoe bomber, harder-to-counterfeit money in response to better counterfeiting technologies, better antivirus software to combat new computer viruses, and so on. The attacker's clear advantage increases the scope of defection even further.

Of course, there are exceptions. There are technologies that immediately benefit the defender and are of no use at all to the attacker—for example, fingerprint technology allowed police to identify suspects after they left the crime scene and didn't provide any corresponding benefit to criminals. The same thing happened with immobilizing technology for cars, alarm systems for houses, and computer authentication technologies. Some technologies benefit both but still give more advantage to the defenders. The radio allowed street policemen to communicate remotely, which increased our level of safety more than the corresponding downside of criminals communicating remotely endangers us.

Still, we tend to be reactive in security, and only implement new measures in response to an increased scope of defection. We're slow about doing it and even slower about getting it right.

The Importance of Security Engineering

Originally published in Schneier on Security, *August 28, 2012*

A shorter version of this essay appeared in the September/October 2012 issue of IEEE Security & Privacy.

In May, neuroscientist and popular author Sam Harris and I debated the issue of profiling Muslims at airport security. We each wrote essays, then went back and forth on the issue. I don't recommend reading the entire discussion; we spent 14,000 words talking past each other. But what's interesting is how our debate illustrates the differences between a security engineer and an intelligent layman. Harris was uninterested in the detailed analysis required to understand a security system and unwilling to accept that security engineering is a specialized discipline with a body of knowledge and relevant expertise. He trusted his intuition.

Many people have researched how intuition fails us in security: Paul Slovic and Bill Burns on risk perception, Daniel Kahneman on cognitive biases in general, Rick Walsh on folk computer-security models. I've written about the psychology of security, and Daniel Gartner has written more. Basically, our intuitions are based on things like antiquated fight-or-flight models, and these increasingly fail in our technological world.

This problem isn't unique to computer security, or even security in general. But this misperception about security matters now more than it ever has. We're no longer asking people to make security choices only for themselves and their businesses; we need them to make security choices as a matter of public policy. And getting it wrong has increasingly bad consequences.

Computers and the Internet have collided with public policy. The entertainment industry wants to enforce copyright. Internet companies want to continue freely spying on users. Law-enforcement wants its own laws imposed on the Internet: laws that make surveillance easier, prohibit anonymity, mandate the removal of objectionable images and texts, and require ISPs to retain data about their customers' Internet activities. Militaries want laws regarding cyber weapons, laws enabling wholesale surveillance, and laws mandating an Internet kill switch. "Security" is now a catch-all excuse for all sorts of authoritarianism, as well as for boondoggles and corporate profiteering.

Cory Doctorow recently spoke about the coming war on general-purpose computing. I talked about it in terms of the entertainment industry and Jonathan Zittrain discussed it more generally, but Doctorow sees it as a much broader issue. Preventing people from copying digital files is only the first skirmish; just wait until the DEA wants to prevent chemical printers from making certain drugs, or the FBI wants to prevent 3D printers from making guns.

I'm not here to debate the merits of any of these policies, but instead to point out that people will debate them. Elected officials will be expected to understand security implications, both good and bad, and will make laws based on that understanding. And if they aren't able to understand security engineering, or even accept that there is such a thing, the result will be ineffective and harmful policies.

So what do we do? We need to establish security engineering as a valid profession in the minds of the public and policy makers. This is less about certifications and (heaven forbid) licensing, and more about perception—and cultivating a security mindset. Amateurs produce amateur security, which costs more in dollars, time, liberty, and dignity while giving us less—or even no—security. We need everyone to know that.

We also need to engage with real-world security problems, and apply our expertise to the variety of technical and socio-technical systems that affect broader society. Everything involves computers, and almost everything involves the Internet. More and more, computer security *is* security.

Finally, and perhaps most importantly, we need to learn how to talk about security engineering to a non-technical audience. We need to convince policy makers to follow a logical approach instead of an emotional one—an approach that includes threat modeling, failure analysis, searching for unintended consequences, and everything else in an engineer's approach to design. Powerful lobbying forces are attempting to force security policies on society, largely for non-security reasons, and sometimes in secret. We need to stand up for security.

Technologies of Surveillance

Originally published in Schneier on Security, *March 5, 2013*

An edited version of this essay appeared in the New York Daily News.

It's a new day for the New York Police Department, with technology increasingly informing the way cops do their jobs. With innovation comes new possibilities but also new concerns.

For one, the NYPD is testing a new type of security apparatus that uses terahertz radiation to detect guns under clothing from a distance. As Police Commissioner Ray Kelly explained to the *Daily News* back in January, If something is obstructing the flow of that radiation—a weapon, for example—the device will highlight that object.

Ignore, for a moment, the glaring constitutional concerns, which make the stop-and-frisk debate pale in comparison: virtual strip-searching, evasion of probable cause, potential racial profiling. Organizations like the American Civil Liberties Union are all over those, even though their opposition probably won't make a difference. We're scared of both terrorism and crime, even as the risks decrease; and when we're scared, we're willing to give up all sorts of freedoms to assuage our fears. Often, the courts go along.

A more pressing question is the effectiveness of technologies that are supposed to make us safer. These include the NYPD's Domain Awareness System, developed by Microsoft, which aims to integrate massive quantities of data to alert cops when a crime may be taking place. Other innovations are surely in the pipeline, all promising to make the city safer. But are we being sold a bill of goods?

For example, press reports make the gun-detection machine look good. We see images from the camera that pretty clearly show a gun outlined under someone's clothing. From that, we can imagine how this technology can spot gun-toting criminals as they enter government buildings or terrorize neighborhoods. Given the right inputs, we naturally construct these stories in our heads. The technology seems like a good idea, we conclude.

The reality is that we reach these conclusions much in the same way we decide that, say, drinking Mountain Dew makes you look cool. These are, after all, the products of for-profit companies, pushed by vendors looking to make sales. As such, they're marketed no less aggressively than soda pop and deodorant. Those images of criminals with concealed weapons were carefully created both to demonstrate maximum effectiveness and push our fear buttons. These companies deliberately craft stories of their effectiveness, both through advertising and placement on television and movies, where police are often showed using high-powered tools to catch high-value targets with minimum complication.

The truth is that many of these technologies are nowhere near as reliable as claimed. They end up costing us gazillions of dollars and open the door for significant abuse. Of course, the vendors hope that by the time we realize this, they're too embedded in our security culture to be removed.

The current poster child for this sort of morass is the airport full-body scanner. Rushed into airports after the underwear bomber Umar Farouk Abdulmutallab nearly blew up a Northwest Airlines flight in 2009, they made us feel better, even though they don't work very well and, ironically, wouldn't have caught Abdulmutallab with his underwear bomb. Both the Transportation Security Administration and vendors repeatedly lied about their effectiveness, whether they stored images, and how safe they were. In January, finally, backscatter X-ray scanners were removed from airports because the company who made them couldn't sufficiently blur the images so they didn't show travelers naked. Now, only millimeter-wave full-body scanners remain.

Another example is closed-circuit television (CCTV) cameras. These have been marketed as a technological solution to both crime and understaffed police and security organizations. London, for example, is rife with them, and New York has plenty of its own. To many, it seems apparent that they make us safer, despite cries of Big Brother. The problem is that in study after study, researchers have concluded that they don't.

Counterterrorist data mining and fusion centers: nowhere near as useful as those selling the technologies claimed. It's the same with DNA testing and fingerprint technologies: both are far less accurate than most people believe. Even torture has been oversold as a security system—this time by a government instead of a company—despite decades of evidence that it doesn't work and makes us all less safe.

It's not that these technologies are totally useless. It's that they're expensive, and none of them is a panacea. Maybe there's a use for a terahertz radar, and maybe the benefits of the technology are worth the costs. But we should not forget that there's a profit motive at work, too.

When Technology Overtakes Security

Originally published in Wired, *March 14, 2013*

A core, not side, effect of technology is its ability to magnify power and multiply force—for both attackers and defenders. One side creates ceramic handguns, laser-guided missiles, and new-identity theft techniques, while the other side creates anti-missile defense systems, fingerprint databases, and automatic facial recognition systems.

The problem is that it's not balanced: Attackers generally benefit from new security technologies before defenders do. They have a first-mover advantage. They're more nimble and adaptable than defensive institutions like police forces. They're not limited by bureaucracy, laws, or ethics. They can evolve faster. And entropy is on their side—it's easier to destroy something than it is to prevent, defend against, or recover from that destruction.

For the most part, though, society still wins. The bad guys simply can't do enough damage to destroy the underlying social system. The question for us is: can society still maintain security as technology becomes more advanced?

I don't think it can.

Because the damage attackers can cause becomes greater as technology becomes more powerful. Guns become more harmful, explosions become bigger, malware becomes more pernicious… and so on. A single attacker, or small group of attackers, can cause more destruction than ever before.

This is exactly why the whole post-9/11 weapons-of-mass-destruction debate was so overwrought: Terrorists are scary, terrorists flying airplanes into buildings are even scarier, and the thought of a terrorist with a nuclear bomb is absolutely terrifying.

As the destructive power of individual actors and fringe groups increases, so do the calls for—and society's acceptance of—increased security.

Rethinking Security

Traditional security largely works "after the fact." We tend not to ban or restrict the objects that can do harm; instead, we punish the people who do harm with objects. There are exceptions, of course, but they're exactly that: exceptions. This system works as long as society can tolerate the destructive effects of those objects (for example, allowing people to own baseball bats and arresting them after they use them in a riot is only viable if society can tolerate the potential for riots).

When that isn't enough, we resort to "before-the-fact" security measures. These come in two basic varieties: **general surveillance** of people in an effort to stop them before they do damage, and **specific interdictions** in an effort to stop people from using those technologies to do damage.

But these measures work better at keeping dangerous technologies out of the hands of amateurs than at keeping them out of the hands of professionals.

And in the global interconnected world we live in, they're not anywhere close to foolproof. Still, a climate of fear causes governments to try. Lots of technologies are already restricted: entire classes of drugs, entire classes of munitions, explosive materials, biological agents. There are age restrictions on vehicles and training restrictions on complex systems like aircraft. We're already almost entirely living in a surveillance state, though we don't realize it or won't admit it to ourselves. This will only get worse as technology advances... today's Ph.D. theses are tomorrow's high-school science-fair projects.

Increasingly, broad prohibitions on technologies, constant ubiquitous surveillance, and *Minority Report*-like preemptive security will become the norm. We can debate the effectiveness of various security measures in different circumstances. But the problem isn't that these security measures won't work—even as they shred our freedoms and liberties—it's that no security is perfect.

Because sooner or later, the technology will exist for a hobbyist to explode a nuclear weapon, print a lethal virus from a bio-printer, or turn our electronic infrastructure into a vehicle for large-scale murder. We'll have the technology eventually to annihilate ourselves in great numbers, and sometime after, that technology will become cheap enough to be easy.

As it gets easier for one member of a group to destroy the entire group, and the group size gets larger, the odds of *someone* in the group doing it approaches certainty. Our global interconnectedness means that our group size encompasses everyone on the planet, and since government hasn't kept up, we have to worry about the weakest-controlled member of the weakest-controlled country. Is this a fundamental limitation of technological advancement, one that could end civilization? First our fears grip us so strongly that, thinking about the short term, we willingly embrace a police state in a desperate attempt to keep us safe; then, someone goes off and destroys us anyway?

If security won't work in the end, what is the solution?

Resilience—building systems able to survive unexpected and devastating attacks—is the best answer we have right now. We need to recognize that large-scale attacks will happen, that society can survive more than we give it credit for, and that we can design systems to survive these sorts of attacks. Calling terrorism an existential threat is ridiculous in a country where more people die each month in car crashes than died in the 9/11 terrorist attacks.

If the US can survive the destruction of an entire city—witness New Orleans after Hurricane Katrina or even New York after Sandy—we need to start acting like it, and planning for it. Still, it's hard to see how resilience buys us anything but additional time. Technology will continue to advance, and right now we don't know how to adapt any defenses—including resilience—fast enough.

We need a more flexible and rationally reactive approach to these problems and new regimes of trust for our information-interconnected world. We're going to have to figure this out if we want to survive, and I'm not sure how many decades we have left.

7

Travel and Security

Crossing Borders with Laptops and PDAs ▬

Originally published in the Guardian, *May 15, 2008*

L ast month a US court ruled that border agents can search your laptop, or any other electronic device, when you're entering the country. They can take your computer and download its entire contents, or keep it for several days. Customs and Border Patrol has not published any rules regarding this practice, and I and others have written a letter to Congress urging it to investigate and regulate this practice.

But the US is not alone. British customs agents search laptops for pornography. And there are reports on the Internet of this sort of thing happening at other borders, too. You might not like it, but it's a fact. So how do you protect yourself?

Encrypting your entire hard drive, something you should certainly do for security in case your computer is lost or stolen, won't work here. The border agent is likely to start this whole process with a "please type in your password." Of course you can refuse, but the agent can search you further, detain you longer, refuse you entry into the country and otherwise ruin your day.

You're going to have to hide your data. Set a portion of your hard drive to be encrypted with a different key—even if you also encrypt your entire hard drive—and keep your sensitive data there. Lots of programs allow you to do this. I use PGPDisk (from pgp.com). TrueCrypt (truecrypt.org) is also good, and free.

While customs agents might poke around on your laptop, they're unlikely to find the encrypted partition. (You can make the icon invisible, for some added protection.) And if they download the contents of your hard drive to examine later, you won't care.

Be sure to choose a strong encryption password. Details are too complicated for a quick tip, but basically anything easy to remember is easy to guess. (My advice is at tinyurl.com/4f8z4n.) Unfortunately, this isn't a perfect solution. Your computer might have left a copy of the password on the disk somewhere, and (as I also describe at the above link) smart forensic software will find it.

So your best defense is to clean up your laptop. A customs agent can't read what you don't have. You don't need five years' worth of email and client data. You don't need your old love letters and those photos (you know the ones I'm talking about). Delete everything you don't absolutely need. And use a secure file erasure program to do it. While you're at it, delete your browser's cookies, cache and browsing history. It's nobody's business what websites you've visited. And turn your computer off—don't just put it to sleep—before you go through customs; that deletes other things. Think of all this as the last thing to do before you stow your electronic devices for landing. Some companies now give their employees forensically clean laptops for travel, and have them download any sensitive data over a virtual private network once they've entered the country. They send any work back the same way, and delete everything again before crossing the border to go home. This is a good idea if you can do it.

If you can't, consider putting your sensitive data on a USB drive or even a camera memory card: even 16GB cards are reasonably priced these days. Encrypt it, of course, because it's easy to lose something that small. Slip it in your pocket, and it's likely to remain unnoticed even if the customs agent pokes through your laptop. If someone does discover it, you can try saying: "I don't know what's on there. My boss told me to give it to the head of the New York office." If you've chosen a strong encryption password, you won't care if he confiscates it.

Lastly, don't forget your phone and PDA. Customs agents can search those too: emails, your phone book, your calendar. Unfortunately, there's nothing you can do here except delete things.

I know this all sounds like work, and that it's easier to just ignore everything here and hope you don't get searched. Today, the odds are in your favor. But new forensic tools are making automatic searches easier and easier, and the recent US court ruling is likely to embolden other countries. It's better to be safe than sorry.

The TSA's Useless Photo ID Rules

Originally published in the Los Angeles Times, *August 28, 2008*

The TSA is tightening its photo ID rules at airport security. Previously, people with expired IDs or who claimed to have lost their IDs were subjected to secondary screening. Then the Transportation Security Administration realized that meant someone on the government's no-fly list—the list that is supposed to keep our planes safe from terrorists—could just fly with no ID.

Now, people without ID must also answer personal questions from their credit history to ascertain their identity. The TSA will keep records of who those ID-less people are, too, in case they're trying to probe the system.

This may seem like an improvement, except that the photo ID requirement is a joke. Anyone on the no-fly list can easily fly whenever he wants. Even worse, the whole concept of matching passenger names against a list of bad guys has negligible security value.

How to fly, even if you are on the no-fly list: Buy a ticket in some innocent person's name. At home, before your flight, check in online and print out your boarding pass. Then, save that web page as a PDF and use Adobe Acrobat to change the name on the boarding pass to your own. Print it again. At the airport, use the fake boarding pass and your valid ID to get through security. At the gate, use the real boarding pass in the fake name to board your flight.

The problem is that it is unverified passenger names that get checked against the no-fly list. At security checkpoints, the TSA just matches IDs to whatever is printed on the boarding passes. The airline checks boarding passes against tickets when people board the plane. But because no one checks ticketed names against IDs, the security breaks down.

This vulnerability isn't new. It isn't even subtle. I wrote about it in 2003, and again in 2006. I asked Kip Hawley, who runs the TSA, about it in 2007. Today, any terrorist smart enough to Google "print your own boarding pass" can bypass the no-fly list.

This gaping security hole would bother me more if the very idea of a no-fly list weren't so ineffective. The system is based on the faulty notion that the feds have this master list of terrorists, and all we have to do is keep the people on the list off the planes.

That's just not true. The no-fly list—a list of people so dangerous they are not allowed to fly yet so innocent we can't arrest them—and the less dangerous "watch list" contain a combined 1 million names representing the identities and aliases of an estimated 400,000 people. There aren't that many terrorists out there; if there were, we would be feeling their effects.

Almost all of the people stopped by the no-fly list are false positives. It catches innocents such as Ted Kennedy, whose name is similar to someone's on the list, and Yusuf Islam (formerly Cat Stevens), who was on the list but no one knew why.

The no-fly list is a Kafkaesque nightmare for the thousands of innocent Americans who are harassed and detained every time they fly. Put on the list by unidentified government officials, they can't get off. They can't challenge the TSA about their status or prove their innocence. (The US 9th Circuit Court of Appeals decided this month that no-fly passengers can sue the FBI, but that strategy hasn't been tried yet.)

But even if these lists were complete and accurate, they wouldn't work. Timothy McVeigh, the Unabomber, the D.C. snipers, the London subway bombers and most of the 9/11 terrorists weren't on any list before they committed their terrorist acts. And if a terrorist wants to know if he's on a list, the TSA has approved a convenient, $100 service that allows him to figure it out: the Clear program, which issues IDs to "trusted travelers" to speed them through security lines. Just apply for a Clear card; if you get one, you're not on the list.

In the end, the photo ID requirement is based on the myth that we can somehow correlate identity with intent. We can't. And instead of wasting money trying, we would be far safer as a nation if we invested in intelligence, investigation and emergency response—security measures that aren't based on a guess about a terrorist target or tactic.

That's the TSA: Not doing the right things. Not even doing right the things it does.

The Two Classes of Airport Contraband

Originally published in Wired News, *September 18, 2008*

Airport security found a jar of pasta sauce in my luggage last month. It was a 6-ounce jar, above the limit; the official confiscated it, because allowing it on the airplane with me would have been too dangerous. And to demonstrate how dangerous he really thought that jar was, he blithely tossed it in a nearby bin of similar liquid bottles and sent me on my way.

There are two classes of contraband at airport security checkpoints: the class that will get you in trouble if you try to bring it on an airplane, and the class that will cheerily be taken away from you if you try to bring it on an airplane. This difference is important: Making security screeners confiscate anything from that second class is a waste of time. All it does is harm innocents; it doesn't stop terrorists at all.

Let me explain. If you're caught at airport security with a bomb or a gun, the screeners aren't just going to take it away from you. They're going to call the police, and you're going to be stuck for a few hours answering a lot of awkward questions. You may be arrested, and you'll almost certainly miss your flight. At best, you're going to have a very unpleasant day.

This is why articles about how screeners don't catch every—or even a majority—of guns and bombs that go through the checkpoints don't bother me. The screeners don't have to be perfect; they just have to be good enough. No terrorist is going to base his plot on getting a gun through airport security if there's a decent chance of getting caught, because the consequences of getting caught are too great.

Contrast that with a terrorist plot that requires a 12-ounce bottle of liquid. There's no evidence that the London liquid bombers actually had a workable plot, but assume for the moment they did. If some copycat terrorists try to bring their liquid bomb through airport security and the screeners catch them—like they caught me with my bottle of pasta sauce—the terrorists can simply try again. They can try again and again. They can keep trying until they succeed. Because there are no consequences to trying and failing, the screeners have to be 100 percent effective. Even if they slip up one in a hundred times, the plot can succeed.

The same is true for knitting needles, pocketknives, scissors, corkscrews, cigarette lighters and whatever else the airport screeners are confiscating this week. If there's no consequence to getting caught with it, then confiscating it only hurts innocent people. At best, it mildly annoys the terrorists.

To fix this, airport security has to make a choice. If something is dangerous, treat it as dangerous and treat anyone who tries to bring it on as potentially dangerous. If it's not dangerous, then stop trying to keep it off airplanes. Trying to have it both ways just distracts the screeners from actually making us safer.

Fixing Airport Security

Originally published in the New York Daily News, *June 24, 2009*

It's been months since the Transportation Security Administration has had a permanent director. If, during the job interview (no, I didn't get one), President Obama asked me how I'd fix airport security in one sentence, I would reply: "Get rid of the photo ID check, and return passenger screening to pre-9/11 levels."

Okay, that's a joke. While showing ID, taking your shoes off and throwing away your water bottles isn't making us much safer, I don't expect the Obama administration to roll back those security measures anytime soon. Airport security is more about CYA than anything else: defending against what the terrorists did last time.

But the administration can't risk appearing as if it facilitated a terrorist attack, no matter how remote the possibility, so those annoyances are probably here to stay.

This would be my real answer: "Establish accountability and transparency for airport screening." And if I had another sentence: "Airports are one of the places where Americans, and visitors to America, are most likely to interact with a law enforcement officer—and yet no one knows what rights travelers have or how to exercise those rights."

Obama has repeatedly talked about increasing openness and transparency in government, and it's time to bring transparency to the Transportation Security Administration (TSA).

Let's start with the no-fly and watch lists. Right now, everything about them is secret: You can't find out if you're on one, or who put you there and why, and you can't clear your name if you're innocent. This Kafkaesque scenario is so un-American it's embarrassing. Obama should make the no-fly list subject to judicial review.

Then, move on to the checkpoints themselves. What are our rights? What powers do the TSA officers have? If we're asked "friendly" questions by behavioral detection officers, are we allowed not to answer? If we object to the rough handling of ourselves or our belongings, can the TSA official retaliate against us by putting us on a watch list? Obama should make the rules clear and explicit, and allow people to bring legal action against the TSA for violating those rules; otherwise, airport checkpoints will remain a Constitution-free zone in our country.

Next, Obama should refuse to use unfunded mandates to sneak expensive security measures past Congress. The Secure Flight program is the worst offender. Airlines are being forced to spend billions of dollars redesigning their reservations systems to accommodate the TSA's demands to preapprove every passenger before he or she is allowed to board an airplane. These costs are borne by us, in the form of higher ticket prices, even though we never see them explicitly listed.

Maybe Secure Flight is a good use of our money; maybe it isn't. But let's have debates like that in the open, as part of the budget process, where it belongs.

And finally, Obama should mandate that airport security be solely about terrorism, and not a general-purpose security checkpoint to catch everyone from pot smokers to deadbeat dads.

The Constitution provides us, both Americans and visitors to America, with strong protections against invasive police searches. Two exceptions come into play at airport security checkpoints. The first is "implied consent," which means that you cannot refuse to be searched; your consent is implied when you purchased your ticket. And the second is "plain view," which means that if the TSA officer happens to see something unrelated to airport security while screening you, he is allowed to act on that.

Both of these principles are well established and make sense, but it's their combination that turns airport security checkpoints into police-state-like checkpoints.

The TSA should limit its searches to bombs and weapons and leave general policing to the police—where we know courts and the Constitution still apply.

None of these changes will make airports any less safe, but they will go a long way to de-ratcheting the culture of fear, restoring the presumption of innocence and reassuring Americans, and the rest of the world, that—as Obama said in his inauguration speech—"we reject as false the choice between our safety and our ideals."

Laptop Security while Crossing Borders

Originally published in Wired News, *July 15, 2009*

Last year, I wrote about the increasing propensity for governments, including the US and Great Britain, to search the contents of people's laptops at customs. What we know is still based on anecdote, as no country has clarified the rules about what their customs officers are and are not allowed to do, and what rights people have.

Companies and individuals have dealt with this problem in several ways, from keeping sensitive data off laptops traveling internationally, to storing the data—encrypted, of course—on websites and then downloading it at the destination. I have never liked either solution. I do a lot of work on the road, and need to carry all sorts of data with me all the time. It's a lot of data, and downloading it can take a long time. Also, I like to work on long international flights.

There's another solution, one that works with whole-disk encryption products like PGPDisk (I'm on PGP's advisory board), TrueCrypt, and BitLocker: Encrypt the data to a key you don't know.

It sounds crazy, but stay with me. Caveat: Don't try this at home if you're not very familiar with whatever encryption product you're using. Failure results in a bricked computer. Don't blame me.

Step One: Before you board your plane, add another key to your whole-disk encryption (it'll probably mean adding another "user")—and make it random. By "random," I mean *really* random: Pound the keyboard for a while, like a monkey trying to write Shakespeare. Don't make it memorable. Don't even try to memorize it.

Technically, this key doesn't directly encrypt your hard drive. Instead, it encrypts the key that is used to encrypt your hard drive—that's how the software allows multiple keys.

So now there are two different users named with two different keys: the one you normally use, and some random one you just invented.

Step Two: Send that new random key to someone you trust. Make sure the trusted recipient has it, and make sure it works. You won't be able to recover your hard drive without it.

Step Three: Burn, shred, delete or otherwise destroy all copies of that new random key. Forget it. If it was sufficiently random and non-memorable, this should be easy.

Step Four: Board your plane normally and use your computer for the whole flight.

Step Five: Before you land, delete the key you normally use.

At this point, you will not be able to boot your computer. The only key remaining is the one you forgot in Step Three. There's no need to lie to the customs official; you can even show him a copy of this article if he doesn't believe you.

Step Six: When you're safely through customs, get that random key back from your confidant, boot your computer and re-add the key you normally use to access your hard drive.

And that's it.

This is by no means a magic get-through-customs-easily card. Your computer might be impounded, and you might be taken to court and compelled to reveal who has the random key.

But the purpose of this protocol isn't to prevent all that; it's just to deny any possible access to your computer to customs. You might be delayed. You might have your computer seized. (This will cost you any work you did on the flight, but—honestly—at that point that's the least of your troubles.) You might be turned back or sent home. But when you're back home, you have access to your corporate management, your personal attorneys, your wits after a good night's sleep, and all the rights you normally have in whatever country you're now in.

This procedure not only protects you against the warrantless search of your data at the border, it also allows you to deny a customs official your data without having to lie or pretend—which itself is often a crime.

Now the big question: Who should you send that random key to?

Certainly it should be someone you trust, but—more importantly—it should be someone with whom you have a privileged relationship. Depending on the laws in your country, this could be your spouse, your attorney, your business partner or your priest. In a larger company, the IT department could institutionalize this as a policy, with the help desk acting as the key holder.

You could also send it to yourself, but be careful. You don't want to e-mail it to your webmail account, because then you'd be lying when you tell the customs official that there is no possible way you can decrypt the drive.

You could put the key on a USB drive and send it to your destination, but there are potential failure modes. It could fail to get there in time to be waiting for your arrival, or it might not get there at all. You could airmail the drive with the key on it to yourself a couple of times, in a couple of different ways, and also fax the key to yourself . . . but that's more work than I want to do when I'm traveling.

If you only care about the return trip, you can set it up before you return. Or you can set up an elaborate one-time pad system, with identical lists of keys with you and at home: Destroy each key on the list you have with you as you use it.

Remember that you'll need to have full-disk encryption, using a product such as PGPDisk, TrueCrypt or BitLocker, already installed and enabled to make this work.

I don't think we'll ever get to the point where our computer data is safe when crossing an international border. Even if countries like the US and Britain clarify their rules and institute privacy protections, there will always be other countries that will exercise greater latitude with their authority. And sometimes protecting your data means protecting your data from yourself.

Breaching the Secure Area in Airports

Originally published in Threatpost, *January 5, 2010*

An unidentified man breached airport security at Newark Airport on Sunday, walking into the secured area through the exit, prompting an evacuation of a terminal and flight delays that continued into the next day. This problem isn't common, but it happens regularly. The result is always the same, and it's not obvious that fixing the problem is the right solution.

This kind of security breach is inevitable, simply because human guards are not perfect. Sometimes it's someone going in through the out door, unnoticed by a bored guard. Sometimes it's someone running through the checkpoint and getting lost in the crowd. Sometimes it's an open door that should be locked. Amazing as it seems to frequent fliers, the perpetrator often doesn't even know he did anything wrong.

Basically, whenever there is—or could be—an unscreened person lost within the secure area of an airport, there are two things the TSA can do. They can say, "This isn't a big deal," and ignore it. Or they can evacuate *everyone* inside the secure area, search every nook and cranny—inside the large boxes of napkins at the fast food restaurant, above the false ceilings in the bathrooms, everywhere—looking for anyone hiding, and then rescreen everybody, causing delays of six, eight, twelve hours or more. That's it; those are his options. And there's no way he's choosing to ignore the risk; even if the odds are minuscule that it's a problem, it'll cost him his career if he's wrong.

Several European airports have their security screening organized differently. At Schiphol Airport in Amsterdam, for example, passengers are screened at the gates. This is more expensive and requires a substantially different airport design, but it does mean that if there is a problem only the one gate has to be evacuated and searched and the people rescreened.

American airports can do more to secure against this risk, but I'm reasonably sure it's not worth it. We could double the guards to reduce the risk of inattentiveness, and redesign the airports to make this kind of thing less likely, but that's an expensive solution to an already rare problem. As much as I don't like saying it, the smartest thing is probably to live with this occasional but major inconvenience.

Stop the Panic on Air Security

Originally published in CNN, *January 7, 2010*

The Underwear Bomber failed. And our reaction to the failed plot is failing as well, by focusing on the specifics of this made-for-a-movie plot rather than the broad threat. While our reaction is predictable, it's not going to make us safer.

We're going to beef up airport security, because Umar Farouk AbdulMutallab allegedly snuck a bomb through a security checkpoint. We're going to intensively screen Nigerians, because he is Nigerian. We're going to field full body scanners, because they might have noticed the PETN that authorities say was hidden in his underwear. And so on.

We're doing these things even though security worked. The security checkpoints, even at their pre-9/11 levels, forced whoever made the bomb to construct a much worse bomb than he would have otherwise. Instead of using a timer or a plunger or another reliable detonation mechanism, as would any commercial user of PETN, he had to resort to an ad hoc homebrew—and a much more inefficient one, involving a syringe, and 20 minutes in the lavatory, and we don't know exactly what else—that didn't explode.

At that point, AbdulMutallab's fellow passengers quickly subdued him. Yes, the screeners didn't notice any PETN in his underwear, but the system was never intended to catch that particular tactic. There probably were intelligence failures—why wasn't his father's tip followed up on, and why wasn't his visa revoked?—but it's always easy to connect the dots in hindsight.

We're doing these things even though this particular plot was chosen precisely because we weren't screening for it; future al Qaeda attacks rarely look like past attacks; and the terrorist threat is far broader than attacks against airplanes.

We're doing these things even though airplane terrorism is incredibly rare, the risk is no greater today than it was in previous decades, the taxi to the airport is still more dangerous than the flight, and ten times as many Americans are killed by lightning as by terrorists.

In fact, we're focusing on the specifics of the plot, not despite these facts, but because of them.

The Underwear Bomber is precisely the sort of story we humans tend to overreact to. Our brains aren't very good at probability and risk analysis, especially when it comes to rare events. Our brains are much better at processing the simple risks we've had to deal with throughout most of our species' existence, and much poorer at evaluating the complex risks modern society forces us to face. We exaggerate spectacular rare events, and downplay familiar and common ones.

We can see the effects of this all the time. We fear being murdered, kidnapped, raped and assaulted by strangers, when it's far more likely that the perpetrator of such offenses is a relative or a friend. We fear school shootings, even though a school is almost always the safest place a child can be. We worry about shark attacks instead of fatal dog or pig attacks—both far more common. In the US, over 38,000 people die each year in car crashes; that's as many deaths as 9/11 each and every month, year after year.

Overreacting to the rare and spectacular is natural. We tend to base risk analysis on personal story rather than on data. If a friend gets mugged in a foreign country, that story is more likely to affect how safe you feel in that country than abstract crime statistics.

We give storytellers we have a relationship with more credibility than we give strangers, and stories that are close to us more weight than stories from foreign lands. And who is everyone's major storyteller these days? Television.

I tell people that if it's in the news, don't worry about it. The very definition of "news" is "something that hardly ever happens." It's when something isn't in the news, when it's so common that it's no longer news—car crashes, domestic violence—that you should start worrying.

But that's not the way we think. The more an event is talked about, the more probable we think it is. The more vivid our thoughts about the event are—again, think television—the more easily we remember it and the more convincing it is. So when faced with a very available and highly vivid event like the Underwear Bomber, 9/11, or a child kidnapping in a playground, we overreact. We get scared.

And once we're scared, we need to "do something"—even if that something doesn't make sense and is ineffective. We need to do something directly related to the story that's making us scared. We implement full body scanners at airports. We pass the Patriot Act. We don't let our children go to playgrounds unsupervised. Instead of implementing effective, but more general, security measures to reduce the overall risk, we concentrate on making the fearful story go away. Yes, it's security theater, but it makes us feel safer.

As circular as it sounds, rare events are rare primarily because they don't occur very often, and not because of any preventive security measures. If you want to do something that makes security sense, figure out what's common among a bunch of rare events, and concentrate your countermeasures there.

Focus on the general risk of terrorism, and not the specific threat of airplane bombings using PETN-filled underwear. Focus on the general risk of troubled teens, and not the specific threat of a lone gunman wandering around a school. Ignore the movie-plot threats, and concentrate on the real risks.

A Waste of Money and Time

Originally published in the New York Times Room for Debate *blog, November 23, 2010*

A short history of airport security: We screen for guns and bombs, so the terrorists use box cutters. We confiscate box cutters and corkscrews, so they put explosives in their sneakers. We screen footwear, so they try to use liquids. We confiscate liquids, so they put PETN bombs in their underwear. We roll out full-body scanners, even though they wouldn't have caught the Underwear Bomber, so they put a bomb in a printer cartridge. We ban printer cartridges over 16 ounces—the level of magical thinking here is amazing—and they're going to do something else.

This is a stupid game, and we should stop playing it.

It's not even a fair game. It's not that the terrorist picks an attack and we pick a defense, and we see who wins. It's that we pick a defense, and then the terrorists look at our defense and pick an attack designed to get around it. Our security measures only work if we happen to guess the plot correctly. If we get it wrong, we've wasted our money. This isn't security; it's security theater.

There are two basic kinds of terrorists. There are the sloppy planners, like the guy who crashed his plane into the Internal Revenue Service building in Austin. He's going to be sloppy and stupid, and even pre-9/11 airplane security is going to catch him. The second is the well-planned, well-financed, and much rarer sort of plot. Do you really expect the T.S.A. screeners, who are busy confiscating water bottles and making people take off their belts—and now doing uncomfortable pat-downs—to stop them?

Of course not. Airport security is the last line of defense, and it's not a very good one. What works is investigation and intelligence: security that works regardless of the terrorist tactic or target. Yes, the target matters too; all this airport security is only effective if the terrorists target airports. If they decide to bomb crowded shopping malls instead, we've wasted our money.

That being said, airplanes require a special level of security for several reasons: they're a favored terrorist target; their failure characteristics mean more deaths than a comparable bomb on a bus or train; they tend to be national symbols; and they often fly to foreign countries where terrorists can operate with more impunity.

But all that can be handled with pre-9/11 security. Exactly two things have made airplane travel safer since 9/11: reinforcing the cockpit door, and convincing passengers they need to fight back. Everything else has been a waste of money. Add screening of checked bags and airport workers and we're done. Take all the rest of the money and spend it on investigation and intelligence.

Immediately after the Christmas Day Underwear Bomber's plot failed, Homeland Security Secretary Janet Napolitano called airplane security a success. She was pilloried in the press and quickly backpedaled, but I think it was one of the most sensible things said on the subject. Plane lands safely, terrorist in custody, nobody injured except the terrorist: what more do people want out of a security success?

Look at what succeeded. Because even pre-9/11 security screened for obvious bombs, Abdulmutallab had to construct a far less reliable bomb than he would have otherwise. Instead of using a timer or a plunger or a reliable detonation mechanism, as would any commercial user of PETN, Abdulmutallab had to resort to an ad hoc and much more inefficient detonation mechanism involving a syringe, 20 minutes in the lavatory, and setting his pants on fire. As a result, his actions came to the notice of the other passengers, who subdued him.

Neither the full-body scanners or the enhanced pat-downs are making anyone safer. They're more a result of politicians and government appointees capitulating to a public that demands that "something must be done," even when nothing should be done; and a government bureaucracy that is more concerned about the security of their careers if they fail to secure against the last attack than what happens if they fail to anticipate the next one.

Why the TSA Can't Back Down

Originally published in the Atlantic, *December 2, 2010*

Organizers of National Opt Out Day, the Wednesday before Thanksgiving when air travelers were urged to opt out of the full-body scanners at security checkpoints and instead submit to full-body patdowns—were outfoxed by the TSA. The government pre-empted the protest by turning off the machines in most airports during the Thanksgiving weekend. Everyone went through the metal detectors, just as before.

Now that Thanksgiving is over, the machines are back on and the "enhanced" pat-downs have resumed. I suspect that more people would prefer to have naked images of themselves seen by TSA agents in another room, than have themselves intimately touched by a TSA agent right in front of them.

But now, the TSA is in a bind. Regardless of whatever lobbying came before, or whatever former DHS officials had a financial interest in these scanners, the TSA has spent billions on those scanners, claiming they're essential. But because people can opt out, the alternate manual method must be equally effective; otherwise, the terrorists could just opt out. If they make the pat-downs less invasive, it would be the same as admitting the scanners aren't essential. Senior officials would get fired over that.

So not counting inconsequential modifications to demonstrate they're "listening," the pat-downs will continue. And they'll continue for everyone: children, abuse survivors, rape survivors, urostomy bag wearers, people in wheelchairs. It has to be that way; otherwise, the terrorists could simply adapt. They'd hide their explosives on their children or in their urostomy bags. They'd recruit rape survivors, abuse survivors, or seniors. They'd dress as pilots. They'd sneak their PETN through airport security using the very type of person who isn't being screened.

And PETN is what the TSA is looking for these days. That's pentaerythritol tetranitrate, the plastic explosive that both the Shoe Bomber and the Underwear Bomber attempted but failed to detonate. It's what was mailed from

Yemen. It's in Iraq and Afghanistan. Guns and traditional bombs are passé; PETN is the terrorist tool of the future.

The problem is that no scanners or puffers can detect PETN; only swabs and dogs work. What the TSA hopes is that they will detect the bulge if someone is hiding a wad of it on their person. But they won't catch PETN hidden in a body cavity. That doesn't have to be as gross as you're imagining; you can hide PETN in your mouth. A terrorist can go through the scanners a dozen times with bits in his mouth each time, and assemble a bigger bomb on the other side. Or he can roll it thin enough to be part of a garment, and sneak it through that way. These tricks aren't new. In the days after the Underwear Bomber was stopped, a scanner manufacturer admitted that the machines might not have caught him.

So what's next? Strip searches? Body cavity searches? TSA Administrator John Pistole said there would be no body cavity searches for now, but his reasons make no sense. He said that the case widely reported as being a body cavity bomb might not actually have been. While that appears to be true, what does that have to do with future bombs? He also said that even body cavity bombs would need "external initiators" that the TSA would be able to detect.

Do you think for a minute that the TSA can detect these "external initiators"? Do you think that if a terrorist took a laptop—or better yet, a less-common piece of electronics gear—and removed the insides and replaced them with a timer, a pressure sensor, a simple contact switch, or a radio frequency switch, the TSA guy behind the X-ray machine monitor would detect it? How about if those components were distributed over a few trips through airport security. On the other hand, if we believe the TSA can magically detect these "external initiators" so effectively that they make body-cavity searches unnecessary, why do we need the full-body scanners?

Either PETN is a danger that must be searched for, or it isn't. Pistole was being either ignorant or evasive.

Once again, the TSA is covering their own asses by implementing security-theater measures to prevent the previous attack while ignoring any threats of future attacks. It's the same thinking that caused them to ban box cutters after 9/11, screen shoes after Richard Reid, limit liquids after that London gang, and—I kid you not—ban printer cartridges over 16 ounces after they were used to house package bombs from Yemen. They act like the terrorists are incapable of thinking creatively, while the terrorists repeatedly demonstrate they can always come up with a new approach that circumvents the old measures.

On the plus side, PETN is very hard to get to explode. The pre-9/11 screening procedures, looking for obvious guns and bombs, forced the terrorists to build inefficient fusing mechanisms. We saw this when Abdulmutallab, the Underwear Bomber, used bottles of liquid and a syringe and 20 minutes in the bathroom to assemble his device, then set his pants on fire—and still failed to ignite his PETN-filled underwear. And when he failed, the passengers quickly subdued him.

The truth is that exactly two things have made air travel safer since 9/11: reinforcing cockpit doors and convincing passengers they need to fight back. The TSA should continue to screen checked luggage. They should start screening airport workers. And then they should return airport security to pre-9/11 levels and let the rest of their budget be used for better purposes. Investigation and intelligence is how we're going to prevent terrorism, on airplanes and elsewhere. It's how we caught the liquid bombers. It's how we found the Yemeni printer-cartridge bombs. And it's our best chance at stopping the next serious plot.

Because if a group of well-planned and well-funded terrorist plotters makes it to the airport, the chance is pretty low that those blue-shirted crotch-groping water-bottle-confiscating TSA agents are going to catch them. The agents are trying to do a good job, but the deck is so stacked against them that their job is impossible. Airport security is the last line of defense, and it's not a very good one.

We have a job here, too, and it's to be indomitable in the face of terrorism. The goal of terrorism is to terrorize us: to make us afraid, and make our government do exactly what the TSA is doing. When we react out of fear, the terrorists succeed even when their plots fail. But if we carry on as before, the terrorists fail—even when their plots succeed.

The Trouble with Airport Profiling

Originally published in Forbes, *May 9, 2012*

Why do otherwise rational people think it's a good idea to profile people at airports? Recently, neuroscientist and best-selling author Sam Harris related a story of an elderly couple being given the twice-over by the TSA, pointed out how these two were obviously not a threat, and recommended that the TSA focus on the actual threat: "Muslims, or anyone who looks like he or she could conceivably be Muslim."

This is a bad idea. It doesn't make us any safer—and it actually puts us all at risk.

The right way to look at security is in terms of cost-benefit trade-offs. If adding profiling to airport checkpoints allowed us to detect more threats at a lower cost, than we should implement it. If it didn't, we'd be foolish to do so. Sometimes profiling works. Consider a sheep in a meadow, happily munching on grass. When he spies a wolf, he's going to judge that individual wolf based on a bunch of assumptions related to the past behavior of its species. In short, that sheep is going to profile . . . and then run away. This makes perfect sense, and is why evolution produced sheep—and other animals—that react this way. But this sort of profiling doesn't work with humans at airports, for several reasons.

First, in the sheep's case the profile is accurate, in that all wolves are out to eat sheep. Maybe a particular wolf isn't hungry at the moment, but enough wolves are hungry enough of the time to justify the occasional false alarm. However, it isn't true that almost all Muslims are out to blow up airplanes. In fact, almost none of them are. Post 9/11, we've had 2 Muslim terrorists on US airplanes: the shoe bomber and the underwear bomber. If you assume 0.8% (that's one estimate of the percentage of Muslim Americans) of the 630 million annual airplane fliers are Muslim and triple it to account for others who look Semitic, then the chances any profiled flier will be a Muslim terrorist is 1 in 80 million. Add the 19 9/11 terrorists—arguably a singular event—that number drops to 1 in 8 million. Either way, because the number of actual terrorists is so low, almost everyone selected by the profile will be innocent. This is called the "base rate fallacy," and dooms any type of broad terrorist profiling, including the TSA's behavioral profiling.

Second, sheep can safely ignore animals that don't look like the few predators they know. On the other hand, to assume that only Arab-appearing people are terrorists is dangerously naive. Muslims are black, white, Asian, and everything else—most Muslims are not Arab. Recent terrorists have been European, Asian, African, Hispanic, and Middle Eastern; male and female; young and old. Underwear bomber Umar Farouk Abdul Mutallab was Nigerian. Shoe bomber Richard Reid was British with a Jamaican father. One of the London subway bombers, Germaine Lindsay, was Afro-Caribbean. Dirty bomb suspect Jose Padilla was Hispanic-American. The 2002 Bali terrorists were Indonesian. Both Timothy McVeigh and the Unabomber were white Americans. The Chechen terrorists who blew up two Russian planes in 2004 were female. Focusing on a profile increases the risk that TSA agents will miss those who don't match it.

Third, wolves can't deliberately try to evade the profile. A wolf in sheep's clothing is just a story, but humans are smart and adaptable enough to put the concept into practice. Once the TSA establishes a profile, terrorists will take steps to avoid it. The Chechens deliberately chose female suicide bombers because Russian security was less thorough with women. Al Qaeda has tried to recruit non-Muslims. And terrorists have given bombs to innocent—and innocent-looking—travelers. Randomized secondary screening is more effective, especially since the goal isn't to catch every plot but to create enough uncertainty that terrorists don't even try.

And fourth, sheep don't care if they offend innocent wolves; the two species are never going to be friends. At airports, though, there is an enormous social and political cost to the millions of false alarms. Beyond the societal harms of deliberately harassing a minority group, singling out Muslims alienates the very people who are in the best position to discover and alert authorities about Muslim plots before the terrorists even get to the airport. This alone is reason enough not to profile.

I too am incensed—but not surprised—when the TSA singles out four-year old girls, children with cerebral palsy, pretty women, the elderly, and wheelchair users for humiliation, abuse, and sometimes theft. Any bureaucracy that processes 630 million people per year will generate stories like this. When people propose profiling, they are really asking for a security system that can apply judgment. Unfortunately, that's really hard. Rules are easier to explain and train. Zero tolerance is easier to justify and defend. Judgment requires better-educated, more expert, and much-higher-paid screeners. And the personal career risks to a TSA agent of being wrong when exercising judgment far outweigh any benefits from being sensible.

The proper reaction to screening horror stories isn't to subject only "those people" to it; it's to subject no one to it. (Can anyone even explain what hypothetical terrorist plot could successfully evade normal security, but would be discovered during secondary screening?) Invasive TSA screening is nothing more than security theater. It doesn't make us safer, and it's not worth the cost. Even more strongly, security isn't our society's only value. Do we really want the full power of government to act out our stereotypes and prejudices? Have we Americans ever done something like this and not been ashamed later? This is what we have a Constitution for: to help us live up to our values and not down to our fears.

8 Security, Policy, Liberty, and Law

Memo to Next President: How to Get Cybersecurity Right

Originally published in Wired News, *August 7, 2008*

O bama has a cybersecurity plan.

It's basically what you would expect: Appoint a national cybersecurity adviser, invest in math and science education, establish standards for critical infrastructure, spend money on enforcement, establish national standards for securing personal data and data-breach disclosure, and work with industry and academia to develop a bunch of needed technologies.

I could comment on the plan, but with security, the devil is always in the details—and, of course, at this point there are few details. But since he brought up the topic—McCain supposedly is "working on the issues" as well—I have three pieces of policy advice for the next president, whoever he is. They're too detailed for campaign speeches or even position papers, but they're essential for improving information security in our society. Actually, they apply to national security in general. And they're things only government can do.

One, use your immense buying power to improve the security of commercial products and services. One property of technological products is that most of the cost is in the development of the product rather than the production. Think software: The first copy costs millions, but the second copy is free.

You have to secure your own government networks, military and civilian. You have to buy computers for all your government employees. Consolidate those contracts, and start putting explicit security requirements into the RFPs. You have the buying power to get your vendors to make serious security improvements in the products and services they sell to the government, and then we all benefit because they'll include those improvements in the same products and services they sell to the rest of us. We're all safer if information technology is more secure, even though the bad guys can use it, too.

Two, legislate results and not methodologies. There are a lot of areas in security where you need to pass laws, where the security externalities are such that the market fails to provide adequate security. For example, software companies who sell insecure products are exploiting an externality just as much as chemical plants that dump waste into the river. But a bad law is worse than no law. A law requiring companies to secure personal data is good; a law specifying what technologies they should use to do so is not. Mandating software liabilities for software failures is good; detailing how is not. Legislate for the results you want and implement the appropriate penalties; let the market figure out how—that's what markets are good at.

Three, broadly invest in research. Basic research is risky; it doesn't always pay off. That's why companies have stopped funding it. Bell Labs is gone because nobody could afford it after the AT&T breakup, but the root cause was a desire for higher efficiency and short-term profitability—not unreasonable in an unregulated business. Government research can be used to balance that by funding long-term research.

Spread those research dollars wide. Lately, most research money has been redirected through DARPA to near-term military-related projects; that's not good. Keep the earmark-happy Congress from dictating how the money is spent. Let the NSF, NIH and other funding agencies decide how to spend the money and don't try to micromanage. Give the national laboratories lots of freedom, too. Yes, some research will sound silly to a layman. But you can't predict what will be useful for what, and if funding is really peer-reviewed, the average results will be much better. Compared with corporate tax breaks and other subsidies, this is chump change.

If our research capability is to remain vibrant, we need more science and math students with decent elementary and high school preparation. The declining interest is partly from the perception that scientists don't get rich like lawyers and dentists and stockbrokers, but also because science isn't valued in a country full of creationists. One way the president can help is by trusting scientific advisers and not overruling them for political reasons.

Oh, and get rid of those post-9/11 restrictions on student visas that are causing so many top students to do their graduate work in Canada, Europe and

Asia instead of in the United States. Those restrictions will hurt us immensely in the long run.

Those are the three big ones; the rest is in the details. And it's the details that matter. There are lots of serious issues that you're going to have to tackle: data privacy, data sharing, data mining, government eavesdropping, government databases, use of Social Security numbers as identifiers, and so on. It's not enough to get the broad policy goals right. You can have good intentions and enact a good law, and have the whole thing completely gutted by two sentences sneaked in during rulemaking by some lobbyist.

Security is both subtle and complex, and—unfortunately—it doesn't readily lend itself to normal legislative processes. You're used to finding consensus, but security by consensus rarely works. On the Internet, security standards are much worse when they're developed by a consensus body, and much better when someone just does them. This doesn't always work—a lot of crap security has come from companies that have "just done it"—but nothing but mediocre standards come from consensus bodies. The point is that you won't get good security without pissing someone off: The information-broker industry, the voting-machine industry, the telcos. The normal legislative process makes it hard to get security right, which is why I don't have much optimism about what you can get done.

And if you're going to appoint a cybersecurity czar, you have to give him actual budgetary authority—otherwise he won't be able to get anything done, either.

CRB Checking

Originally published in Schneier on Security, *November 8, 2008*

Since the UK's Criminal Records Bureau (CRB) was established in 2002, an ever-increasing number of people are required to undergo a "CRB check" before they can interact with children. It's not only teachers and daycare providers, but football coaches, scoutmasters and Guiders, church volunteers, bus drivers, and school janitors—3.4 million checks in 2007, 15 million since 2002. In 2009, it will include anyone who works or volunteers in a position where he or she comes into contact with children: 11.3 million people, or a quarter of the adult population.

This might make sense if it worked, but it doesn't. CRB checks don't keep child predators away from children. And even worse, this bureaucratic process fosters an atmosphere of mistrust among parents, teaches parents to ignore their own intuitions about other adults, and limits children's activities as organizations find CRB checks too cumbersome.

Effectiveness first. CRB checking does not guarantee that only non-predatory adults interact with children. At best, it only protects children from recidivist predators. This is a real risk but less than first-time predators, predatory relatives, or predators they come into casual contact with.

The CRB cites statistics like "Since 2004 the CRB has stopped 80,000 unsuitable people working with vulnerable groups," but that's just false. In the first place, there are only 30,000 people on the list. Also, denying someone a CRB approval isn't the correct metric—protecting children is. Before CRB checks, there weren't 20,000 repeat-offender child-predatory crimes annually. The effectiveness of this program is the difference between the small handful in 2001 and the smaller handful today.

The Home Office admits that 9,000 potential predators who should be on the list are not, and their error rate means that 2,000 innocent people will be falsely labeled as child predators in 2009. But it's more than the errors; the list is filled with people who shouldn't be on it. For example, underage teenagers could be put on the list for having consensual sex—nothing that should prevent them from taking a summer job around kids.

CRB checking might not be effective at stopping child predators, but it's effective at instilling fear in parents. Sociology professor Frank Furedi wrote the book *License to Hug* about the issue, chronicles some examples: a mother who couldn't kiss her child goodbye on a school trip, another barred from taking her child to a school event, and a father who gets "filthy looks" when he takes his child swimming. The most horrific example is the story of a bricklayer who did not help a lost two-year-old because he feared being thought an abductor. The girl later drowned.

Pervasive CRB checking also teaches parents to ignore their own parenting instincts. As Furedi says, "If adults are not expected to respond to problems in accordance with their experience and intuition they will have little incentive to develop the kind of skills required to manage children and young people."

The assumption—contrary to all data—that everyone is a child predator unless checked by the police poisons the natural relationship between children and adults, and directly affects their welfare. Half of all adults fear being falsely accused of being abusers and 13% of men don't volunteer as a result.

At the same time, 50,000 girls can't join the Guides because of a shortage of CRB-checked adults, and kids' sports leagues are drastically cutting back.

A parent's natural reaction is "If it were your child, you'd do anything . . . ." This is natural—we're all predisposed to exaggerate risks that are extreme, that are from strangers, and that are against our children. Over several generations, children have had less freedom than their parents, even though the data doesn't warrant it. When evaluating risks, we respond more to stories than to data.

This enormous government hydra, first proposed in 1996 and which Furedi estimates has cost half a billion pounds since it was implemented 2002, seems to have been sold primarily on two stories: the 1997 murder of ten-year-old Scott Simpson by convicted sex offender Stephen Leisk, and the 2002 murders of 10-year-olds Jessica Chapman and Holly Wells by school caretaker Ian Huntley. As gruesome as these stories are, they're don't make a basis for sound policy. Government database checking is no substitute for alert parenting.

State Data Breach Notification Laws: Have They Helped?

Originally published in Information Security, *January 2009*

This essay appeared as the second half of a point/counterpoint with Marcus Ranum.

There are three reasons for breach notification laws. One, it's common politeness that when you lose something of someone else's, you tell him. The prevailing corporate attitude before the law—"They won't notice, and if they do notice they won't know it's us, so we are better off keeping quiet about the whole thing"—is just wrong. Two, it provides statistics to security researchers as to how pervasive the problem really is. And three, it forces companies to improve their security.

That last point needs a bit of explanation. The problem with companies protecting your data is that it isn't in their financial best interest to do so. That is, the companies are responsible for protecting your data, but bear none of the costs if your data is compromised. You suffer the harm, but you have no control—or even knowledge—of the company's security practices. The idea behind such laws, and how they were sold to legislators, is that they would increase the cost—both in bad publicity and the actual notification—of security breaches, motivating companies to spend more to prevent them. In economic terms, the law reduces the externalities and forces companies to deal with the true costs of these data breaches.

So how has it worked?

Earlier this year, three researchers at the Heinz School of Public Policy and Management at Carnegie Mellon University—Sasha Romanosky, Rahul Telang and Alessandro Acquisti—tried to answer that question. They looked at reported data breaches and rates of identity theft from 2002 to 2007, comparing states with a law to states without one. If these laws had their desired effects, people in states with notification laws should experience fewer incidences of identity theft. The result: not so much. The researchers found data breach notification laws reduced identity theft by just 2 percent on average.

I think there's a combination of things going on. Identity theft is being reported far more today than five years ago, so it's difficult to compare identity theft rates before and after the state laws were enacted. Most identity theft occurs when someone's home or work computer is compromised, not from theft of large corporate databases, so the effect of these laws is small. Most of the security improvements companies made didn't make much of a difference, reducing the effect of these laws.

The laws rely on public shaming. It's embarrassing to have to admit to a data breach, and companies should be willing to spend to avoid this PR expense. The problem is, in order for this to work well, public shaming needs the cooperation of the press. And there's an attenuation effect going on. The first major breach after the first state disclosure law was in February 2005 in California, when ChoicePoint sold personal data on 145,000 people to criminals. The event was big news, ChoicePoint's stock tanked, and it was shamed into improving its security.

Next, LexisNexis exposed personal data on 300,000 individuals, and then Citigroup lost data on 3.9 million. The law worked; the only reason we knew about these security breaches was because of the law. But the breaches came in increasing numbers, and in larger quantities. Data breach stories felt more like "crying wolf" and soon, data breaches were no longer news.

Today, the remaining cost is that of the direct mail campaign to notify customers, which often turns into a marketing opportunity.

I'm still a fan of these laws, if only for the first two reasons I listed. Disclosure is important, but it's not going to solve identity theft. As I've written previously, the reason theft of personal information is common is that the data is valuable once stolen. The way to mitigate the risk of fraud due to impersonation is not to make personal information difficult to steal, it's to make it difficult to use.

Disclosure laws only deal with the economic externality of data owners protecting your personal information. What we really need are laws prohibiting financial institutions from granting credit to someone using your name with only a minimum of authentication.

How to Ensure Police Database Accuracy

Originally published in the Wall Street Journal, *January 27, 2009*

Earlier this month, the Supreme Court ruled that evidence gathered as a result of errors in a police database is admissible in court. Their narrow decision is wrong, and will only ensure that police databases remain error-filled in the future.

The specifics of the case are simple. A computer database said there was a felony arrest warrant pending for Bennie Herring when there actually wasn't. When the police came to arrest him, they searched his home and found illegal drugs and a gun. The Supreme Court was asked to rule whether the police had the right to arrest him for possessing those items, even though there was no legal basis for the search and arrest in the first place.

What's at issue here is the exclusionary rule, which basically says that unconstitutionally or illegally collected evidence is inadmissible in court. It might seem like a technicality, but excluding what is called "the fruit of the poisonous tree" is a security system designed to protect us all from police abuse.

We have a number of rules limiting what the police can do: rules governing arrest, search, interrogation, detention, prosecution, and so on. And one of the ways we ensure that the police follow these rules is by forbidding the police to receive any benefit from breaking them. In fact, we design the system so that the police actually harm their own interests by breaking them, because all evidence that stems from breaking the rules is inadmissible.

And that's what the exclusionary rule does. If the police search your home without a warrant and find drugs, they can't arrest you for possession. Since the police have better things to do than waste their time, they have an incentive to get a warrant.

The Herring case is more complicated, because the police thought they did have a warrant. The error was not a police error, but a database error. And, in fact, Judge Roberts wrote for the majority: "The exclusionary rule serves to deter deliberate, reckless, or grossly negligent conduct, or in some circumstances recurring or systemic negligence. The error in this case does not rise to that level."

Unfortunately, Roberts is wrong. Government databases are filled with errors. People often can't see data about themselves, and have no way to correct the errors if they do learn of any. And more and more databases are trying to exempt themselves from the Privacy Act of 1974, and specifically the provisions that require data accuracy. The legal argument for excluding this evidence was best made by an amicus curiae filed by the Electronic Privacy Information Center, but in short, the court should exclude the evidence because it's the only way to ensure police database accuracy.

We are protected from becoming a police state by limits on police power and authority. This is not a trade-off we make lightly: we deliberately hamper law enforcement's ability to do its job because we recognize that these limits make us safer. Without the exclusionary rule, your only remedy against an illegal search is to bring legal action against the police—and that can be very difficult. We, the people, would rather have you go free than motivate the police to ignore the rules that limit their power.

By not applying the exclusionary rule in the Herring case, the Supreme Court missed an important opportunity to motivate the police to purge errors from their databases. Constitutional lawyers have written many articles about this ruling, but the most interesting idea comes from George Washington University professor Daniel J. Solove, who proposes this compromise: "If a particular database has reasonable protections and deterrents against errors, then the Fourth Amendment exclusionary rule should not apply. If not, then the exclusionary rule should apply. Such a rule would create an incentive for law enforcement officials to maintain accurate databases, to avoid all errors, and would ensure that there would be a penalty or consequence for errors."

Increasingly, we are being judged by the trail of data we leave behind us. Increasingly, data accuracy is vital to our personal safety and security. And if errors made by police databases aren't held to the same legal standard as errors made by policemen, then more and more innocent Americans will find themselves the victims of incorrect data.

How Perverse Incentives Drive Bad Security Decisions

Originally published in Wired News, *February 26, 2009*

An employee of Whole Foods in Ann Arbor, Michigan, was fired in 2007 for apprehending a shoplifter. More specifically, he was fired for touching a customer, even though that customer had a backpack filled with stolen groceries and was running away with them.

I regularly see security decisions that, like the Whole Foods incident, seem to make absolutely no sense. However, in every case, the decisions actually make perfect sense once you understand the underlying incentives driving the decision. All security decisions are trade-offs, but the motivations behind them are not always obvious: They're often subjective, and driven by external incentives. And often security trade-offs are made for nonsecurity reasons.

Almost certainly, Whole Foods has a no-touching-the-customer policy because its attorneys recommended it. "No touching" is a security measure as well, but it's security against customer lawsuits. The cost of these lawsuits would be much, much greater than the $346 worth of groceries stolen in this instance. Even applied to suspected shoplifters, the policy makes sense: The cost of a lawsuit resulting from tackling an innocent shopper by mistake would be far greater than the cost of letting actual shoplifters get away. As perverse as it may seem, the result is completely reasonable given the corporate incentives—Whole Foods wrote a corporate policy that benefited itself.

At least, it works as long as the police and other factors keep society's shoplifter population down to a reasonable level.

Incentives explain much that is perplexing about security trade-offs. Why does King County, Washington, require one form of ID to get a concealed-carry permit, but two forms of ID to pay for the permit by check? Making a mistake on a gun permit is an abstract problem, but a bad check actually costs some department money.

In the decades before 9/11, why did the airlines fight every security measure except the photo-ID check? Increased security annoys their customers, but the photo-ID check solved a security problem of a different kind: the resale of nonrefundable tickets. So the airlines were on board for that one.

And why does the TSA confiscate liquids at airport security, on the off chance that a terrorist will try to make a liquid explosive instead of using the more common solid ones? Because the officials in charge of the decision used CYA security measures to prevent specific, known tactics rather than broad, general ones.

The same misplaced incentives explain the ongoing problem of innocent prisoners spending years in places like Guantanamo and Abu Ghraib. The solution might seem obvious: Release the innocent ones, keep the guilty ones, and figure out whether the ones we aren't sure about are innocent or guilty. But the incentives are more perverse than that. Who is going to sign the order releasing one of those prisoners? Which military officer is going to accept the risk, no matter how small, of being wrong?

I read almost five years ago that prisoners were being held by the United States far longer than they should, because "no one wanted to be responsible for releasing the next Osama bin Laden." That incentive to do nothing hasn't changed. It might have even gotten stronger, as these innocents languish in prison.

In all these cases, the best way to change the trade-off is to change the incentives. Look at why the Whole Foods case works. Store employees don't have to apprehend shoplifters, because society created a special organization specifically authorized to lay hands on people the grocery store points to as shoplifters: the police. If we want more rationality out of the TSA, there needs to be someone with a broader perspective willing to deal with general threats rather than specific targets or tactics.

For prisoners, society has created a special organization specifically entrusted with the role of judging the evidence against them and releasing them if appropriate: the judiciary. It's only because the George W. Bush administration decided to remove the Guantanamo prisoners from the legal system that we are now stuck with these perverse incentives. Our country would be smart to move as many of these people through the court system as we can.

It's Time to Drop the "Expectation of Privacy" Test

Originally published in Wired News, *March 26, 2009*

In the United States, the concept of "expectation of privacy" matters because it's the constitutional test, based on the Fourth Amendment, that governs when and how the government can invade your privacy.

Based on the 1967 *Katz v. United States* Supreme Court decision, this test actually has two parts. First, the government's action can't contravene an individual's subjective expectation of privacy; and second, that expectation of privacy must be one that society in general recognizes as reasonable. That second part isn't based on anything like polling data; it is more of a normative idea of what level of privacy people should be allowed to expect, given the competing importance of personal privacy on one hand and the government's interest in public safety on the other.

The problem is, in today's information society, that definition test will rapidly leave us with no privacy at all.

In *Katz*, the Court ruled that the police could not eavesdrop on a phone call without a warrant: Katz expected his phone conversations to be private and this expectation resulted from a reasonable balance between personal privacy and societal security. Given NSA's large-scale warrantless eavesdropping, and the previous administration's continual insistence that it was necessary to keep America safe from terrorism, is it still reasonable to expect that our phone conversations are private?

Between the NSA's massive Internet eavesdropping program and Gmail's content-dependent advertising, does anyone actually expect their e-mail to be private? Between calls for ISPs to retain user data and companies serving content-dependent web ads, does anyone expect their web browsing to be private? Between the various computer-infecting malware, and world governments increasingly demanding to see laptop data at borders, hard drives are barely private. I certainly don't believe that my SMSs, any of my telephone data, or anything I say on LiveJournal or Facebook—regardless of the privacy settings—is private.

Aerial surveillance, data mining, automatic face recognition, terahertz radar that can "see" through walls, wholesale surveillance, brain scans, RFID, "life recorders" that save everything: Even if society still has some small expectation of digital privacy, that will change as these and other technologies become ubiquitous. In short, the problem with a normative expectation of privacy is that it changes with perceived threats, technology and large-scale abuses.

Clearly, something has to change if we are to be left with any privacy at all. Three legal scholars have written law review articles that wrestle with the problems of applying the Fourth Amendment to cyberspace and to our computer-mediated world in general.

George Washington University's Daniel Solove, who blogs at Concurring Opinions, has tried to capture the byzantine complexities of modern privacy.

He points out, for example, that the following privacy violations—all real—are very different: A company markets a list of 5 million elderly incontinent women; reporters deceitfully gain entry to a person's home and secretly photograph and record the person; the government uses a thermal sensor device to detect heat patterns in a person's home; and a newspaper reports the name of a rape victim. Going beyond simple definitions such as the divulging of a secret, Solove has developed a taxonomy of privacy, and the harms that result from their violation.

His 16 categories are: surveillance, interrogation, aggregation, identification, insecurity, secondary use, exclusion, breach of confidentiality, disclosure, exposure, increased accessibility, blackmail, appropriation, distortion, intrusion and decisional interference. Solove's goal is to provide a coherent and comprehensive understanding of what is traditionally an elusive and hard-to-explain concept: privacy violations. (This taxonomy is also discussed in Solove's book, *Understanding Privacy.*)

Orin Kerr, also a law professor at George Washington University, and a blogger at Volokh Conspiracy, has attempted to lay out general principles for applying the Fourth Amendment to the Internet. First, he points out that the traditional inside/outside distinction—the police can watch you in a public place without a warrant, but not in your home—doesn't work very well with regard to cyberspace. Instead, he proposes a distinction between content and non-content information: the body of an e-mail versus the header information, for example. The police should be required to get a warrant for the former, but not for the latter. Second, he proposes that search warrants should be written for particular individuals and not for particular Internet accounts.

Meanwhile, Jed Rubenfeld of Yale Law School has tried to reinterpret the Fourth Amendment not in terms of privacy, but in terms of security. Pointing out that the whole "expectations" test is circular—what the government does affects what the government can do—he redefines everything in terms of security: the security that our private affairs are private.

This security is violated when, for example, the government makes widespread use of informants, or engages in widespread eavesdropping—even if no one's privacy is actually violated. This neatly bypasses the whole individual privacy versus societal security question—a balancing that the individual usually loses—by framing both sides in terms of personal security.

I have issues with all of these articles. Solove's taxonomy is excellent, but the sense of outrage that accompanies a privacy violation—"How could they know/do/say that!?"—is an important part of the harm resulting from a privacy violation. The non-content information that Kerr believes should be collectible without a warrant can be very private and personal: URLs can be very personal, and it's possible to figure out browsed content just from the size of encrypted SSL traffic. Also, the ease with which the government can collect all of it—the calling and called party of every phone call in the country—makes the balance very different. I believe these need to be protected with a warrant requirement. Rubenfeld's reframing is interesting, but the devil is in the details. Reframing privacy in terms of security still results in a balancing of competing rights. I'd rather take the approach of stating the—obvious to me—individual and societal value of privacy, and giving privacy its rightful place as a fundamental human right. (There's additional commentary on Rubenfeld's thesis at ArsTechnica.)

The trick here is to realize that a normative definition of the expectation of privacy doesn't need to depend on threats or technology, but rather on what we—as society—decide it should be. Sure, today's technology makes it easier than ever to violate privacy. But it doesn't necessarily follow that we have to violate privacy. Today's guns make it easier than ever to shoot virtually anyone for any reason. That doesn't mean our laws have to change.

No one knows how this will shake out legally. These three articles are from law professors; they're not judicial opinions. But clearly something has to change, and ideas like these may someday form the basis of new Supreme Court decisions that brings legal notions of privacy into the 21st century.

Who Should Be in Charge of Cybersecurity?

Originally published in the Wall Street Journal, *March 31, 2009*

US government cybersecurity is an insecure mess, and fixing it is going to take considerable attention and resources. Trying to make sense of this, President Barack Obama ordered a 60-day review of government cybersecurity initiatives. Meanwhile, the US House Subcommittee on Emerging Threats, Cybersecurity, Science and Technology is holding hearings on the same topic.

One of the areas of contention is who should be in charge. The FBI, DHS and DoD—specifically, the NSA—all have interests here. Earlier this month, Rod Beckström resigned from his position as director of the DHS's National Cybersecurity Center, warning of a power grab by the NSA.

Putting national cybersecurity in the hands of the NSA is an incredibly bad idea. An entire parade of people, ranging from former FBI director Louis Freeh to Microsoft's Trusted Computing Group Vice President and former Justice Department computer crime chief Scott Charney, have told Congress the same thing at this month's hearings.

Cybersecurity isn't a military problem, or even a government problem—it's a universal problem. All networks, military, government, civilian and commercial, use the same computers, the same networking hardware, the same Internet protocols and the same software packages. We all are the targets of the same attack tools and tactics. It's not even that government targets are somehow more important; these days, most of our nation's critical IT infrastructure is in commercial hands. Government-sponsored Chinese hackers go after both military and civilian targets.

Some have said that the NSA should be in charge because it has specialized knowledge. Earlier this month, Director of National Intelligence Admiral Dennis Blair made this point, saying "There are some wizards out there at Ft. Meade who can do stuff." That's probably not true, but if it is, we'd better get them out of Ft. Meade as soon as possible—they're doing the nation little good where they are now.

Not that government cybersecurity failings require any specialized wizardry to fix. GAO reports indicate that government problems include insufficient access controls, a lack of encryption where necessary, poor network management, failure to install patches, inadequate audit procedures, and incomplete or ineffective information security programs. These aren't super-secret NSA-level security issues; these are the same managerial problems that every corporate CIO wrestles with.

We've all got the same problems, so solutions must be shared. If the government has any clever ideas to solve its cybersecurity problems, certainly a lot of us could benefit from those solutions. If it has an idea for improving network security, it should tell everyone. The best thing the government can do for cybersecurity world-wide is to use its buying power to improve the security of the IT products everyone uses. If it imposes significant security requirements on its IT vendors, those vendors will modify their products to meet those requirements. And those same products, now with improved security, will become available to all of us as the new standard.

Moreover, the NSA's dual mission of providing security and conducting surveillance means it has an inherent conflict of interest in cybersecurity. Inside the NSA, this is called the "equities issue." During the Cold War, it was easy; the NSA used its expertise to protect American military information and communications, and eavesdropped on Soviet information and communications. But what happens when both the good guys the NSA wants to protect, and the bad guys the NSA wants to eavesdrop on, use the same systems? They all use Microsoft Windows, Oracle databases, Internet email, and Skype. When the NSA finds a vulnerability in one of those systems, does it alert the manufacturer and fix it—making both the good guys and the bad guys more secure? Or does it keep quiet about the vulnerability and not tell anyone—making it easier to spy on the bad guys but also keeping the good guys insecure? Programs like the NSA's warrantless wiretapping program have created additional vulnerabilities in our domestic telephone networks.

Testifying before Congress earlier this month, former DHS National Cyber Security division head Amit Yoran said "the intelligence community has always and will always prioritize its own collection efforts over the defensive and protection mission of our government's and nation's digital systems."

Maybe the NSA could convince us that it's putting cybersecurity first, but its culture of secrecy will mean that any decisions it makes will be suspect. Under current law, extended by the Bush administration's extravagant invocation of the "state secrets" privilege when charged with statutory and constitutional violations, the NSA's activities are not subject to any meaningful public oversight. And the NSA's tradition of military secrecy makes it harder for it to coordinate with other government IT departments, most of which don't have clearances, let alone coordinate with local law enforcement or the commercial sector.

We need transparent and accountable government processes, using commercial security products. We need government cybersecurity programs that improve security for everyone. The NSA certainly has an advisory and a coordination role in national cybersecurity, and perhaps a more supervisory role in DoD cybersecurity—both offensive and defensive—but it should not be in charge.

Coordinate, but Distribute Responsibility

Originally published in NYTimes.com, *May 29, 2009*

This essay appeared as part of a round table about Obama's cybersecurity speech on the New York Times Room for Debate *blog.*

I am optimistic about President Obama's new cybersecurity policy and the appointment of a new "cybersecurity coordinator," though much depends on the details. What we do know is that the threats are real, from identity theft to Chinese hacking to cyberwar.

His principles were all welcome—securing government networks, coordinating responses, working to secure the infrastructure in private hands (the power grid, the communications networks, and so on), although I think he's overly optimistic that legislation won't be required. I was especially heartened to hear his commitment to funding research. Much of the technology we currently use to secure cyberspace was developed from university research, and the more of it we finance today the more secure we'll be in a decade.

Education is also vital, although sometimes I think my parents need more cybersecurity education than my grandchildren do. I also appreciate the president's commitment to transparency and privacy, both of which are vital for security.

But the details matter. Centralizing security responsibilities has the downside of making security more brittle by instituting a single approach and a uniformity of thinking. Unless the new coordinator distributes responsibility, cybersecurity won't improve.

As the administration moves forward on the plan, two principles should apply. One, security decisions need to be made as close to the problem as possible. Protecting networks should be done by people who understand those networks, and threats needs to be assessed by people close to the threats. But distributed responsibility has more risk, so oversight is vital.

Two, security coordination needs to happen at the highest level possible, whether that's evaluating information about different threats, responding to an Internet worm or establishing guidelines for protecting personal information. The whole picture is larger than any single agency.

"Zero Tolerance" Really Means Zero Discretion

Originally published in MPR NewsQ, *November 4, 2009*

Recent stories have documented the ridiculous effects of zero-tolerance weapons policies in a Delaware school district: a first-grader expelled for taking a camping utensil to school, a 13-year-old expelled after another student dropped a pocketknife in his lap, and a seventh-grader expelled for cutting paper with a utility knife for a class project. Where's the common sense? the editorials cry.

These so-called zero-tolerance policies are actually zero-discretion policies. They're policies that must be followed, no situational discretion allowed. We encounter them whenever we go through airport security: no liquids, gels or aerosols. Some workplaces have them for sexual harassment incidents; in some sports a banned substance found in a urine sample means suspension, even if it's for a real medical condition. Judges have zero discretion when faced with mandatory sentencing laws: three strikes for drug offences and you go to jail, mandatory sentencing for statutory rape (underage sex), etc. A national restaurant chain won't serve hamburgers rare, even if you offer to sign a waiver. Whenever you hear "that's the rule, and I can't do anything about it"—and they're not lying to get rid of you—you're butting against a zero discretion policy.

These policies enrage us because they are blind to circumstance. Editorial after editorial denounced the suspensions of elementary school children for offenses that anyone with any common sense would agree were accidental and harmless. The Internet is filled with essays demonstrating how the TSA's rules are nonsensical and sometimes don't even improve security. I've written some of them. What we want is for those involved in the situations to have discretion.

However, problems with discretion were the reason behind these mandatory policies in the first place. Discretion is often applied inconsistently. One school principal might deal with knives in the classroom one way, and another principal another way. Your drug sentence could depend considerably on how sympathetic your judge is, or on whether she's having a bad day.

Even worse, discretion can lead to discrimination. Schools had weapons bans before zero-tolerance policies, but teachers and administrators enforced the rules disproportionally against African-American students. Criminal sentences varied by race, too. The benefit of zero-discretion rules and laws is that they ensure that everyone is treated equally.

Zero-discretion rules also protect against lawsuits. If the rules are applied consistently, no parent, air traveler or defendant can claim he was unfairly discriminated against.

So that's the choice. Either we want the rules enforced fairly across the board, which means limiting the discretion of the enforcers at the scene at the time, or we want a more nuanced response to whatever the situation is, which means we give those involved in the situation more discretion.

Of course, there's more to it than that. The problem with the zero-tolerance weapons rules isn't that they're rigid, it's that they're poorly written.

What constitutes a weapon? Is it any knife, no matter how small? Should the penalties be the same for a first grader and a high school student? Does intent matter? When an aspirin carried for menstrual cramps becomes "drug possession," you know there's a badly written rule in effect.

It's the same with airport security and criminal sentencing. Broad and simple rules may be simpler to follow—and require less thinking on the part of those enforcing them—but they're almost always far less nuanced than our complex society requires. Unfortunately, the more complex the rules are, the more they're open to interpretation and the more discretion the interpreters have.

The solution is to combine the two, rules and discretion, with procedures to make sure they're not abused. Provide rules, but don't make them so rigid that there's no room for interpretation. Give the people in the situation—the teachers, the airport security agents, the policemen, the judges—discretion to apply the rules to the situation. But—and this is the important part—allow people to appeal the results if they feel they were treated unfairly. And regularly audit the results to ensure there is no discrimination or favoritism. It's the combination of the four that work: rules plus discretion plus appeal plus audit.

All systems need some form of redress, whether it be open and public like a courtroom or closed and secret like the TSA. Giving discretion to those at the scene just makes for a more efficient appeals process, since the first level of appeal can be handled on the spot.

Zachary, the Delaware first grader suspended for bringing a combination fork, spoon and knife camping utensil to eat his lunch with, had his punishment unanimously overturned by the school board. This was the right decision; but what about all the other students whose parents weren't as forceful or media-savvy enough to turn their child's plight into a national story? Common sense in applying rules is important, but so is equal access to that common sense.

US Enables Chinese Hacking of Google

Originally published in CNN, January 23, 2010

Google made headlines when it went public with the fact that Chinese hackers had penetrated some of its services, such as Gmail, in a politically motivated attempt at intelligence gathering. The news here isn't that Chinese hackers engage in these activities or that their attempts are technically sophisticated—we knew that already—it's that the US government inadvertently aided the hackers.

In order to comply with government search warrants on user data, Google created a backdoor access system into Gmail accounts. This feature is what the Chinese hackers exploited to gain access.

Google's system isn't unique. Democratic governments around the world—in Sweden, Canada and the UK, for example—are rushing to pass laws giving their police new powers of Internet surveillance, in many cases requiring communications system providers to redesign products and services they sell.

Many are also passing data retention laws, forcing companies to retain information on their customers. In the US, the 1994 Communications Assistance for Law Enforcement Act required phone companies to facilitate FBI eavesdropping, and since 2001, the National Security Agency has built substantial eavesdropping systems with the help of those phone companies.

Systems like these invite misuse: criminal appropriation, government abuse and stretching by everyone possible to apply to situations that are applicable only by the most tortuous logic. The FBI illegally wiretapped the phones of Americans, often falsely invoking terrorism emergencies, 3,500 times between 2002 and 2006 without a warrant. Internet surveillance and control will be no different.

Official misuses are bad enough, but it's the unofficial uses that worry me more. Any surveillance and control system must itself be secured. An infrastructure conducive to surveillance and control invites surveillance and control, both by the people you expect and by the people you don't.

China's hackers subverted the access system Google put in place to comply with US intercept orders. Why does anyone think criminals won't be able to use the same system to steal bank account and credit card information, use it to launch other attacks or turn it into a massive spam-sending network? Why does anyone think that only authorized law enforcement can mine collected Internet data or eavesdrop on phone and IM conversations?

These risks are not merely theoretical. After September 11, the NSA built a surveillance infrastructure to eavesdrop on telephone calls and e-mails within the US Although procedural rules stated that only non-Americans and international phone calls were to be listened to, actual practice didn't match those rules. NSA analysts collected more data than they were authorized to and used the system to spy on wives, girlfriends and notables such as President Clinton.

But that's not the most serious misuse of a telecommunications surveillance infrastructure. In Greece, between June 2004 and March 2005, someone wiretapped more than 100 cell phones belonging to members of the Greek government: the prime minister and the ministers of defense, foreign affairs and justice.

Ericsson built this wiretapping capability into Vodafone's products and enabled it only for governments that requested it. Greece wasn't one of those governments, but someone still unknown—A rival political party? Organized crime? Foreign intelligence?—figured out how to surreptitiously turn the feature on.

And surveillance infrastructure can be exported, which also aids totalitarianism around the world. Western companies like Siemens and Nokia built Iran's surveillance. US companies helped build China's electronic police state. Just last year, Twitter's anonymity saved the lives of Iranian dissidents, anonymity that many governments want to eliminate.

In the aftermath of Google's announcement, some members of Congress are reviving a bill banning US tech companies from working with governments that digitally spy on their citizens. Presumably, those legislators don't understand that their own government is on the list.

This problem isn't going away. Every year brings more Internet censorship and control, not just in countries like China and Iran but in the US, the UK, Canada, and other free countries, egged on by both law enforcement trying to catch terrorists, child pornographers and other criminals, and by media companies trying to stop file sharers.

The problem is that such control makes us all less safe. Whether the eavesdroppers are the good guys or the bad guys, these systems put us all at greater risk. Communications systems that have no inherent eavesdropping capabilities are more secure than systems with those capabilities built in. And it's bad civic hygiene to build technologies that could someday be used to facilitate a police state.

Should the Government Stop Outsourcing Code Development?

Originally published in Information Security, *March 2010*

This essay appeared as the second half of a point/counterpoint with Marcus Ranum.

Information technology is increasingly everywhere, and it's the same technologies everywhere. The same operating systems are used in corporate and government computers. The same software controls critical infrastructure and home shopping. The same networking technologies are used in every country. The same digital infrastructure underpins the small and the large, the important and the trivial, the local and the global; the same vendors, the same standards, the same protocols, the same applications.

With all of this sameness, you'd think these technologies would be designed to the highest security standard, but they're not. They're designed to the lowest or, at best, somewhere in the middle. They're designed sloppily, in an ad hoc manner, with efficiency in mind. Security is a requirement, more or less, but it's a secondary priority. It's far less important than functionality, and security is what gets compromised when schedules get tight.

Should the government—ours, someone else's?—stop outsourcing code development? That's the wrong question to ask. Code isn't magically more secure when it's written by someone who receives a government paycheck than when it's written by someone who receives a corporate paycheck. It's not magically less secure when it's written by someone who speaks a foreign language, or is paid by the hour instead of by salary. Writing all your code in-house isn't even a viable option anymore; we're all stuck with software written by who-knows-whom in who-knows-which-country. And we need to figure out how to get security from that.

The traditional solution has been defense in depth: layering one mediocre security measure on top of another mediocre security measure. So we have the security embedded in our operating system and applications software, the security embedded in our networking protocols, and our additional security products such as antivirus and firewalls. We hope that whatever security flaws—either found and exploited, or deliberately inserted—there are in one layer are counteracted by the security in another layer, and that when they're not, we can patch our systems quickly enough to avoid serious long-term damage. That is a lousy solution when you think about it, but we've been more-or-less managing with it so far.

Bringing all software—and hardware, I suppose—development in-house under some misconception that proximity equals security is not a better solution. What we need is to improve the software development process, so we can have some assurance that our software is secure—regardless of what coder, employed by what company, and living in what country, writes it. The key word here is "assurance."

Assurance is less about developing new security techniques than about using the ones we already have. It's all the things described in books on secure coding practices. It's what Microsoft is trying to do with its Security Development Lifecycle. It's the Department of Homeland Security's Build Security In program. It's what every aircraft manufacturer goes through before it fields a piece of avionics software. It's what the NSA demands before it purchases a piece of security equipment. As an industry, we know how to provide security assurance in software and systems. But most of the time, we don't care; commercial software, as insecure as it is, is good enough for most purposes.

Assurance is expensive, in terms of money and time, for both the process and the documentation. But the NSA needs assurance for critical military systems and Boeing needs it for its avionics. And the government needs it more and more: for voting machines, for databases entrusted with our personal information, for electronic passports, for communications systems, for the computers and systems controlling our critical infrastructure. Assurance requirements should be more common in government IT contracts.

The software used to run our critical infrastructure—government, corporate, everything—isn't very secure, and there's no hope of fixing it anytime soon. Assurance is really our only option to improve this, but it's expensive and the market doesn't care. Government has to step in and spend the money where its requirements demand it, and then we'll all benefit when we buy the same software.

Punishing Security Breaches

Originally published in Schneier on Security, *April 26, 2009*

The editor of the Freakonomics blog asked me to write about this topic. The idea was that they would get several opinions, and publish them all. They spiked the story, but I'd already written my piece. So here it is.

In deciding what to do with Gray Powell, the Apple employee who accidentally left a secret prototype 4G iPhone in a California bar, Apple needs to figure out how much of the problem is due to an employee not following the rules, and how much of the problem is due to unclear, unrealistic, or just plain bad rules.

If Powell sneaked the phone out of the Apple building in a flagrant violation of the rules—maybe he wanted to show it to a friend—he should be disciplined, perhaps even fired. Some military installations have rules like that. If someone wants to take something classified out of a top secret military compound, he might have to secrete it on his person and deliberately sneak it past a guard who searches briefcases and purses. He might be committing a crime by doing so, by the way. Apple isn't the military, of course, but if its corporate security policy is that strict, it may very well have rules like that. And the only way to ensure rules are followed is by enforcing them, and that means severe disciplinary action against those who bypass the rules.

Even if Powell had authorization to take the phone out of Apple's labs— presumably someone has to test drive the new toys sooner or later—the corporate rules might have required him to pay attention to it at all times. We've all heard of military attachés who carry briefcases chained to their wrists. It's an extreme example, but demonstrates how a security policy can allow for objects to move around town—or around the world—without getting lost. Apple almost certainly doesn't have a policy as rigid as that, but its policy might explicitly prohibit Powell from taking that phone into a bar, putting it down on a counter, and participating in a beer tasting. Again, if Apple's rules and Powell's violation were both that clear, Apple should enforce them.

On the other hand, if Apple doesn't have clear-cut rules, if Powell wasn't prohibited from taking the phone out of his office, if engineers routinely ignore or bypass security rules and—as long as nothing bad happens—no one complains, then Apple needs to understand that the system is more to blame than the individual. Most corporate security policies have this sort of problem. Security is important, but it's quickly jettisoned when there's an important job to be done. A common example is passwords: people aren't supposed to share them, unless it's really important and they have to. Another example is guest accounts. And doors that are supposed to remain locked but rarely are. People routinely bypass security policies if they get in the way, and if no one complains, those policies are effectively meaningless.

Apple's unfortunately public security breach has given the company an opportunity to examine its policies and figure out how much of the problem is Powell and how much of it is the system he's a part of. Apple needs to fix its security problem, but only after it figures out where the problem is.

Three Reasons to Kill the Internet Kill Switch Idea

Originally published in AOL News, July 9, 2010

Last month, Sen. Joe Lieberman, I-Conn., introduced a bill that might—we're not really sure—give the president the authority to shut down all or portions of the Internet in the event of an emergency. It's not a new idea. Sens. Jay Rockefeller, D-W.Va., and Olympia Snowe, R-Maine, proposed the same thing last year, and some argue that the president can already do something like this. If this or a similar bill ever passes, the details will change considerably and repeatedly. So let's talk about the idea of an Internet kill switch in general.

It's a bad one.

Security is always a trade-off: costs versus benefits. So the first question to ask is: What are the benefits? There is only one possible use of this sort of capability, and that is in the face of a warfare-caliber enemy attack. It's the primary reason lawmakers are considering giving the president a kill switch. They know that shutting off the Internet, or even isolating the US from the rest of the world, would cause damage, but they envision a scenario where not doing so would cause even more.

That reasoning is based on several flawed assumptions.

Internet without Borders

The first flawed assumption is that cyberspace has traditional borders, and we could somehow isolate ourselves from the rest of the world using an electronic Maginot Line. We can't.

Yes, we can cut off almost all international connectivity, but there are lots of ways to get out onto the Internet: satellite phones, obscure ISPs in Canada and Mexico, long-distance phone calls to Asia.

The Internet is the largest communications system mankind has ever created, and it works because it is distributed. There is no central authority. No nation is in charge. Plugging all the holes isn't possible.

Even if the president ordered all US Internet companies to block, say, all packets coming from China, or restrict non-military communications, or just shut down access in the greater New York area, it wouldn't work. You can't figure out what packets do just by looking at them; if you could, defending against worms and viruses would be much easier.

And packets that come with return addresses are easy to spoof. Remember the cyberattack July 4, 2009, that probably came from North Korea, but might have come from England, or maybe Florida? On the Internet, disguising traffic is easy. And foreign cyberattackers could always have dial-up accounts via US phone numbers and make long-distance calls to do their misdeeds.

Unpredictable Side Effects

The second flawed assumption is that we can predict the effects of such a shutdown. The Internet is the most complex machine mankind has ever built, and shutting down portions of it would have all sorts of unforeseen ancillary effects.

Would ATMs work? What about the stock exchanges? Which emergency services would fail? Would trucks and trains be able to route their cargo? Would airlines be able to route their passengers? How much of the military's logistical system would fail?

That's to say nothing of the variety of corporations that rely on the Internet to function, let alone the millions of Americans who would need to use it to communicate with their loved ones in a time of crisis.

Even worse, these effects would spill over internationally. The Internet is international in complex and surprising ways, and it would be impossible to ensure that the effects of a shutdown stayed domestic and didn't cause similar disasters in countries we're friendly with.

Security Flaws

The third flawed assumption is that we could build this capability securely. We can't.

Once we engineered a selective shutdown switch into the Internet, and implemented a way to do what Internet engineers have spent decades making sure never happens, we would have created an enormous security vulnerability. We would make the job of any would-be terrorist intent on bringing down the Internet much easier.

Computer and network security is hard, and every Internet system we've ever created has security vulnerabilities. It would be folly to think this one wouldn't as well. And given how unlikely the risk is, any actual shutdown would be far more likely to be a result of an unfortunate error or a malicious hacker than of a presidential order.

But the main problem with an Internet kill switch is that it's too coarse a hammer.

Yes, the bad guys use the Internet to communicate, and they can use it to attack us. But the good guys use it, too, and the good guys far outnumber the bad guys.

Shutting the Internet down, either the whole thing or just a part of it, even in the face of a foreign military attack would do far more damage than it could possibly prevent. And it would hurt others whom we don't want to hurt.

For years we've been bombarded with scare stories about terrorists wanting to shut the Internet down. They're mostly fairy tales, but they're scary precisely because the Internet is so critical to so many things.

Why would we want to terrorize our own population by doing exactly what we don't want anyone else to do? And a national emergency is precisely the worst time to do it.

Just implementing the capability would be very expensive; I would rather see that money going toward securing our nation's critical infrastructure from attack.

Defending his proposal, Sen. Lieberman pointed out that China has this capability. It's debatable whether or not it actually does, but it's actively pursuing the capability because the country cares less about its citizens.

Here in the US, it is both wrong and dangerous to give the president the power and ability to commit Internet suicide and terrorize Americans in this way.

Web Snooping Is a Dangerous Move

Originally published in CNN, *September 29, 2010*

On Monday, the *New York Times* reported that President Obama will seek sweeping laws enabling law enforcement to more easily eavesdrop on the Internet. Technologies are changing, the administration argues, and modern digital systems aren't as easy to monitor as traditional telephones.

The government wants to force companies to redesign their communications systems and information networks to facilitate surveillance, and to provide law enforcement with back doors that enable them to bypass any security measures.

The proposal may seem extreme, but—unfortunately—it's not unique. Just a few months ago, the governments of the United Arab Emirates and Saudi

Arabia threatened to ban BlackBerry devices unless the company made eavesdropping easier. China has already built a massive Internet surveillance system to better control its citizens.

Formerly reserved for totalitarian countries, this wholesale surveillance of citizens has moved into the democratic world as well. Governments like Sweden, Canada and the United Kingdom are debating or passing laws giving their police new powers of Internet surveillance, in many cases requiring communications system providers to redesign products and services they sell. More are passing data retention laws, forcing companies to retain customer data in case they might need to be investigated later.

Obama isn't the first US president to seek expanded digital eavesdropping. The 1994 CALEA law required phone companies to build ways to better facilitate FBI eavesdropping into their digital phone switches. Since 2001, the National Security Agency has built substantial eavesdropping systems within the United States.

These laws are dangerous, both for citizens of countries like China and citizens of Western democracies. Forcing companies to redesign their communications products and services to facilitate government eavesdropping reduces privacy and liberty; that's obvious. But the laws also make us less safe. Communications systems that have no inherent eavesdropping capabilities are more secure than systems with those capabilities built in.

Any surveillance system invites both criminal appropriation and government abuse. Function creep is the most obvious abuse: New police powers, enacted to fight terrorism, are already used in situations of conventional non-terrorist crime. Internet surveillance and control will be no different.

Official misuses are bad enough, but the unofficial uses are far more worrisome. An infrastructure conducive to surveillance and control invites surveillance and control, both by the people you expect and the people you don't. Any surveillance and control system must itself be secured, and we're not very good at that. Why does anyone think that only authorized law enforcement will mine collected Internet data or eavesdrop on Skype and IM conversations?

These risks are not theoretical. After 9/11, the National Security Agency built a surveillance infrastructure to eavesdrop on telephone calls and e-mails within the United States. Although procedural rules stated that only non-Americans and international phone calls were to be listened to, actual practice didn't always match those rules. NSA analysts collected more data than they were authorized to and used the system to spy on wives, girlfriends and famous people like former President Bill Clinton.

The most serious known misuse of a telecommunications surveillance infrastructure took place in Greece. Between June 2004 and March 2005, someone wiretapped more than 100 cell phones belonging to members of the Greek government—the prime minister and the ministers of defense, foreign affairs and justice—and other prominent people. Ericsson built this wiretapping capability into Vodafone's products, but enabled it only for governments that requested it. Greece wasn't one of those governments, but some still unknown party—a rival political group? organized crime?—figured out how to surreptitiously turn the feature on.

Surveillance infrastructure is easy to export. Once surveillance capabilities are built into Skype or Gmail or your BlackBerry, it's easy for more totalitarian countries to demand the same access; after all, the technical work has already been done.

Western companies such as Siemens, Nokia and Secure Computing built Iran's surveillance infrastructure, and US companies like L-1 Identity Solutions helped build China's electronic police state. The next generation of worldwide citizen control will be paid for by countries like the United States.

We should be embarrassed to export eavesdropping capabilities. Secure, surveillance-free systems protect the lives of people in totalitarian countries around the world. They allow people to exchange ideas even when the government wants to limit free exchange. They power citizen journalism, political movements and social change. For example, Twitter's anonymity saved the lives of Iranian dissidents—anonymity that many governments want to eliminate.

Yes, communications technologies are used by both the good guys and the bad guys. But the good guys far outnumber the bad guys, and it's far more valuable to make sure they're secure than it is to cripple them on the off chance it might help catch a bad guy. It's like the FBI demanding that no automobiles drive above 50 mph, so they can more easily pursue getaway cars. It might or might not work—but, regardless, the cost to society of the resulting slowdown would be enormous.

It's bad civic hygiene to build technologies that could someday be used to facilitate a police state. No matter what the eavesdroppers say, these systems cost too much and put us all at greater risk.

The Plan to Quarantine Infected Computers

Originally published in Forbes, *November 11, 2010*

Last month, Scott Charney of Microsoft proposed that infected computers be quarantined from the Internet. Using a public health model for Internet security, the idea is that infected computers spreading worms and viruses are a risk to the greater community and thus need to be isolated. Internet service providers would administer the quarantine, and would also clean up and update users' computers so they could rejoin the greater Internet.

This isn't a new idea. Already there are products that test computers trying to join private networks, and only allow them access if their security patches are up-to-date and their antivirus software certifies them as clean. Computers denied access are sometimes shunned to a limited-capability sub-network where all they can do is download and install the updates they need to regain access. This sort of system has been used with great success at universities and end-user-device-friendly corporate networks. They're happy to let you log in with any device you want—this is the consumerization trend in action—as long as your security is up to snuff.

Charney's idea is to do that on a larger scale. To implement it we have to deal with two problems. There's the technical problem—making the quarantine work in the face of malware designed to evade it, and the social problem—ensuring that people don't have their computers unduly quarantined. Understanding the problems requires us to understand quarantines in general.

Quarantines have been used to contain disease for millennia. In general several things need to be true for them to work. One, the thing being quarantined needs to be easily recognized. It's easier to quarantine a disease if it has obvious physical characteristics: fever, boils, etc. If there aren't any obvious physical effects, or if those effects don't show up while the disease is contagious, a quarantine is much less effective.

Similarly, it's easier to quarantine an infected computer if that infection is detectable. As Charney points out, his plan is only effective against worms and viruses that our security products recognize, not against those that are new and still undetectable.

Two, the separation has to be effective. The leper colonies on Molokai and Spinalonga both worked because it was hard for the quarantined to leave. Quarantined medieval cities worked less well because it was too easy to leave, or—when the diseases spread via rats or mosquitoes—because the quarantine was targeted at the wrong thing.

Computer quarantines have been generally effective because the users whose computers are being quarantined aren't sophisticated enough to break out of the quarantine, and find it easier to update their software and rejoin the network legitimately.

Three, only a small section of the population must need to be quarantined. The solution works only if it's a minority of the population that's affected, either with physical diseases or computer diseases. If most people are infected, over-all infection rates aren't going to be slowed much by quarantining. Similarly, a quarantine that tries to isolate most of the Internet simply won't work.

Fourth, the benefits must outweigh the costs. Medical quarantines are expensive to maintain, especially if people are being quarantined against their will. Determining who to quarantine is either expensive (if it's done correctly) or arbitrary, authoritative and abuse-prone (if it's done badly). It could even be both. The value to society must be worth it.

It's the last point that Charney and others emphasize. If Internet worms were only damaging to the infected, we wouldn't need a societally imposed quarantine like this. But they're damaging to everyone else on the Internet, spreading and infecting others. At the same time, we can implement systems that quarantine cheaply. The value to society far outweighs the cost.

That makes sense, but once you move quarantines from isolated private networks to the general Internet, the nature of the threat changes. Imagine an intelligent and malicious infectious disease: That's what malware is. The current crop of malware ignores quarantines; they're few and far enough between not to affect their effectiveness.

If we tried to implement Internet-wide—or even countrywide—quarantining, worm-writers would start building in ways to break the quarantine. So instead of nontechnical users not bothering to break quarantines because they don't know how, we'd have technically sophisticated virus-writers trying to break quarantines. Implementing the quarantine at the ISP level would help, and if the ISP monitored computer behavior, not just specific virus signatures, it would be somewhat effective even in the face of evasion tactics. But evasion would be possible, and we'd be stuck in another computer security arms race.

This isn't a reason to dismiss the proposal outright, but it is something we need to think about when weighing its potential effectiveness.

Additionally, there's the problem of who gets to decide which computers to quarantine. It's easy on a corporate or university network: the owners of the network get to decide. But the Internet doesn't have that sort of hierarchical control, and denying people access without due process is fraught with danger. What are the appeal mechanisms? The audit mechanisms? Charney proposes that ISPs administer the quarantines, but there would have to be some central authority that decided what degree of infection would be sufficient to impose the quarantine. Although this is being presented as a wholly technical solution, it's these social and political ramifications that are the most difficult to determine and the easiest to abuse.

Once we implement a mechanism for quarantining infected computers, we create the possibility of quarantining them in all sorts of other circumstances. Should we quarantine computers that don't have their patches up to date, even if they're uninfected? Might there be a legitimate reason for someone to avoid patching his computer? Should the government be able to quarantine someone for something he said in a chat room, or a series of search queries he made? I'm sure we don't think it should, but what if that chat and those queries revolved around terrorism? Where's the line?

Microsoft would certainly like to quarantine any computers it feels are not running legal copies of its operating system or applications software. The music and movie industry will want to quarantine anyone it decides is downloading or sharing pirated media files—they're already pushing similar proposals.

A security measure designed to keep malicious worms from spreading over the Internet can quickly become an enforcement tool for corporate business models. Charney addresses the need to limit this kind of function creep, but I don't think it will be easy to prevent; it's an enforcement mechanism just begging to be used.

Once you start thinking about implementation of quarantine, all sorts of other social issues emerge. What do we do about people who need the Internet? Maybe VoIP is their only phone service. Maybe they have an Internet-enabled medical device. Maybe their business requires the Internet to run. The effects of quarantining these people would be considerable, even potentially life-threatening. Again, where's the line?

What do we do if people feel they are quarantined unjustly? Or if they are using nonstandard software unfamiliar to the ISP? Is there an appeals process? Who administers it? Surely not a for-profit company.

Public health is the right way to look at this problem. This conversation—between the rights of the individual and the rights of society—is a valid one to have, and this solution is a good possibility to consider.

There are some applicable parallels. We require drivers to be licensed and cars to be inspected not because we worry about the danger of unlicensed drivers and uninspected cars to themselves, but because we worry about their danger to other drivers and pedestrians. The small number of parents who don't vaccinate their kids have already caused minor outbreaks of whooping cough and measles among the greater population. We all suffer when someone on the Internet allows his computer to get infected. How we balance that with individuals' rights to maintain their own computers as they see fit is a discussion we need to start having.

Close the Washington Monument

Originally published in New York Daily News, *December 2, 2010*

The published version of this essay was heavily edited. This is the complete version.

Securing the Washington Monument from terrorism has turned out to be a surprisingly difficult job. The concrete fence around the building protects it from attacking vehicles, but there's no visually appealing way to house the airport-level security mechanisms the National Park Service has decided are a must for visitors. It is considering several options, but I think we should close the monument entirely. Let it stand, empty and inaccessible, as a monument to our fears.

An empty Washington Monument would serve as a constant reminder to those on Capitol Hill that they are afraid of the terrorists and what they could do. They're afraid that by speaking honestly about the impossibility of attaining absolute security or the inevitability of terrorism—or that some American ideals are worth maintaining even in the face of adversity—they will be branded as "soft on terror." And they're afraid that Americans would vote them out of office if another attack occurred. Perhaps they're right, but what has happened to leaders who aren't afraid? What has happened to "the only thing we have to fear is fear itself"?

An empty Washington Monument would symbolize our lawmakers' inability to take that kind of stand—and their inability to truly lead.

Some of them call terrorism an "existential threat" against our nation. It's not. Even the events of 9/11, as horrific as they were, didn't make an existential dent in our nation. Automobile-related fatalities—at 42,000 per year, more deaths each month, on average, than 9/11—aren't, either. It's our reaction to terrorism that threatens our nation, not terrorism itself. The empty monument would symbolize the empty rhetoric of those leaders who preach fear and then use that fear for their own political ends.

The day after Umar Farouk Abdulmutallab failed to blow up a Northwest jet with a bomb hidden in his underwear, Homeland Security Secretary Janet Napolitano said "The system worked." I agreed. Plane lands safely, terrorist in custody, nobody injured except the terrorist. Seems like a working system to me. The empty monument would represent the politicians and press who pilloried her for her comment, and Napolitano herself, for backing down.

The empty monument would symbolize our war on the unexpected,—our overreaction to anything different or unusual—our harassment of photographers, and our probing of airline passengers. It would symbolize our "show me your papers" society, rife with ID checks and security cameras. As long as we're willing to sacrifice essential liberties for a little temporary safety, we should keep the Washington Monument empty.

Terrorism isn't a crime against people or property. It's a crime against our minds, using the death of innocents and destruction of property to make us fearful. Terrorists use the media to magnify their actions and further spread fear. And when we react out of fear, when we change our policy to make our country less open, the terrorists succeed—even if their attacks fail. But when we refuse to be terrorized, when we're indomitable in the face of terror, the terrorists fail—even if their attacks succeed.

We can reopen the monument when every foiled or failed terrorist plot causes us to praise our security, instead of redoubling it. When the occasional terrorist attack succeeds, as it inevitably will, we accept it, as we accept the murder rate and automobile-related death rate; and redouble our efforts to remain a free and open society.

The grand reopening of the Washington Monument will not occur when we've won the war on terror, because that will never happen. It won't even occur when we've defeated al Qaeda. Militant Islamic terrorism has fractured into small, elusive groups. We can reopen the Washington Monument when we've defeated our fears, when we've come to accept that placing safety above all other virtues cedes too much power to government and that liberty is worth the risks, and that the price of freedom is accepting the possibility of crime.

I would proudly climb to the top of a monument to those ideals.

Whitelisting and Blacklisting

Originally published in Information Security, *January 2011*

This essay appeared as the second half of a point/counterpoint with Marcus Ranum.

The whitelist/blacklist debate is far older than computers, and it's instructive to recall what works where. Physical security works generally on a whitelist model: if you have a key, you can open the door; if you know the combination, you can open the lock. We do it this way not because it's easier—although it is generally much easier to make a list of people who should be allowed through your office door than a list of people who shouldn't—but because it's a security system that can be implemented automatically, without people.

To find blacklists in the real world, you have to start looking at environments where almost everyone is allowed. Casinos are a good example: everyone can come in and gamble except those few specifically listed in the casino's black book or the more general Griffin book. Some retail stores have the same model—a Google search on "banned from Wal-Mart" results in 1.5 million hits, including Megan Fox—although you have to wonder about enforcement. Does Wal-Mart have the same sort of security manpower as casinos?

National borders certainly have that kind of manpower, and Marcus is correct to point to passport control as a system with both a whitelist and a blacklist. There are people who are allowed in with minimal fuss, people who are summarily arrested with as minimal a fuss as possible, and people in the middle who receive some amount of fussing. Airport security works the same way: the no-fly list is a blacklist, and people with redress numbers are on the whitelist.

Computer networks share characteristics with your office and Wal-Mart: sometimes you only want a few people to have access, and sometimes you want almost everybody to have access. And you see whitelists and blacklists at work in computer networks. Access control is whitelisting: if you know the password, or have the token or biometric, you get access. Antivirus is blacklisting: everything coming into your computer from the Internet is assumed to be safe unless it appears on a list of bad stuff. On computers, unlike the real world, it takes no extra manpower to implement a blacklist—the software can do it largely for free.

Traditionally, execution control has been based on a blacklist. Computers are so complicated and applications so varied that it just doesn't make sense to limit users to a specific set of applications. The exception is constrained environments, such as computers in hotel lobbies and airline club lounges. On those, you're often limited to an Internet browser and a few common business applications.

Lately, we're seeing more whitelisting on closed computing platforms. The iPhone works on a whitelist: if you want a program to run on the phone, you need to get it approved by Apple and put in the iPhone store. Your Wii game machine works the same way. This is done primarily because the manufacturers want to control the economic environment, but it's being sold partly as a security measure. But in this case, more security equals less liberty; do you really want your computing options limited by Apple, Microsoft, Google, Facebook, or whoever controls the particular system you're using?

Turns out that many people do. Apple's control over its apps hasn't seemed to hurt iPhone sales, and Facebook's control over its apps hasn't seemed to affect Facebook's user numbers. And honestly, quite a few of us would have had an easier time over the Christmas holidays if we could have implemented a whitelist on the computers of our less-technical relatives.

For these two reasons, I think the whitelist model will continue to make inroads into our general purpose computers. And those of us who want control over our own environments will fight back—perhaps with a whitelist we maintain personally, but more probably with a blacklist.

Securing Medical Research: a Cybersecurity Point of View

Originally published in Science, *June 22, 2012*

This article was based on a talk given at the meeting on H5N1 Research, Biosafety, Biosecurity, and Bioethics, Royal Society, London, April 3, 2012.

Science and *Nature* have each published papers on the H5N1 virus in humans after considerable debate about whether the research results in those papers could help terrorists create a bioweapon. This notion of "dual use" research is an important one for the community, and one that will sooner or later become critical. Perhaps these two papers are not dangerous in the wrong hands, but eventually there will be research results that are.

My background is in cryptography and computer security. I cannot comment on the potential value or harm from any particular piece of biological research, but I can discuss what works and what does not to keep research data secure. The cryptography and computer security communities have been wrestling for decades now with dual-use research: for example, whether to publish new Windows (Microsoft Corporation) vulnerabilities that can be immediately used to attack computers but whose publication helps us make the operating system more secure in the long run. From this experience, I offer five points to the virology community.

First, security based on secrecy is inherently fragile. The more secrets a system has, the less secure it is. A door lock that has a secret but unchangeable locking mechanism is less secure than a commercially purchased door lock with an easily changeable key. In cryptography, this is known as Kerckhoffs' principle: Put all your secrecy into the key and none into the cryptographic algorithm. The key is unique and easily changeable; the algorithm is system-wide and much more likely to become public. In fact, algorithms are deliberately published so that they get analyzed broadly. The lesson for dual-use virology research is that it is risky to base your security on keeping research secret. Militaries spend an enormous amount of money trying to maintain secret research laboratories, and even they do not always get security right. Once secret data become public, there is no way to go back.

Second, omitting technical details from published research is a poor security measure. We tried this in computer security with regard to vulnerabilities, announcing general information but not publishing specifics. The problem is that once the general information is announced, it is much easier for another researcher to replicate the results and generate the details. This is probably even more true in virology research than in computer security research, where the very existence of a result can provide much of the road map to that result.

Third, technical difficulty as a security measure has only short-term value. Technology only gets better; it never gets worse. To believe that some research cannot be replicated by amateurs because it requires equipment only available to state-of-the-art research institutions is short-sighted at best. What is impossible today will be a Ph.D. thesis in 20 years, and what was a Ph.D. thesis 20 years ago is a high-school science fair project today.

Fourth, securing research data in computer networks is risky at best. If you read newspapers, you know the current state of the art in computer security: Everything gets hacked. Cyber criminals steal money from banks. Cyber spies steal data from military computers. Although people talk about H5N1 research in terms of securing the research papers, that is largely a red herring; even if no papers existed, the research data would still be on a network-connected computer somewhere.

Not all computers are hacked and not all data gets stolen, but the risks are there. There are two basic types of threats in cyberspace. There are the opportunists: for example, criminals who want to break into a retail merchant's system and steal a thousand credit card numbers. Against these attackers, relative security is what matters. Because the criminals do not care whom they attack, you are safe if you are more secure than other networks. The other type of threat is a targeted attack. These are attackers who, for whatever reason, want to attack a particular network. The buzzword in Internet security for this is "advanced persistent threat." It is almost impossible to secure a network against a sufficiently skilled and tenacious adversary. All we can do is make the attacker's job harder.

This does not mean that all virology data will be stolen via computer networks, but it does mean that, once the existence of that data becomes public knowledge, you should assume that the bad guys will be able to get their hands on it.

Lastly, national measures that prohibit publication will not work in an international community, especially in the Internet age. If either *Science* or *Nature* had refused to publish the H5N1 papers, they would have been published somewhere else. Even if some countries stop funding—or ban—this sort of research, it will still happen in another country.

The US cryptography community saw this in the 1970s and early 1980s. At that time, the National Security Agency (NSA) controlled cryptography research, which included denying funding for research, classifying results after the fact, and using export-control laws to limit what ended up in products. This was the pre-Internet world, and it worked for a while. In the 1980s they gave up on classifying research, because an international community arose. The limited ability for US researchers to get funding for block-cipher cryptanalysis merely moved that research to Europe and Asia. The NSA continued to limit the spread of cryptography via export-control laws; the US-centric nature of the computer industry meant that this was effective. In the 1990s they gave up on controlling software because the international online community became mainstream; this period was called "the Crypto Wars." Export-control laws did prevent Microsoft from embedding cryptography into Windows for over a decade, but it did nothing to prevent products made in other countries from filling the market gaps.

Today, there are no restrictions on cryptography, and many US government standards are the result of public international competitions. Right now the National Institute of Standards and Technology is working on a new Secure

Hash Algorithm standard. When it is announced next year, it will be the product of a public call for algorithms that resulted in 64 submissions from over a dozen countries and then years of international analysis. The practical effects of unrestricted research are seen in the computer security you use today: on your computer, as you browse the Internet and engage in commerce, and on your cell phone and other smart devices. Sure, the bad guys make use of this research, too, but the beneficial uses far outweigh the malicious ones.

The computer security community has also had to wrestle with these dual-use issues. In the early days of public computing, researchers who discovered vulnerabilities would quietly tell the product vendors so as to not also alert hackers. But all too often, the vendors would ignore the researchers. Because the vulnerability was not public, there was no urgency to fix it. Fixes might go into the next product release. Researchers, tired of this, started publishing the existence of vulnerabilities but not the details. Vendors, in response, tried to muzzle the researchers. They threatened them with lawsuits and belittled them in the press, calling the vulnerabilities only theoretical and not practical. The response from the researchers was predictable: They started publishing full details, and sometimes even code, demonstrating the vulnerabilities they found. This was called "full disclosure" and is the primary reason vendors now patch vulnerabilities quickly. Faced with published vulnerabilities that they could not pretend did not exist and that the hackers could use, they started building internal procedures to quickly issue patches. If you use Microsoft Windows, you know about "patch Tuesday," the once-a-month automatic download and installation of security patches.

Once vendors started taking security patches seriously, the research community (university researchers, security consultants, and informal hackers) moved to something called "responsible disclosure." Now it is common for researchers to alert vendors before publication, giving them a month or two head start to release a security patch. But without the threat of full disclosure, responsible disclosure would not work, and vendors would go back to ignoring security vulnerabilities.

Could a similar process work for viruses? That is, could the makers work in concert with people who develop vaccines so that vaccines become available at the same time as the original results are released? Certainly this is not easy in practice, but perhaps it is a goal to work toward.

Limiting research, either through government classification or legal threats from venders, has a chilling effect. Why would professors or graduate students choose cryptography or computer security if they were going to be prevented from publishing their results? Once these sorts of research slow down, the increasing ignorance hurts us all.

On the other hand, the current vibrant fields of cryptography and computer security are a direct result of our willingness to publish methods of attack. Making and breaking systems are one and the same; you cannot learn one without the other. (Some universities even offer classes in computer virus writing.) Cryptography is better, and computers and networks are more secure, because our communities openly publish details on how to attack systems.

Virology is not computer science. A biological virus is not the same as a computer virus. A vulnerability that affects every individual copy of Windows is not as bad as a vulnerability that affects every individual person. Still, the lessons from computer security are valuable to anyone considering policies intended to encourage life-saving research in virology while at the same time prevent that research from being used to cause harm. This debate will not go away; it will only get more urgent.

Fear Pays the Bills, but Accounts Must Be Settled

Originally published in the New York Times Room for Debate *blog, October 19, 2012*

A lot of the debate around President Obama's cybersecurity initiative centers on how much of a burden it would be on industry, and how that should be financed. As important as that debate is, it obscures some of the larger issues surrounding cyberwar, cyberterrorism, and cybersecurity in general.

It's difficult to have any serious policy discussion amongst the fear-mongering. Secretary Panetta's recent comments are just the latest; search the Internet for "cyber 9/11," "cyber Pearl-Harbor," "cyber Katrina," or—my favorite—"cyber Armageddon."

There's an enormous amount of money and power that results from pushing cyberwar and cyberterrorism: power within the military, the Department of Homeland Security, and the Justice Department; and lucrative government contracts supporting those organizations. As long as cyber remains a prefix that scares, it'll continue to be used as a bugaboo.

But while scare stories are more movie-plot than actual threat, there are real risks. The government is continually poked and probed in cyberspace, from attackers ranging from kids playing politics to sophisticated national intelligence gathering operations. Hackers can do damage, although nothing like the cyberterrorism rhetoric would lead you to believe. Cybercrime continues to rise, and still poses real risks to those of us who work, shop, and play on the Internet. And cyberdefense needs to be part of our military strategy.

Industry has definitely not done enough to protect our nation's critical infrastructure, and federal government may need more involvement. This should come as no surprise; the economic externalities in cybersecurity are so great that even the freest free market would fail.

For example, the owner of a chemical plant will protect that plant from cyberattack up to the value of that plant to the owner; the residual risk to the community around the plant will remain. Politics will color how government involvement looks: market incentives, regulation, or outright government takeover of some aspects of cybersecurity.

None of this requires heavy-handed regulation. Over the past few years we've heard calls for the military to better control Internet protocols; for the United States to be able to "kill" all or part of the Internet, or to cut itself off from the greater Internet; for increased government surveillance; and for limits on anonymity. All of those would be dangerous, and would make us less secure. The world's first military cyberweapon, Stuxnet, was used by the United States and Israel against Iran.

In all of this government posturing about cybersecurity, the biggest risk is a cyber-war arms race; and that's where remarks like Panetta's lead us. Increased government spending on cyberweapons and cyberdefense, and an increased militarization of cyberspace, are both expensive and destabilizing. Fears lead to weapons buildups, and weapons beg to be used.

I would like to see less fear-mongering, and more reasoned discussion about the actual threats and reasonable countermeasures. Pushing the fear button benefits no one.

Power and the Internet ━━━━━━━━━━━━━━━━

Originally published in Edge, *January 23, 2013*

This essay appeared as a response to Edge's *annual question,* "What Should We Be Worried About?"

All disruptive technologies upset traditional power balances, and the Internet is no exception. The standard story is that it empowers the powerless, but that's only half the story. The Internet empowers everyone. Powerful institutions might be slow to make use of that new power, but since they are powerful, they can use it more effectively. Governments and corporations have woken up to the fact that not only can they use the Internet, they can control it for their interests. Unless we start deliberately debating the future we want to live in, and information technology in enabling that world, we will end up with an Internet that benefits existing power structures and not society in general.

We've all lived through the Internet's disruptive history. Entire industries, like travel agencies and video rental stores, disappeared. Traditional publishing—books, newspapers, encyclopedias, music—lost power, while Amazon and others gained. Advertising-based companies like Google and Facebook gained a lot of power. Microsoft lost power (as hard as that is to believe).

The Internet changed political power as well. Some governments lost power as citizens organized online. Political movements became easier, helping to topple governments. The Obama campaign made revolutionary use of the Internet, both in 2008 and 2012.

And the Internet changed social power, as we collected hundreds of "friends" on Facebook, tweeted our way to fame, and found communities for the most obscure hobbies and interests. And some crimes became easier: impersonation fraud became identity theft, copyright violation became file sharing, and accessing censored materials—political, sexual, cultural— became trivially easy.

Now powerful interests are looking to deliberately steer this influence to their advantage. Some corporations are creating Internet environments that maximize their profitability: Facebook and Google, among many others. Some industries are lobbying for laws that make their particular business models more profitable: telecom carriers want to be able to discriminate between different types of Internet traffic, entertainment companies want to crack down on file sharing, advertisers want unfettered access to data about our habits and preferences.

On the government side, more countries censor the Internet—and do so more effectively—than ever before. Police forces around the world are using Internet data for surveillance, with less judicial oversight and sometimes in advance of any crime. Militaries are fomenting a cyberwar arms race. Internet surveillance—both governmental and commercial—is on the rise, not just in totalitarian states but in Western democracies as well. Both companies and governments rely more on propaganda to create false impressions of public opinion.

In 1996, cyber-libertarian John Perry Barlow issued his "Declaration of the Independence of Cyberspace." He told governments: "You have no moral right to rule us, nor do you possess any methods of enforcement that we have true reason to fear." It was a utopian ideal, and many of us believed him. We believed that the Internet generation, those quick to embrace the social changes this new technology brought, would swiftly outmaneuver the more ponderous institutions of the previous era.

Reality turned out to be much more complicated. What we forgot is that technology magnifies power in both directions. When the powerless found the Internet, suddenly they had power. But while the unorganized and nimble were the first to make use of the new technologies, eventually the powerful behemoths woke up to the potential—and they have more power to magnify. And not only does the Internet change power balances, but the powerful can also change the Internet. Does anyone else remember how incompetent the FBI was at investigating Internet crimes in the early 1990s? Or how Internet users ran rings around China's censors and Middle Eastern secret police? Or how digital cash was going to make government currencies obsolete, and Internet organizing was going to make political parties obsolete? Now all that feels like ancient history.

It's not all one-sided. The masses can occasionally organize around a specific issue—SOPA/PIPA, the Arab Spring, and so on—and can block some actions by the powerful. But it doesn't last. The unorganized go back to being unorganized, and powerful interests take back the reins.

Debates over the future of the Internet are morally and politically complex. How do we balance personal privacy against what law enforcement needs to prevent copyright violations? Or child pornography? Is it acceptable to be judged by invisible computer algorithms when being served search results? When being served news articles? When being selected for additional scrutiny by airport security? Do we have a right to correct data about us? To delete it? Do we want computer systems that forget things after some number of years? These are complicated issues that require meaningful debate, international cooperation, and iterative solutions. Does anyone believe we're up to the task?

We're not, and that's the worry. Because if we're not trying to understand how to shape the Internet so that its good effects outweigh the bad, powerful interests will do all the shaping. The Internet's design isn't fixed by natural laws. Its history is a fortuitous accident: an initial lack of commercial interests, governmental benign neglect, military requirements for survivability and resilience, and the natural inclination of computer engineers to build open systems that work simply and easily. This mix of forces that created yesterday's Internet will not be trusted to create tomorrow's. Battles over the future of the Internet are going on right now: in legislatures around the world, in international organizations like the International Telecommunications Union and the World Trade Organization, and in Internet standards bodies. The Internet is what we make it, and is constantly being re-created by organizations, companies, and countries with specific interests and agendas. Either we fight for a seat at the table, or the future of the Internet becomes something that is done to us.

Danger Lurks in Growing New Internet Nationalism

Originally published in MIT Technology Review, *March 11, 2013*

For technology that was supposed to ignore borders, bring the world closer together, and sidestep the influence of national governments, the Internet is fostering an awful lot of nationalism right now. We've started to see increased concern about the country of origin of IT products and services; US companies are worried about hardware from China; European companies are worried about cloud services in the US; no one is sure whether to trust hardware and software from Israel; Russia and China might each be building their own operating systems out of concern about using foreign ones.

I see this as an effect of all the cyberwar saber-rattling that's going on right now. The major nations of the world are in the early years of a cyberwar arms race, and we're all being hurt by the collateral damage.

Our nationalist worries have recently been fueled by a media frenzy surrounding attacks from China. These attacks aren't new—cyber-security experts have been writing about them for at least a decade, and the popular media reported about similar attacks in 2009 and again in 2010—and the current allegations aren't even very different than what came before. This isn't to say that the Chinese attacks aren't serious. The country's espionage campaign is sophisticated, and ongoing. And because they're in the news, people are understandably worried about them.

But it's not just China. International espionage works in both directions, and I'm sure we are giving just as good as we're getting. China is certainly worried about the US Cyber Command's recent announcement that it was expanding from 900 people to almost 5,000, and the NSA's massive new data center in Utah. The US even admits that it can spy on non-US citizens freely.

The fact is that governments and militaries have discovered the Internet; everyone is spying on everyone else, and countries are ratcheting up offensive actions against other countries.

At the same time, many nations are demanding more control over the Internet within their own borders. They reserve the right to spy and censor, and to limit the ability of others to do the same. This idea is now being called the "cyber sovereignty movement," and gained traction at the International Telecommunications Union meeting last December in Dubai. One analyst called that meeting the "Internet Yalta," where the Internet split between liberal-democratic and authoritarian countries. I don't think he's exaggerating.

Not that this is new, either. Remember 2010, when the governments of the UAE, Saudi Arabia, and India demanded that RIM give them the ability to spy on BlackBerry PDAs within their borders? Or last year, when Syria used the Internet to surveil its dissidents? Information technology is a surprisingly powerful tool for oppression: not just surveillance, but censorship and propaganda as well. And countries are getting better at using that tool.

But remember: none of this is cyberwar. It's all espionage, something that's been going on between countries ever since countries were invented. What moves public opinion is less the facts and more the rhetoric, and the rhetoric of war is what we're hearing.

The result of all this saber-rattling is a severe loss of trust, not just amongst nation-states but between people and nation-states. We know we're nothing more than pawns in this game, and we figure we'll be better off sticking with our own country.

Unfortunately, both the reality and the rhetoric play right into the hands of the military and corporate interests that are behind the cyberwar arms race in the first place. There is an enormous amount of power at stake here: not only power within governments and militaries, but power and profit amongst the corporations that supply the tools and infrastructure for cyber-attack and cyber-defense. The more we believe we are "at war" and believe the jingoistic rhetoric, the more willing we are to give up our privacy, freedoms, and control over how the Internet is run.

Arms races are fueled by two things: ignorance and fear. We don't know the capabilities of the other side, and we fear that they are more capable than we are. So we spend more, just in case. The other side, of course, does the same. That spending will result in more cyber weapons for attack and more cyber-surveillance for defense. It will result in more government control over the protocols of the Internet, and less free-market innovation over the same. At its worst, we might be about to enter an information-age Cold War: one with more than two "superpowers." Aside from this being a bad future for the Internet, this is inherently destabilizing. It's just too easy for this amount of antagonistic power and advanced weaponry to get used: for a mistaken attribution to be reacted to with a counterattack, for a misunderstanding to become a cause for offensive action, or for a minor skirmish to escalate into a full-fledged cyberwar.

Nationalism is rife on the Internet, and it's getting worse. We need to damp down the rhetoric and—more importantly—stop believing the propaganda from those who profit from this Internet nationalism. Those who are beating the drums of cyberwar don't have the best interests of society, or the Internet, at heart.

IT for Oppression

Originally published in IEEE Security & Privacy, *March/April 2013*

Whether it's Syria using Facebook to help identify and arrest dissidents or China using its "Great Firewall" to limit access to international news throughout the country, repressive regimes all over the world are using the Internet to more efficiently implement surveillance, censorship, propaganda, and control. They're getting really good at it, and the IT industry is helping. We're helping by creating business applications—categories of applications, really—that are being repurposed by oppressive governments for their own use:

- What is called censorship when practiced by a government is content filtering when practiced by an organization. Many companies want to keep their employees from viewing porn or updating their Facebook pages while at work. In the other direction, data loss prevention software keeps employees from sending proprietary corporate information outside the network and also serves as a censorship tool. Governments can use these products for their own ends.

- Propaganda is really just another name for marketing. All sorts of companies offer social media-based marketing services designed to fool consumers into believing there is "buzz" around a product or brand. The only thing different in a government propaganda campaign is the content of the messages.

- Surveillance is necessary for personalized marketing, the primary profit stream of the Internet. Companies have built massive Internet surveillance systems designed to track users' behavior all over the Internet and closely monitor their habits. These systems track not only individuals but also relationships between individuals, to deduce their interests so as to advertise to them more effectively. It's a totalitarian's dream.

- Control is how companies protect their business models by limiting what people can do with their computers. These same technologies can easily be co-opted by governments that want to ensure that only certain computer programs are run inside their countries or that their citizens never see particular news programs.

Technology magnifies power, and there's no technical difference between a government and a corporation wielding it. This is how commercial security equipment from companies like BlueCoat and Sophos end up being used by the Syrian and other oppressive governments to surveil—in order to arrest—and censor their citizens. This is how the same face-recognition technology that Disney uses in its theme parks ends up identifying protesters in China and Occupy Wall Street protesters in New York.

There are no easy technical solutions, especially because these four applications—censorship, propaganda, surveillance, and control—are intertwined; it can be hard to affect one without also affecting the others. Anonymity helps prevent surveillance, but it also makes propaganda easier. Systems that block propaganda can facilitate censorship. And giving users the ability to run untrusted software on their computers makes it easier for governments—and criminals—to install spyware.

We need more research into how to circumvent these technologies, but it's a hard sell to both the corporations and governments that rely on them. For example, law enforcement in the US wants drones that can identify and track people, even as we decry China's use of the same technology. Indeed, the battleground is often economic and political rather than technical; sometimes circumvention research is itself illegal.

The social issues are large. Power is using the Internet to increase its power, and we haven't yet figured out how to correct the imbalances among government, corporate, and individual interests in our digital world. Cyberspace is still waiting for its Gandhi, its Martin Luther King, and a convincing path from the present to a better future.

The Public/Private Surveillance Partnership

Originally published in the Atlantic, *April 30, 2013*

Our government collects a lot of information about us. Tax records, legal records, license records, records of government services received—it's all in databases that are increasingly linked and correlated. Still, there's a lot of personal information the government can't collect. Either they're prohibited by law from asking without probable cause and a judicial order, or they simply have no cost-effective way to collect it. But the government has figured out how to get around the laws, and collect personal data that has been historically denied to them: ask corporate America for it.

It's no secret that we're monitored continuously on the Internet. Some of the company names you know, such as Google and Facebook. Others hide in the background as you move about the Internet. There are browser plugins that show you who is tracking you. One Atlantic editor found 105 companies tracking him during one 36-hour period. Add data from your cell phone (who you talk to, your location), your credit cards (what you buy, from whom you buy it), and the dozens of other times you interact with a computer daily, we live in a surveillance state beyond the dreams of Orwell.

It's all corporate data, compiled and correlated, bought and sold. And increasingly, the government is doing the buying. Some of this is collected using National Security Letters (NSLs). These give the government the ability to demand an enormous amount of personal data about people for very speculative reasons, with neither probable cause nor judicial oversight. Data on these secretive orders is obviously scant, but we know that the FBI has issued hundreds of thousands of them in the past decade—for reasons that go far beyond terrorism.

NSLs aren't the only way the government can get at corporate data. Sometimes they simply purchase it, just as any other company might. Sometimes they can get it for free, from corporations that want to stay on the government's good side.

CISPA, a bill currently wending its way through Congress, codifies this sort of practice even further. If signed into law, CISPA will allow the government to collect all sorts of personal data from corporations, without any oversight at all, and will protect corporations from lawsuits based on their handing over that data. Without hyperbole, it's been called the death of the 4th Amendment. Right now, it's mainly the FBI and the NSA who are getting this data, but—all sorts of government agencies have administrative subpoena power.

Data on this scale has all sorts of applications. From finding tax cheaters by comparing data brokers' estimates of income and net worth with what's reported on tax returns, to compiling a list of gun owners from Web browsing habits, instant messaging conversations, and locations—did you have your iPhone turned on when you visited a gun store?—the possibilities are endless.

Government photograph databases form the basis of any police facial recognition system. They're not very good today, but they'll only get better. But the government no longer needs to collect photographs. Experiments demonstrate that the Facebook database of tagged photographs is surprisingly effective at identifying people. As more places follow Disney's lead in fingerprinting people at its theme parks, the government will be able to use that to identify people as well.

In a few years, the whole notion of a government-issued ID will seem quaint. Among facial recognition, the unique signature from your smart phone, the RFID chips in your clothing and other items you own, and whatever new technologies that will broadcast your identity, no one will have to ask to see ID. When you walk into a store, they'll already know who you are. When you interact with a policeman, she'll already have your personal information displayed on her Internet-enabled glasses.

Soon, governments won't have to bother collecting personal data. We're willingly giving it to a vast network of for-profit data collectors, and they're more than happy to pass it on to the government without our knowledge or consent.

Transparency and Accountability Don't Hurt Security—They're Crucial to It

Originally published in the Atlantic, *May 8, 2013*

As part of the fallout of the Boston bombings, we're probably going to get some new laws that give the FBI additional investigative powers. As with the Patriot Act after 9/11, the debate over whether these new laws are helpful will be minimal, but the effects on civil liberties could be large. Even though most people are skeptical about sacrificing personal freedoms for security, it's hard for politicians to say no to the FBI right now, and it's politically expedient to demand that *something* be done.

If our leaders can't say no—and there's no reason to believe they can—there are two concepts that need to be part of any new counterterrorism laws, and investigative laws in general: transparency and accountability.

Long ago, we realized that simply trusting people and government agencies to always do the right thing doesn't work, so we need to check up on them. In a democracy, transparency and accountability are how we do that. It's how we ensure that we get both effective and cost-effective government. It's how we prevent those we trust from abusing that trust, and protect ourselves when they do. And it's especially important when security is concerned.

First, we need to ensure that the stuff we're paying money for actually works and has a measureable impact. Law-enforcement organizations regularly invest in technologies that don't make us any safer. The TSA, for example, could devote an entire museum to expensive but ineffective systems: puffer machines, body scanners, FAST behavioral screening, and so on. Local police departments have been wasting lots of post-9/11 money on unnecessary high-tech weaponry and equipment. The occasional high-profile success aside, police surveillance cameras have been shown to be a largely ineffective police tool.

Sometimes honest mistakes led organizations to invest in these technologies. Sometimes there's self-deception and mismanagement—and far too often lobbyists are involved. Given the enormous amount of security money post-9/11, you inevitably end up with an enormous amount of waste. Transparency and accountability are how we keep all of this in check.

Second, we need to ensure that law enforcement does what we expect it to do and nothing more. Police powers are invariably abused. Mission creep is inevitable, and it results in laws designed to combat one particular type of crime being used for an ever-widening array of crimes. Transparency is the only way we have of knowing when this is going on.

For example, that's how we learned that the FBI is abusing National Security Letters. Traditionally, we use the warrant process to protect ourselves from police overreach. It's not enough for the police to want to conduct a search; they also need to convince a neutral third party—a judge—that the search is in the public interest and will respect the rights of those searched. That's accountability, and it's the very mechanism that NSLs were exempted from.

When laws are broken, accountability is how we punish those who abused their power. It's how, for example, we correct racial profiling by police departments. And it's a lack of accountability that permits the FBI to get away with massive data collection until exposed by a whistleblower or noticed by a judge.

Third, transparency and accountability keep both law enforcement and politicians from lying to us. The Bush Administration lied about the extent of the NSA's warrantless wiretapping program. The TSA lied about the ability of full-body scanners to save naked images of people. We've been lied to about the lethality of Tasers, when and how the FBI eavesdrops on cell-phone calls, and about the existence of surveillance records. Without transparency, we would never know.

A decade ago, the FBI was heavily lobbying Congress for a law to give it new wiretapping powers: a law known as CALEA. One of its key justifications was that existing law didn't allow it to perform speedy wiretaps during kidnapping investigations. It sounded plausible—and who wouldn't feel sympathy for kidnapping victims?—but when civil-liberties organizations analyzed the actual data, they found that it was just a story; there were no instances of wiretapping in kidnapping investigations. Without transparency, we would never have known that the FBI was making up stories to scare Congress.

If we're going to give the government any new powers, we need to ensure that there's oversight. Sometimes this oversight is before action occurs. Warrants are a great example. Sometimes they're after action occurs: public reporting, audits by inspector generals, open hearings, notice to those affected, or some other mechanism. Too often, law enforcement tries to exempt itself from this principle by supporting laws that are specifically excused from oversight. . . or by establishing secret courts that just rubber-stamp government wiretapping requests.

Furthermore, we need to ensure that mechanisms for accountability have teeth and are used.

As we respond to the threat of terrorism, we must remember that there are other threats as well. A society without transparency and accountability is the very definition of a police state. And while a police state might have a low crime rate—especially if you don't define police corruption and other abuses of power as crime—and an even lower terrorism rate, it's not a society that most of us would willingly choose to live in.

We already give law enforcement enormous power to intrude into our lives. We do this because we know they need this power to catch criminals, and we're all safer thereby. But because we recognize that a powerful police force is itself a danger to society, we must temper this power with transparency and accountability.

It's Smart Politics to Exaggerate Terrorist Threats

Originally published in CNN, *May 20, 2013*

Terrorism causes fear, and we overreact to that fear. Our brains aren't very good at probability and risk analysis. We tend to exaggerate spectacular, strange and rare events, and downplay ordinary, familiar and common ones. We think rare risks are more common than they are, and we fear them more than probability indicates we should.

Our leaders are just as prone to this overreaction as we are. But aside from basic psychology, there are other reasons that it's smart politics to exaggerate terrorist threats, and security threats in general.

The first is that we respond to a strong leader. Bill Clinton famously said: "When people feel uncertain, they'd rather have somebody that's strong and wrong than somebody who's weak and right." He's right.

The second is that doing something—anything—is good politics. A politician wants to be seen as taking charge, demanding answers, fixing things. It just doesn't look as good to sit back and claim that there's nothing to do. The logic is along the lines of: "Something must be done. This is something. Therefore, we must do it."

The third is that the "fear preacher" wins, regardless of the outcome. Imagine two politicians today. One of them preaches fear and draconian security measures. The other is someone like me, who tells people that terrorism is a negligible risk, that risk is part of life, and that while some security is necessary, we should mostly just refuse to be terrorized and get on with our lives.

Fast-forward 10 years. If I'm right and there have been no more terrorist attacks, the fear preacher takes credit for keeping us safe. But if a terrorist attack has occurred, my government career is over. Even if the incidence of terrorism is as ridiculously low as it is today, there's no benefit for a politician to take my side of that gamble.

The fourth and final reason is money. Every new security technology, from surveillance cameras to high-tech fusion centers to airport full-body scanners, has a for-profit corporation lobbying for its purchase and use. Given the three other reasons above, it's easy—and probably profitable—for a politician to make them happy and say yes.

For any given politician, the implications of these four reasons are straightforward. Overestimating the threat is better than underestimating it. Doing something about the threat is better than doing nothing. Doing something that is explicitly reactive is better than being proactive. (If you're proactive and you're wrong, you've wasted money. If you're proactive and you're right but no longer in power, whoever is in power is going to get the credit for what you did.) Visible is better than invisible. Creating something new is better than fixing something old.

Those last two maxims are why it's better for a politician to fund a terrorist fusion center than to pay for more Arabic translators for the National Security Agency. No one's going to see the additional appropriation in the NSA's secret budget. On the other hand, a high-tech computerized fusion center is going to make front page news, even if it doesn't actually do anything useful.

This leads to another phenomenon about security and government. Once a security system is in place, it can be very hard to dislodge it. Imagine a politician who objects to some aspect of airport security: the liquid ban, the shoe removal, something. If he pushes to relax security, he gets the blame if something bad happens as a result. No one wants to roll back a police power and have the lack of that power cause a well-publicized death, even if it's a one-in-a-billion fluke.

We're seeing this force at work in the bloated terrorist no-fly and watch lists; agents have lots of incentive to put someone on the list, but absolutely no incentive to take anyone off. We're also seeing this in the Transportation Security Administration's attempt to reverse the ban on small blades on airplanes. Twice it tried to make the change, and twice fearful politicians prevented it from going through with it.

Lots of unneeded and ineffective security measures are perpetrated by a government bureaucracy that is primarily concerned about the security of its members' careers. They know the voters are more likely to punish them more if they fail to secure against a repetition of the last attack, and less if they fail to anticipate the next one.

What can we do? Well, the first step toward solving a problem is recognizing that you have one. These are not iron-clad rules; they're tendencies. If we can keep these tendencies and their causes in mind, we're more likely to end up with sensible security measures that are commensurate with the threat, instead of a lot of security theater and draconian police powers that are not.

Our leaders' job is to resist these tendencies. Our job is to support politicians who do resist.

References

Consolidation: Plague or Progress
http://searchsecurity.techtarget.com/
    magazineFeature/0,296894,sid14_gci1303850_idx2,00.html

Prediction: RSA Conference Will Shrink Like a Punctured Balloon
http://www.wired.com/politics/security/news/2008/04/
    securitymatters_0417

How to Sell Security
http://www.cio.com/article/367913

Why Do We Accept Signatures by Fax?
http://www.wired.com/politics/security/commentary/
    securitymatters/2008/05/securitymatters_0529

The Pros and Cons of LifeLock
http://www.wired.com/politics/security/commentary/
    securitymatters/2008/06/securitymatters_0612

The Problem Is Information Insecurity
https://www.schneier.com/essay-233.html

Security ROI: Fact or Fiction?
http://www.csoonline.com/article/446866/
    Security_ROI_Fact_or_Fiction_

Social Networking Risks
http://searchsecurity.techtarget.com/magazineContent/
    Schneier-Ranum-debate-social-networking-risks

Do You Know Where Your Data Are?
http://online.wsj.com/article/SB123997522418329223.html

Be Careful When You Come to Put Your Trust in the Clouds
http://www.guardian.co.uk/technology/2009/jun/04/
    bruce-schneier-cloud-computing

Is Perfect Access Control Possible?
http://searchsecurity.techtarget.com/
    magazineFeature/0,296894,sid14_gci1365957,00.html

News Media Strategies for Survival for Journalists
http://www.tcdailyplanet.net/news/2009/11/11/
    opinion-news-media-strategies-survival

Security and Function Creep
https://www.schneier.com/essay-307.html

Weighing the Risk of Hiring Hackers
http://searchsecurity.techtarget.com/magazinePrintFriendly/
    0,296905,sid14_gci1514250,00.html

Should Enterprises Give In to IT Consumerization at the Expense of
Security?
http://searchsecurity.techtarget.com/
    magazineFeature/0,296894,sid14_gci1519679,00.html

The Vulnerabilities Market and the Future of Security
http://www.forbes.com/sites/bruceschneier/2012/05/30/
    the-vulnerabilities-market-and-the-future-of-security/

So You Want to Be a Security Expert
http://krebsonsecurity.com/2012/07/
    how-to-break-into-security-schneier-edition/

When It Comes to Security, We're Back to Feudalism
http://www.wired.com/opinion/2012/11/feudal-security/

You Have No Control Over Security on the Feudal Internet
http://blogs.hbr.org/cs/2013/06/you_have_no_control_over_s.html

America's Dilemma: Close Security Holes, or Exploit Them Ourselves
http://www.wired.com/politics/security/commentary/
    securitymatters/2008/05/blog_securitymatters_0501

Are Photographers Really a Threat?
http://www.guardian.co.uk/technology/2008/jun/05/news.terrorism

CCTV Doesn't Keep Us Safe, yet the Cameras Are Everywhere
http://www.guardian.co.uk/technology/2008/jun/26/politics.ukcrime

Chinese Cyberattacks: Myth or Menace?
http://searchsecurity.techtarget.com/
magazineFeature/0,296894,sid14_gci1321716,00.html

How a Classic Man-in-the-Middle Attack Saved Colombian Hostages
http://www.wired.com/politics/security/commentary/
securitymatters/2008/07/securitymatters_0710

How to Create the Perfect Fake Identity
http://www.wired.com/politics/security/commentary/
securitymatters/2008/09/securitymatters_0904

A Fetishistic Approach to Security Is a Perverse Way to Keep Us Safe
http://www.guardian.co.uk/technology/2008/sep/04/terrorism
.terrorismandtravel

The Seven Habits of Highly Ineffective Terrorists
http://www.wired.com/politics/security/commentary/
securitymatters/2008/10/securitymatters_1002

Why Society Should Pay the True Costs of Security
http://www.guardian.co.uk/technology/2008/oct/02/chemicals
.terrorism

Why Technology Won't Prevent Identity Theft
http://online.wsj.com/article/SB123125633551557469.html

Terrorists May Use Google Earth, but Fear Is No Reason to Ban It
http://www.guardian.co.uk/technology/2009/jan/29/
read-me-first-google-earth

Thwarting an Internal Hacker
http://online.wsj.com/article/SB123447990459779609.html

An Enterprising Criminal Has Spotted a Gap in the Market
http://www.guardian.co.uk/technology/2009/apr/02/
google-earth-censorship-crime-comodities

We Shouldn't Poison Our Minds with Fear of Bioterrorism
http://www.guardian.co.uk/technology/2009/may/14/
bruce-schneier-bioterrorism

Raising the Cost of Paperwork Errors Will Improve Accuracy
http://www.guardian.co.uk/technology/2009/jun/24/
read-me-first-identity-fraud

So-Called Cyberattack Was Overblown
http://minnesota.publicradio.org/display/web/2009/07/10/schneier/

Why Framing Your Enemies Is Now Virtually Child's Play
http://www.guardian.co.uk/technology/2009/oct/15/
    bruce-schneier-internet-security

Beyond Security Theater
https://www.schneier.com/essay-292.html

Cold War Encryption Is Unrealistic in Today's Trenches
http://search.japantimes.co.jp/cgi-bin/nc20091230a2.html

Profiling Makes Us Less Safe
http://roomfordebate.blogs.nytimes.com/2010/01/04/
    will-profiling-make-a-difference/

Fixing Intelligence Failures
http://www.sfgate.com/cgi-bin/article.cgi?f=/c/a/2010/01/14/
    EDOL1BIFK6.DTL

Spy Cameras Won't Make Us Safer
http://www.cnn.com/2010/OPINION/02/25/schneier.security.cameras/
    index.html

Scanners, Sensors Are Wrong Way to Secure the Subway
http://www.nydailynews.com/opinions/2010/04/07/2010-04-07
    _scanners_sensors_are_wrong_way_to_secure_the_subway.html

Preventing Terrorist Attacks in Crowded Areas
http://roomfordebate.blogs.nytimes.com/2010/05/03/
    times-square-bombs-and-big-crowds/?src=tptw#bruce

Where Are All the Terrorist Attacks?
http://www.aolnews.com/2010/05/04/
    opinion-where-are-all-the-terrorist-attacks/

Worst-Case Thinking Makes Us Nuts, Not Safe
http://www.cnn.com/2010/OPINION/05/12/schneier.worst.case
    .thinking/

Threat of "Cyberwar" Has Been Hugely Hyped
http://www.cnn.com/2010/OPINION/07/07/schneier.cyberwar.hyped/

Cyberwar and the Future of Cyber Conflict
http://www.ft.com/cms/s/0/f863fb4c-fe53-11df-abac-00144feab49a
    .html

Why Terror Alert Codes Never Made Sense
http://www.cnn.com/2011/OPINION/01/28/schneier.terror.threat
    .level/

Debate Club: An International Cyberwar Treaty Is the Only Way to Stem the
   Threat
http://www.usnews.com/debate-club/should-there-be-an
   -international-treaty-on-cyberwarfare/an-international
   -cyberwar-treaty-is-the-only-way-to-stem-the-threat

Overreaction and Overly Specific Reactions to Rare Risks
http://www.cnn.com/2012/07/31/opinion/schneier-aurora-aftermath/
   index.html

Militarizing Cyberspace Will Do More Harm Than Good
http://www.irishtimes.com/newspaper/
   finance/2012/1129/1224327257946.html

Rhetoric of Cyber War Breeds Fear—And More Cyber War
https://www.schneier.com/essay-421.html

The Boston Marathon Bombing: Keep Calm and Carry On
http://www.theatlantic.com/national/archive/2013/04/
   the-boston-marathon-bombing-keep-calm-and-carry-on/275014/

Why FBI and CIA Didn't Connect the Dots
http://www.cnn.com/2013/05/02/opinion/schneier-boston-bombing/
   index.html

The FBI's New Wiretapping Plan Is Great News for Criminals
http://www.foreignpolicy.com/articles/2013/05/29/
   the_fbi_s_new_wiretapping_plan_is_great_news_for_criminals

US Offensive Cyberwar Policy
http://www.cnn.com/2013/06/18/opinion/schneier-cyberwar-policy/
   index.html

Secret Questions Blow a Hole in Security
http://www.computerweekly.com/Articles/2008/04/04/230137/
   secret-questions-blow-a-hole-in-security.htm

When You Lose a Piece of Kit, the Real Loss Is the Data It Contains
http://www.guardian.co.uk/technology/2008/dec/04/
   computer-security-mobile-phones

The Kindness of Strangers
http://online.wsj.com/article/SB123567809587886053.html

Blaming the User Is Easy—But It's Better to Bypass Them Altogether
http://www.guardian.co.uk/technology/2009/mar/12/read-me-first

The Value of Self-Enforcing Protocols
http://threatpost.com/blogs/value-self-enforcing-protocols

Reputation is Everything in IT Security
http://www.guardian.co.uk/technology/2009/nov/11/
    schneier-reputation-it-security

When to Change Passwords
http://www.darkreading.com/hacked-off/
    when-to-change-passwords/228201016

The Big Idea: Bruce Schneier
http://whatever.scalzi.com/2012/02/16/the-big-idea-bruce-schneier/

High-Tech Cheats in a World of Trust
http://www.newscientist.com/article/
    mg21328530.400-foiling-the-cheats-in-a-world-of-hightech-
    trust.html

Detecting Cheaters
https://www.schneier.com/essay-337.html

Lance Armstrong and the Prisoner's Dilemma of Doping in Professional
    Sports
http://www.wired.com/opinion/2012/10/
    lance-armstrong-and-the-prisoners-dilemma-of-doping-in-
    professional-sports/

Trust and Society
http://www.themontrealreview.com/2009/
    Liars-and-Outliers-Bruce-Schneier.php

How Secure Is the Papal Election?
http://www.cnn.com/2013/02/20/opinion/
    schneier-papal-election-secure/index.html

The Court of Public Opinion
http://www.wired.com/opinion/2013/02/court-of-public-opinion/

On Security Awareness Training
http://www.darkreading.com/blog/240151108/
    on-security-awareness-training.html

Our New Regimes of Trust
https://www.schneier.com/essay-410.html

https://www.schneier.com/essay-253.html
https://www.schneier.com/blog/archives/2013/02/our_new_regimes
    .html

The Myth of the "Transparent Society"
http://www.wired.com/politics/security/commentary/
    securitymatters/2008/03/securitymatters_0306

Our Data, Ourselves
http://www.wired.com/politics/security/commentary/
    securitymatters/2008/05/securitymatters_0515

The Future of Ephemeral Conversation
http://online.wsj.com/article/SB122722381368945937.html

How to Prevent Digital Snooping
http://online.wsj.com/article/SB122877438178489235.html

Architecture of Privacy
https://www.schneier.com/essay-253.html

Privacy in the Age of Persistence
http://news.bbc.co.uk/1/hi/technology/7897892.stm

Should We Have an Expectation of Online Privacy?
http://searchsecurity.techtarget.com/magazinePrintFriendly/
    0,296905,sid14_gci1354832,00.html

Offhand but On Record
http://www.japantimes.co.jp/life/2009/08/19/life/
    offhand-but-on-record/

Google's and Facebook's Privacy Illusion
http://www.forbes.com/2010/04/05/
        google-facebook-twitter-technology-security-10-privacy
    .html

The Internet: Anonymous Forever
http://www.forbes.com/2010/05/12/
        privacy-hackers-internet-technology-security-anonymity
    .html

A Taxonomy of Social Networking Data
https://www.schneier.com/essay-322.html

The Difficulty of Surveillance Crowdsourcing
http://threatpost.com/en_us/blogs/
        difficulty-surveillance-crowdsourcing-110810

The Difficulty of Surveillance Crowdsourcing
http://threatpost.com/en_us/blogs/
    difficulty-surveillance-crowdsourcing-110810

The Internet Is a Surveillance State
http://www.cnn.com/2013/03/16/opinion/
    schneier-internet-surveillance/index.html

Surveillance and the Internet of Things
http://www.guardian.co.uk/technology/2013/may/16/
    internet-of-things-privacy-google

Government Secrets and the Need for Whistleblowers
http://www.theatlantic.com/politics/archive/2013/06/
    what-we-dont-know-about-spying-on-citizens-scarier
    -than-what-we-know/276607/

Before Prosecuting, Investigate the Government
http://www.nytimes.com/roomfordebate/2013/06/11/
    in-nsa-leak-case-a-whistle-blower-or-a-criminal/
    before-prosecuting-snowden-investigate-the-government

The Security Mindset
http://www.wired.com/politics/security/commentary/
    securitymatters/2008/03/securitymatters_0320

The Difference between Feeling and Reality in Security
http://www.wired.com/politics/security/commentary/
    securitymatters/2008/04/securitymatters_0403

How the Human Brain Buys Security
http://ieeexplore.ieee.org/xpl/login
    .jsp?tp=&arnumber=4588238&isnumber=4588217&url=http%3A%2F%
    2Fieeexplore.ieee.org%2Fxpls%2Fabs_all
    .jsp%3Farnumber%3D4588238%26isnumber%3D4588217

Does Risk Management Make Sense?
http://searchsecurity.techtarget.com/
    magazineFeature/0,296894,sid14_gci1332745_idx2,00.html

How the Great Conficker Panic Hacked into Human Credulity
http://www.guardian.co.uk/technology/2009/apr/23/conficker-panic

How Science Fiction Writers Can Help, or Hurt, Homeland Security
http://www.wired.com/politics/security/commentary/
    securitymatters/2009/06/securitymatters_0619

Privacy Salience and Social Networking Sites
http://www.guardian.co.uk/technology/2009/jul/15/
     privacy-internet-facebook

Security, Group Size, and the Human Brain
https://www.schneier.com/essay-275.html July/August 2009

People Understand Risks—But Do Security Staff Understand People?
http://www.guardian.co.uk/technology/2009/aug/05/
     bruce-schneier-risk-security

Nature's Fears Extend to Online Behavior
http://www.japantimes.co.jp/text/nc20091118a1.html

The Ethics of Vulnerability Research
http://searchsecurity.techtarget.com/
     magazineFeature/0,296894,sid14_gci1313268,00.html

I've Seen the Future, and It Has a Kill Switch
http://www.wired.com/politics/security/commentary/
     securitymatters/2008/06/securitymatters_0626

Software Makers Should Take Responsibility
http://www.guardian.co.uk/technology/2008/jul/17/internet
     .security

Lesson from the DNS Bug: Patching Isn't Enough
http://www.wired.com/politics/security/commentary/
     securitymatters/2008/07/securitymatters_0723

Why Being Open about Security Makes Us All Safer in the Long Run
http://www.guardian.co.uk/technology/2008/aug/07/hacking.security

Boston Court's Meddling with "Full Disclosure" Is Unwelcome
http://www.wired.com/politics/security/commentary/
     securitymatters/2008/08/securitymatters_0821

Quantum Cryptography: As Awesome As It Is Pointless
http://www.wired.com/politics/security/commentary/
     securitymatters/2008/10/securitymatters_1016

Passwords Are Not Broken, but How We Choose Them Sure Is
http://www.guardian.co.uk/technology/2008/nov/13/
     internet-passwords

America's Next Top Hash Function Begins
http://www.wired.com/politics/security/commentary/
     securitymatters/2008/11/securitymatters_1120

Tigers Use Scent, Birds Use Calls—Biometrics Are Just Animal Instinct
http://www.guardian.co.uk/technology/2009/jan/08/
　　identity-fraud-security-biometrics-schneier-id

The Secret Question Is: Why Do IT Systems Use Insecure Passwords?
http://www.guardian.co.uk/technology/2009/feb/19/
　　insecure-passwords-conflickerb-worm

The Pros and Cons of Password Masking
http://www.schneier.com/blog/archives/2009/07/the_pros_and_co.html

Technology Shouldn't Give Big Brother a Head Start
http://minnesota.publicradio.org/display/web/2009/07/30/schneier/

Lockpicking and the Internet
http://www.darkreading.com/hacked-off/
　　lockpicking-and-the-internet/227700647

The Battle Is On against Facebook and Co. to Regain Control of Our Files
http://www.guardian.co.uk/technology/2009/sep/09/
　　bruce-schneier-file-deletion

The Difficulty of Un-Authentication
http://threatpost.com/difficulty-un-authentication-092809/72267

Is Antivirus Dead?
http://searchsecurity.techtarget.com/magazinePrintFriendly/
　　0,296905,sid14_gci1373562,00.html

Virus and Protocol Scares Happen Every Day—But Don't Let Them Worry
You
http://www.guardian.co.uk/technology/blog/2009/dec/09/
　　virus-protocol-scares-every-day

The Failure of Cryptography to Secure Modern Networks
http://www.darkreading.com/blog/227700878/
　　the-failure-of-cryptography-to-secure-modern-networks.html

The Story behind The Stuxnet Virus
http://www.forbes.com/2010/10/06/
　　iran-nuclear-computer-technology-security-stuxnet-worm
　　.html

The Dangers of a Software Monoculture
http://searchsecurity.techtarget.com/
　　magazineFeature/0,296894,sid14_gci1522895,00.html

How Changing Technology Affects Security
https://www.schneier.com/essay-392.html

The Importance of Security Engineering
http://www.schneier.com/blog/archives/2012/08/the_importance_1
    .html

Technologies of Surveillance
http://www.schneier.com/blog/archives/2013/03/technologies_of.html

When Technology Overtakes Security
http://www.wired.com/opinion/2013/03/
    security-when-the-bad-guys-have-technology-too-how-do-we-
    survive/

Memo to Next President: How to Get Cybersecurity Right
http://www.wired.com/politics/security/commentary/
    securitymatters/2008/08/securitymatters_0807

CRB Checking
https://www.schneier.com/essay-277.html

State Data Breach Notification Laws: Have They Helped?
http://searchsecurity.techtarget.com/
    magazineFeature/0,296894,sid14_gci1344729_idx2,00.html

How to Ensure Police Database Accuracy
http://online.wsj.com/article/SB123301316511017419.html

How Perverse Incentives Drive Bad Security Decisions
http://www.wired.com/politics/security/commentary/
    securitymatters/2009/02/securitymatters_0226

It's Time to Drop the "Expectation of Privacy" Test
http://www.wired.com/politics/security/commentary/
    securitymatters/2009/03/securitymatters_0326

Who Should Be in Charge of Cybersecurity?
http://online.wsj.com/article/SB123844579753370907.html

Coordinate, but Distribute Responsibility
http://roomfordebate.blogs.nytimes
    .com/2009/05/29/a-plan-of-attack-in-cyberspace/#bruce

"Zero Tolerance" Really Means Zero Discretion
http://minnesota.publicradio.org/display/web/2009/11/03/schneier/

US Enables Chinese Hacking of Google
http://www.cnn.com/2010/OPINION/01/23/schneier.google.hacking/

Should the Government Stop Outsourcing Code Development?
http://searchsecurity.techtarget.com/
    magazineFeature/0,296894,sid14_gci1507396,00.html

Punishing Security Breaches
https://www.schneier.com/blog/archives/2010/04/punishing_secur
    .html

Three Reasons to Kill the Internet Kill Switch Idea
https://www.schneier.com/essay-321.html

Web Snooping Is a Dangerous Move
http://www.cnn.com/2010/OPINION/09/29/schneier.web.surveillance/
    index.html?iref=allsearch

The Plan to Quarantine Infected Computers
http://www.forbes.com/2010/11/10/
    microsoft-viruses-security-technology-quarantine.html

Close the Washington Monument
https://www.schneier.com/essay-332.html
http://www.nydailynews.com/opinions/2010/12/02/2010-12-02
    _washington_monument_security_debate_is_the_height_of
    _irrational_fearmongering.html

Whitelisting and Blacklisting
http://searchsecurity.techtarget.com/
    magazineFeature/0,296894,sid14_gci1526425,00.html

Securing Medical Research: A Cybersecurity Point of View
http://www.sciencemag.org/content/336/6088/1527.full

Fear Pays the Bills, but Accounts Must Be Settled
http://www.nytimes.com/roomfordebate/2012/10/17/
    should-industry-face-more-cybersecurity-mandates/
    fear-pays-the-bills-but-accounts-must-be-settled

Power And The Internet
http://edge.org/response-detail/23818

IT for Oppression
https://www.schneier.com/essay-420.html

The Public/Private Surveillance Partnership
http://www.theatlantic.com/technology/archive/13/04/
governments-wont-need-to-issue-ids-data-brokers-
will-identify-you-for-them/275431/

Transparency and Accountability Don't Hurt Security—
They're Crucial to It
http://www.theatlantic.com/politics/archive/2013/05/
transparency-and-accountability-dont-hurt
-security-theyre-crucial-to-it/275662/

It's Smart Politics to Exaggerate Terrorist Threats
http://www.cnn.com/2013/05/20/opinion/schneier-security-politics/
index.html

State Data Breach Notification Laws: Have They Helped?
http://searchsecurity.techtarget.com/
magazineFeature/0,296894,sid14_gci1344729_idx2,00.html

How to Ensure Police Database Accuracy
http://online.wsj.com/article/SB123301316511017419.html

Crossing Borders with Laptops and PDAs
http://www.guardian.co.uk/technology/2008/may/15/computing
.security

The TSA's Useless Photo ID Rules
http://www.latimes.com/news/opinion/
la-oe-schneier28-2008aug28,0,3099808.story

The Two Classes of Airport Contraband
http://www.wired.com/politics/security/commentary/
securitymatters/2008/09/securitymatters_0918

Fixing Airport Security
http://www.nydailynews.com/opinions/2009/06/24/2009-06-24
_clear_common_sense_for_takeoff_how_the_tsa_can_make
_airport_security_work_for_pa.html

Fixing Airport Security

http://www.nydailynews.com/opinions/2009/06/24/2009-06-24
_clear_common_sense_for_takeoff_how_the_tsa_can_make
_airport_security_work_for_pa.html

Laptop Security while Crossing Borders

http://www.wired.com/politics/security/commentary/
securitymatters/2009/07/securitymatters_0715

Breaching the Secure Area in Airports

http://threatpost.com/en_us/blogs/
fixing-security-problem-isnt-always-right-answer-010510

Stop the Panic on Air Security

http://www.cnn.com/2010/OPINION/01/07/schneier.security/

A Waste of Money and Time

http://www.nytimes.com/roomfordebate/2010/11/22/
do-body-scanners-make-us-safer/a-waste-of-money-and-time

Why the TSA Can't Back Down

http://www.theatlantic.com/national/archive/2010/12/
why-the-tsa-cant-back-down/67337/

The Trouble with Airport Profiling

http://www.forbes.com/sites/bruceschneier/2012/05/09/
the-trouble-with-airport-profiling/

Index